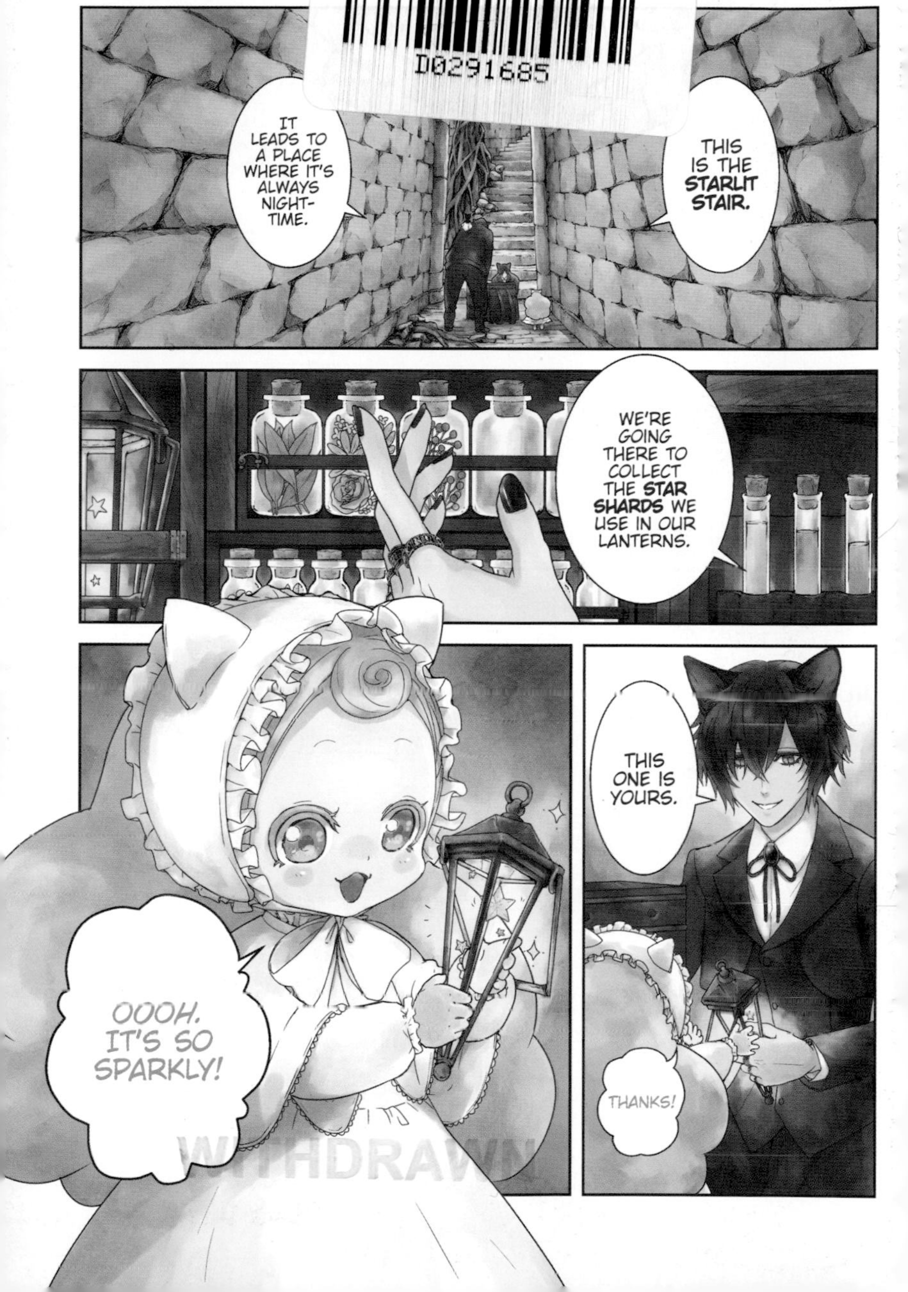
THIS IS THE **STARLIT STAIR.**
IT LEADS TO A PLACE WHERE IT'S ALWAYS NIGHT-TIME.
WE'RE GOING THERE TO COLLECT THE **STAR SHARDS** WE USE IN OUR LANTERNS.
THIS ONE IS YOURS.
THANKS!
OOOH. IT'S SO SPARKLY!

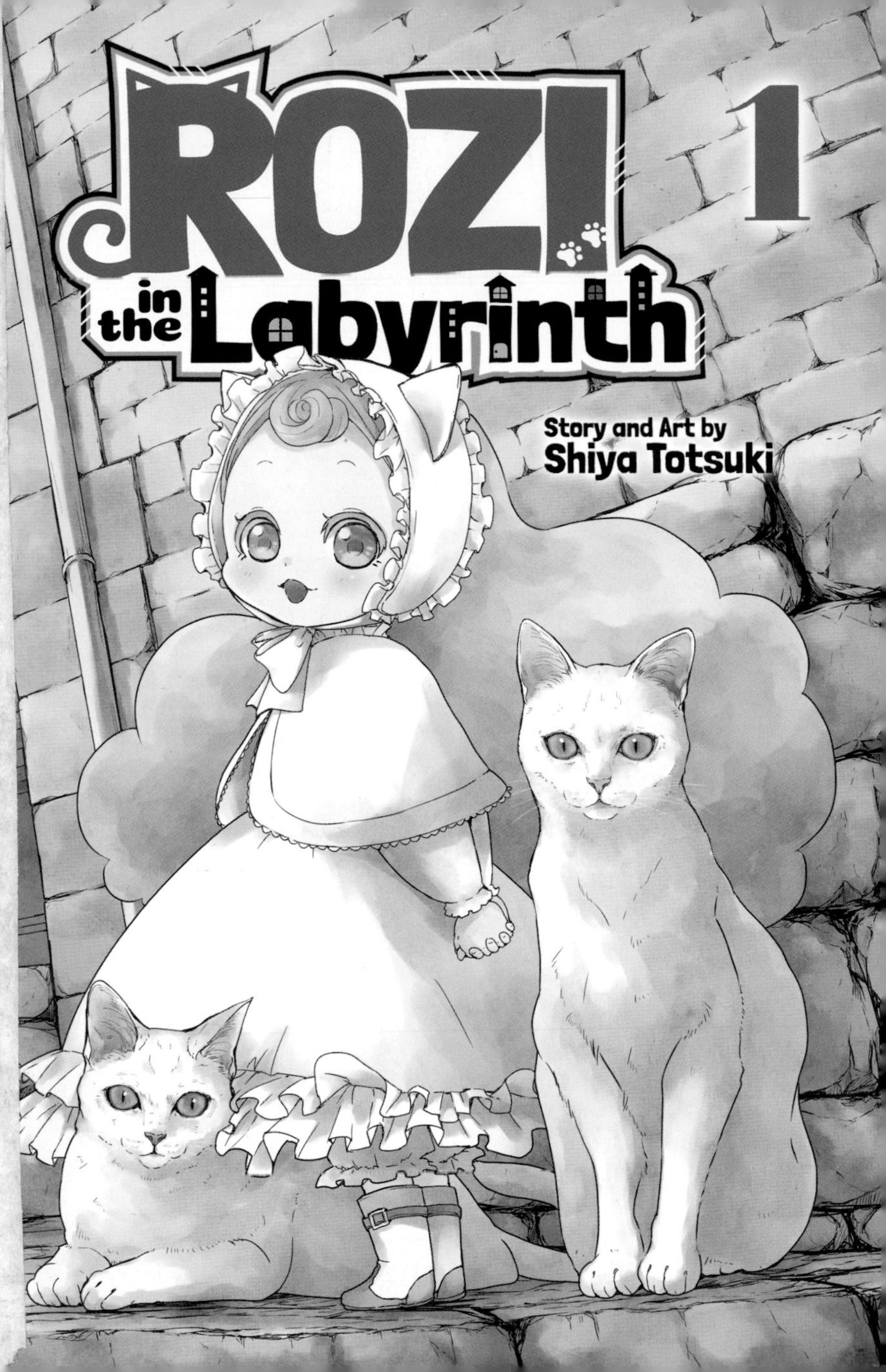
ROZI in the Labyrinth
1
Story and Art by
Shiya Totsuki

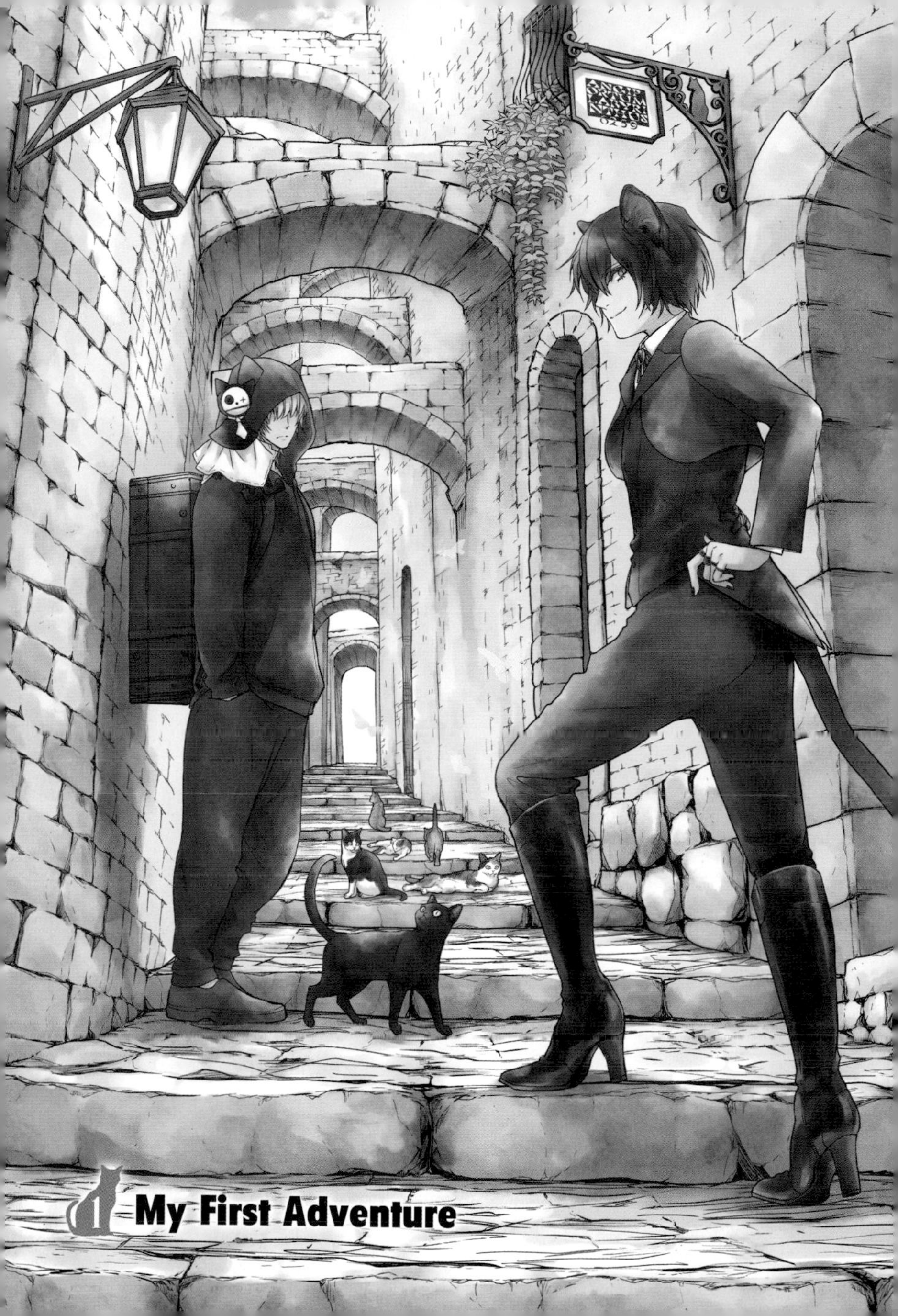

1 My First Adventure

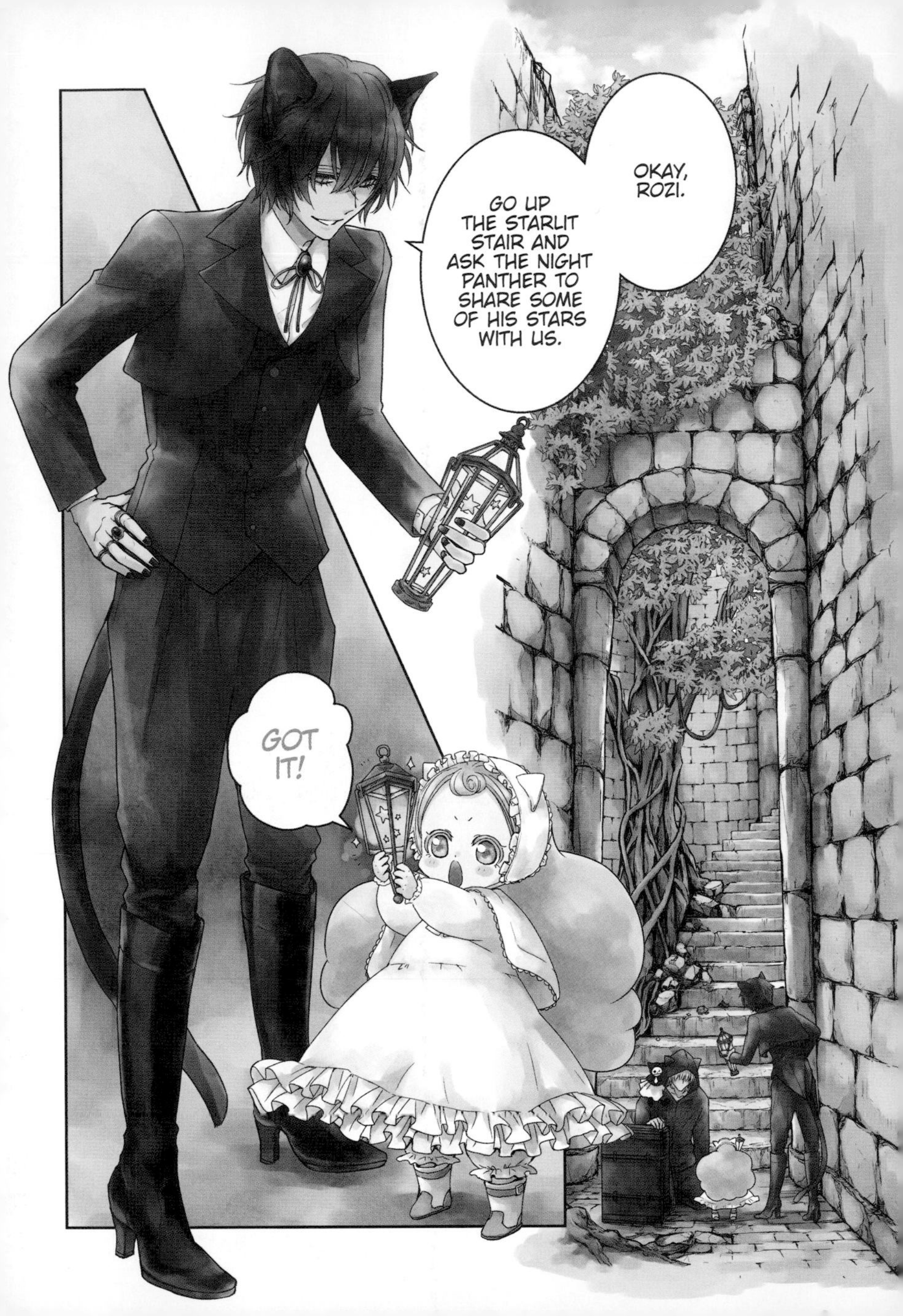
OKAY, ROZI.
GO UP THE STARLIT STAIR AND ASK THE NIGHT PANTHER TO SHARE SOME OF HIS STARS WITH US.
GOT IT!

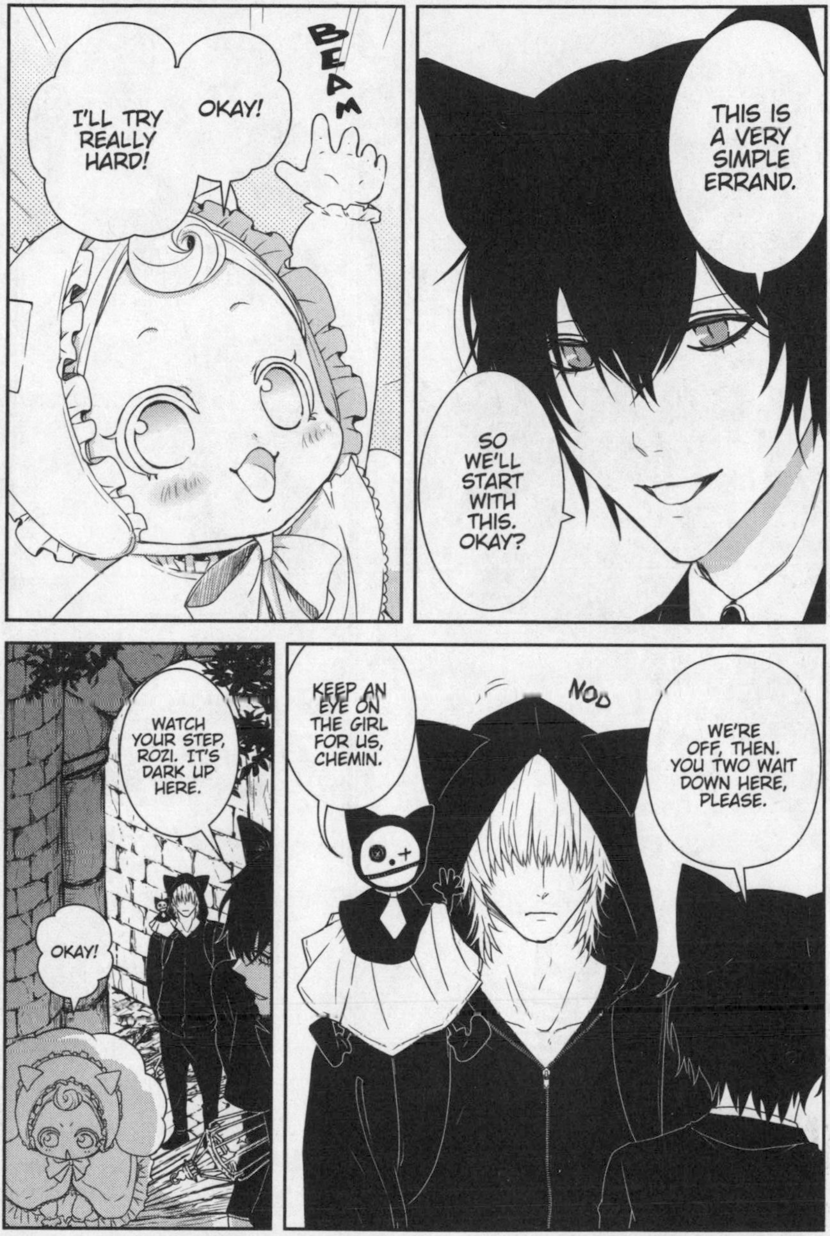
THIS IS A VERY SIMPLE ERRAND.
SO WE'LL START WITH THIS. OKAY?
BEAM
OKAY!
I'LL TRY REALLY HARD!
WE'RE OFF, THEN. YOU TWO WAIT DOWN HERE, PLEASE.
NOD
KEEP AN EYE ON THE GIRL FOR US, CHEMIN.
WATCH YOUR STEP, ROZI. IT'S DARK UP HERE.
OKAY!

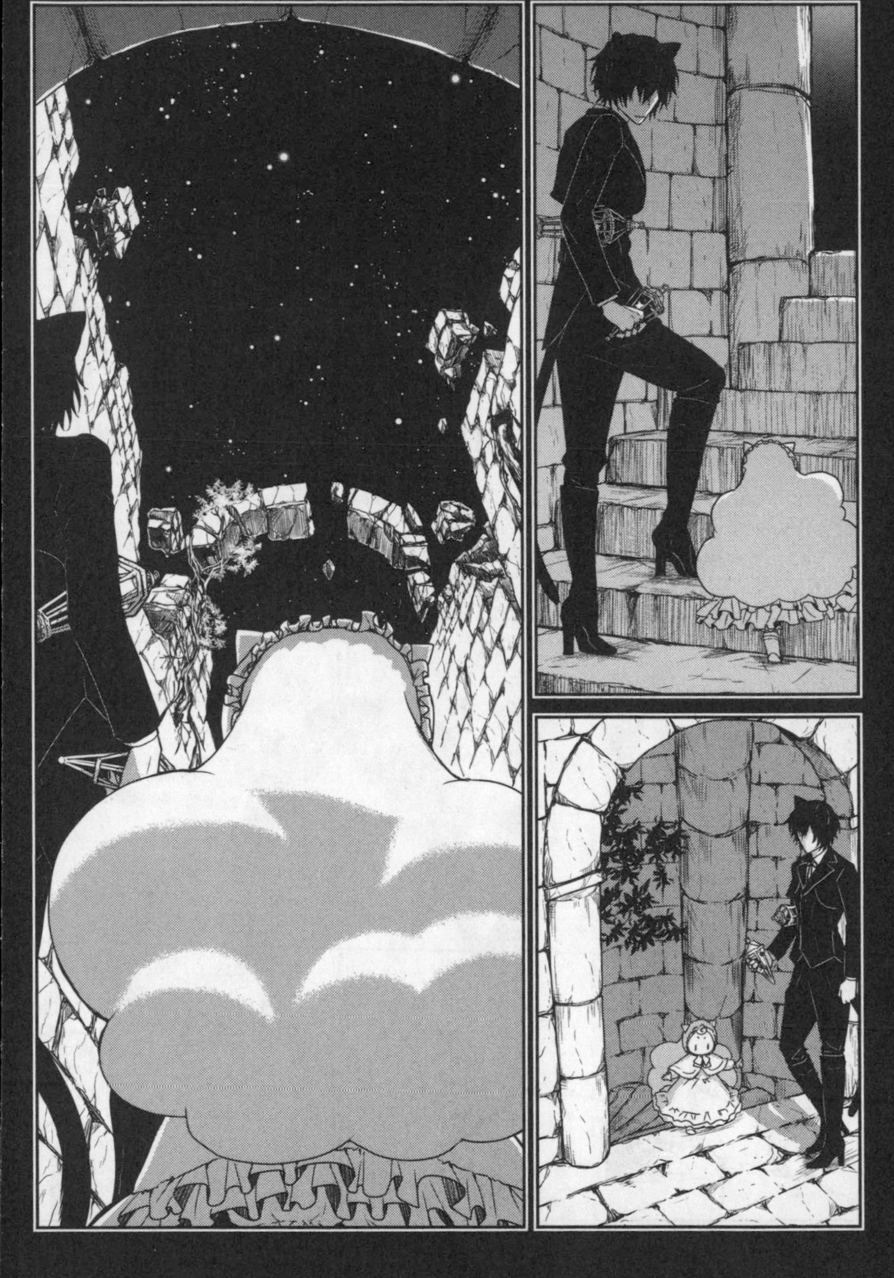

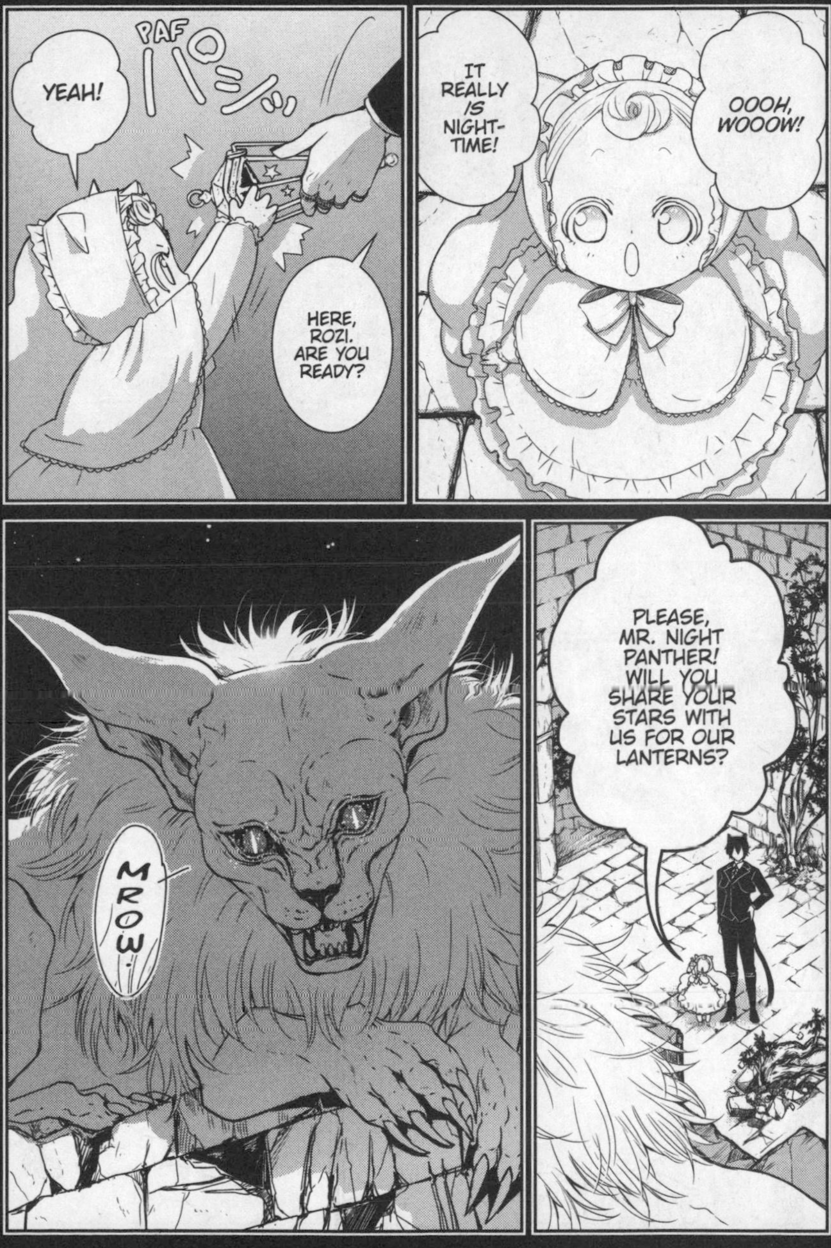
OOOH, WOOOW!
IT REALLY IS NIGHT-TIME!
PAF
YEAH!
HERE, ROZI. ARE YOU READY?
PLEASE, MR. NIGHT PANTHER! WILL YOU SHARE YOUR STARS WITH US FOR OUR LANTERNS?
MROW.

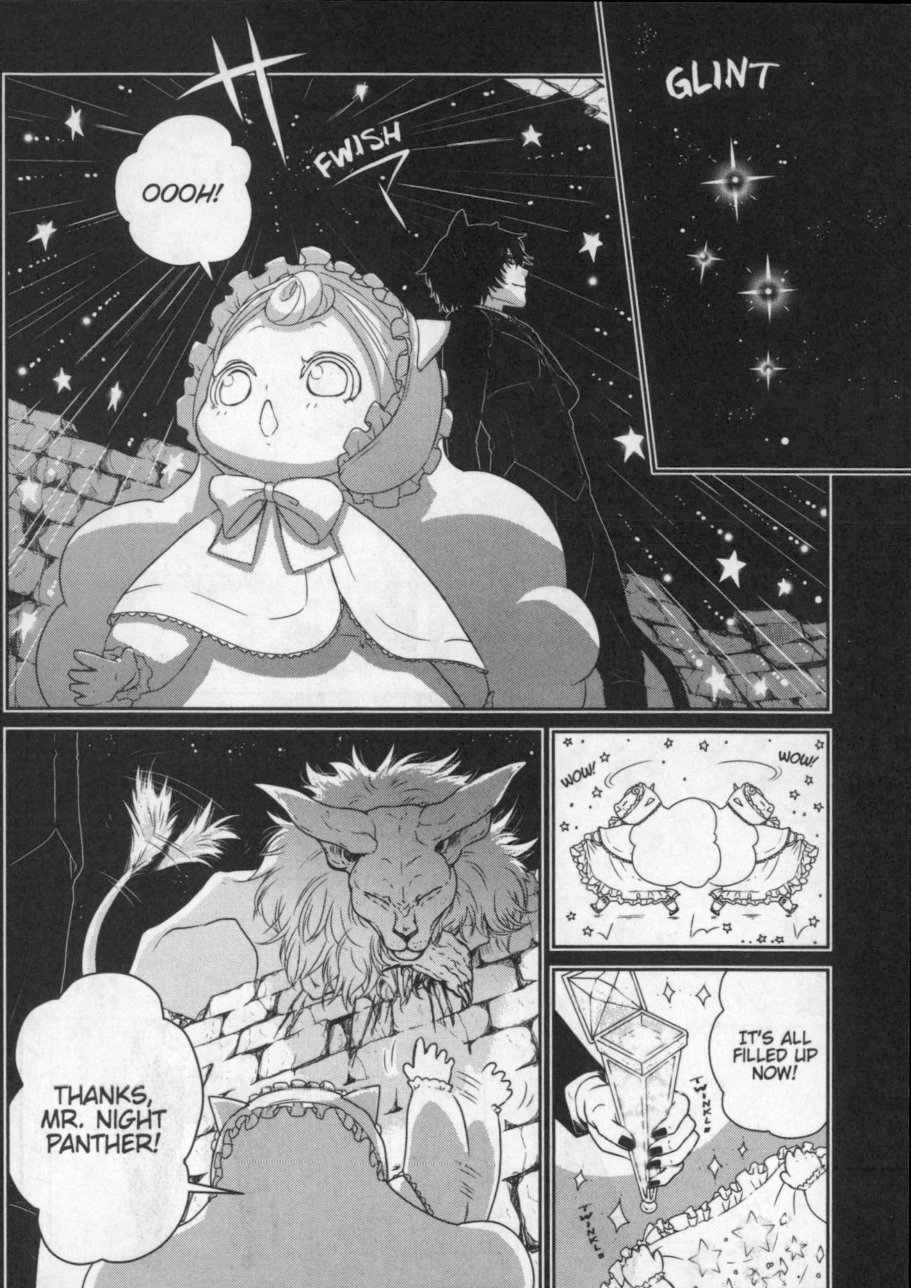
GLINT
FWISH
OOOH!
WOW!
WOW!
IT'S ALL FILLED UP NOW!
TWINKLE
TWINKLE
THANKS, MR. NIGHT PANTHER!

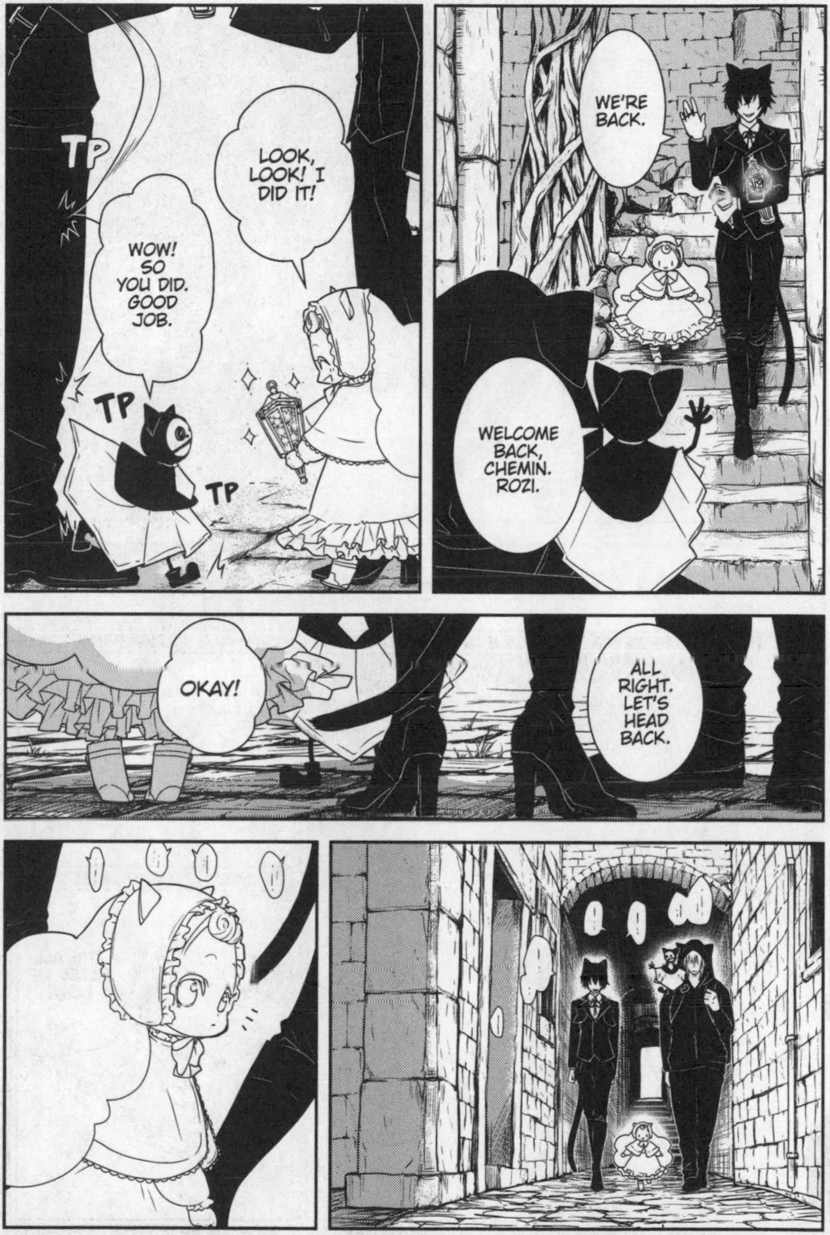

WE'RE BACK.
WELCOME BACK, CHEMIN. ROZI.
LOOK, LOOK! I DID IT!
TP
WOW! SO YOU DID. GOOD JOB.
TP
TP
ALL RIGHT. LET'S HEAD BACK.
OKAY!

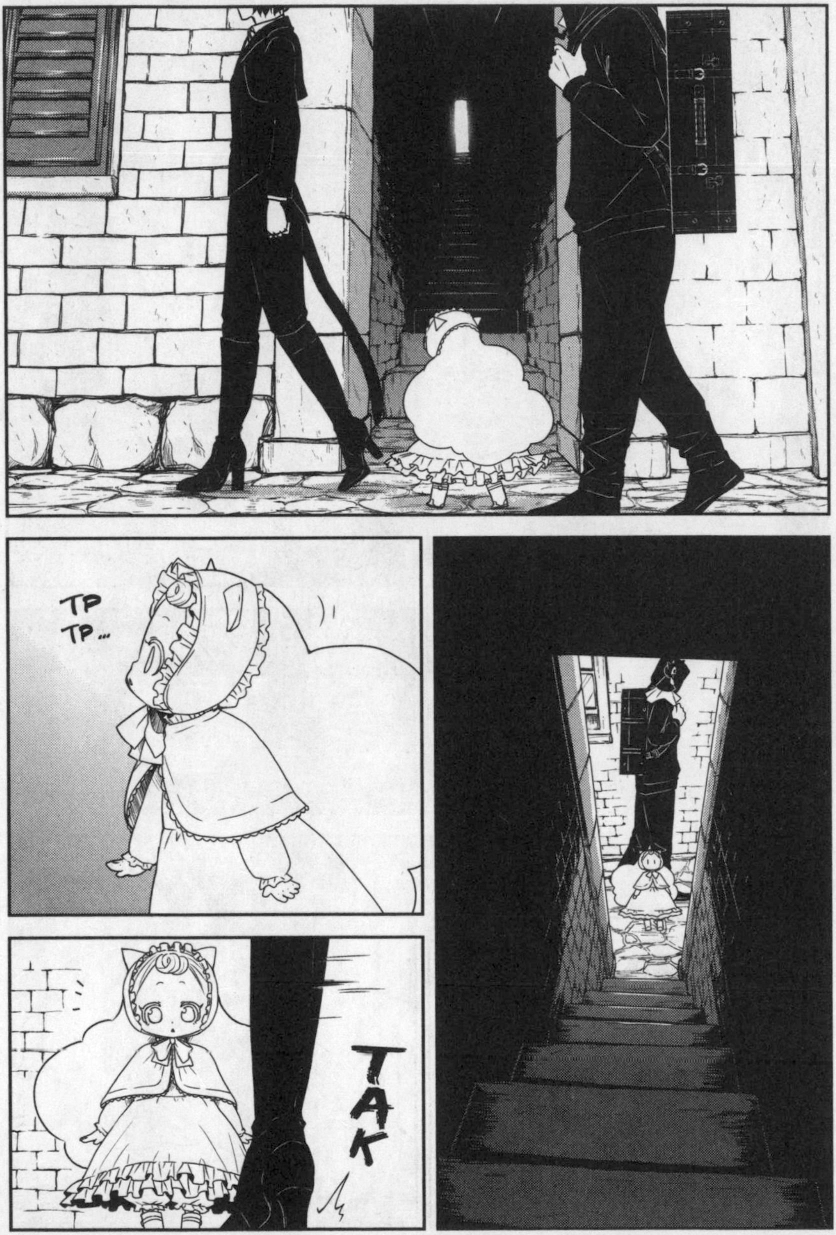
TP
TP...
TAK

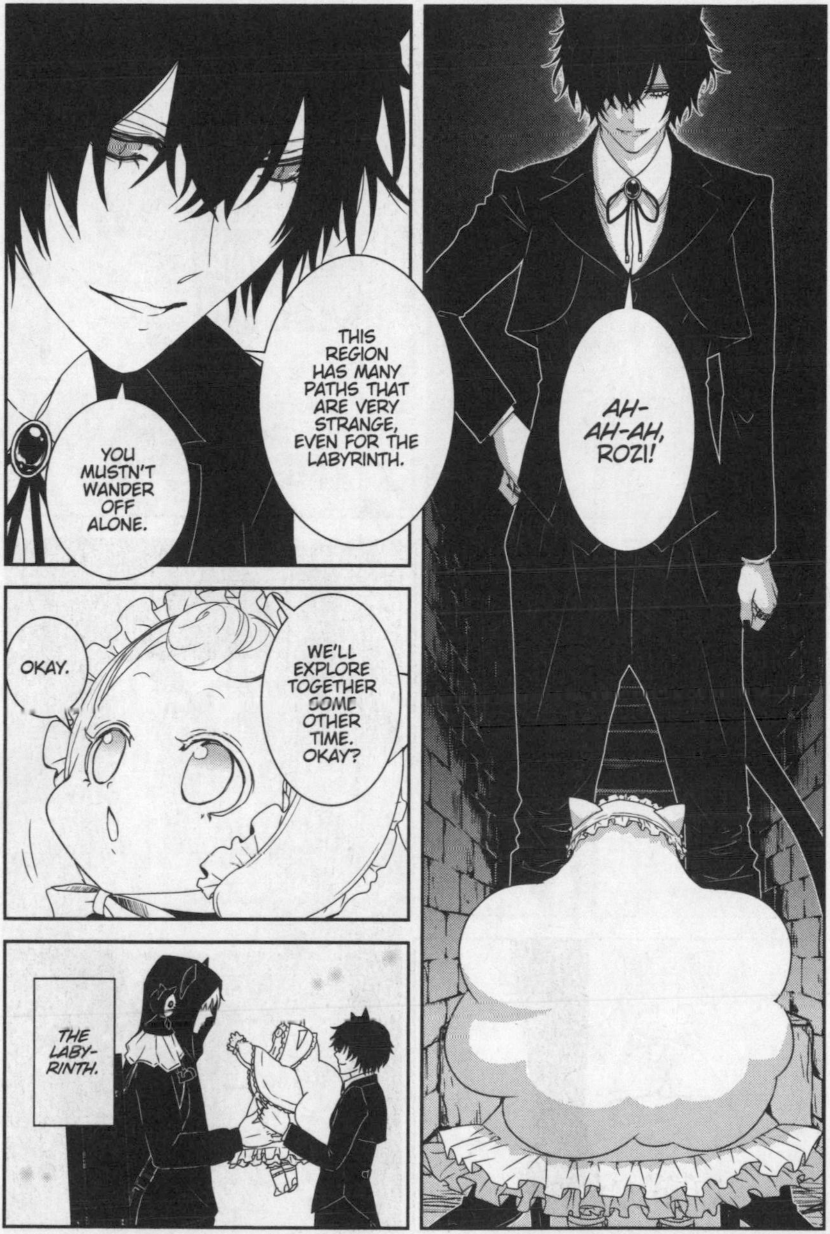
AH-AH-AH, ROZI!
THIS REGION HAS MANY PATHS THAT ARE VERY STRANGE, EVEN FOR THE LABYRINTH.
YOU MUSTN'T WANDER OFF ALONE.
WE'LL EXPLORE TOGETHER SOME OTHER TIME. OKAY?
OKAY.
THE LABY-RINTH.

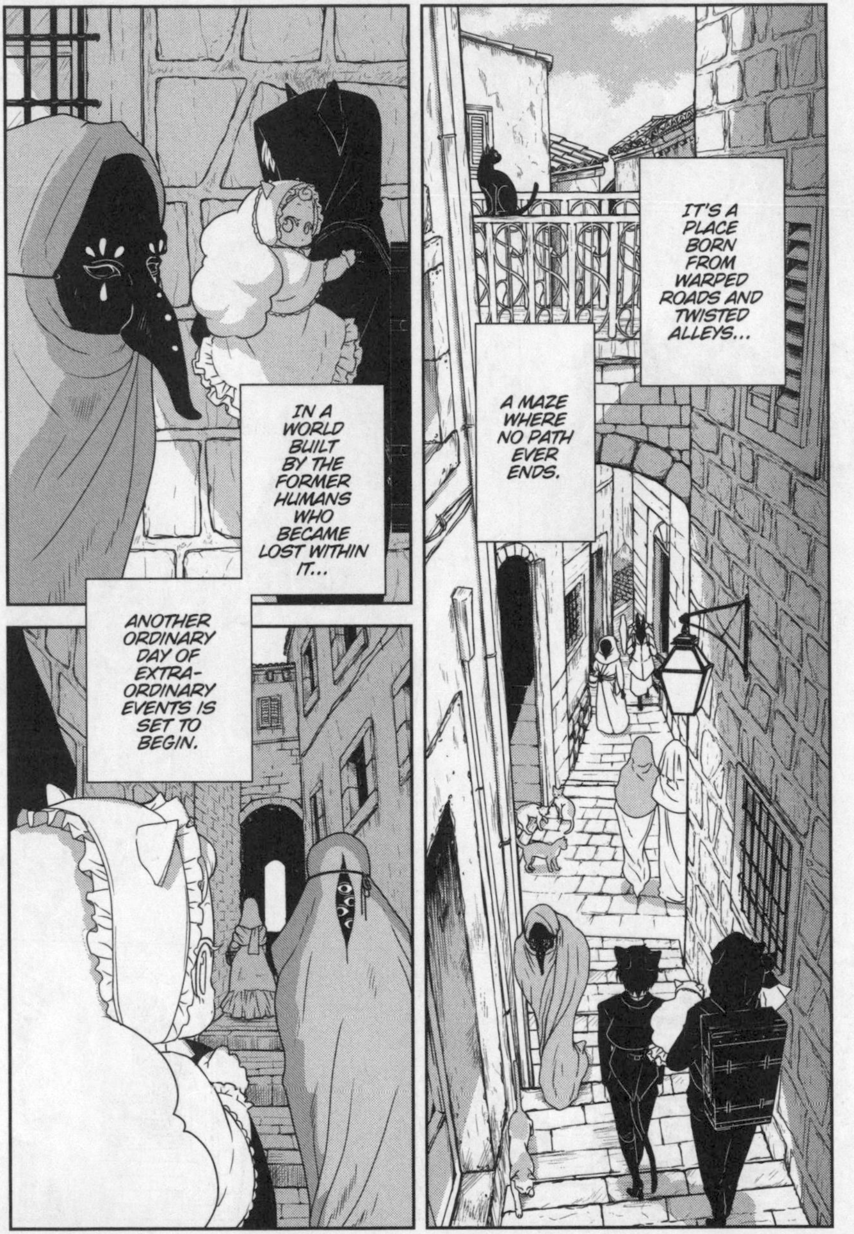
IT'S A PLACE BORN FROM WARPED ROADS AND TWISTED ALLEYS...
A MAZE WHERE NO PATH EVER ENDS.
IN A WORLD BUILT BY THE FORMER HUMANS WHO BECAME LOST WITHIN IT...
ANOTHER ORDINARY DAY OF EXTRA-ORDINARY EVENTS IS SET TO BEGIN.

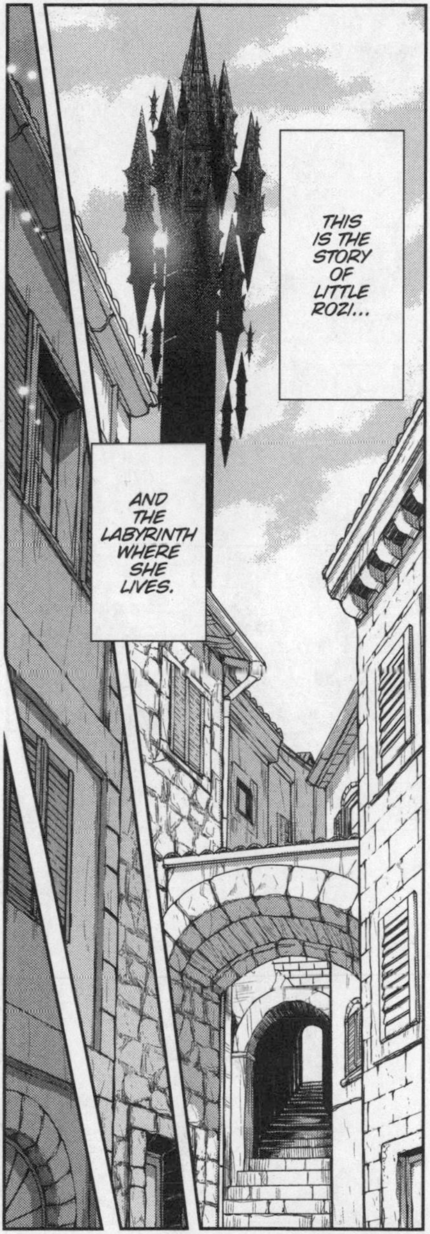
THIS IS THE STORY OF LITTLE ROZI...
AND THE LABYRINTH WHERE SHE LIVES.
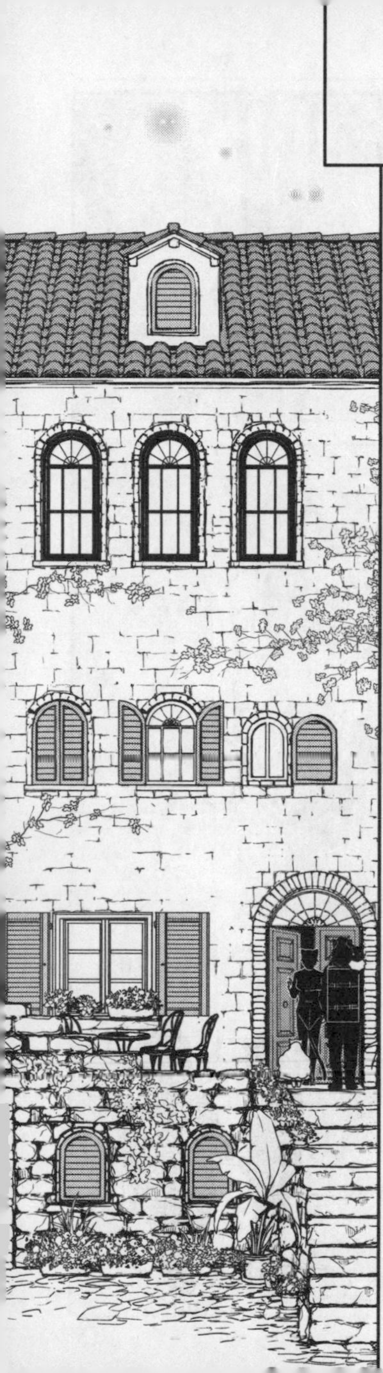

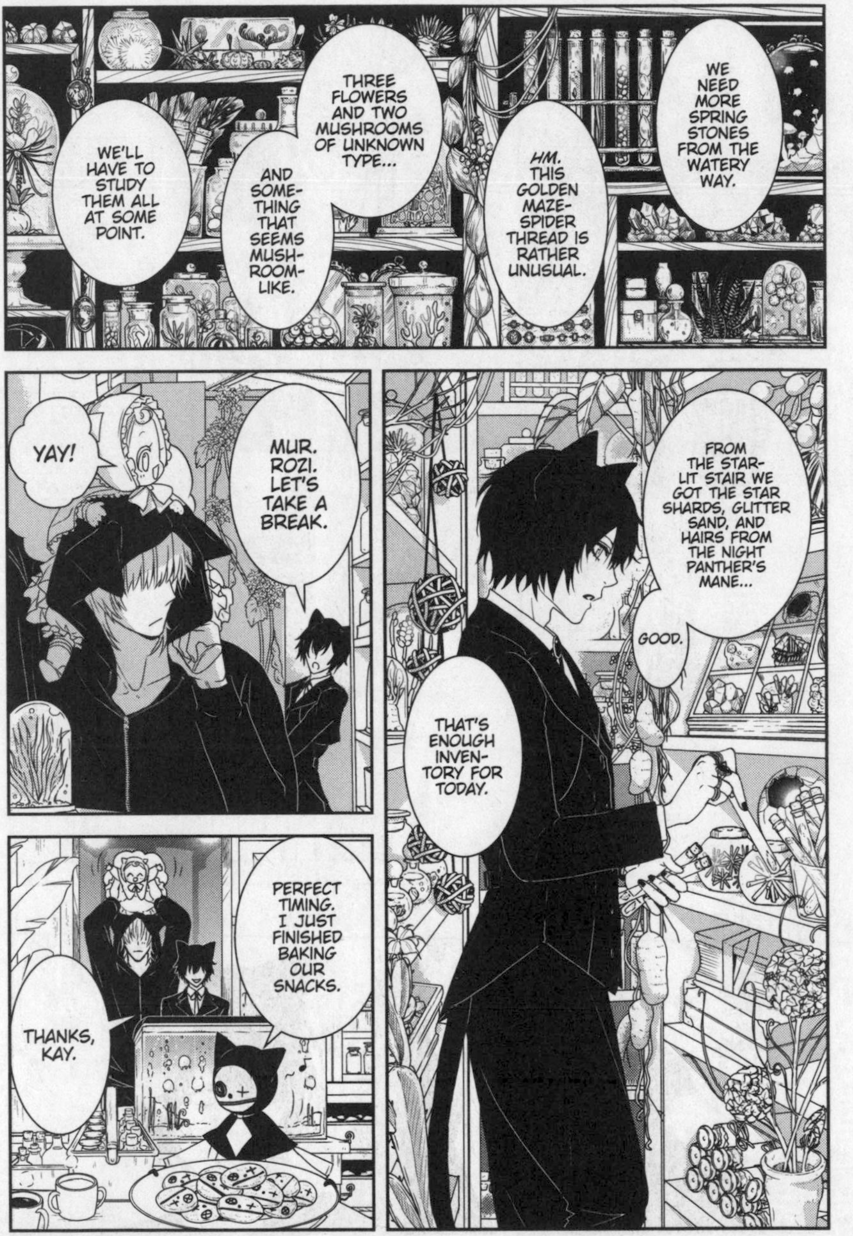

WE NEED MORE SPRING STONES FROM THE WATERY WAY.
HM. THIS GOLDEN MAZE-SPIDER THREAD IS RATHER UNUSUAL.
THREE FLOWERS AND TWO MUSHROOMS OF UNKNOWN TYPE...
AND SOMETHING THAT SEEMS MUSHROOM-LIKE.
WE'LL HAVE TO STUDY THEM ALL AT SOME POINT.
FROM THE STARLIT STAIR WE GOT THE STAR SHARDS, GLITTER SAND, AND HAIRS FROM THE NIGHT PANTHER'S MANE...
GOOD.
THAT'S ENOUGH INVENTORY FOR TODAY.
MUR. ROZI. LET'S TAKE A BREAK.
YAY!
PERFECT TIMING. I JUST FINISHED BAKING OUR SNACKS.
THANKS, KAY.

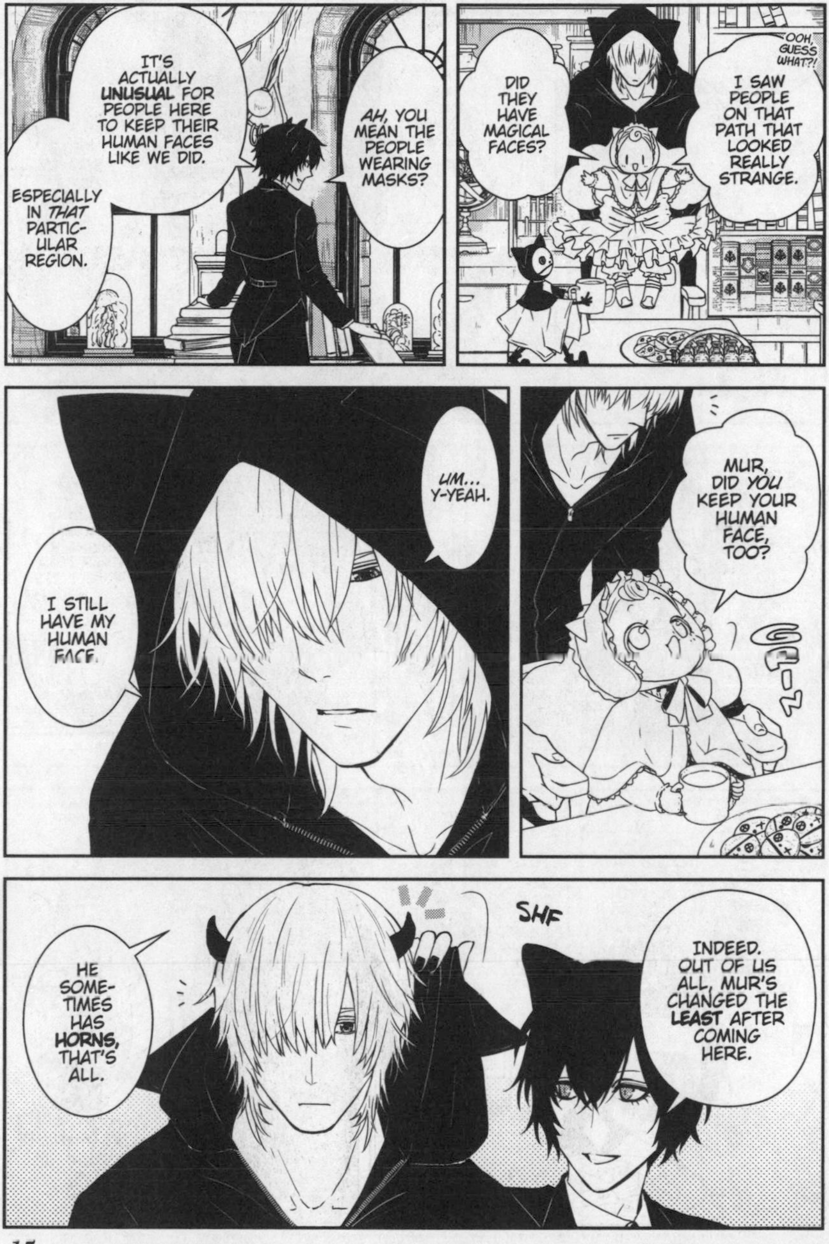
OOH, GUESS WHAT?!
I SAW PEOPLE ON THAT PATH THAT LOOKED REALLY STRANGE.
DID THEY HAVE MAGICAL FACES?
AH, YOU MEAN THE PEOPLE WEARING MASKS?
IT'S ACTUALLY UNUSUAL FOR PEOPLE HERE TO KEEP THEIR HUMAN FACES LIKE WE DID.
ESPECIALLY IN THAT PARTICULAR REGION.
MUR, DID YOU KEEP YOUR HUMAN FACE, TOO?
UM... Y-YEAH.
I STILL HAVE MY HUMAN FACE.
INDEED. OUT OF US ALL, MUR'S CHANGED THE LEAST AFTER COMING HERE.
SHF
HE SOMETIMES HAS HORNS, THAT'S ALL.

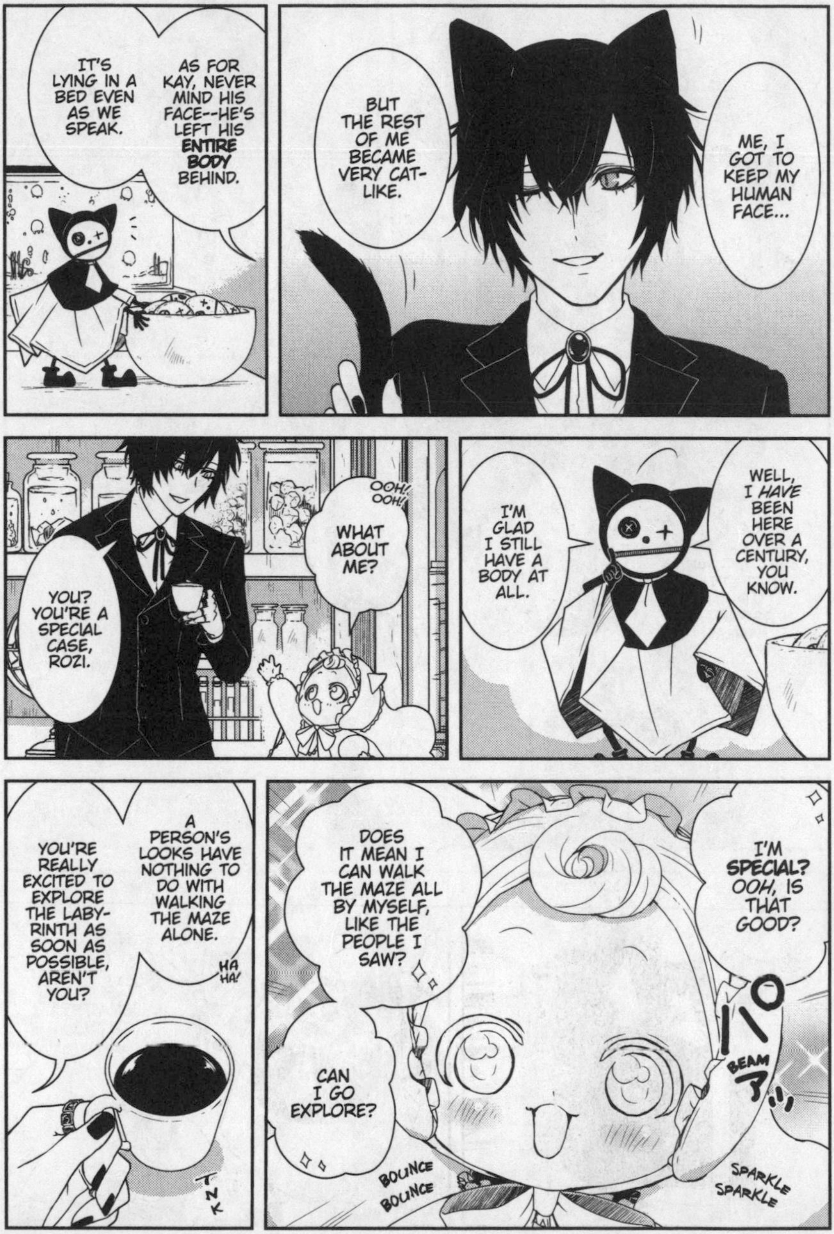
ME, I GOT TO KEEP MY HUMAN FACE...
BUT THE REST OF ME BECAME VERY CAT-LIKE.
AS FOR KAY, NEVER MIND HIS FACE--HE'S LEFT HIS **ENTIRE BODY** BEHIND.
IT'S LYING IN A BED EVEN AS WE SPEAK.
WELL, I *HAVE* BEEN HERE OVER A CENTURY, YOU KNOW.
I'M GLAD I STILL HAVE A BODY AT ALL.
OOH! OOH!
WHAT ABOUT ME?
YOU? YOU'RE A SPECIAL CASE, ROZI.
I'M **SPECIAL?** *OOH,* IS THAT GOOD?
BEAM
SPARKLE SPARKLE
DOES IT MEAN I CAN WALK THE MAZE ALL BY MYSELF, LIKE THE PEOPLE I SAW?
CAN I GO EXPLORE?
BOUNCE BOUNCE
A PERSON'S LOOKS HAVE NOTHING TO DO WITH WALKING THE MAZE ALONE.
YOU'RE REALLY EXCITED TO EXPLORE THE LABYRINTH AS SOON AS POSSIBLE, AREN'T YOU?
HA HA!
TNK

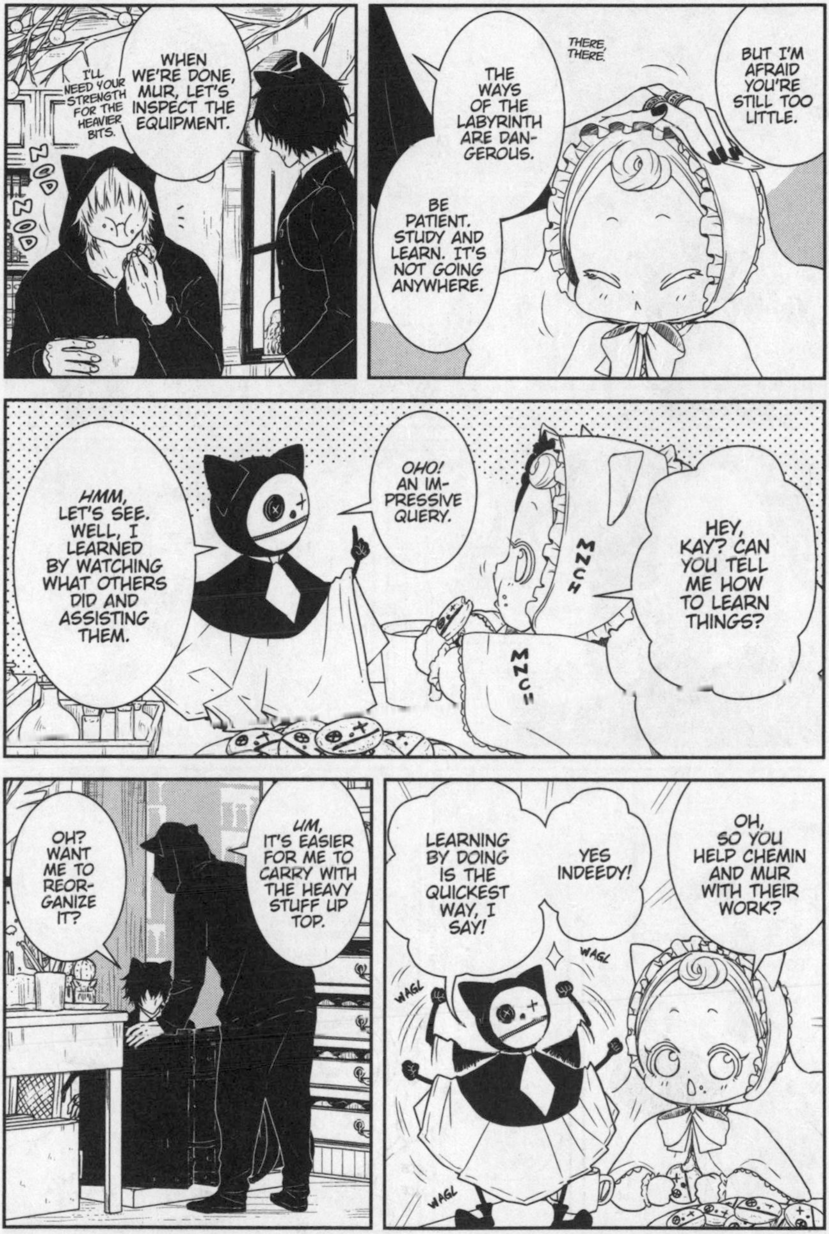
BUT I'M AFRAID YOU'RE STILL TOO LITTLE.
THERE, THERE.
THE WAYS OF THE LABYRINTH ARE DAN-GEROUS.
BE PATIENT. STUDY AND LEARN. IT'S NOT GOING ANYWHERE.
WHEN WE'RE DONE, MUR, LET'S INSPECT THE EQUIPMENT.
I'LL NEED YOUR STRENGTH FOR THE HEAVIER BITS.
NOD NOD
HEY, KAY? CAN YOU TELL ME HOW TO LEARN THINGS?
MNCH
MNCH
OHO! AN IM-PRESSIVE QUERY.
HMM, LET'S SEE. WELL, I LEARNED BY WATCHING WHAT OTHERS DID AND ASSISTING THEM.
OH, SO YOU HELP CHEMIN AND MUR WITH THEIR WORK?
YES INDEEDY!
LEARNING BY DOING IS THE QUICKEST WAY, I SAY!
WAGL
WAGL
WAGL
UM, IT'S EASIER FOR ME TO CARRY WITH THE HEAVY STUFF UP TOP.
OH? WANT ME TO REOR-GANIZE IT?

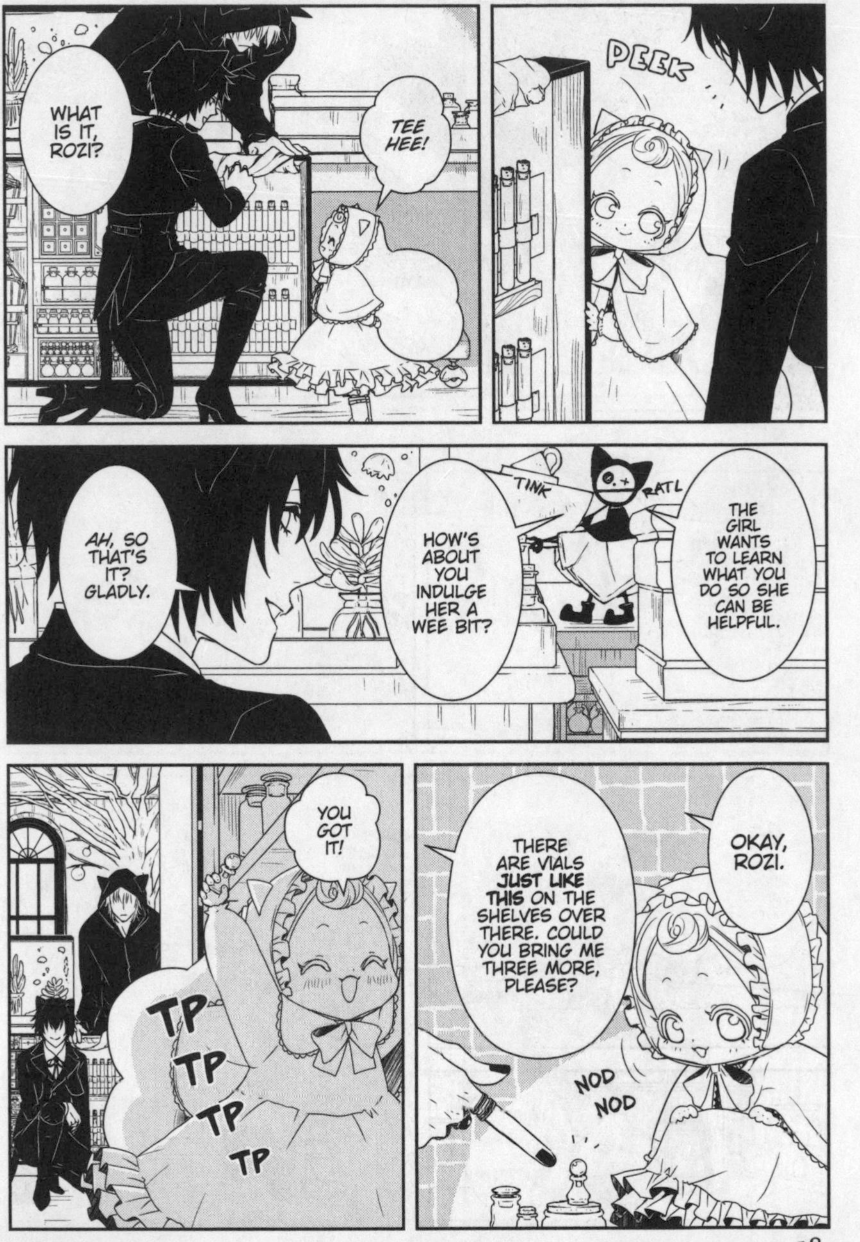
PEEK
...
TEE HEE!
WHAT IS IT, ROZI?
THE GIRL WANTS TO LEARN WHAT YOU DO SO SHE CAN BE HELPFUL.
RATL
TINK
HOW'S ABOUT YOU INDULGE HER A WEE BIT?
AH, SO THAT'S IT? GLADLY.
OKAY, ROZI.
THERE ARE VIALS **JUST LIKE THIS** ON THE SHELVES OVER THERE. COULD YOU BRING ME THREE MORE, PLEASE?
NOD NOD
YOU GOT IT!
TP TP TP TP

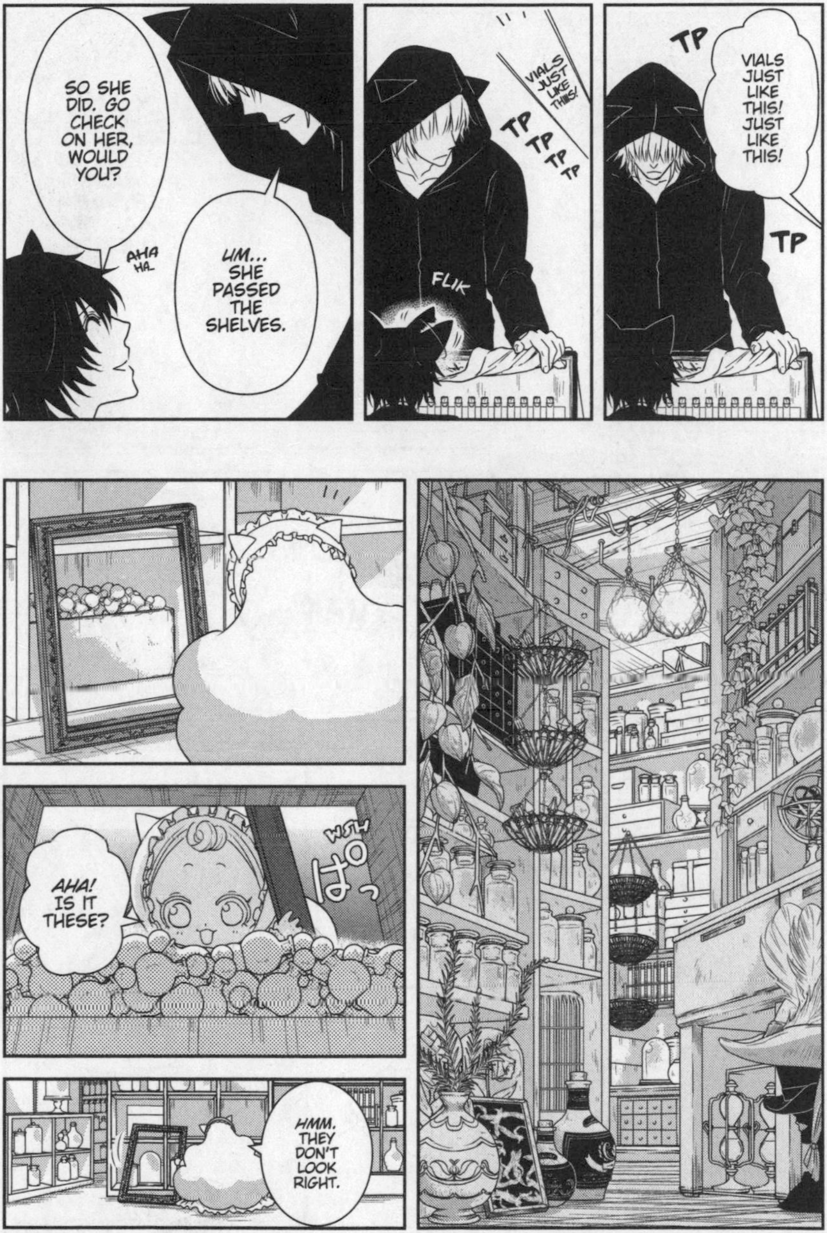
TP
VIALS JUST LIKE THIS! JUST LIKE THIS!
TP
VIALS JUST LIKE THIS!
TP TP TP TP
FLIK
UM... SHE PASSED THE SHELVES.
SO SHE DID. GO CHECK ON HER, WOULD YOU?
AHA HA.
AHA! IS IT THESE?
WSH
ぱっ
HMM. THEY DON'T LOOK RIGHT.

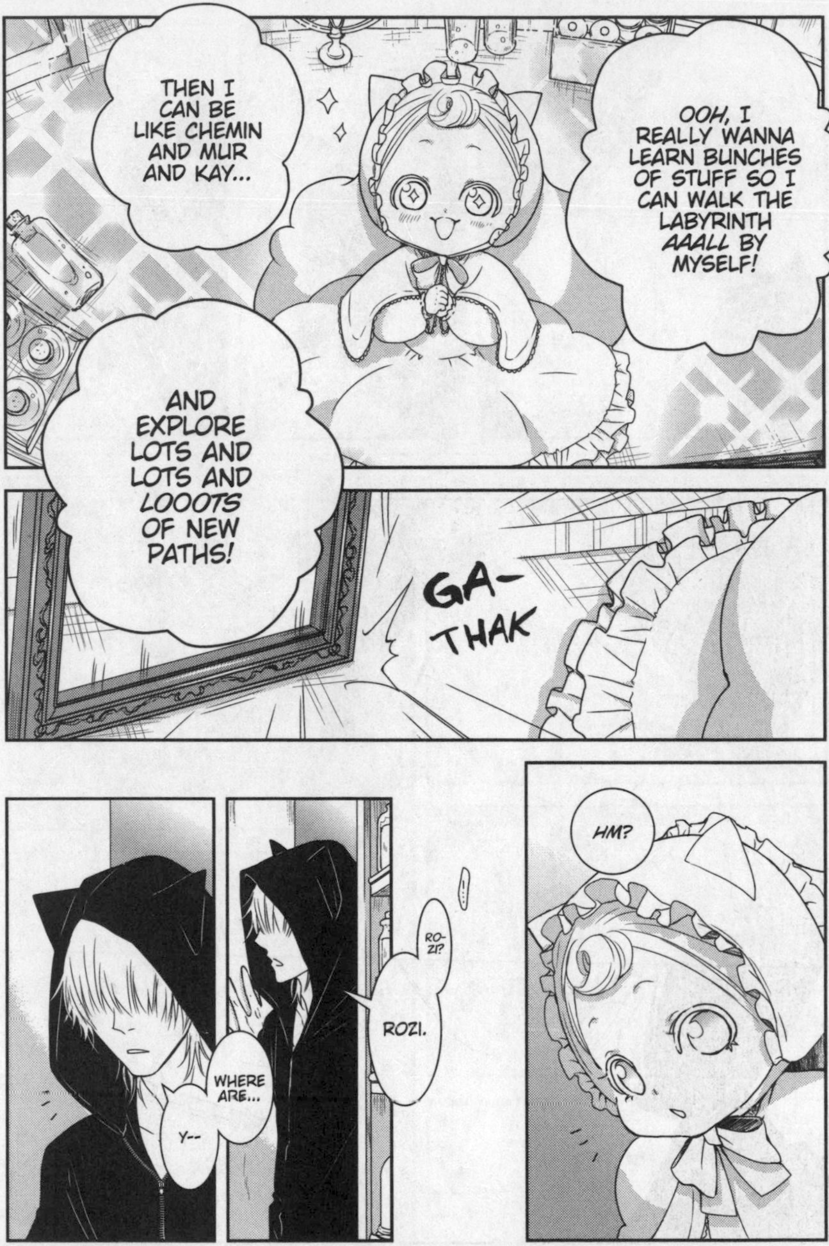
OOH, I REALLY WANNA LEARN BUNCHES OF STUFF SO I CAN WALK THE LABYRINTH AAALL BY MYSELF!
THEN I CAN BE LIKE CHEMIN AND MUR AND KAY...
AND EXPLORE LOTS AND LOTS AND LOOOTS OF NEW PATHS!
GA-THAK
HM?
!
RO-ZI?
ROZI.
WHERE ARE...
Y--

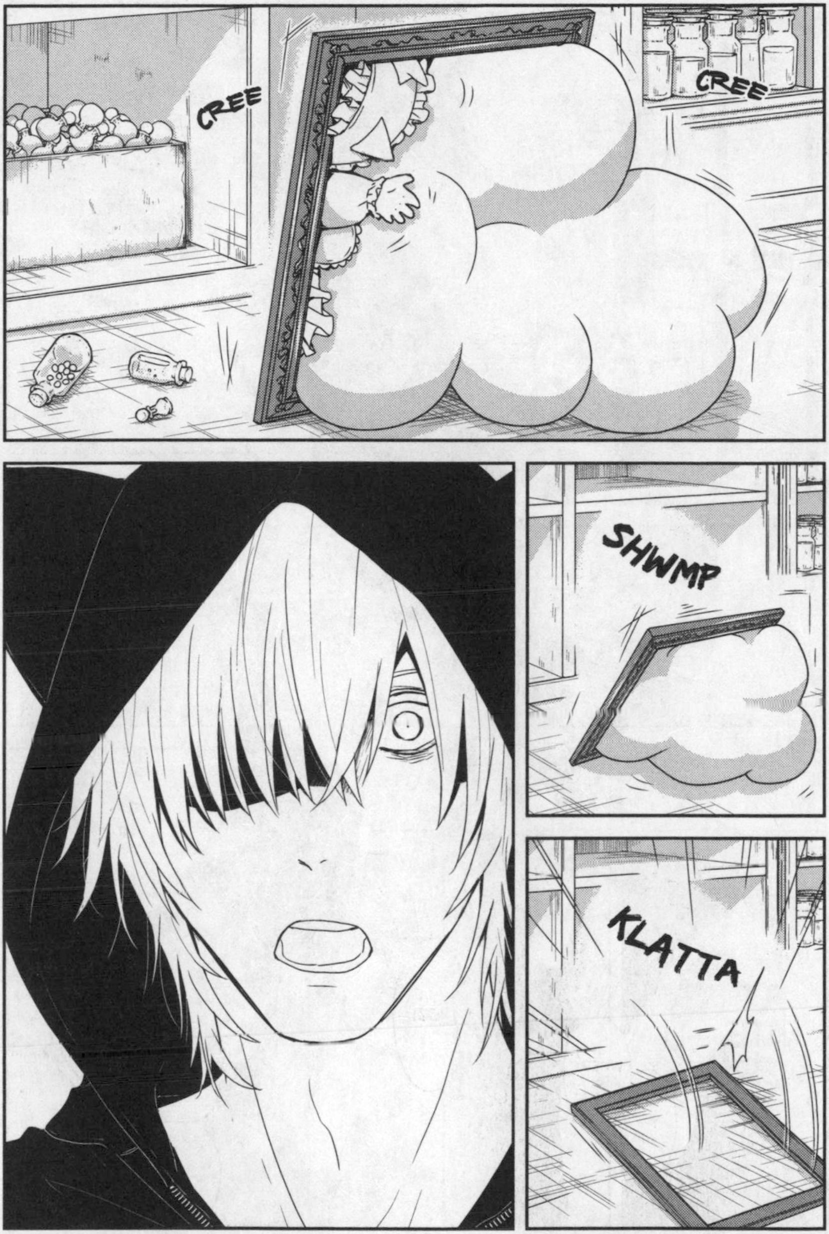
CREE
CREE
SHWMP
KLATTA

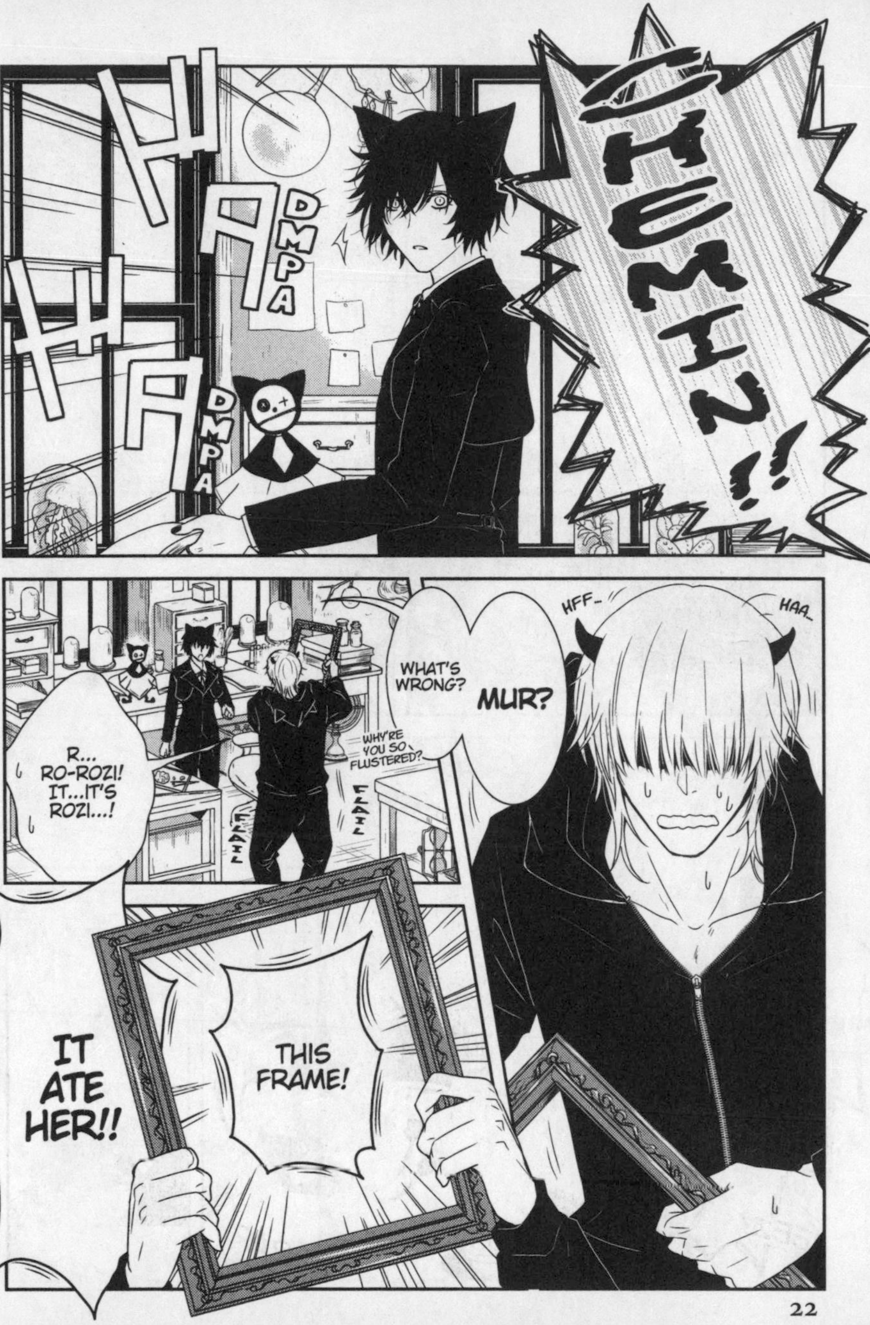
CHEMIN!!
DMPA
HA
HA
DMPA
HFF...
HAA...
MUR?
WHAT'S WRONG?
WHY'RE YOU SO FLUSTERED?
FLAIL
FLAIL
R... RO-ROZI! IT...IT'S ROZI...!
THIS FRAME!
IT ATE HER!!

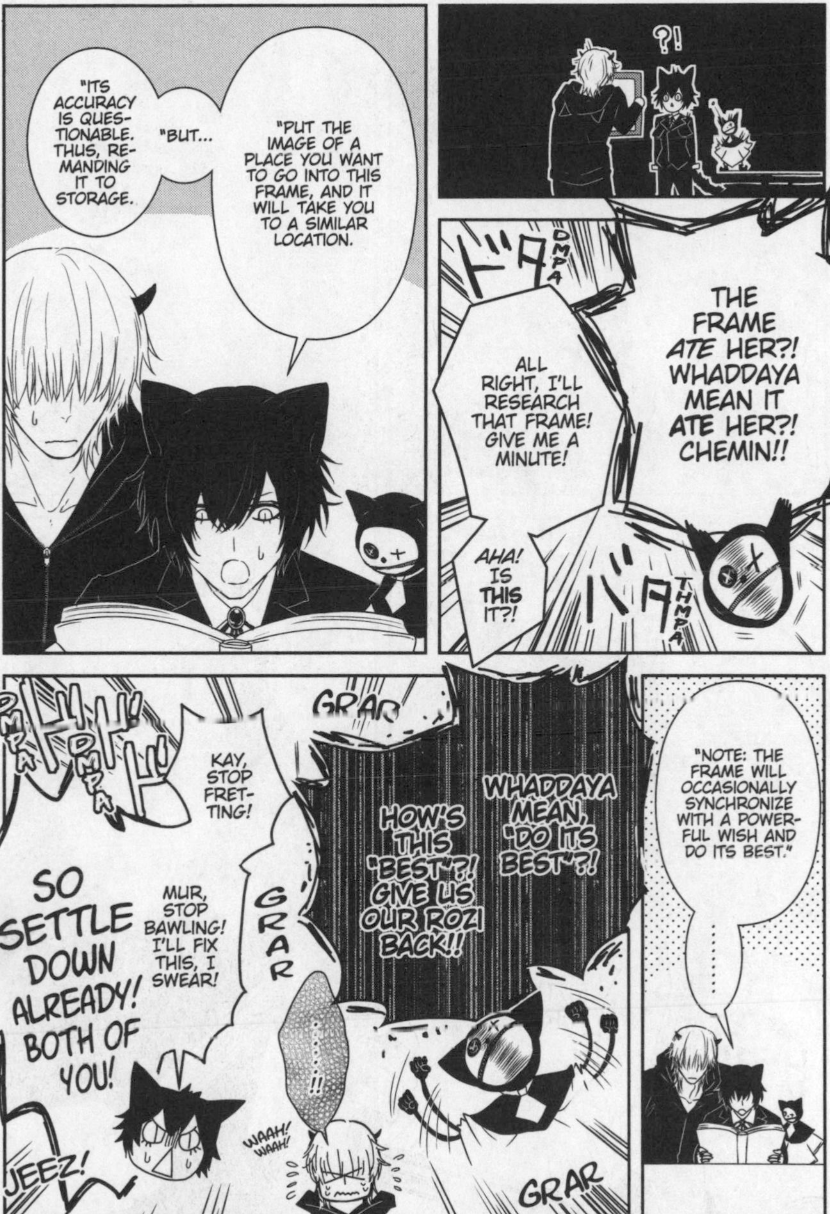
?!
ドタ
DMPA
THE FRAME ATE HER?! WHADDAYA MEAN IT ATE HER?! CHEMIN!!
ALL RIGHT, I'LL RESEARCH THAT FRAME! GIVE ME A MINUTE!
AHA! IS THIS IT?!
バタ
THMPA
"PUT THE IMAGE OF A PLACE YOU WANT TO GO INTO THIS FRAME, AND IT WILL TAKE YOU TO A SIMILAR LOCATION.
"BUT...
"ITS ACCURACY IS QUES-TIONABLE. THUS, RE-MANDING IT TO STORAGE.
"NOTE: THE FRAME WILL OCCASIONALLY SYNCHRONIZE WITH A POWER-FUL WISH AND DO ITS BEST."
GRAR
WHADDAYA MEAN, "DO ITS BEST"?!
HOW'S THIS "BEST"?! GIVE US OUR ROZI BACK!!
GRAR
KAY, STOP FRET-TING!
MUR, STOP BAWLING! I'LL FIX THIS, I SWEAR!
DMPA
DMPA
SO SETTLE DOWN ALREADY! BOTH OF YOU!
WAAH! WAAH!
GRAR
JEEZ!

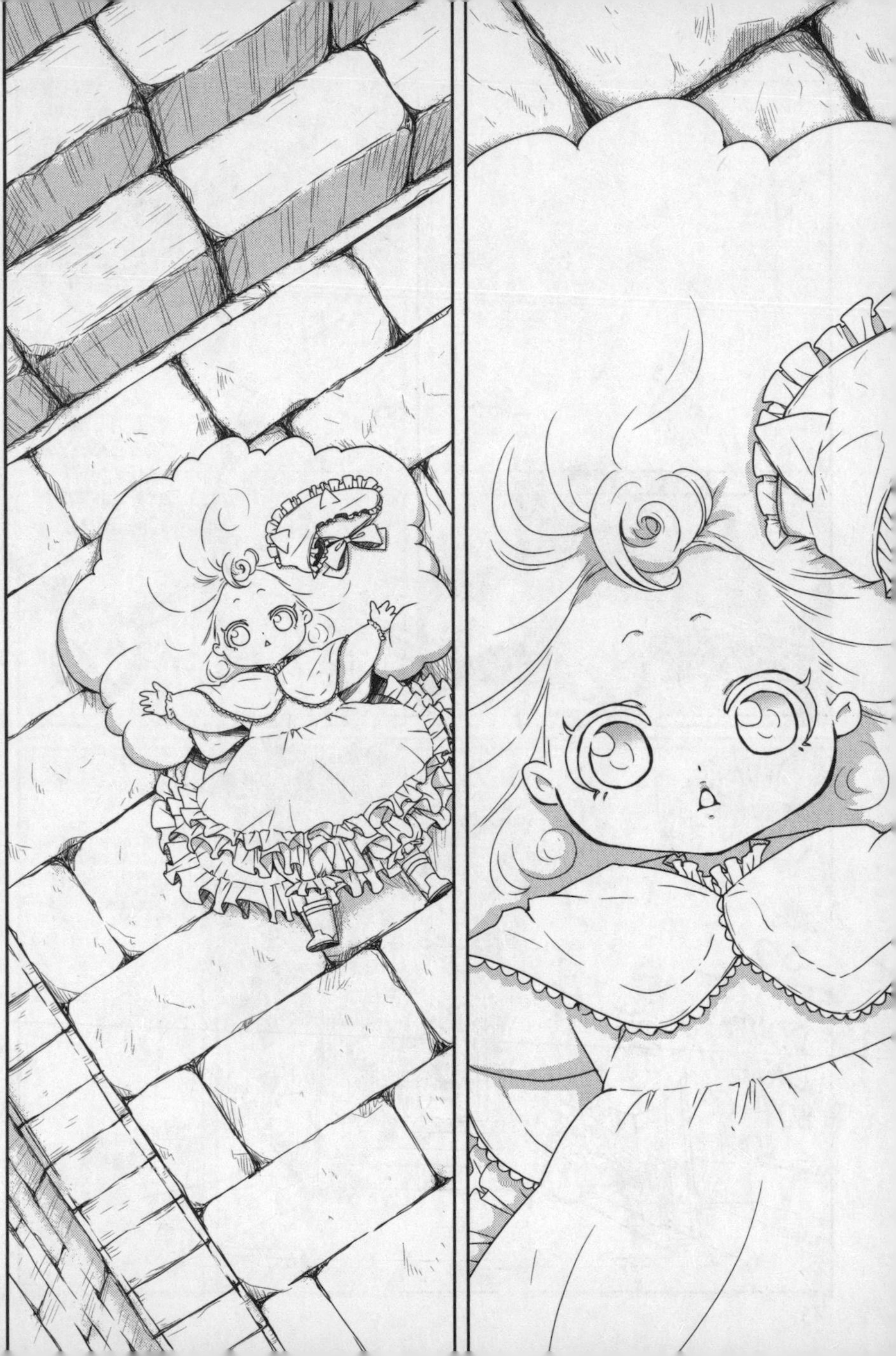

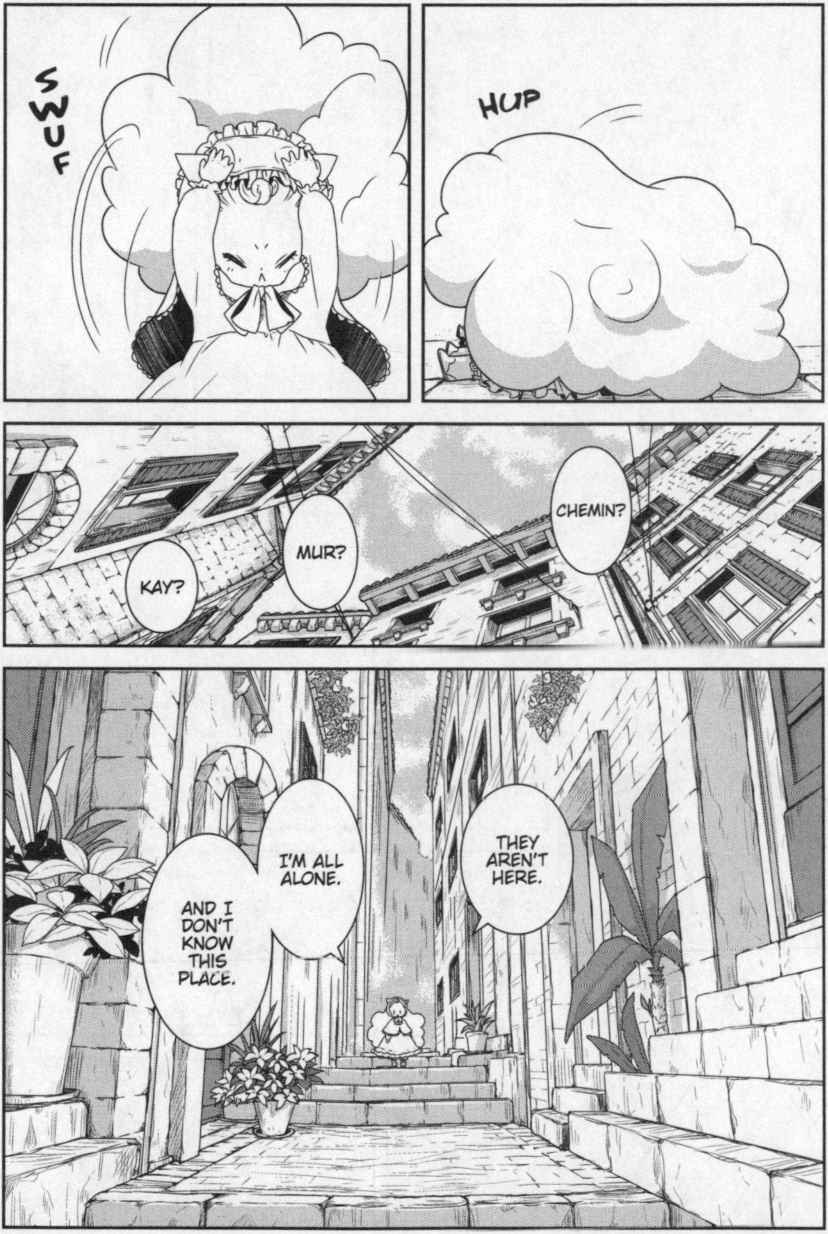
HUP
SWUF
CHEMIN?
MUR?
KAY?
THEY AREN'T HERE.
I'M ALL ALONE.
AND I DON'T KNOW THIS PLACE.

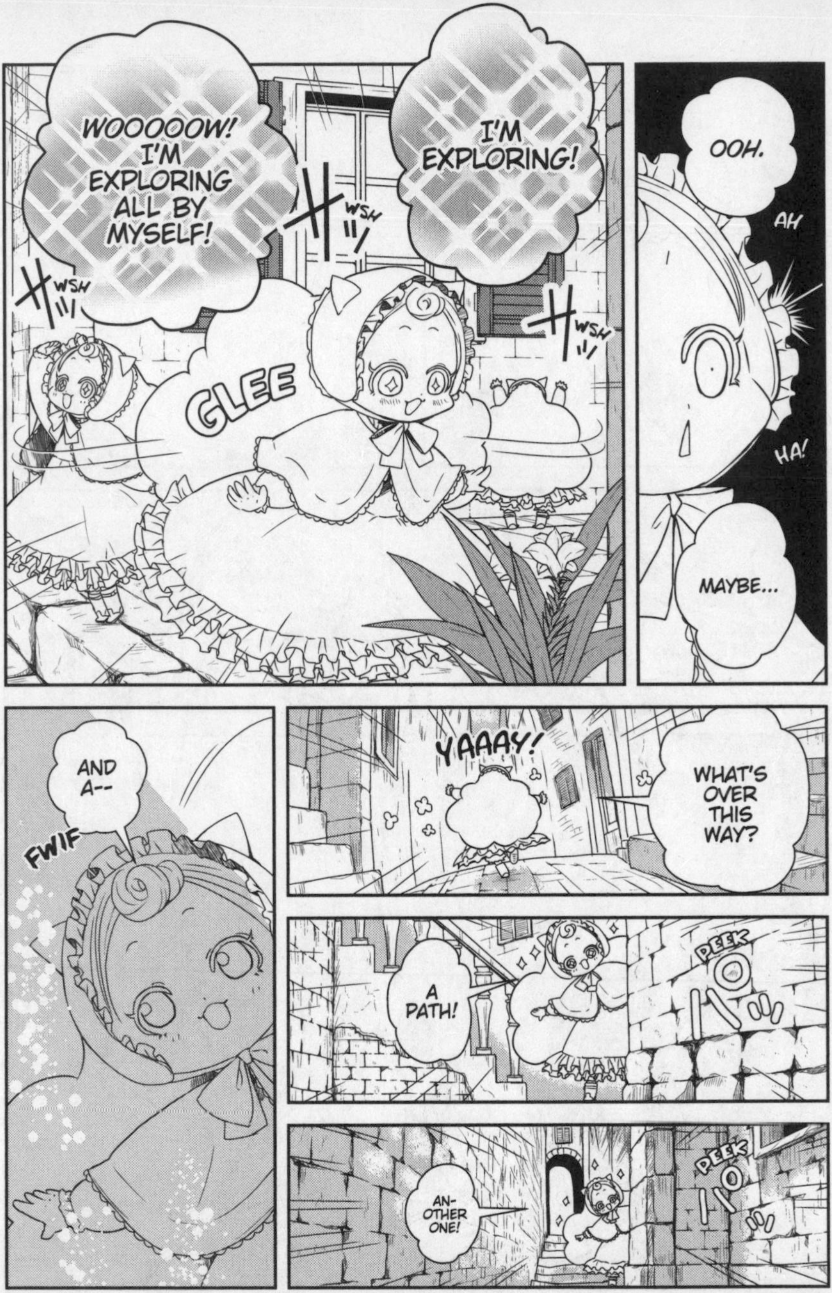
OOH.
AH
HA!
MAYBE...
I'M EXPLORING!
WSH
WOOOOOW! I'M EXPLORING ALL BY MYSELF!
WSH
WSH
GLEE
WHAT'S OVER THIS WAY?
YAAAY!
PEEK
A PATH!
PEEK
AN-OTHER ONE!
AND A--
FWIF

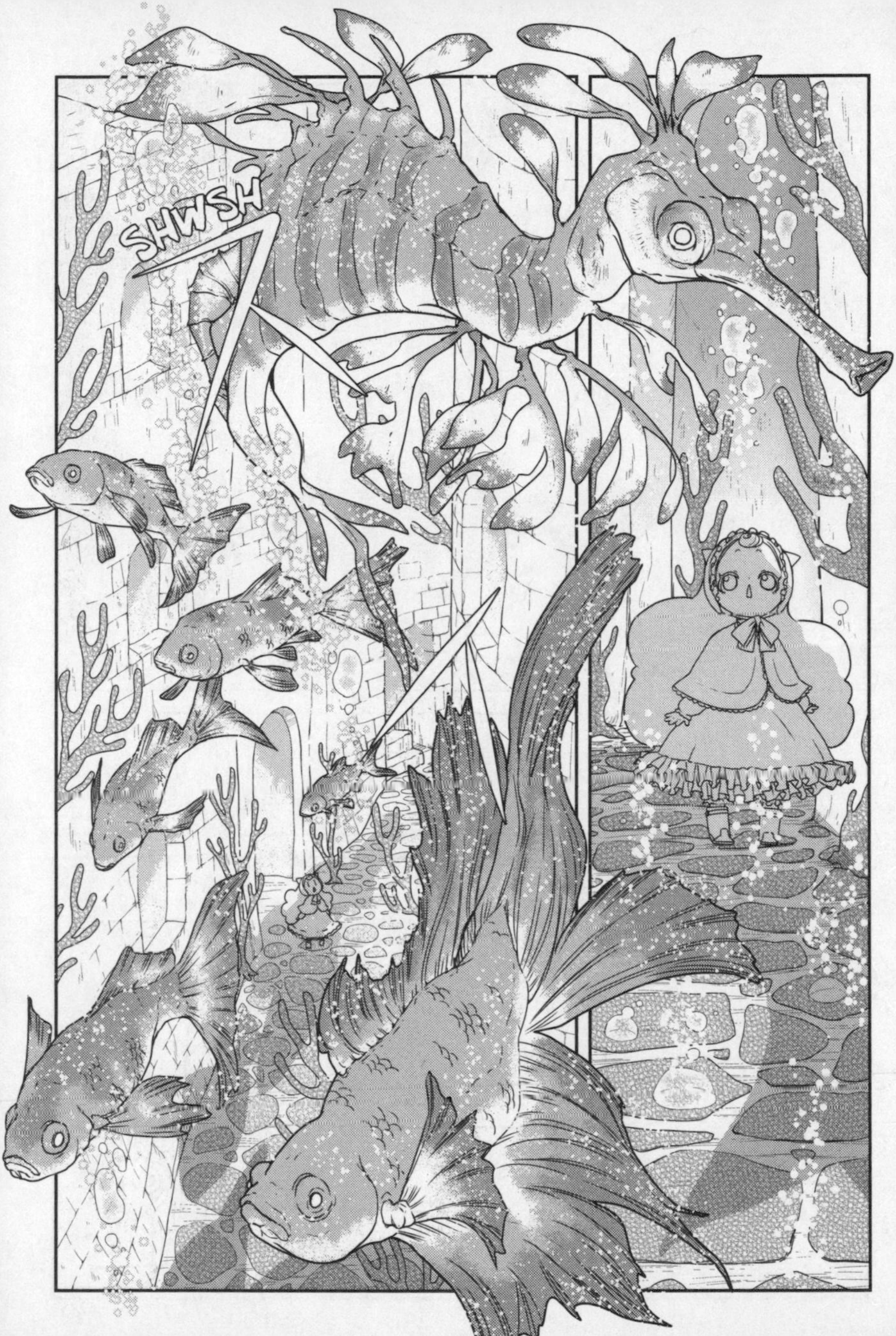
SHWSH

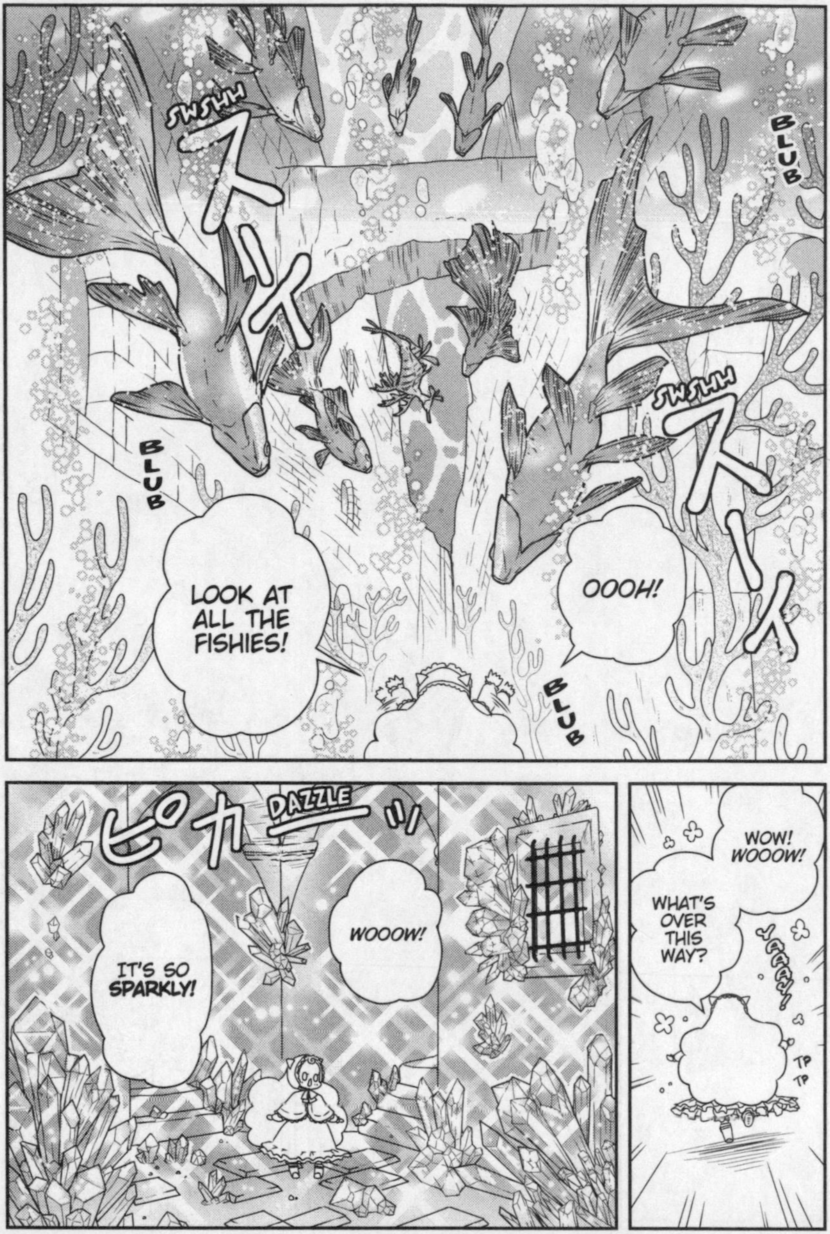
BLUB
SWSHH
スーイ
OOOH!
BLUB
SWSHH
スーイ
BLUB
LOOK AT ALL THE FISHIES!
WOW! WOOOW!
WHAT'S OVER THIS WAY?
YAAAY!
TP TP
ピカーッ
DAZZLE
WOOOW!
IT'S SO SPARKLY!

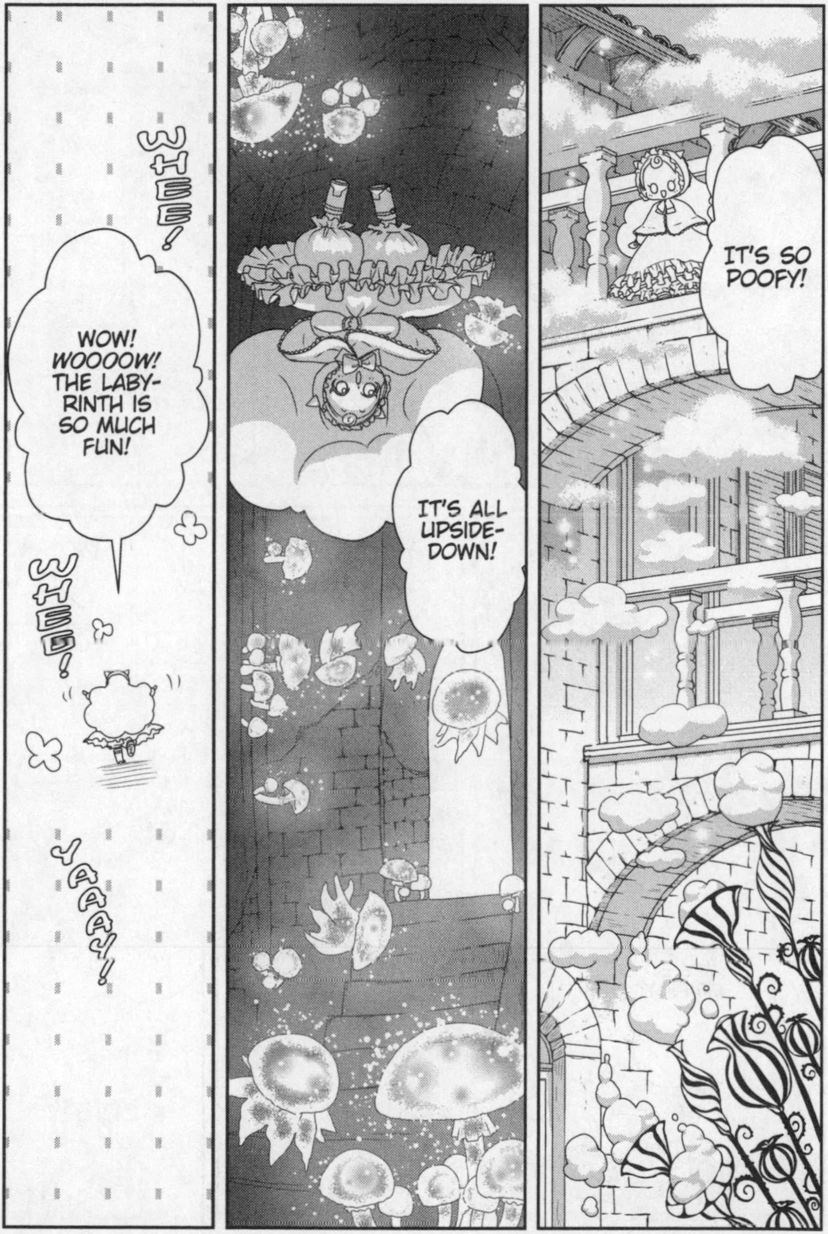
IT'S SO POOFY!
IT'S ALL UPSIDE-DOWN!
WHEE!
WOW! WOOOOW! THE LABY-RINTH IS SO MUCH FUN!
WHEE!
YAAAAY!

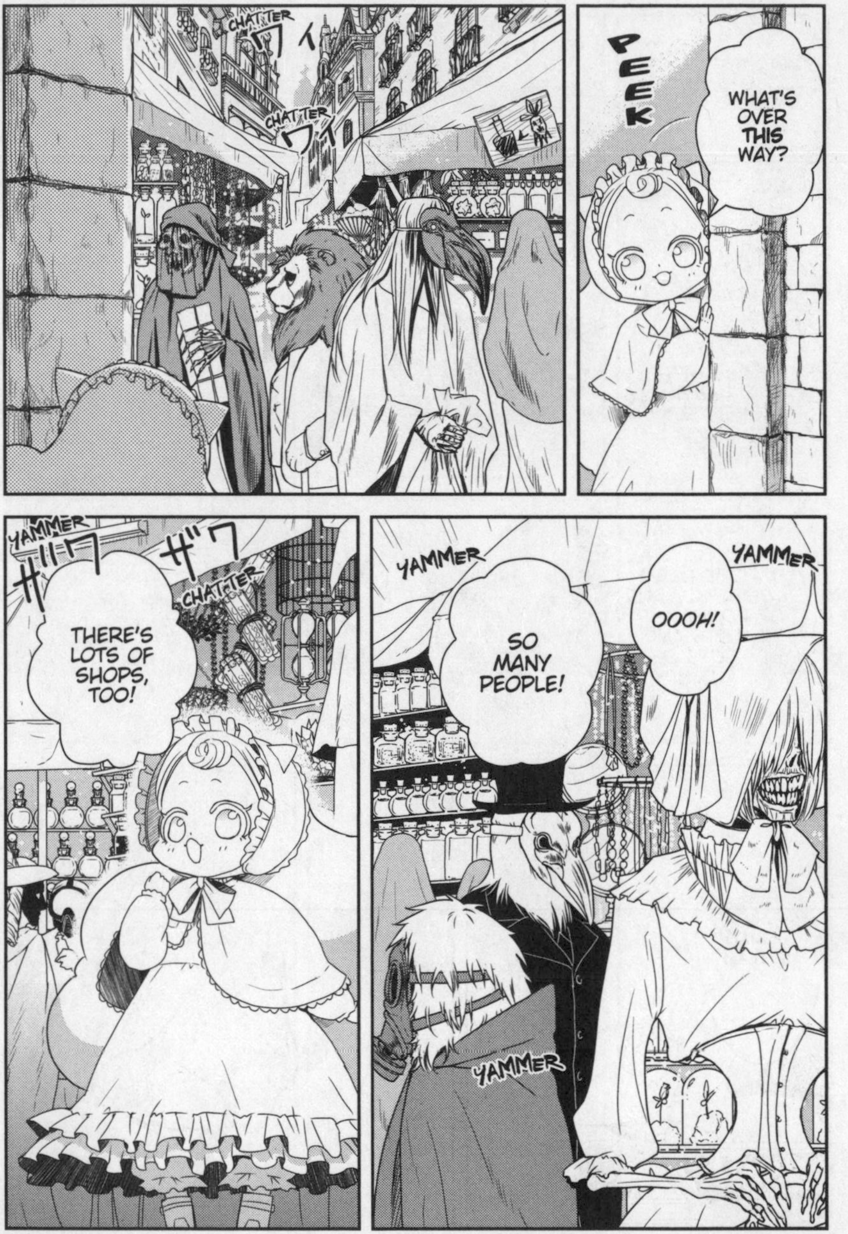
PEEK
WHAT'S OVER THIS WAY?
CHATTER ワイ
CHATTER ワイ
YAMMER
OOOH!
SO MANY PEOPLE!
YAMMER
YAMMER
YAMMER ザワ
ザワ
CHATTER
THERE'S LOTS OF SHOPS, TOO!

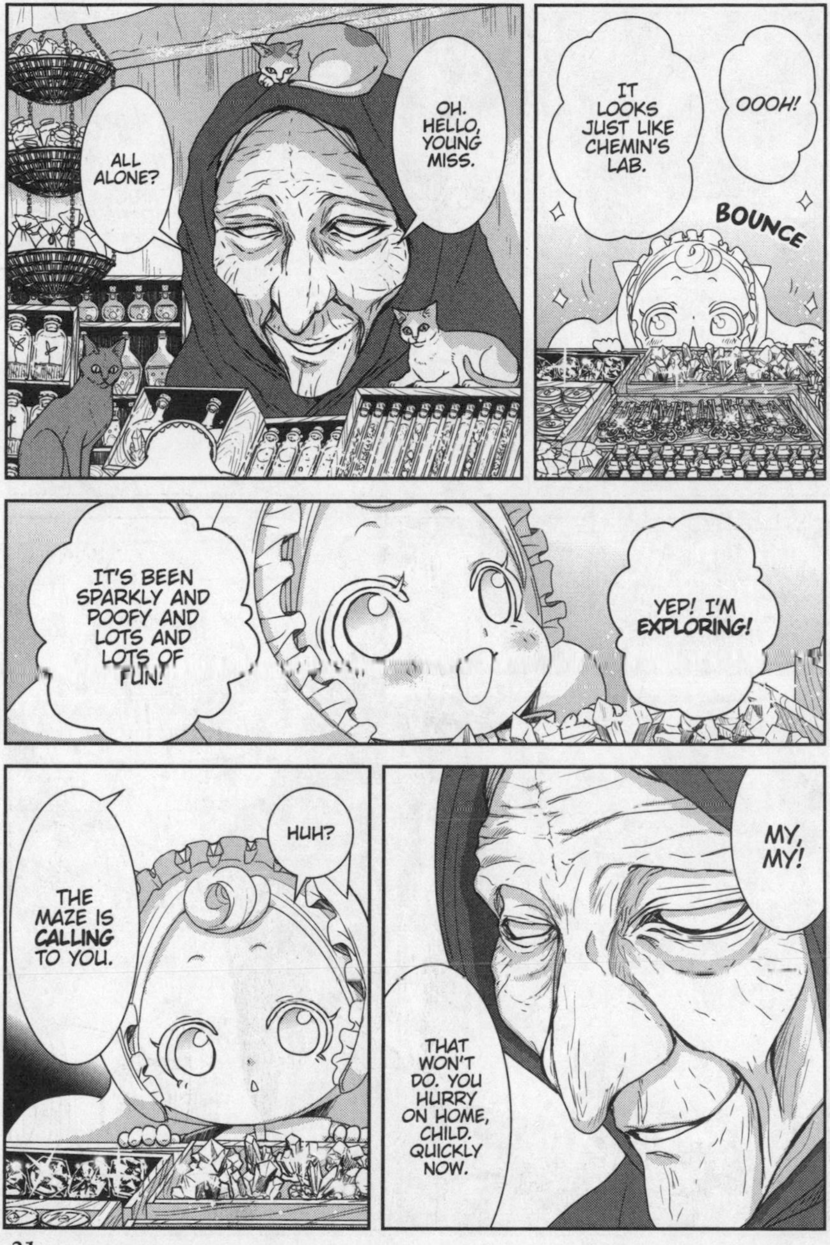
OOOH!
IT LOOKS JUST LIKE CHEMIN'S LAB.
BOUNCE
OH. HELLO, YOUNG MISS.
ALL ALONE?
YEP! I'M **EXPLORING!**
IT'S BEEN SPARKLY AND POOFY AND LOTS AND LOTS OF FUN!
MY, MY!
THAT WON'T DO. YOU HURRY ON HOME, CHILD. QUICKLY NOW.
HUH?
THE MAZE IS **CALLING** TO YOU.

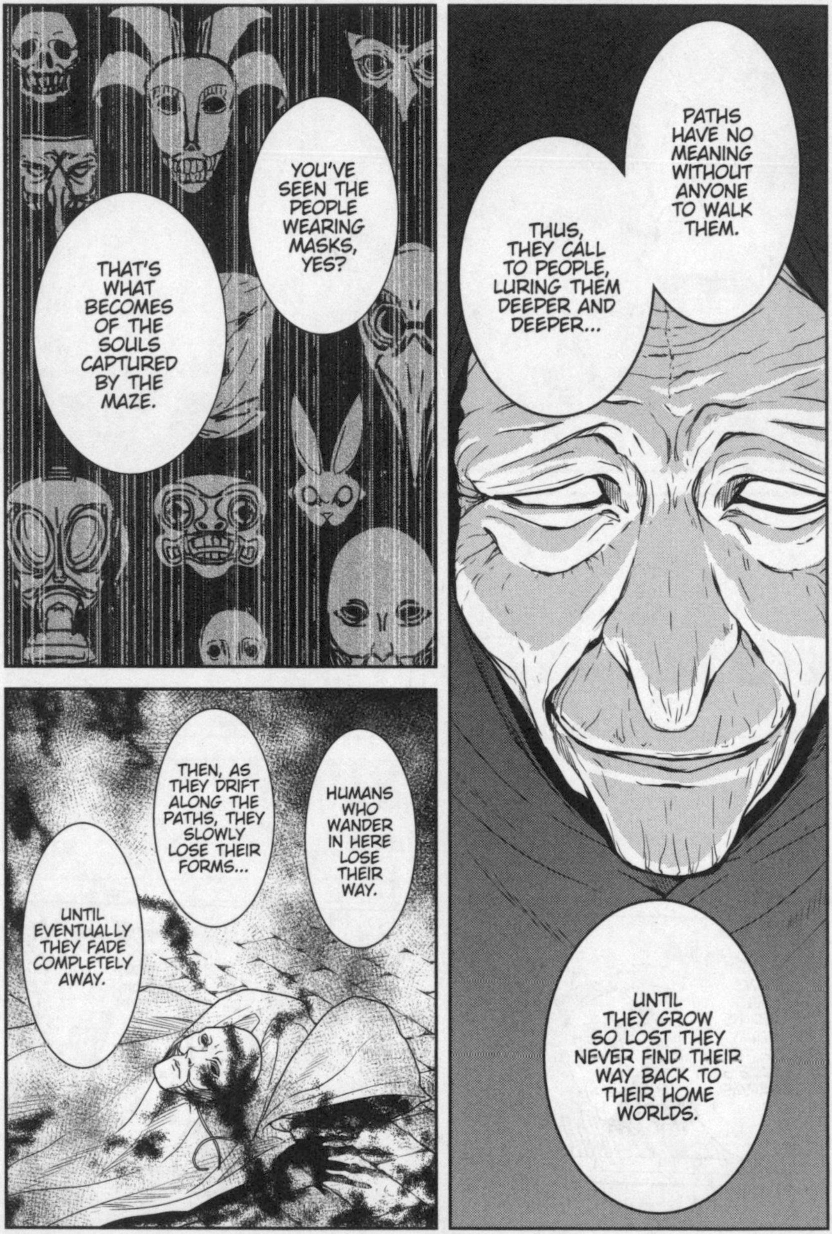
PATHS HAVE NO MEANING WITHOUT ANYONE TO WALK THEM.
THUS, THEY CALL TO PEOPLE, LURING THEM DEEPER AND DEEPER...
UNTIL THEY GROW SO LOST THEY NEVER FIND THEIR WAY BACK TO THEIR HOME WORLDS.
YOU'VE SEEN THE PEOPLE WEARING MASKS, YES?
THAT'S WHAT BECOMES OF THE SOULS CAPTURED BY THE MAZE.
HUMANS WHO WANDER IN HERE LOSE THEIR WAY.
THEN, AS THEY DRIFT ALONG THE PATHS, THEY SLOWLY LOSE THEIR FORMS...
UNTIL EVENTUALLY THEY FADE COMPLETELY AWAY.

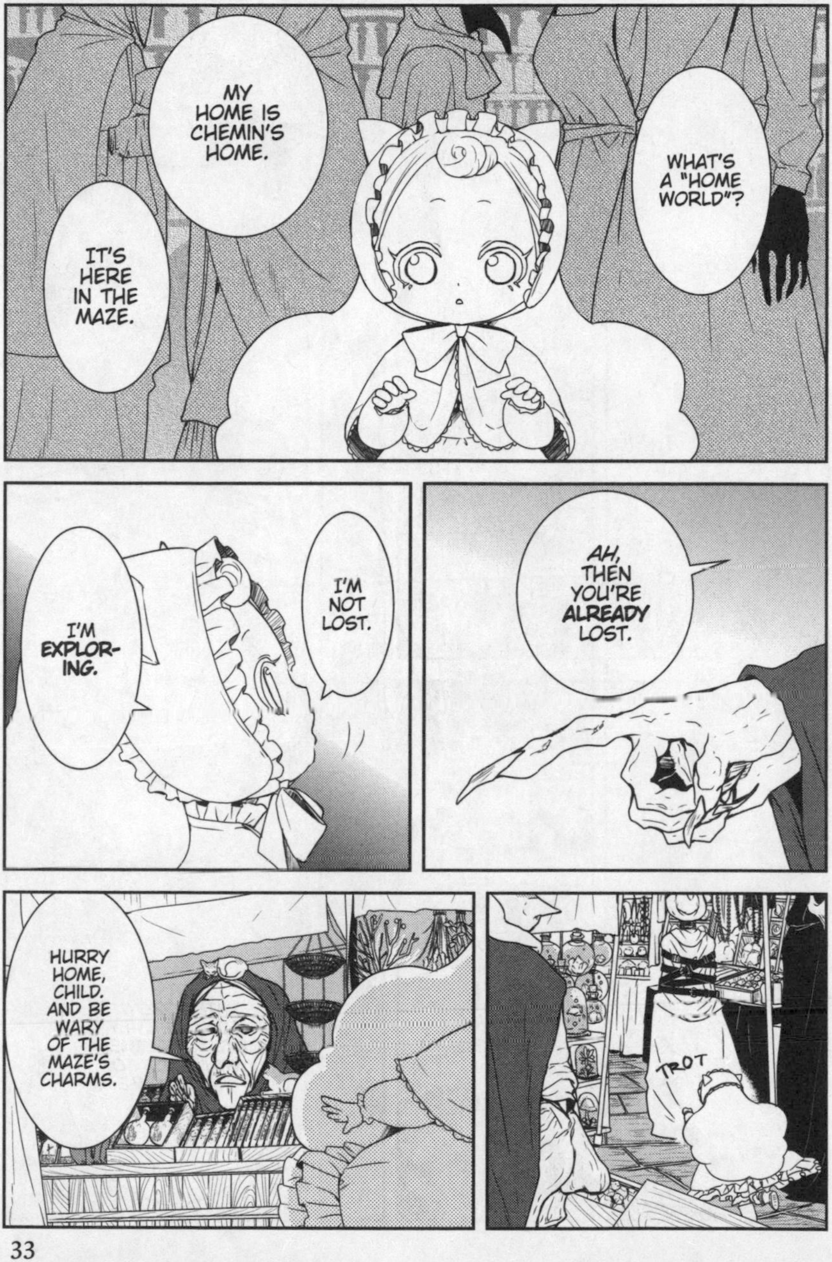
WHAT'S A "HOME WORLD"?
MY HOME IS CHEMIN'S HOME.
IT'S HERE IN THE MAZE.
AH, THEN YOU'RE **ALREADY** LOST.
I'M NOT LOST.
I'M **EXPLORING.**
TROT
HURRY HOME, CHILD. AND BE WARY OF THE MAZE'S CHARMS.

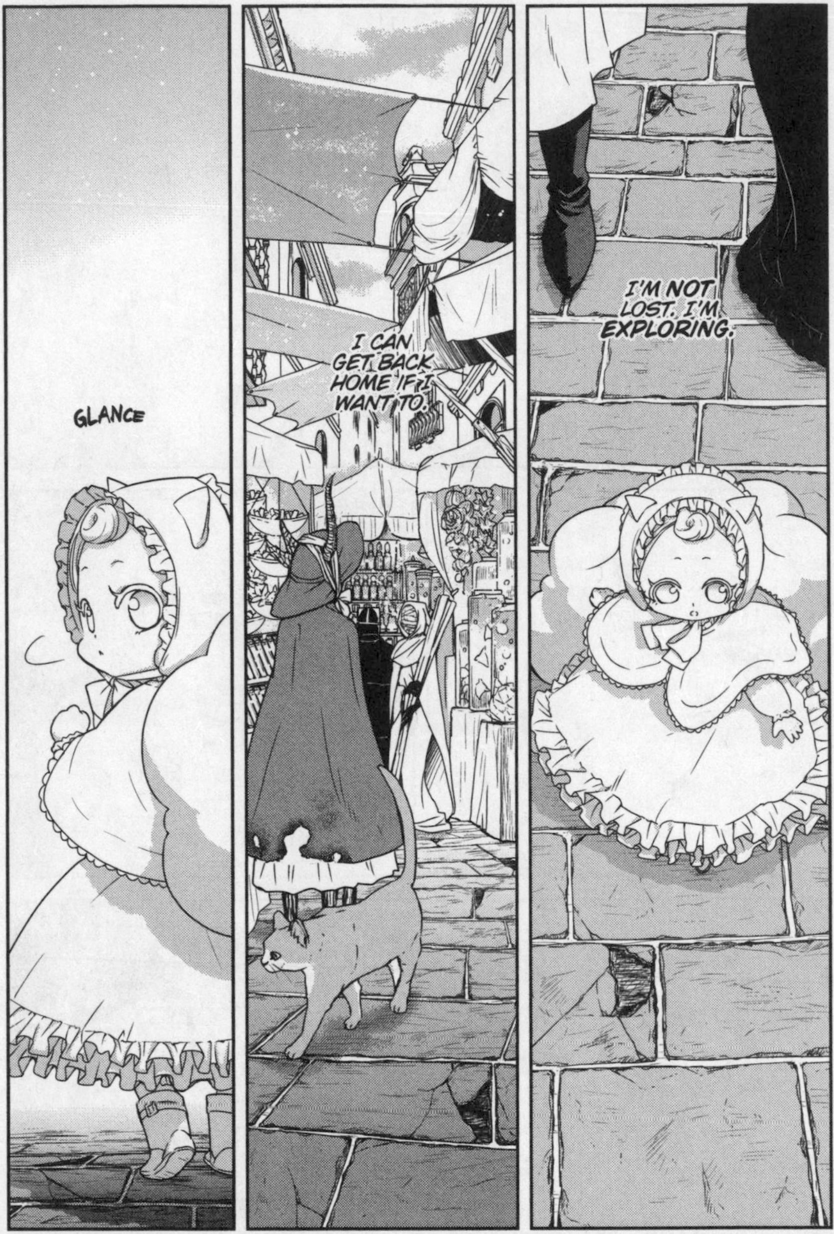
I'M NOT LOST. I'M EXPLORING.
I CAN GET BACK HOME IF I WANT TO.
GLANCE

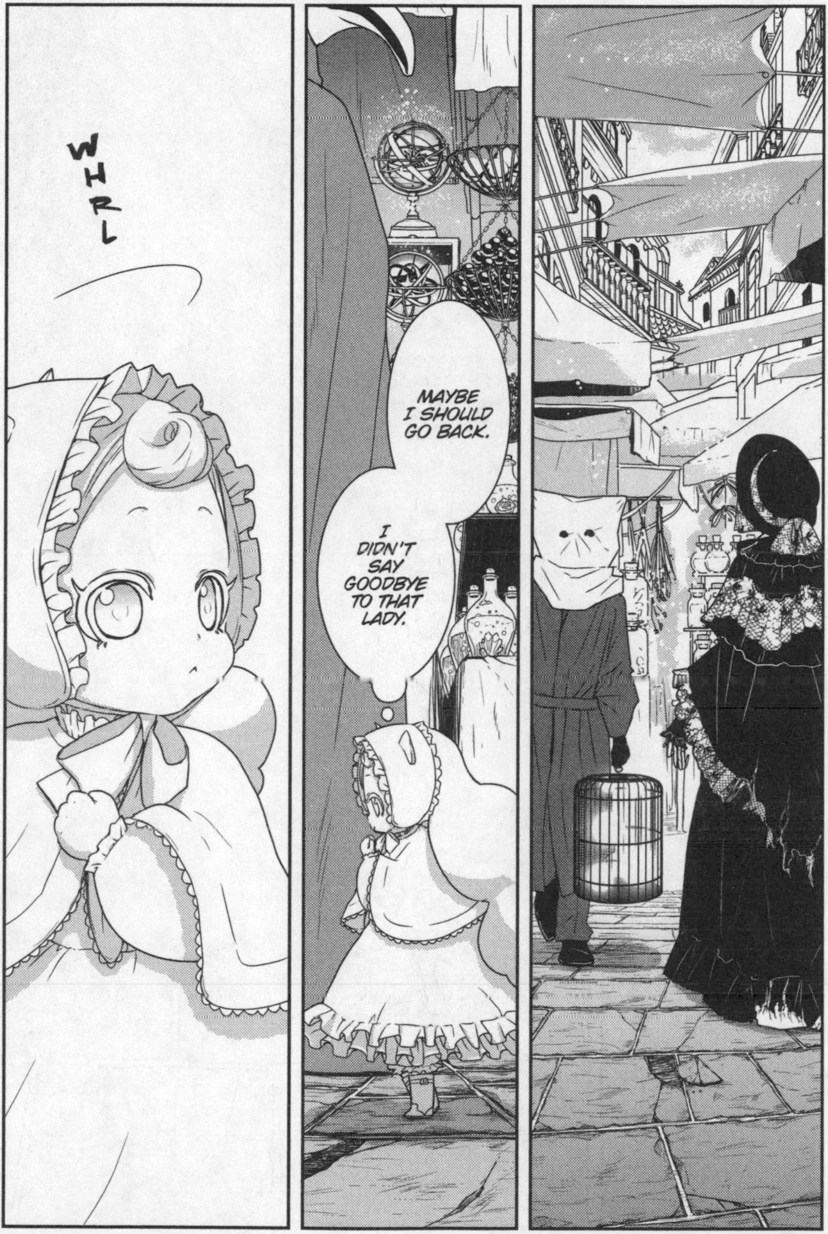
MAYBE I SHOULD GO BACK.
I DIDN'T SAY GOODBYE TO THAT LADY.
WHRL

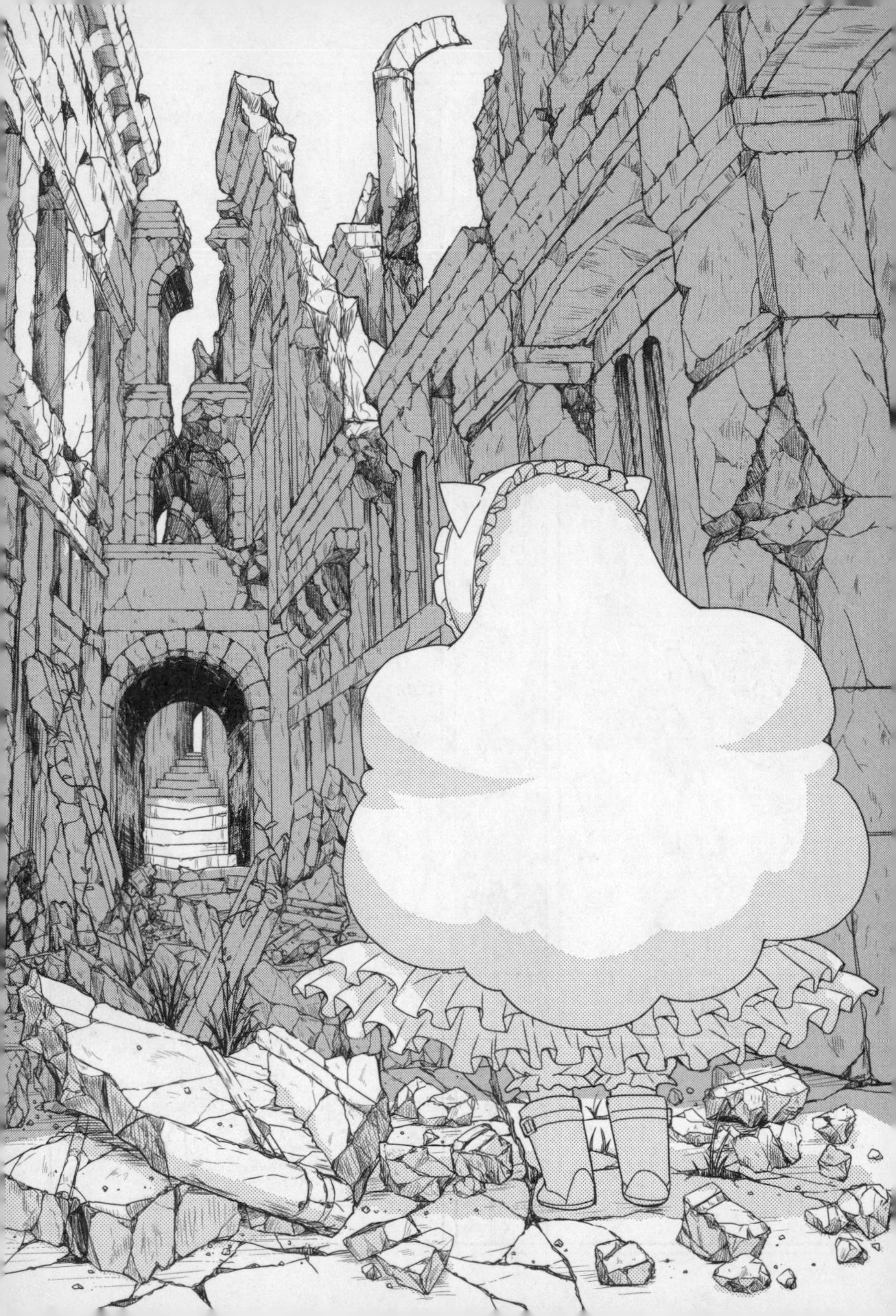

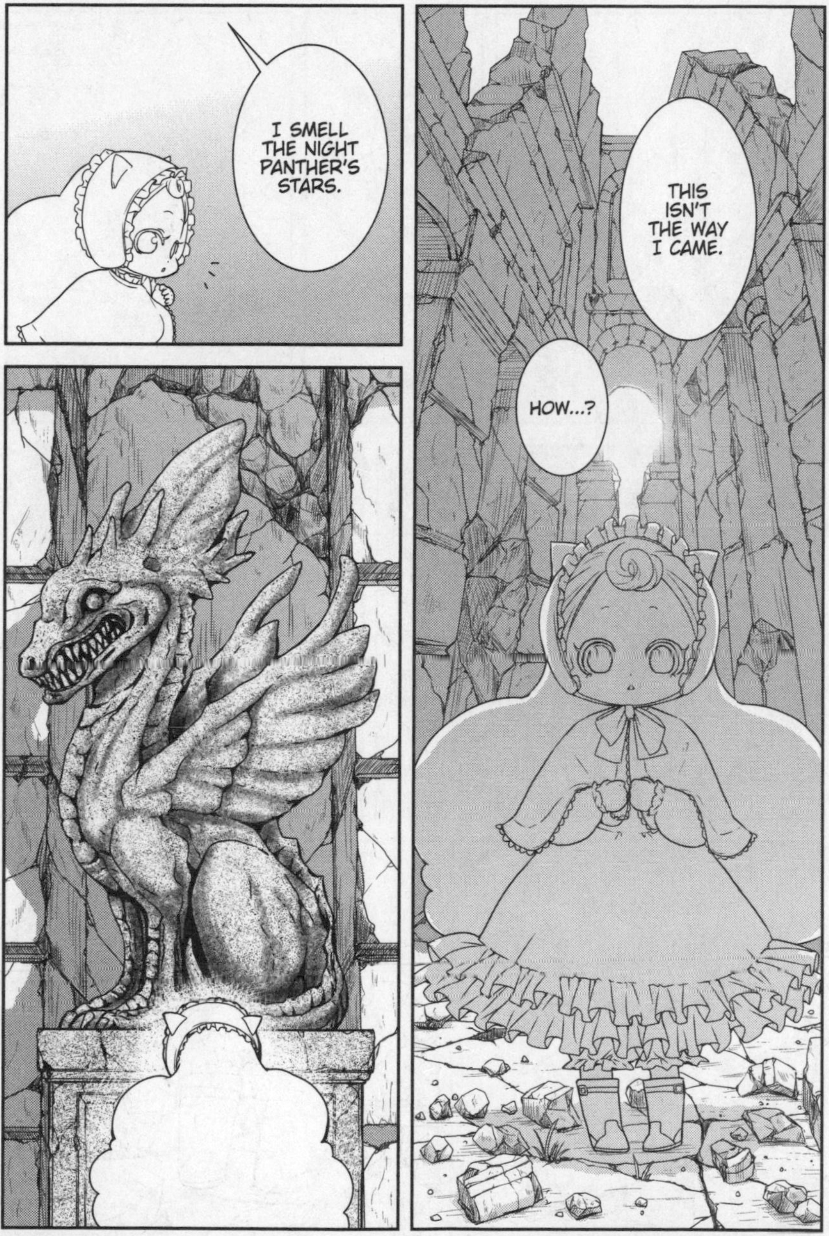
THIS ISN'T THE WAY I CAME.
HOW...?
I SMELL THE NIGHT PANTHER'S STARS.

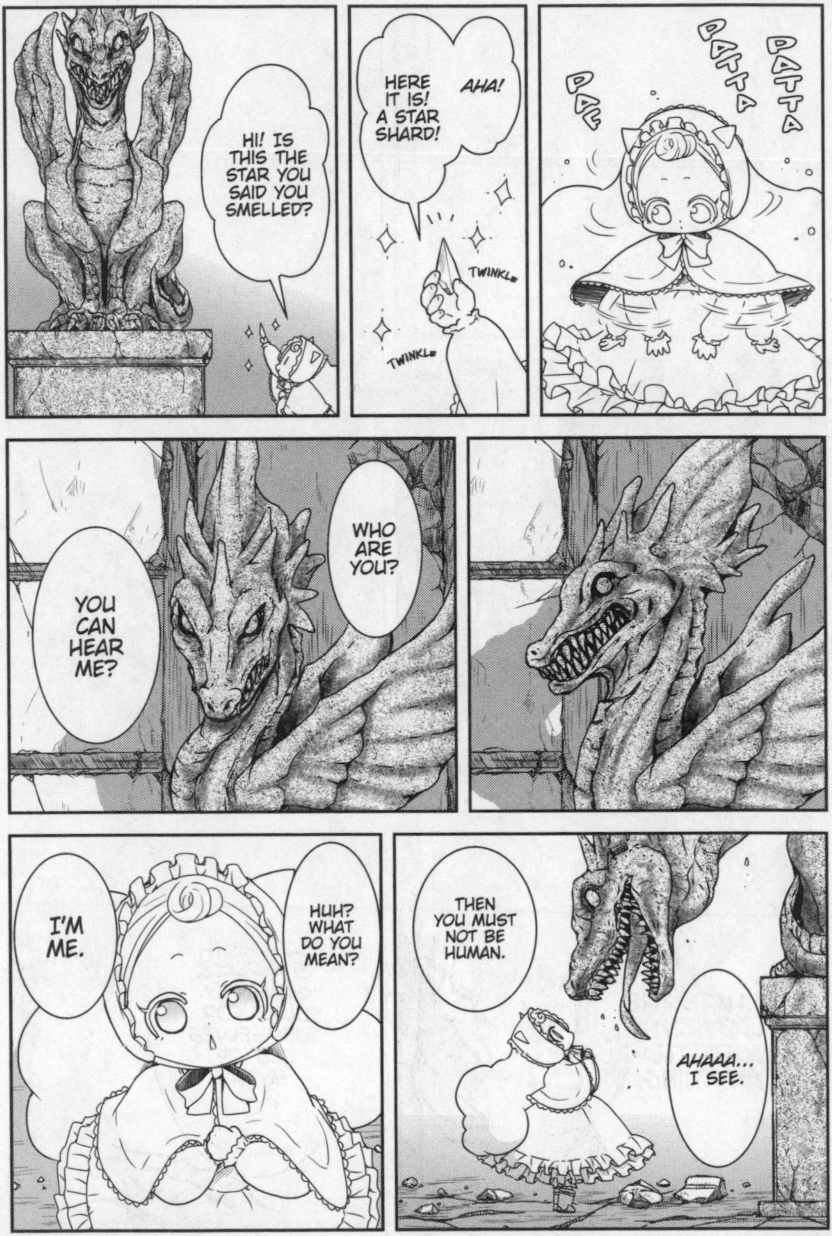
PATTA
PATTA
PA
AHA!
HERE IT IS! A STAR SHARD!
TWINKLE
TWINKLE
HI! IS THIS THE STAR YOU SAID YOU SMELLED?
WHO ARE YOU?
YOU CAN HEAR ME?
THEN YOU MUST NOT BE HUMAN.
AHAAA... I SEE.
HUH? WHAT DO YOU MEAN?
I'M ME.

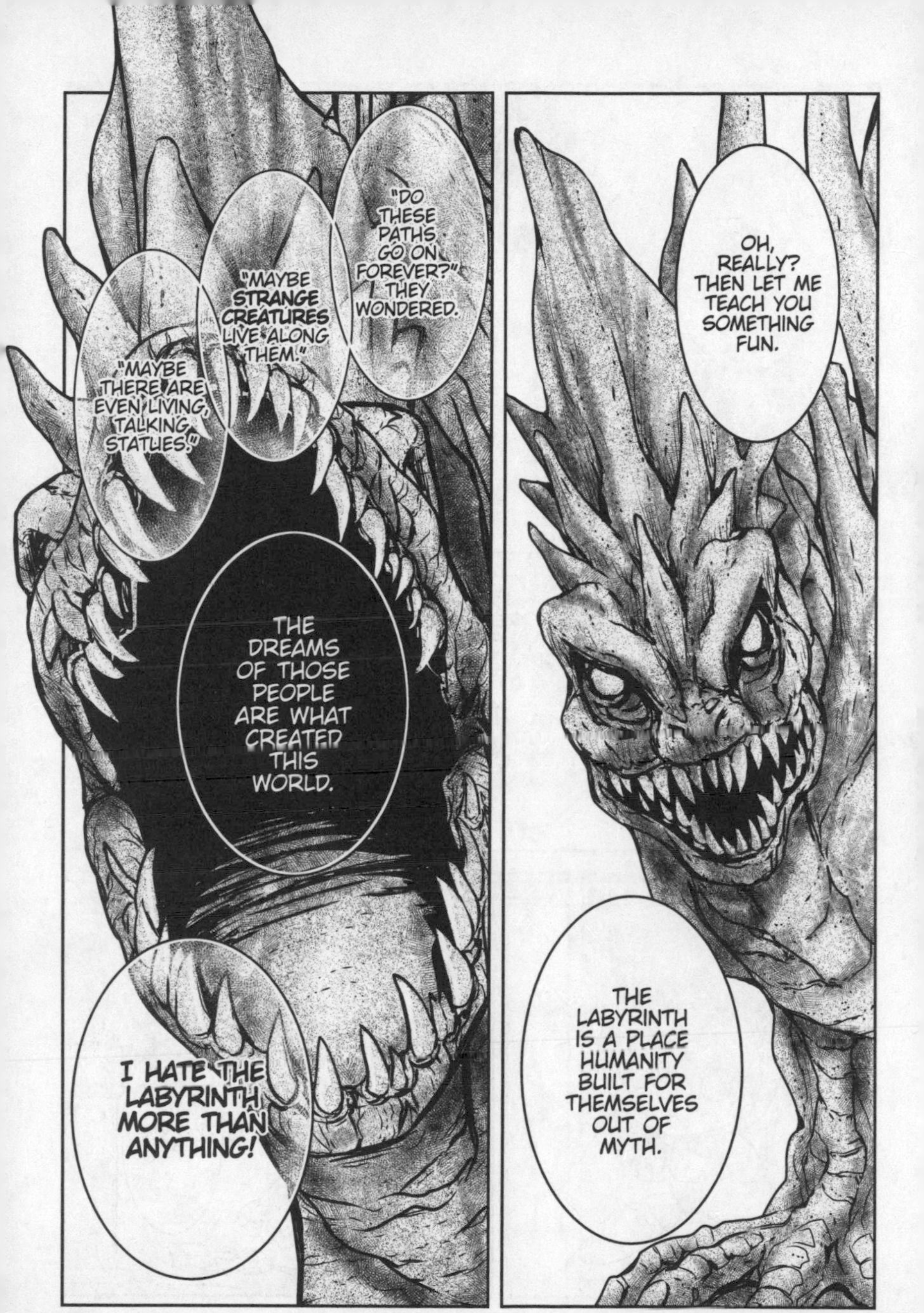
OH, REALLY? THEN LET ME TEACH YOU SOMETHING FUN.
THE LABYRINTH IS A PLACE HUMANITY BUILT FOR THEMSELVES OUT OF MYTH.
"DO THESE PATHS GO ON FOREVER?" THEY WONDERED.
"MAYBE STRANGE CREATURES LIVE ALONG THEM."
"MAYBE THERE ARE EVEN LIVING, TALKING STATUES."
THE DREAMS OF THOSE PEOPLE ARE WHAT CREATED THIS WORLD.
I HATE THE LABYRINTH MORE THAN ANYTHING!

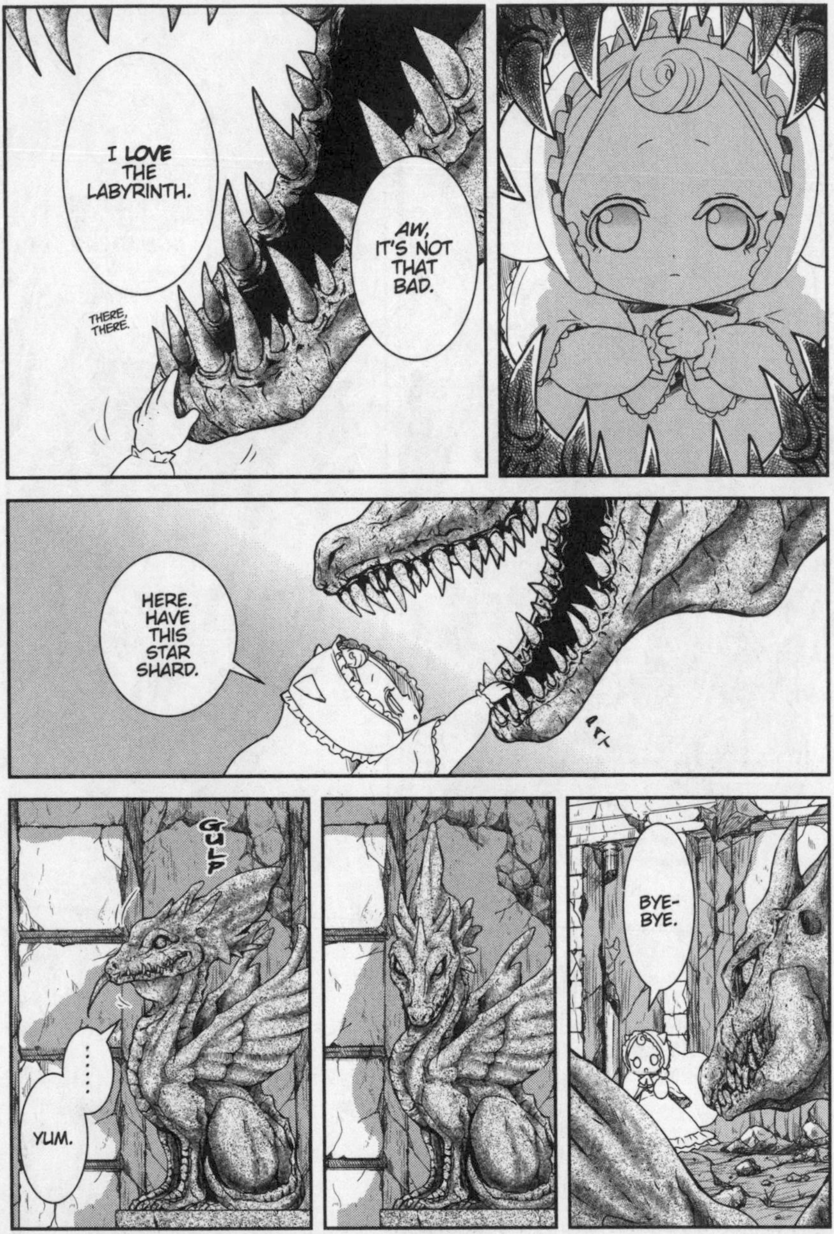
AW, IT'S NOT THAT BAD.
I LOVE THE LABYRINTH.
THERE, THERE.
HERE. HAVE THIS STAR SHARD.
BYE-BYE.
GULP
......
YUM.

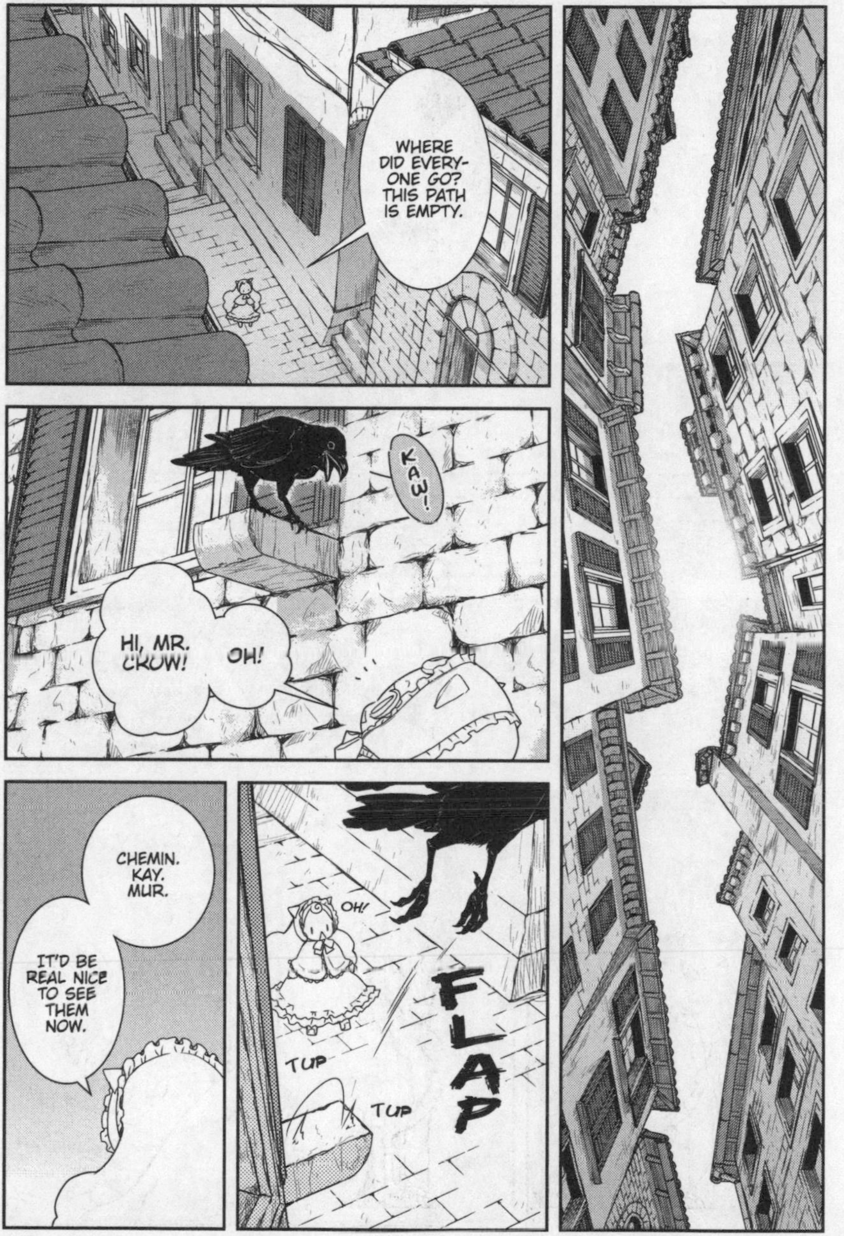
WHERE DID EVERY-ONE GO? THIS PATH IS EMPTY.
KAW!
OH!
HI, MR. CROW!
OH!
FLAP
TUP
TUP
CHEMIN. KAY. MUR.
IT'D BE REAL NICE TO SEE THEM NOW.

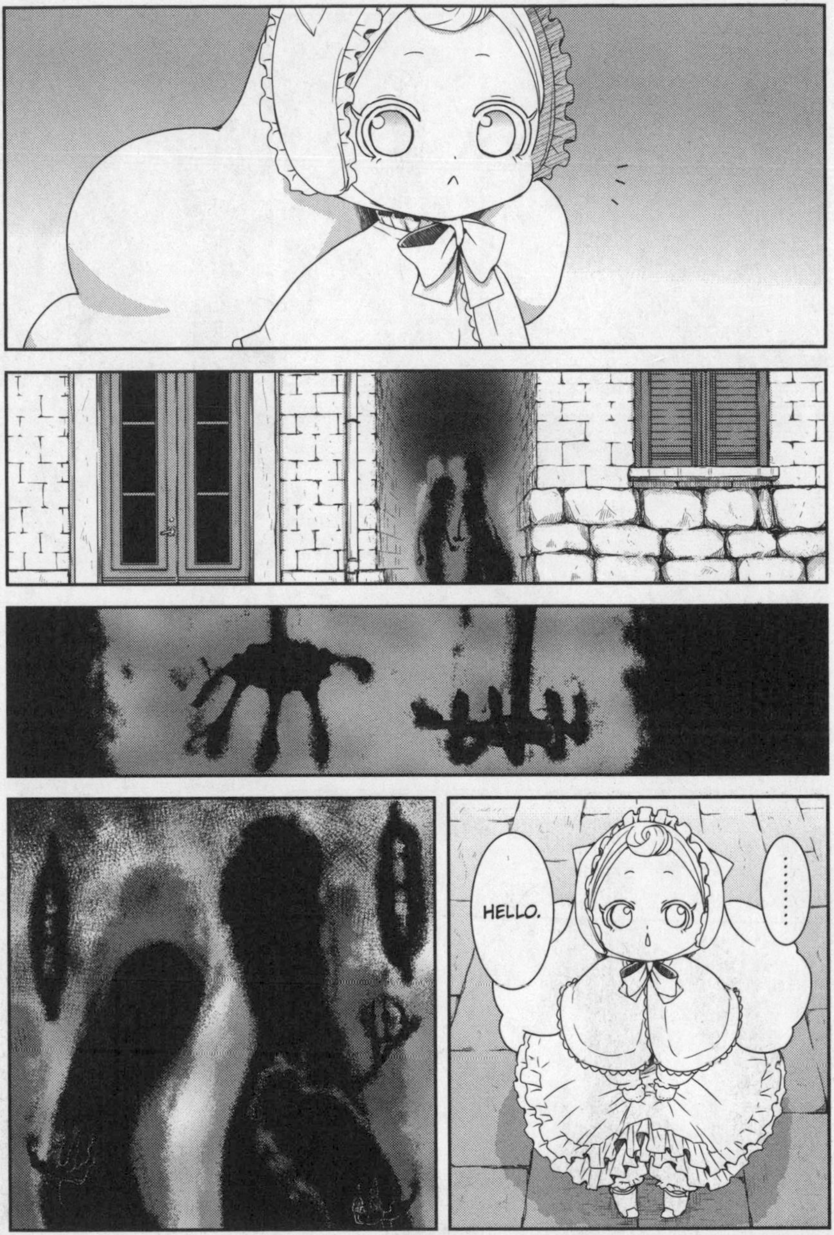
......
HELLO.

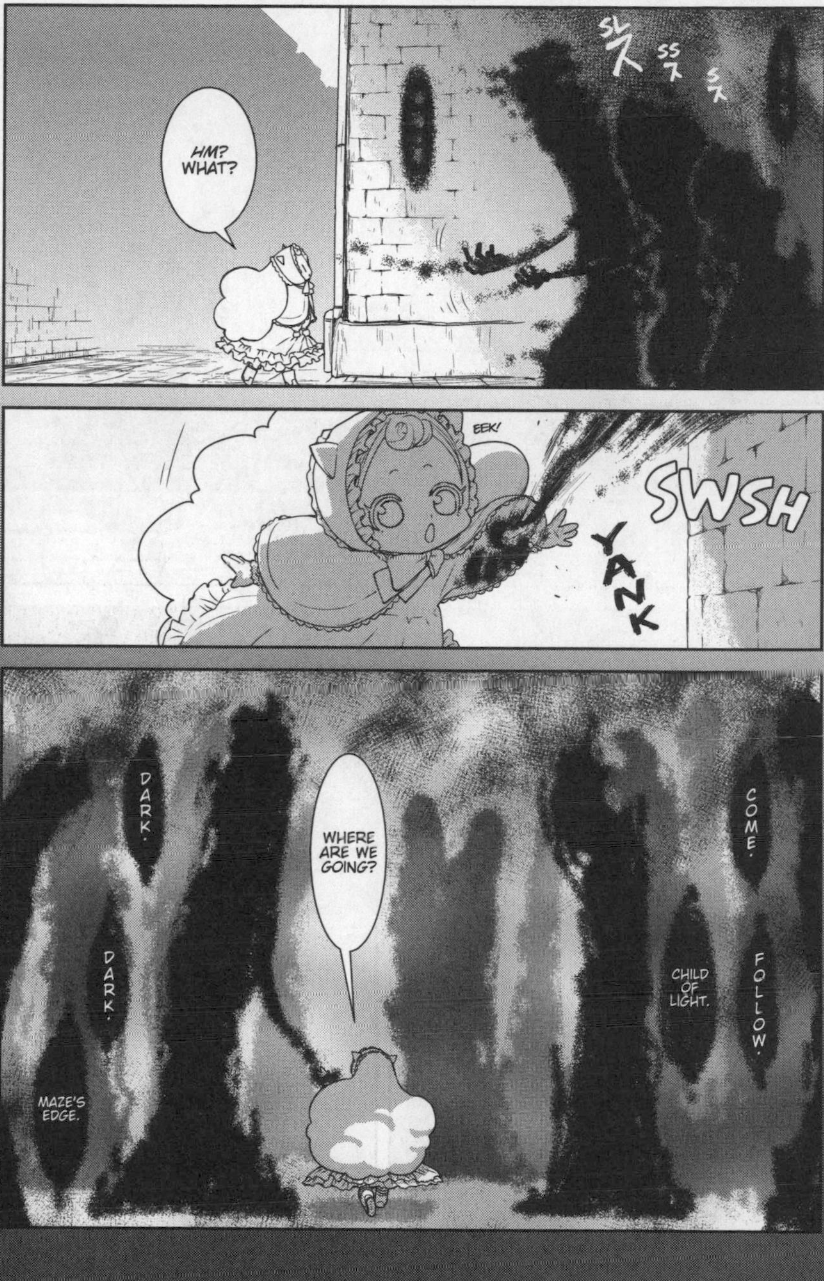
SL ス
SS ス
S ス
HM? WHAT?
EEK!
SWSH
YANK
COME.
FOLLOW.
CHILD OF LIGHT.
WHERE ARE WE GOING?
DARK.
DARK.
MAZE'S EDGE.

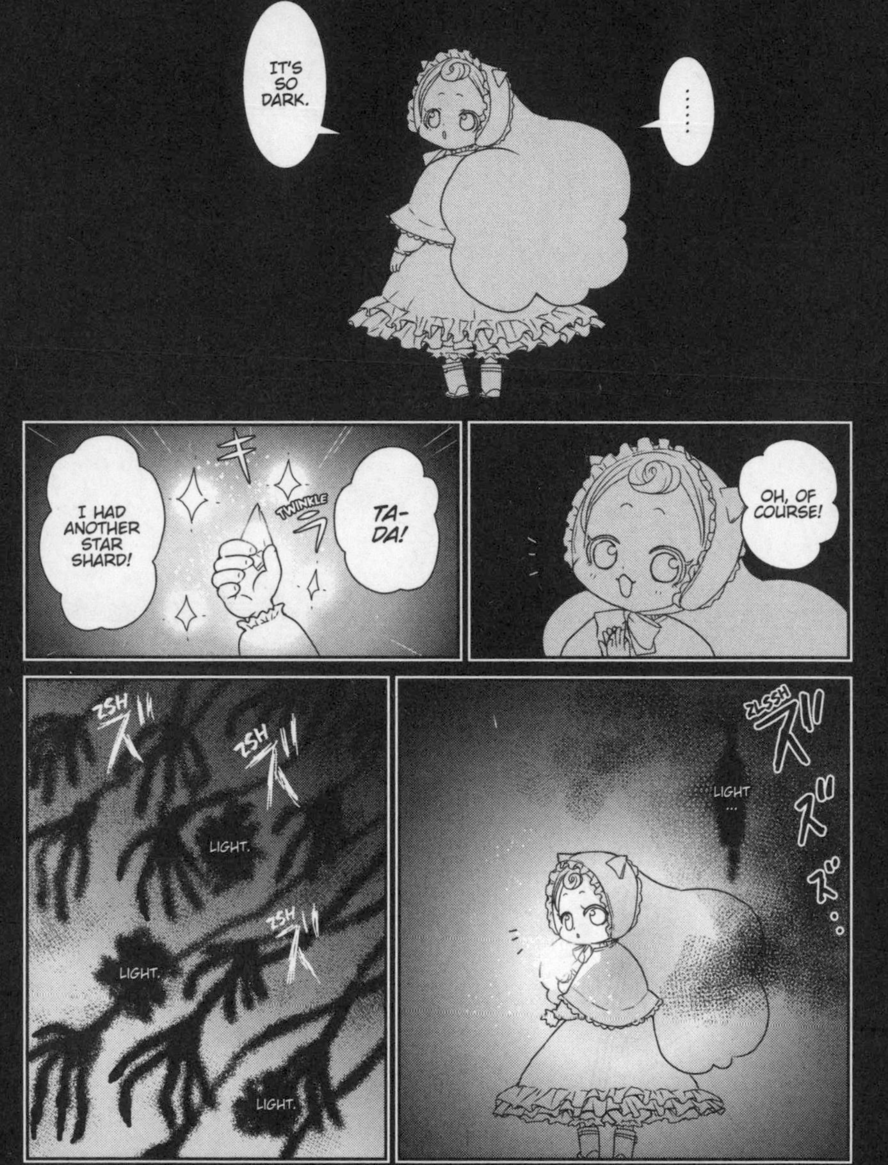
IT'S SO DARK.
......
OH, OF COURSE!
TA-DA!
TWINKLE
I HAD ANOTHER STAR SHARD!
ZLSSH
LIGHT ...
ZSH
ZSH
LIGHT.
ZSH
LIGHT.
LIGHT.

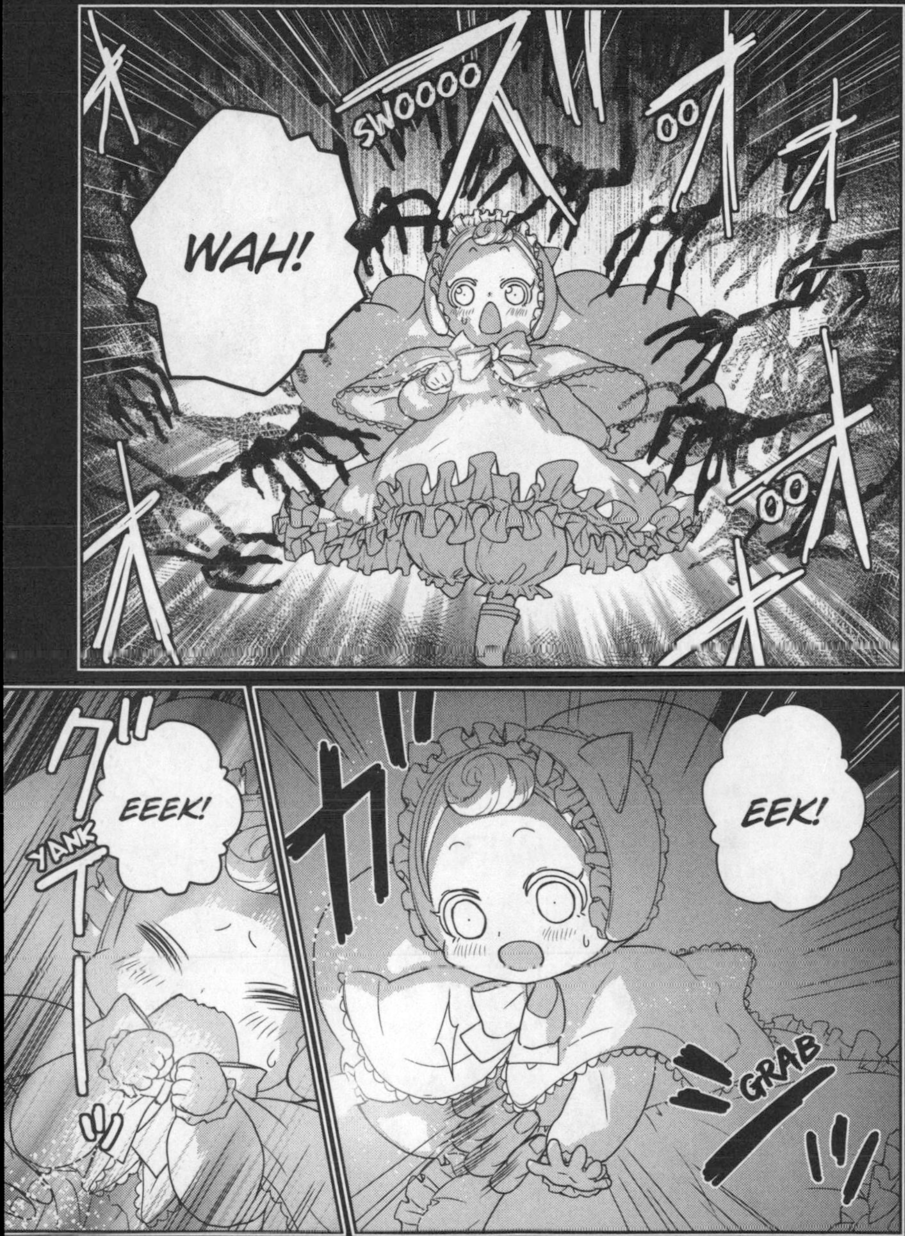
OO
SWOOOO
WAH!
OO
EEK!
GRAB
EEEK!
YANK

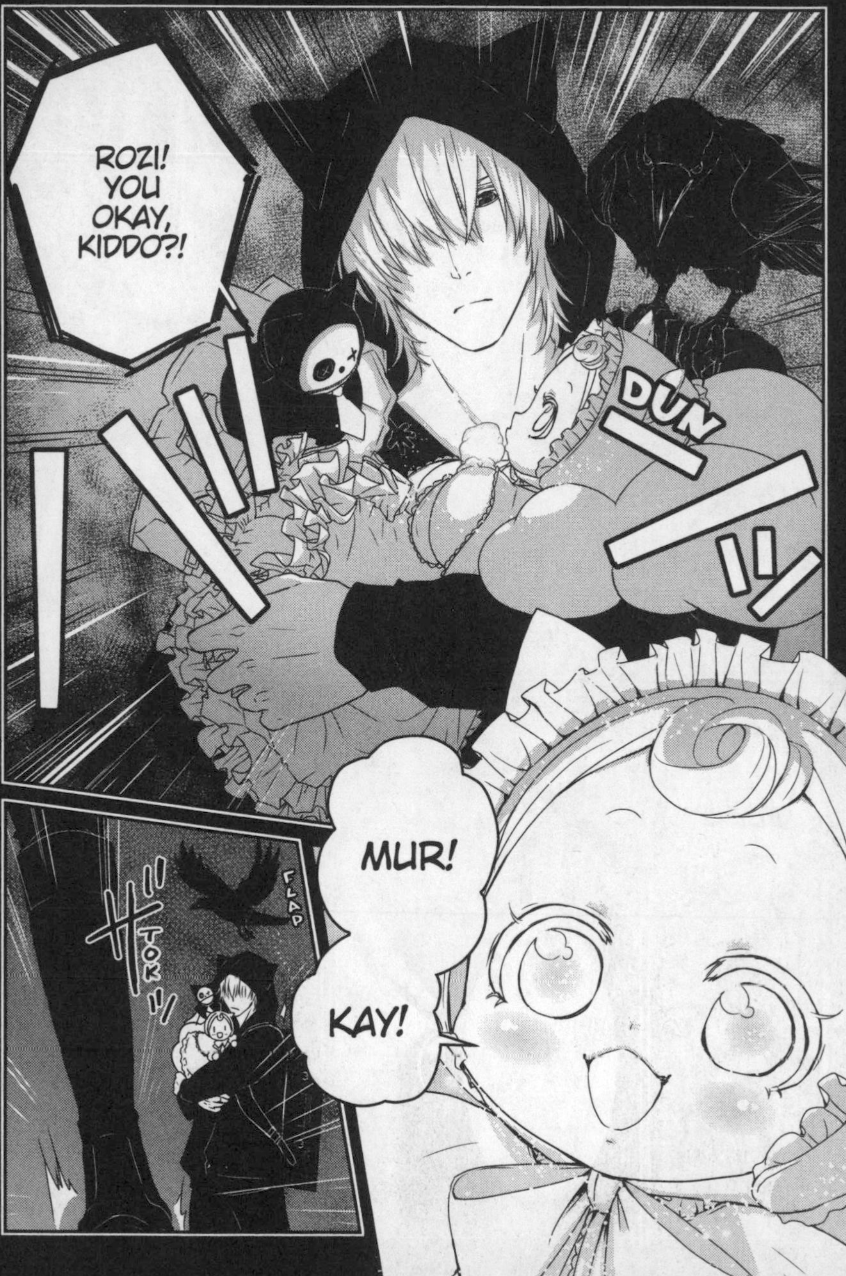
ROZI! YOU OKAY, KIDDO?!
DUN
MUR!
KAY!
FLAP
TOK

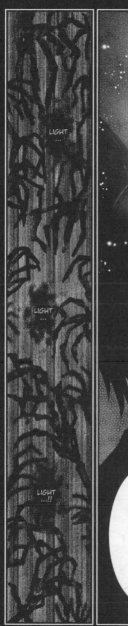

LIGHT
...

LIGHT
...

LIGHT
...!!

HOW IRONIC. THOUGH GIVEN BODIES OF DARKNESS...

YOU STILL YEARN FOR THE LIGHT.

GLEAM

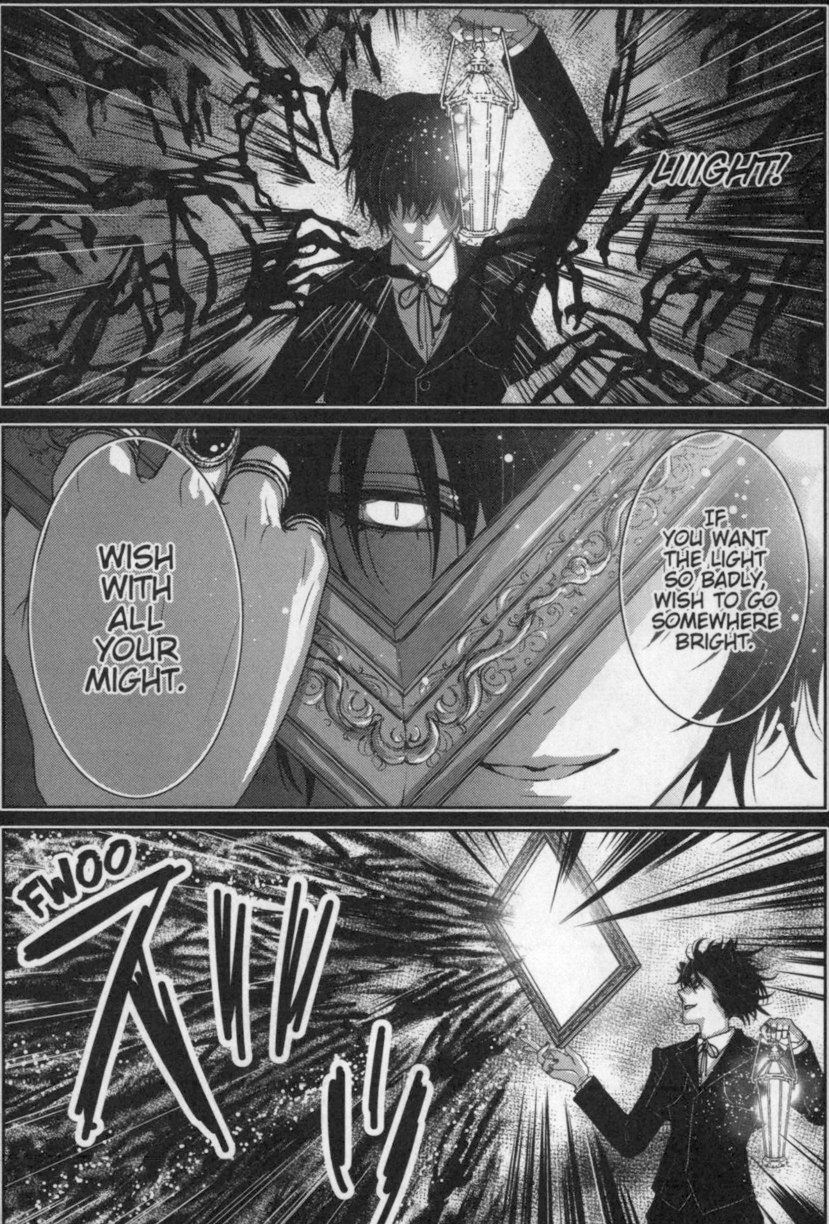
LIIIGHT!
IF YOU WANT THE LIGHT SO BADLY, WISH TO GO SOMEWHERE BRIGHT.
WISH WITH ALL YOUR MIGHT.
FWOO

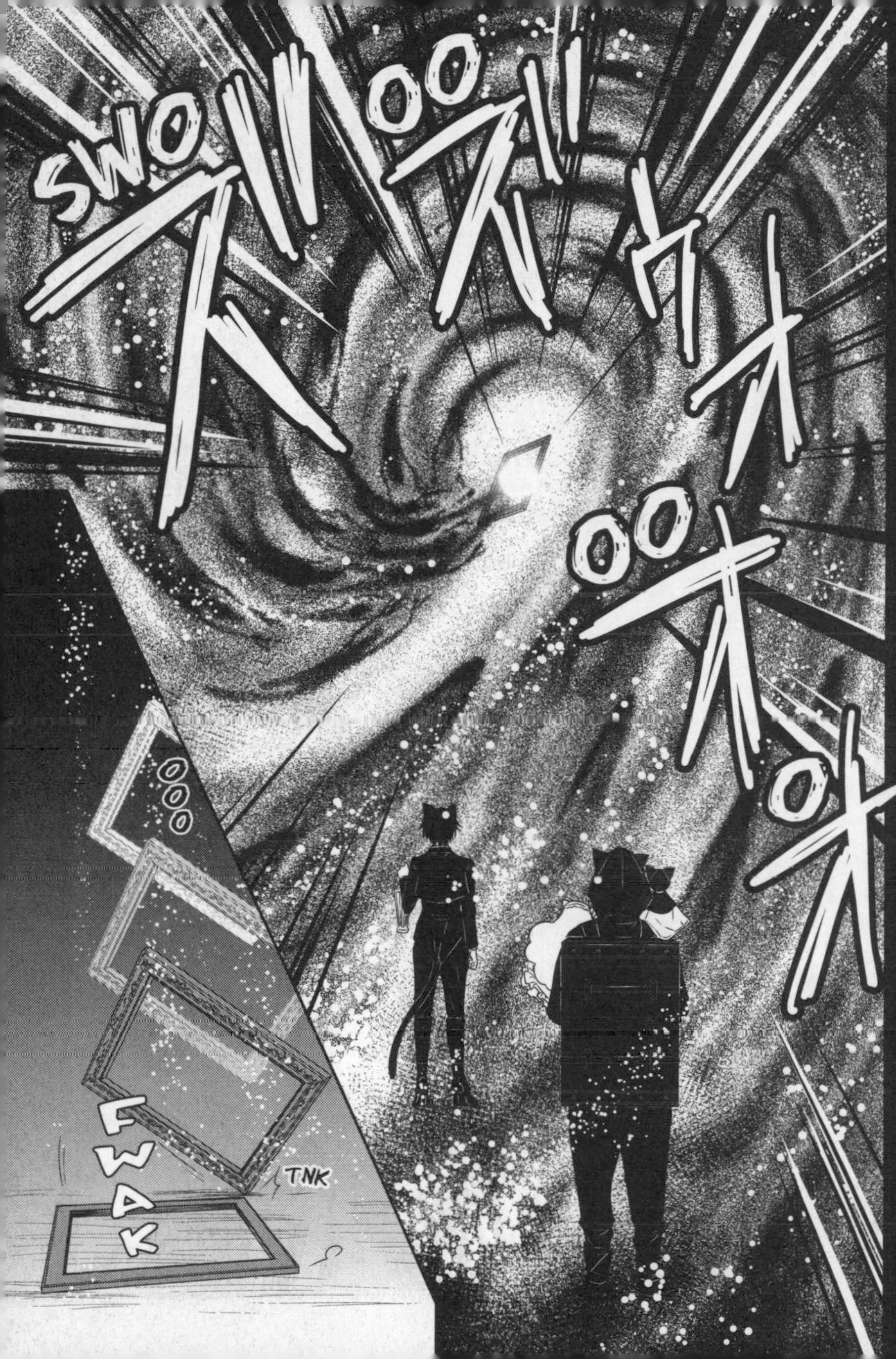
SWOOOOOO
OOO
FWAK
TNK

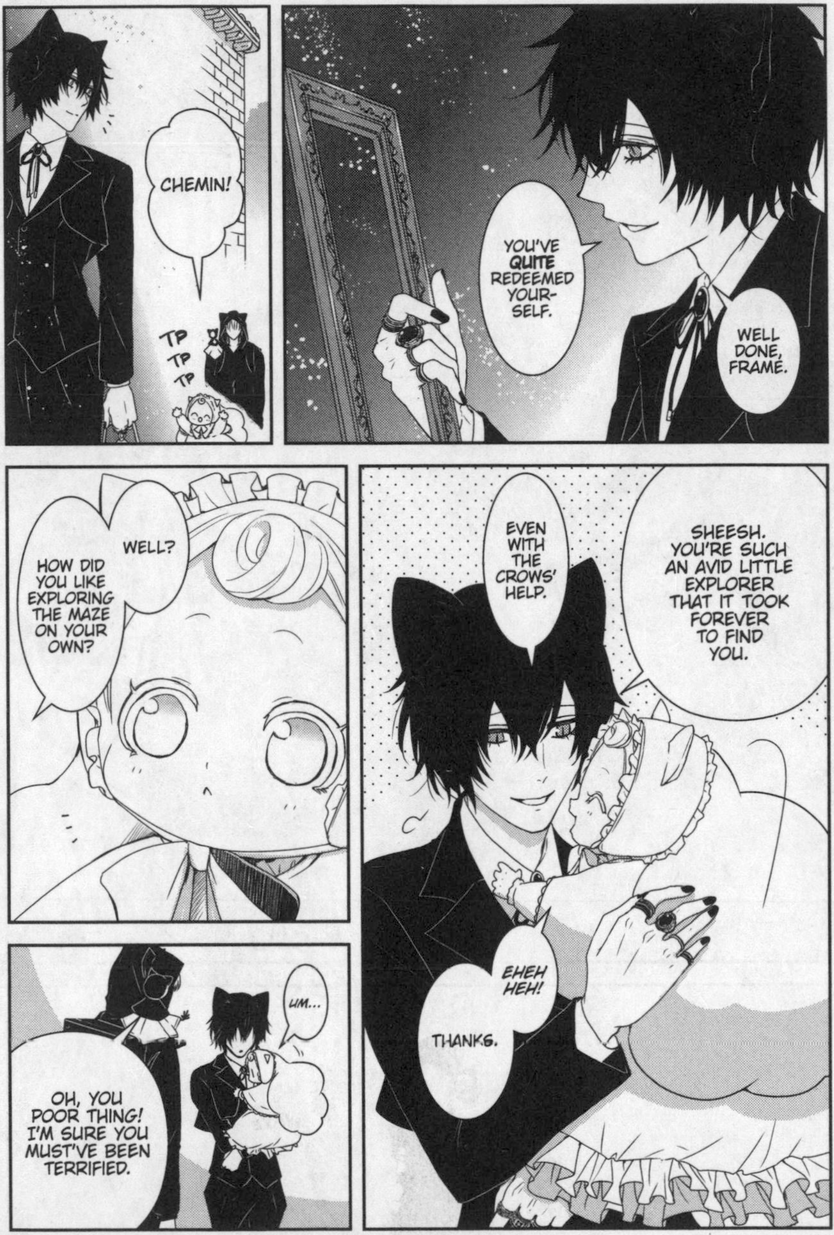
WELL DONE, FRAME.
YOU'VE QUITE REDEEMED YOURSELF.
CHEMIN!
TP TP TP
SHEESH. YOU'RE SUCH AN AVID LITTLE EXPLORER THAT IT TOOK FOREVER TO FIND YOU.
EVEN WITH THE CROWS' HELP.
EHEH HEH!
THANKS.
WELL?
HOW DID YOU LIKE EXPLORING THE MAZE ON YOUR OWN?
UM...
OH, YOU POOR THING! I'M SURE YOU MUST'VE BEEN TERRIFIED.

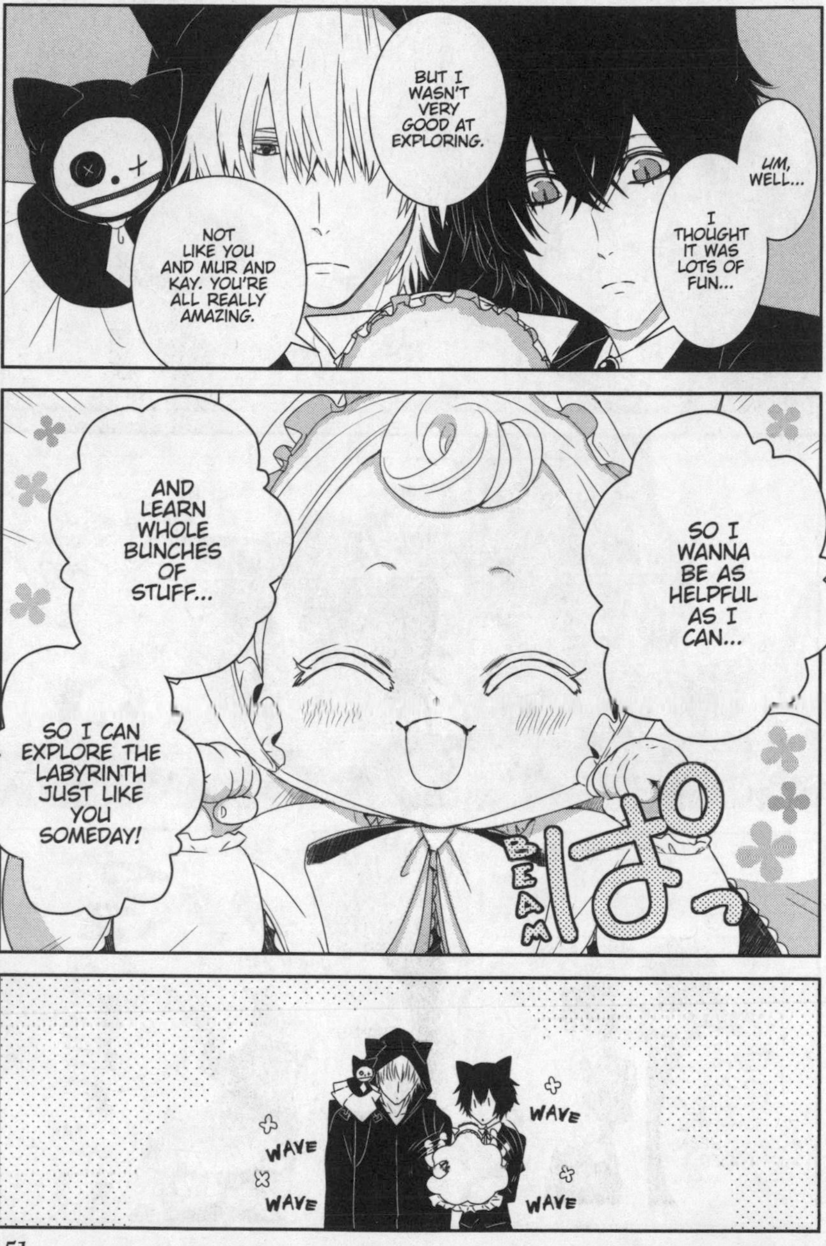
UM, WELL...
I THOUGHT IT WAS LOTS OF FUN...
BUT I WASN'T VERY GOOD AT EXPLORING.
NOT LIKE YOU AND MUR AND KAY. YOU'RE ALL REALLY AMAZING.
SO I WANNA BE AS HELPFUL AS I CAN...
AND LEARN WHOLE BUNCHES OF STUFF...
SO I CAN EXPLORE THE LABYRINTH JUST LIKE YOU SOMEDAY!
ぱっ
BEAM
WAVE
WAVE
WAVE
WAVE

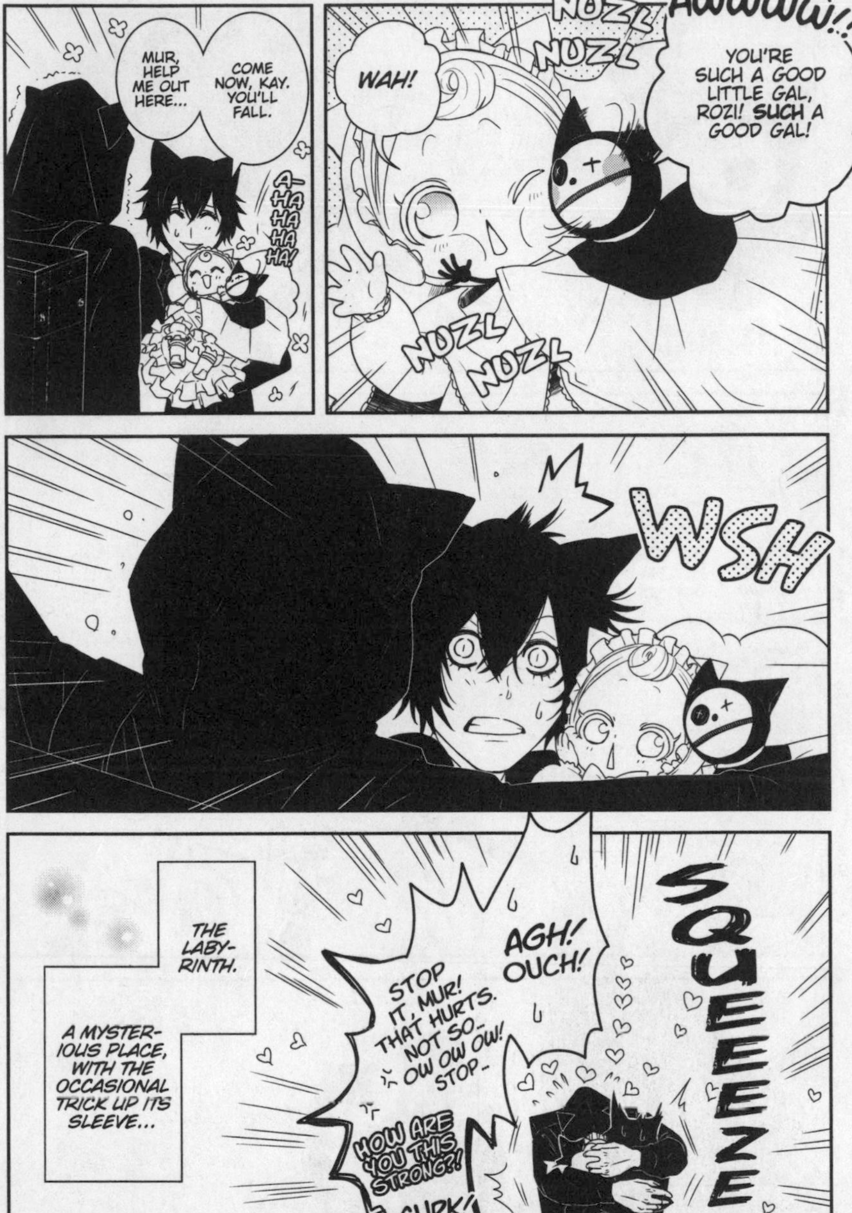
AWWWW!!
NUZL NUZL
YOU'RE SUCH A GOOD LITTLE GAL, ROZI! SUCH A GOOD GAL!
WAH!
NUZL NUZL
COME NOW, KAY. YOU'LL FALL.
MUR, HELP ME OUT HERE...
A-HA HA HA HA!
WSH
SQUEEEZE
AGH! OUCH!
STOP IT, MUR! THAT HURTS. NOT SO... OW OW OW! STOP-
HOW ARE YOU THIS STRONG?!
GURK!
THE LABYRINTH.
A MYSTERIOUS PLACE, WITH THE OCCASIONAL TRICK UP ITS SLEEVE...

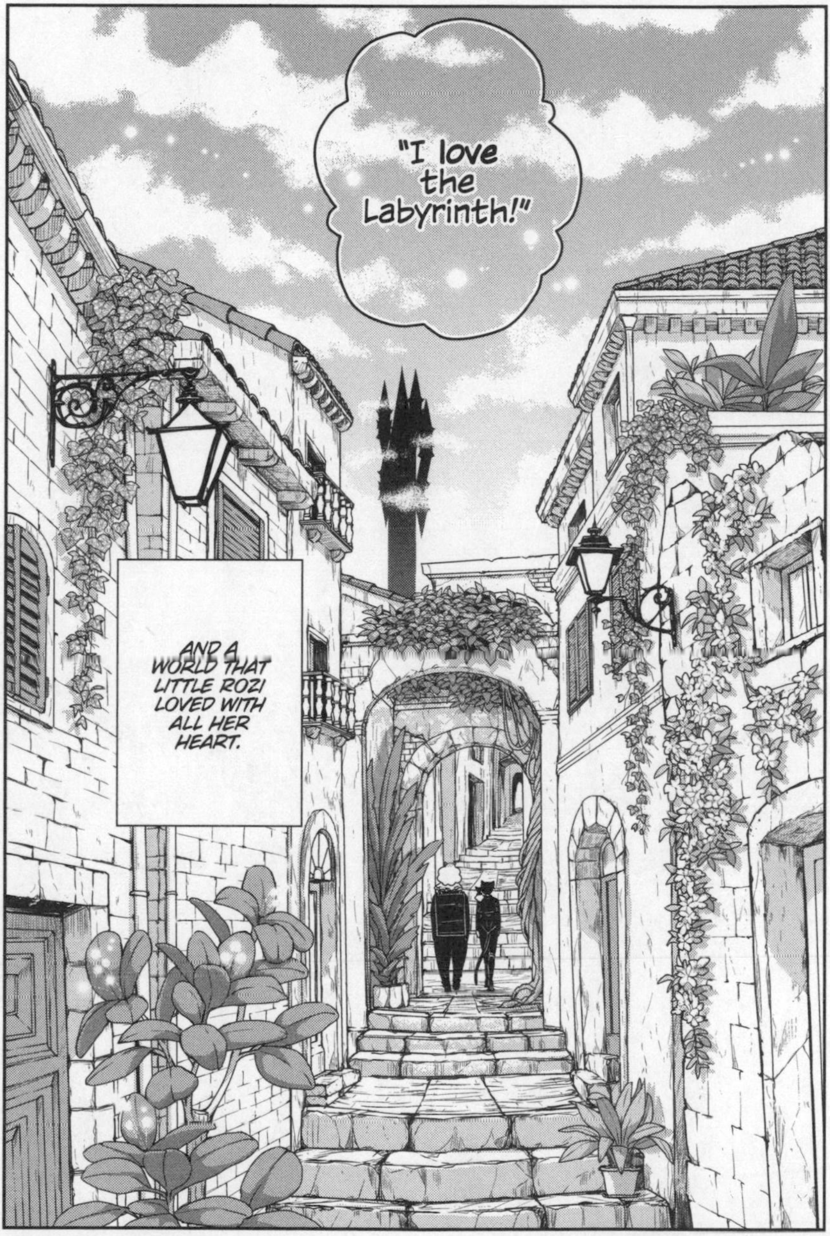
"I love the Labyrinth!"
AND A WORLD THAT LITTLE ROZI LOVED WITH ALL HER HEART.

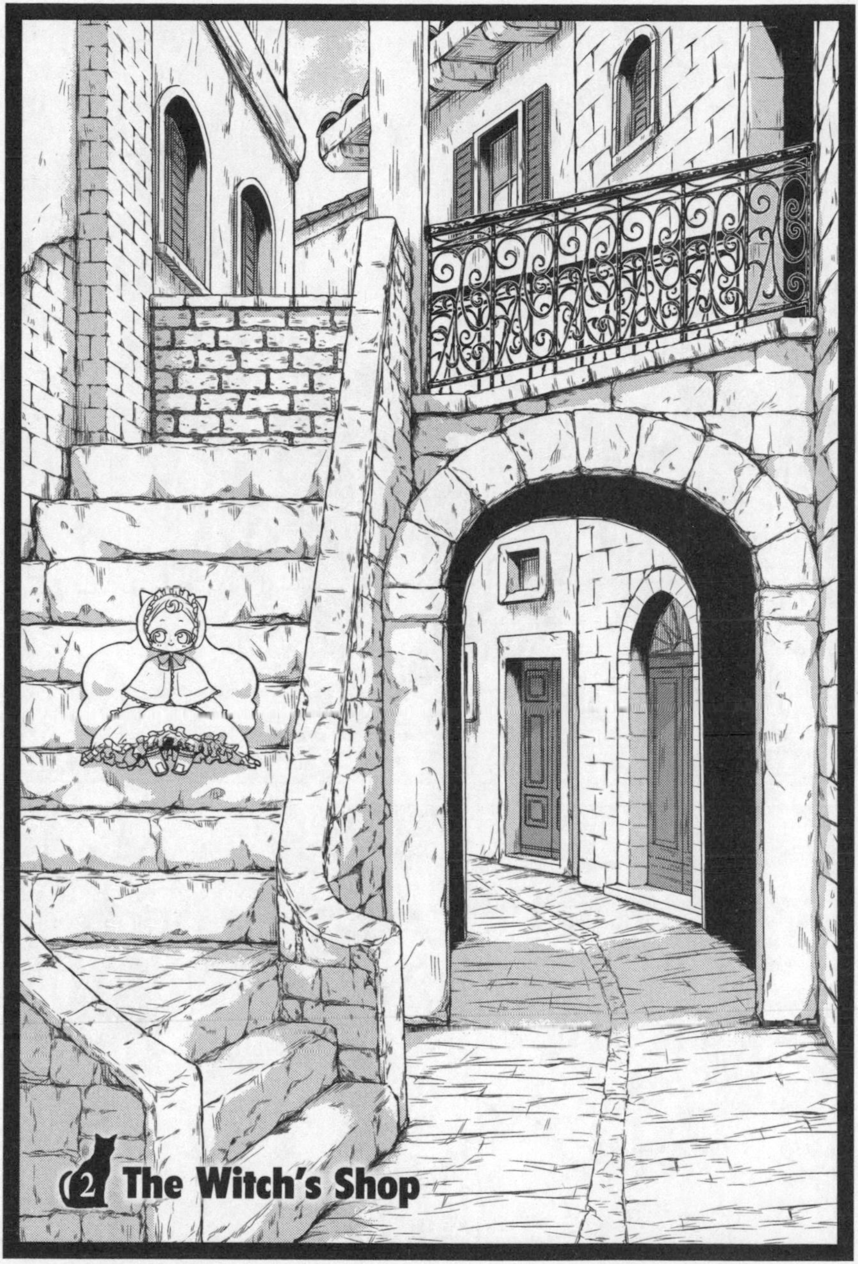
2 The Witch's Shop

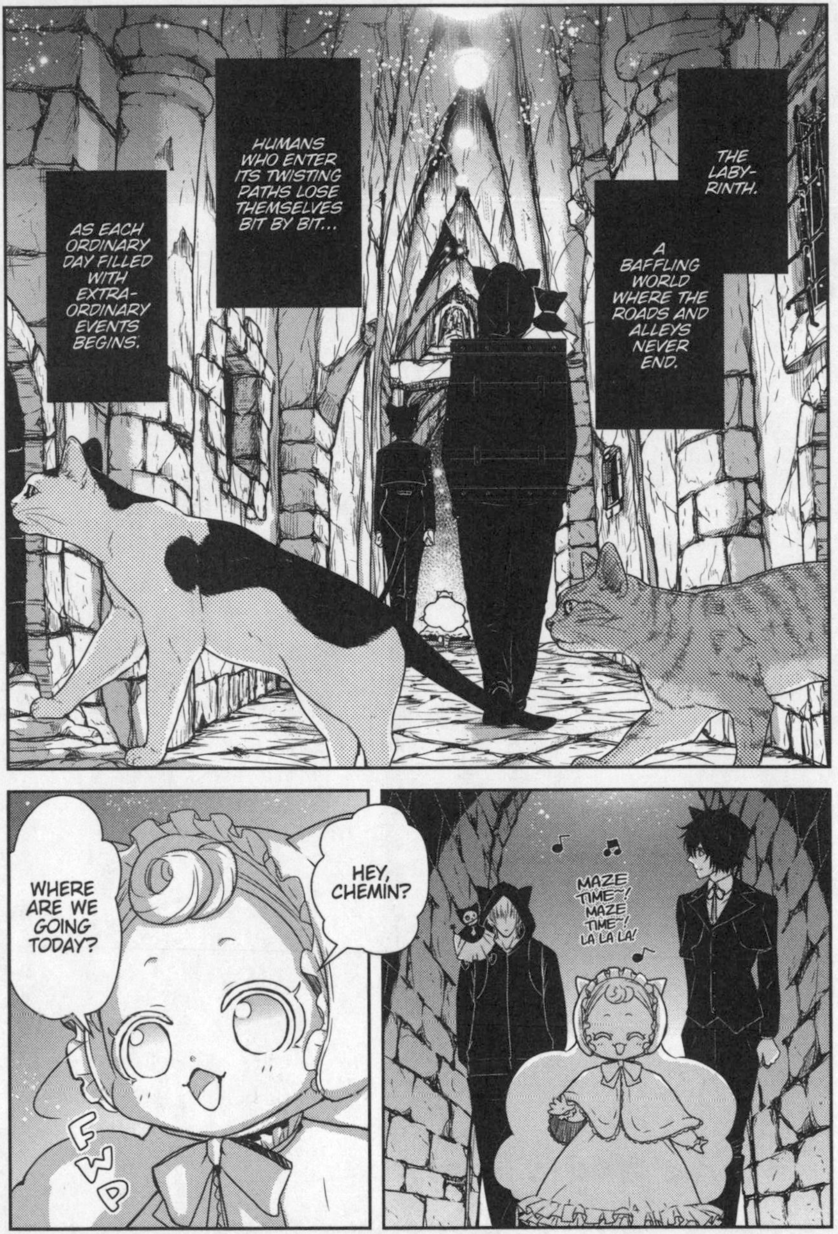
THE LABYRINTH.
A BAFFLING WORLD WHERE THE ROADS AND ALLEYS NEVER END.
HUMANS WHO ENTER ITS TWISTING PATHS LOSE THEMSELVES BIT BY BIT...
AS EACH ORDINARY DAY FILLED WITH EXTRA-ORDINARY EVENTS BEGINS.
MAZE TIME~! MAZE TIME~! LA LA LA!
HEY, CHEMIN?
WHERE ARE WE GOING TODAY?
FWP

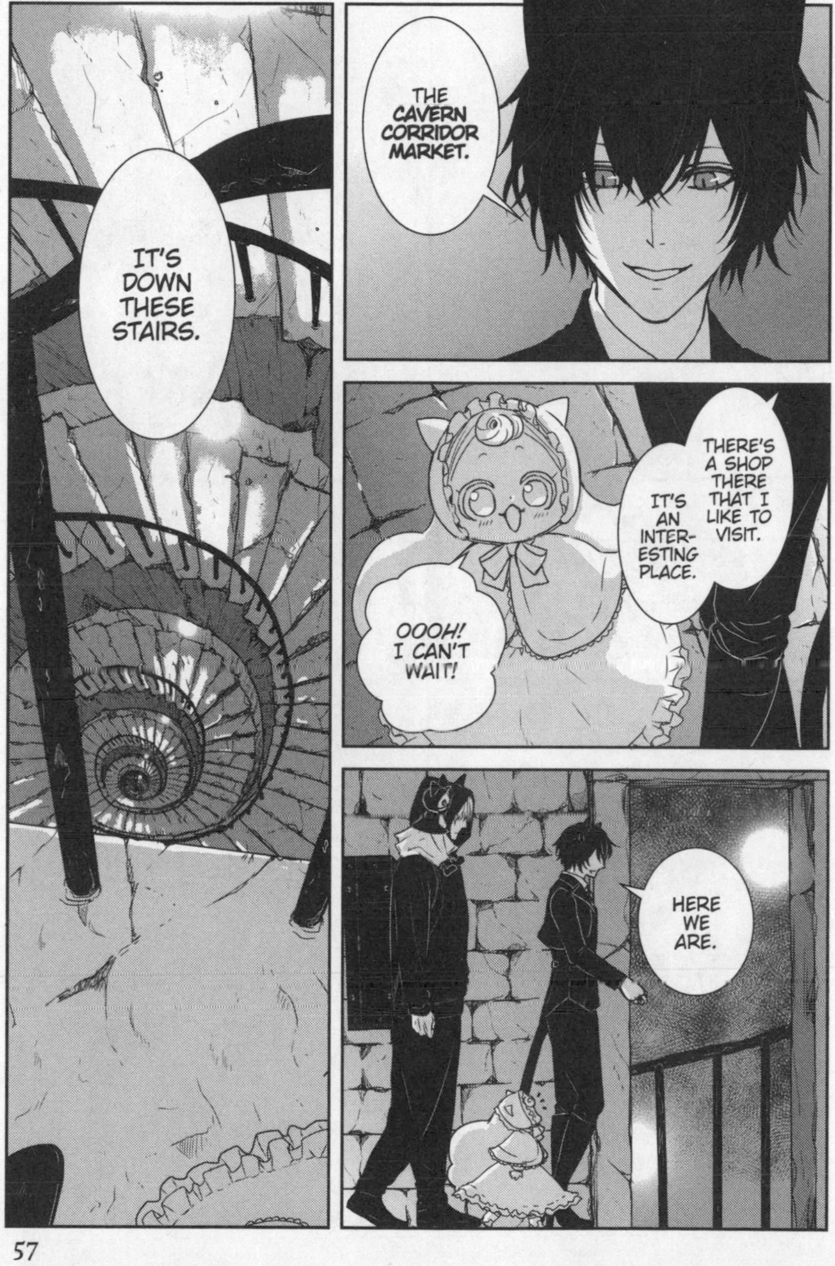
THE CAVERN CORRIDOR MARKET.
THERE'S A SHOP THERE THAT I LIKE TO VISIT.
IT'S AN INTER-ESTING PLACE.
OOOH! I CAN'T WAIT!
HERE WE ARE.
IT'S DOWN THESE STAIRS.

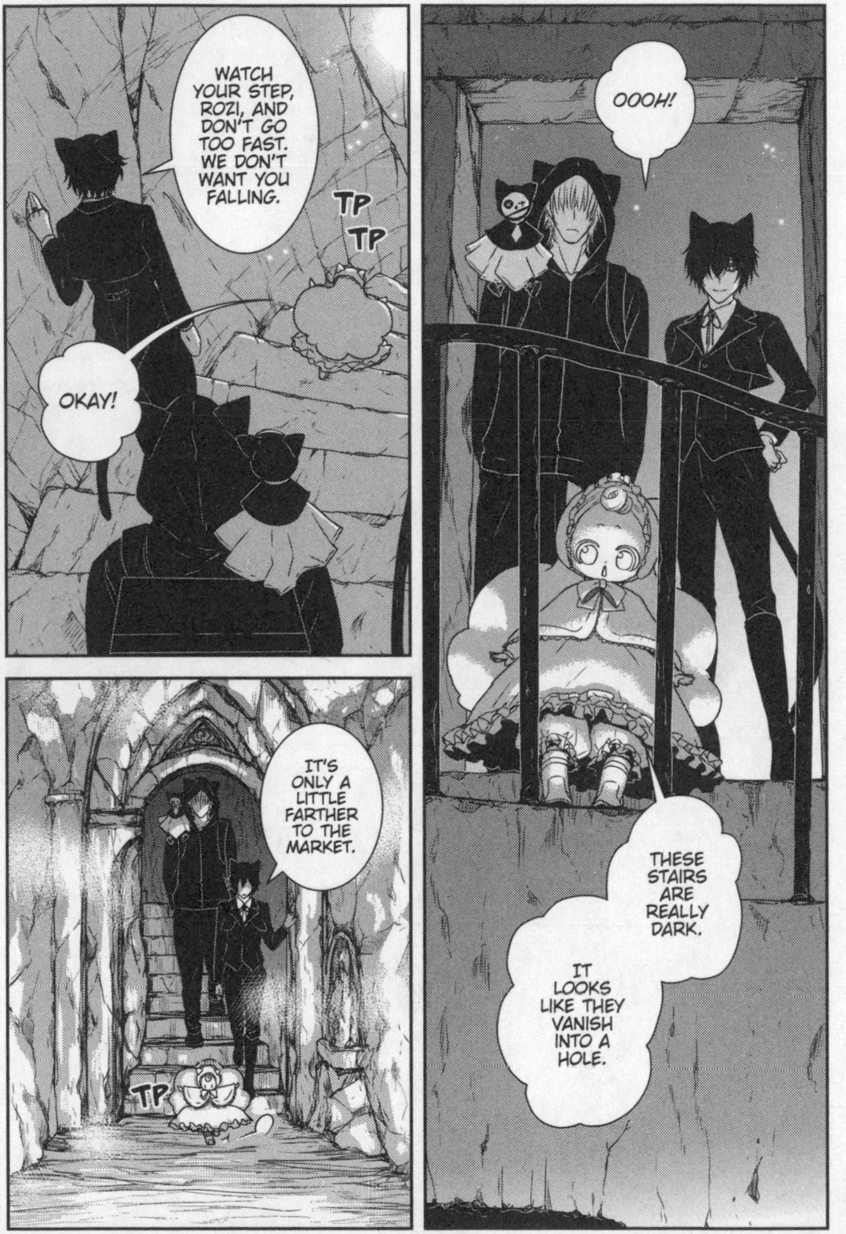
OOOH!
THESE STAIRS ARE REALLY DARK.
IT LOOKS LIKE THEY VANISH INTO A HOLE.
WATCH YOUR STEP, ROZI, AND DON'T GO TOO FAST. WE DON'T WANT YOU FALLING.
TP
TP
OKAY!
IT'S ONLY A LITTLE FARTHER TO THE MARKET.
TP

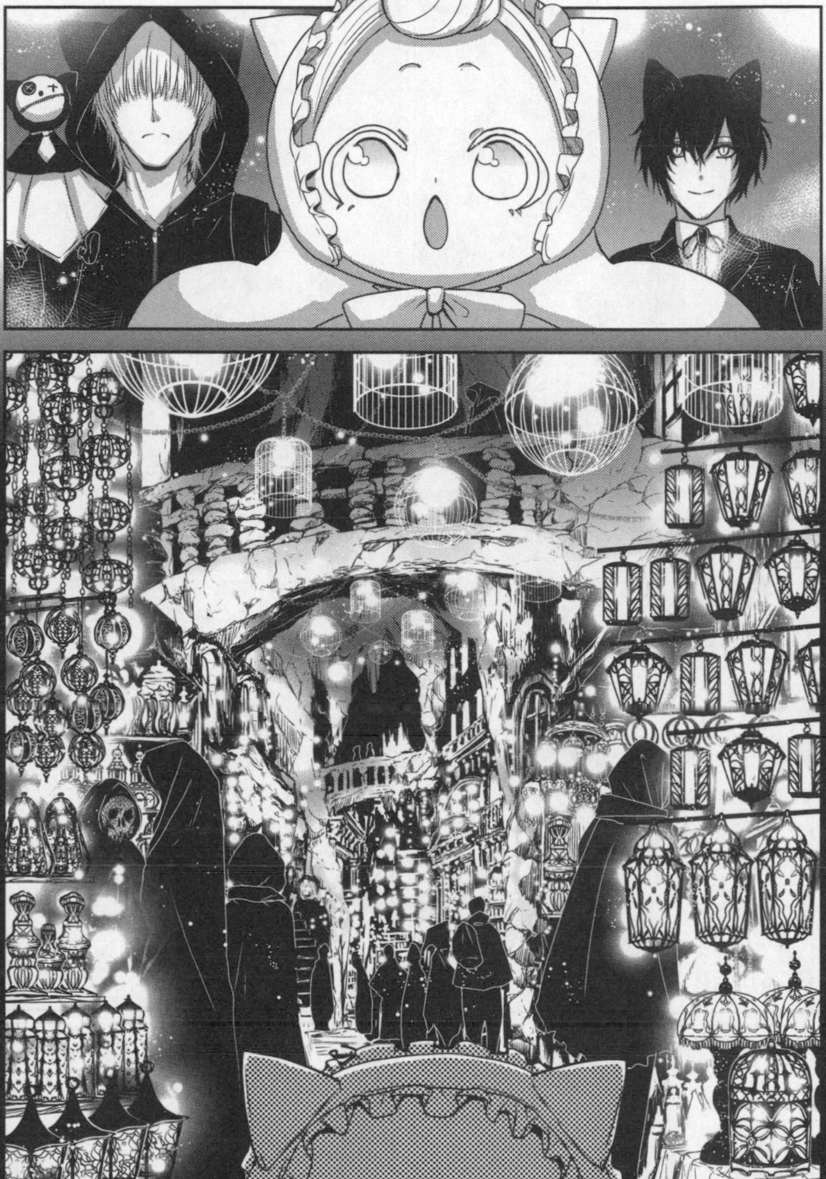

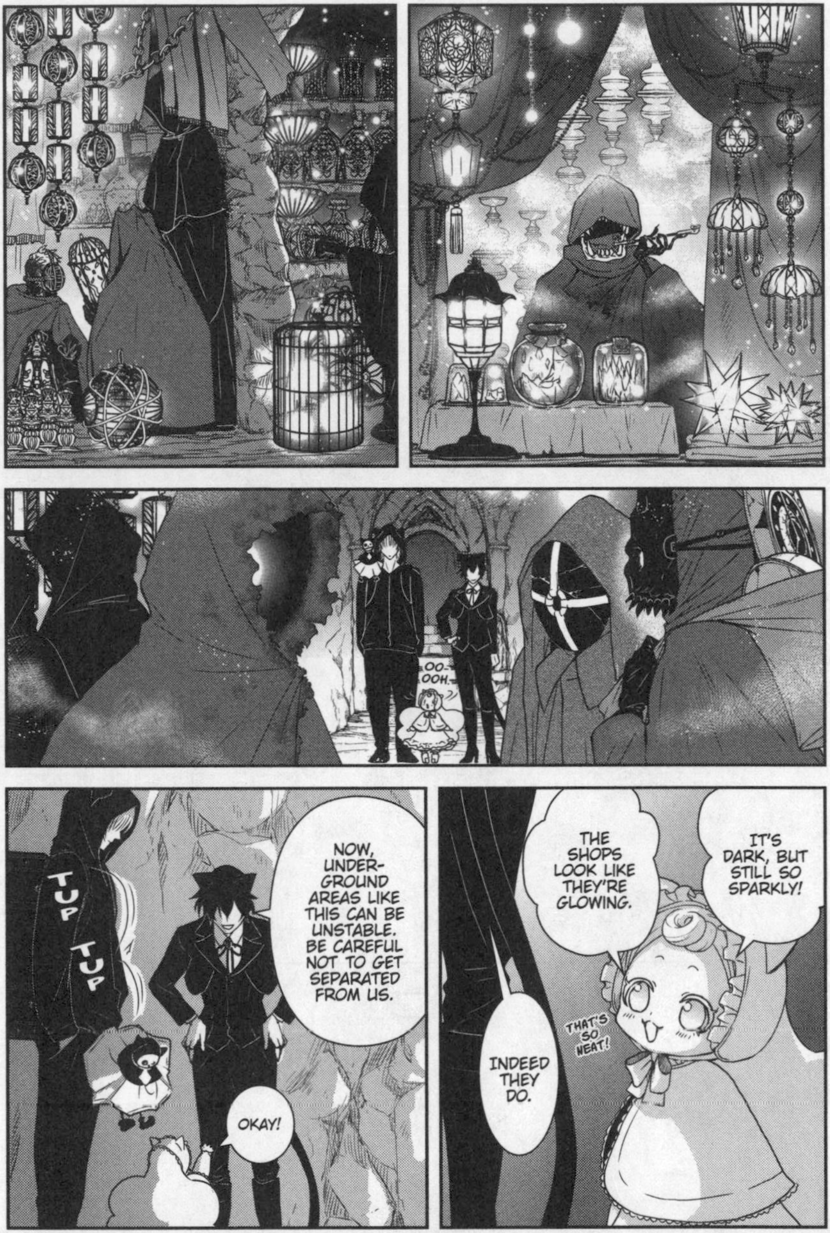
OO-OOH.
IT'S DARK, BUT STILL SO SPARKLY!
THE SHOPS LOOK LIKE THEY'RE GLOWING.
THAT'S SO NEAT!
INDEED THEY DO.
NOW, UNDER-GROUND AREAS LIKE THIS CAN BE UNSTABLE. BE CAREFUL NOT TO GET SEPARATED FROM US.
TUP TUP
OKAY!

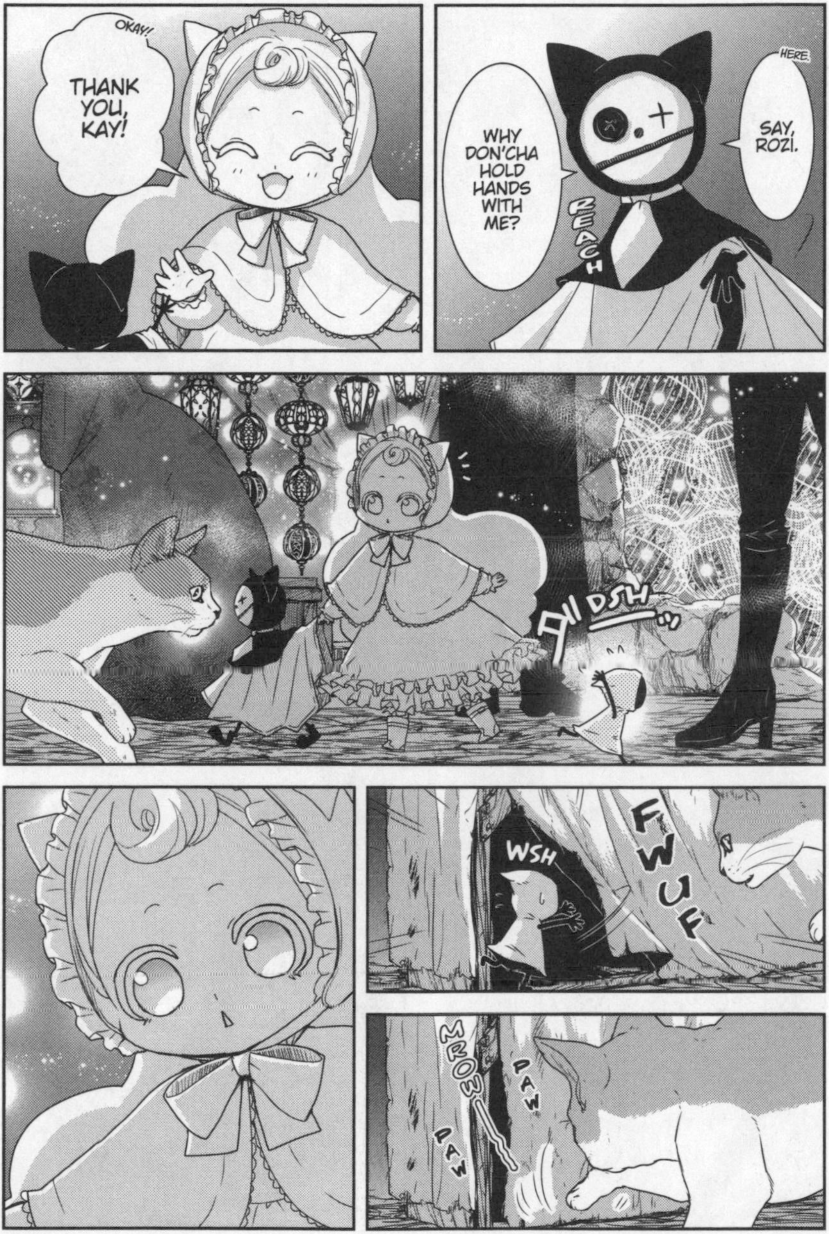
HERE.
SAY, ROZI.
WHY DON'CHA HOLD HANDS WITH ME?
REACH
OKAY!!
THANK YOU, KAY!
DSH
FWUF
WSH
PAW
MROW
PAW
PAW

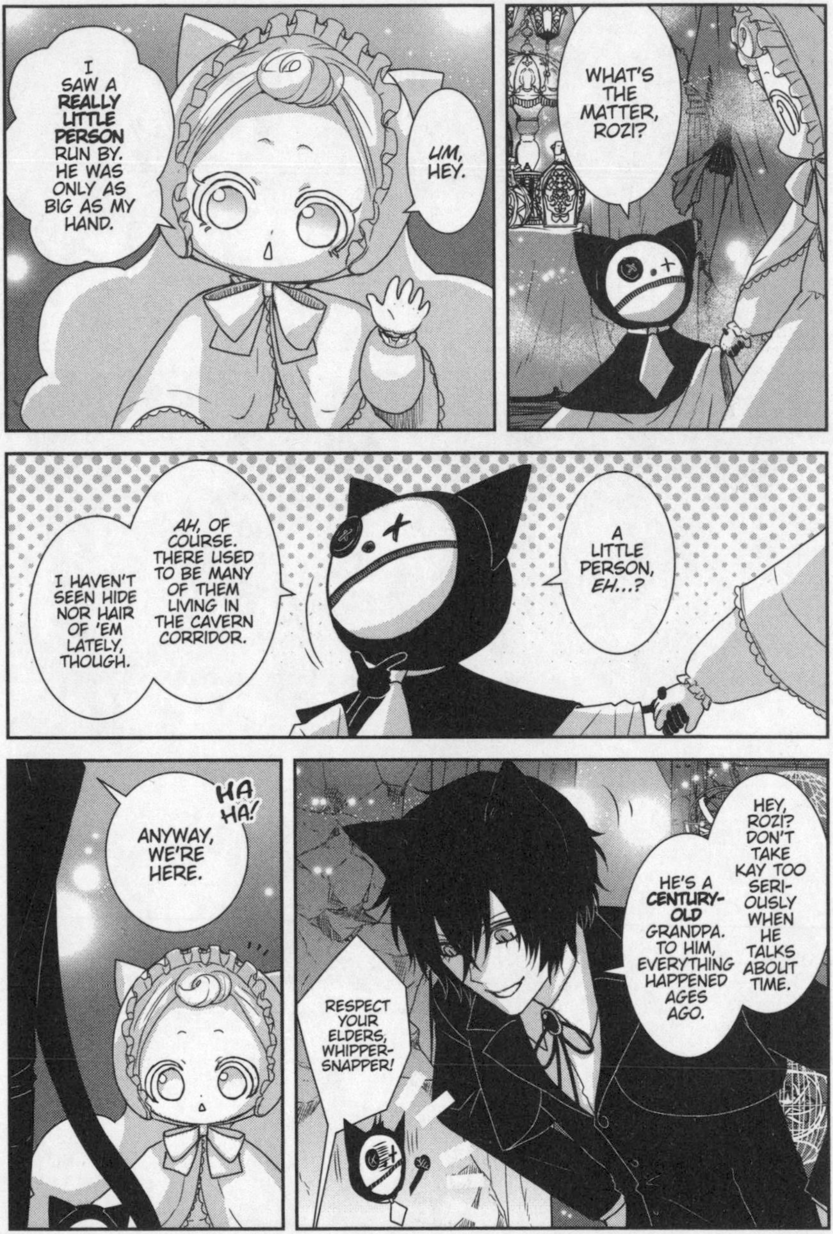
WHAT'S THE MATTER, ROZI?
UM, HEY.
I SAW A **REALLY LITTLE PERSON** RUN BY. HE WAS ONLY AS BIG AS MY HAND.
A LITTLE PERSON, EH...?
AH, OF COURSE. THERE USED TO BE MANY OF THEM LIVING IN THE CAVERN CORRIDOR.
I HAVEN'T SEEN HIDE NOR HAIR OF 'EM LATELY, THOUGH.
HEY, ROZI? DON'T TAKE KAY TOO SERI-OUSLY WHEN HE TALKS ABOUT TIME.
HE'S A **CENTURY-OLD** GRANDPA. TO HIM, EVERYTHING HAPPENED AGES AGO.
RESPECT YOUR ELDERS, WHIPPER-SNAPPER!
HA HA!
ANYWAY, WE'RE HERE.

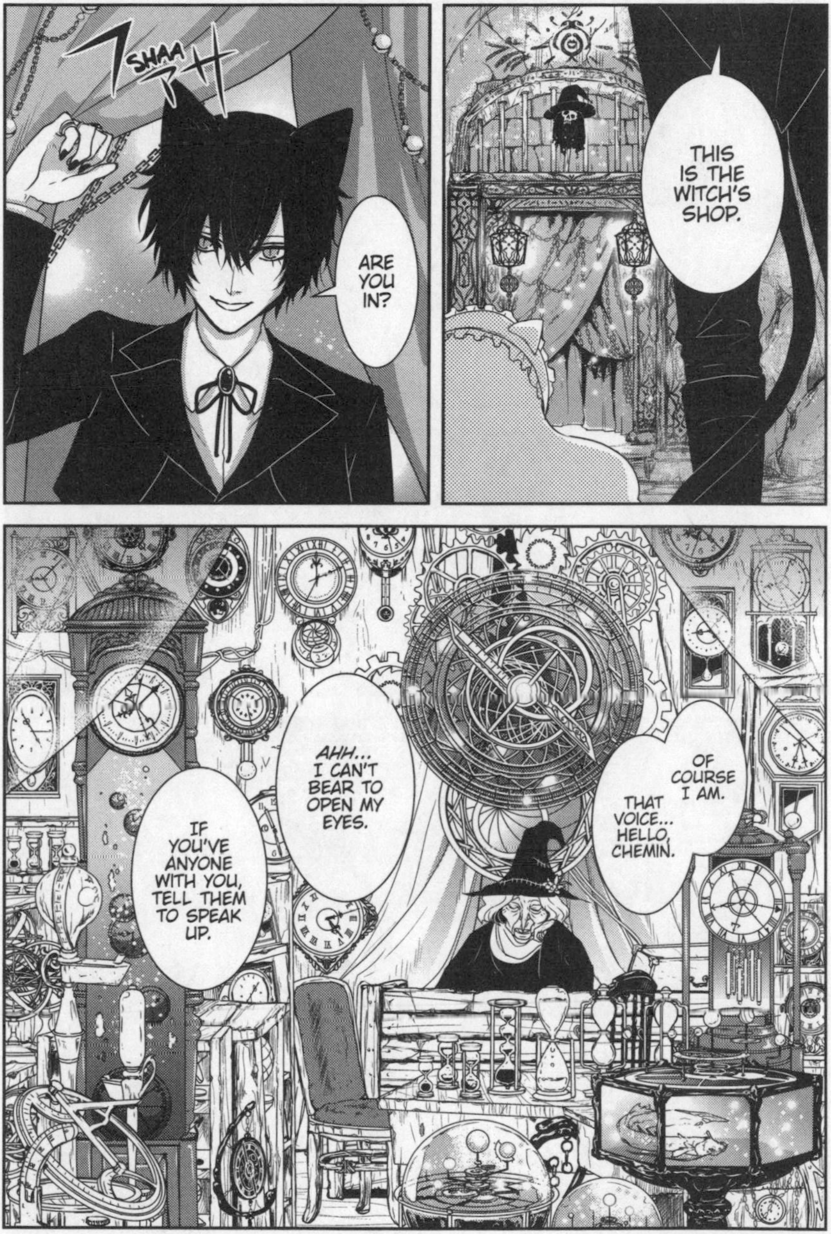
THIS IS THE WITCH'S SHOP.
SHAA
ARE YOU IN?
OF COURSE I AM.
THAT VOICE... HELLO, CHEMIN.
AHH... I CAN'T BEAR TO OPEN MY EYES.
IF YOU'VE ANYONE WITH YOU, TELL THEM TO SPEAK UP.

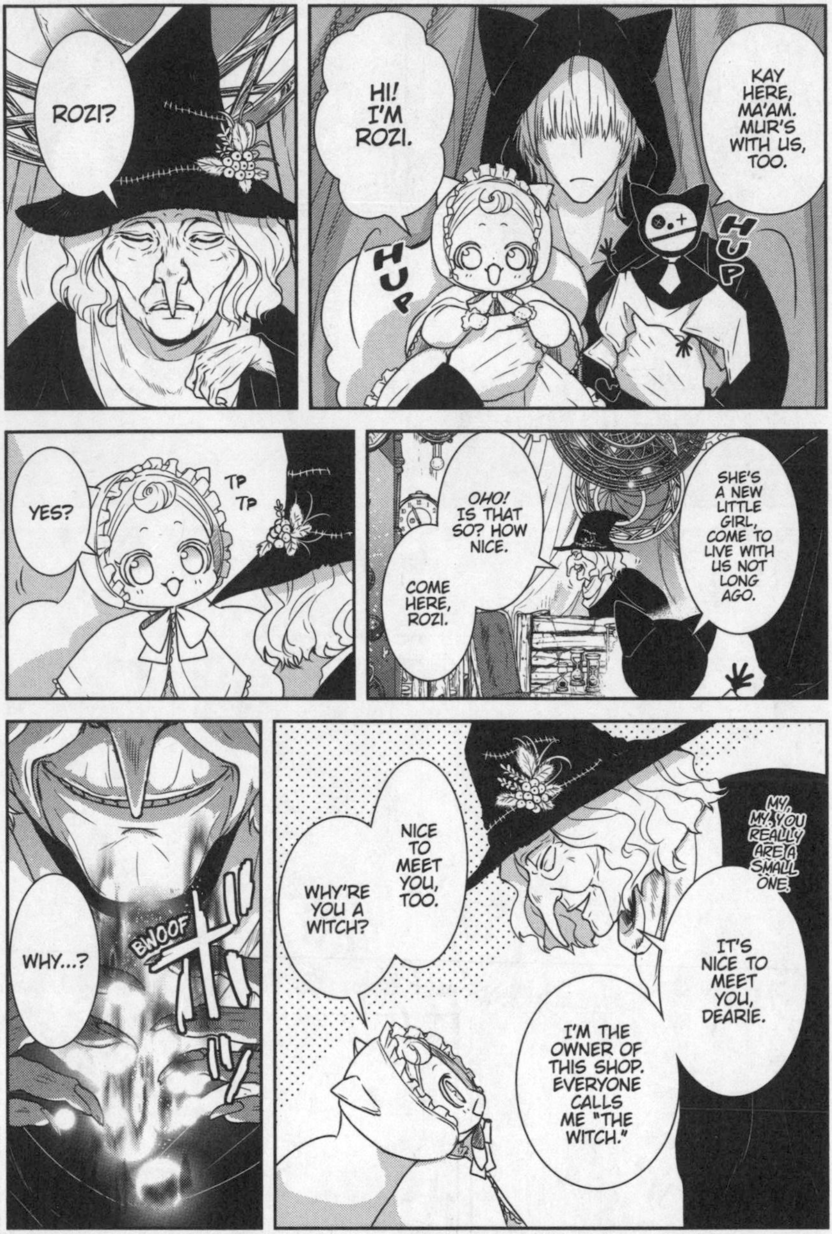
KAY HERE, MA'AM. MUR'S WITH US, TOO.
HUP
HI! I'M ROZI.
HUP
ROZI?
SHE'S A NEW LITTLE GIRL, COME TO LIVE WITH US NOT LONG AGO.
OHO! IS THAT SO? HOW NICE.
COME HERE, ROZI.
TP TP
YES?
MY, MY, YOU REALLY ARE A SMALL ONE.
IT'S NICE TO MEET YOU, DEARIE.
I'M THE OWNER OF THIS SHOP. EVERYONE CALLS ME "THE WITCH."
NICE TO MEET YOU, TOO.
WHY'RE YOU A WITCH?
BWOOF
WHY...?

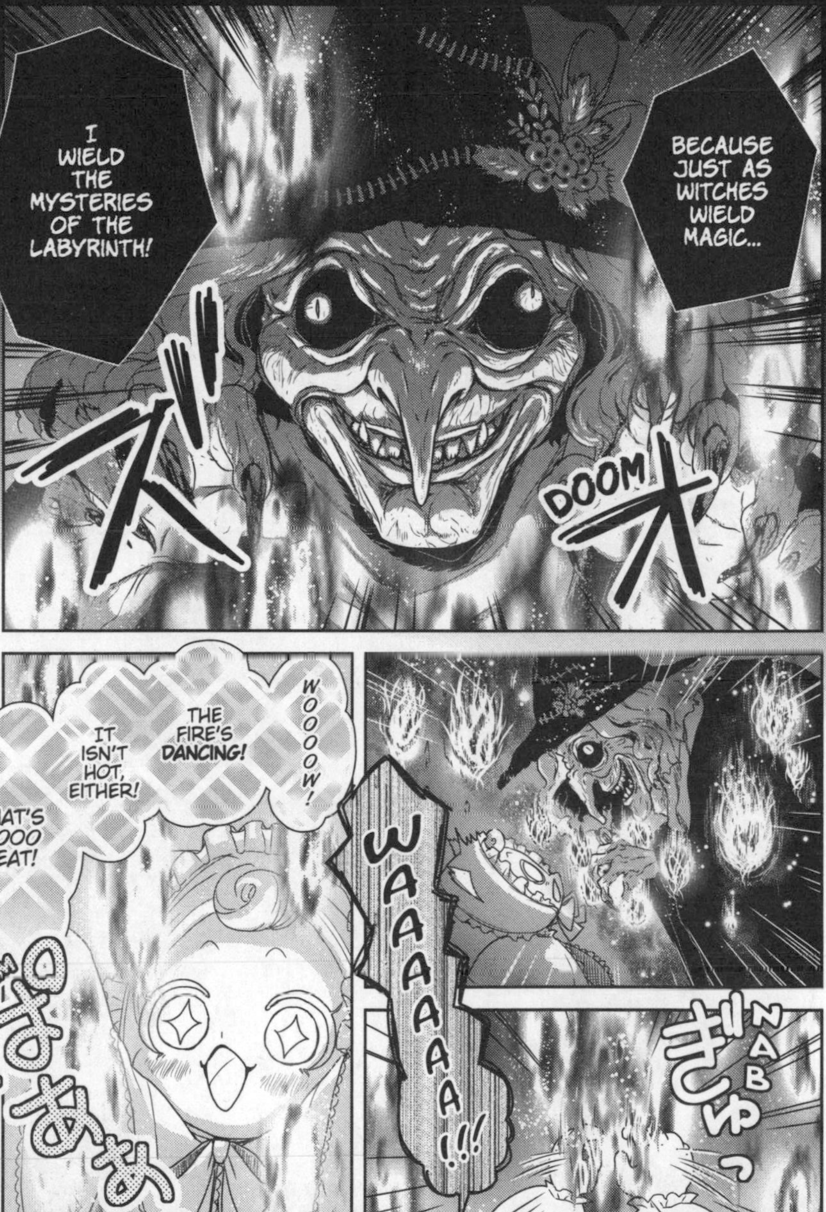
BECAUSE JUST AS WITCHES WIELD MAGIC...
I WIELD THE MYSTERIES OF THE LABYRINTH!
DOOM
WAAAAAAA!!!
NAB
WOOOOOW!
THE FIRE'S DANCING!
IT ISN'T HOT, EITHER!
THAT'S SOOO NEAT!
GLEAM

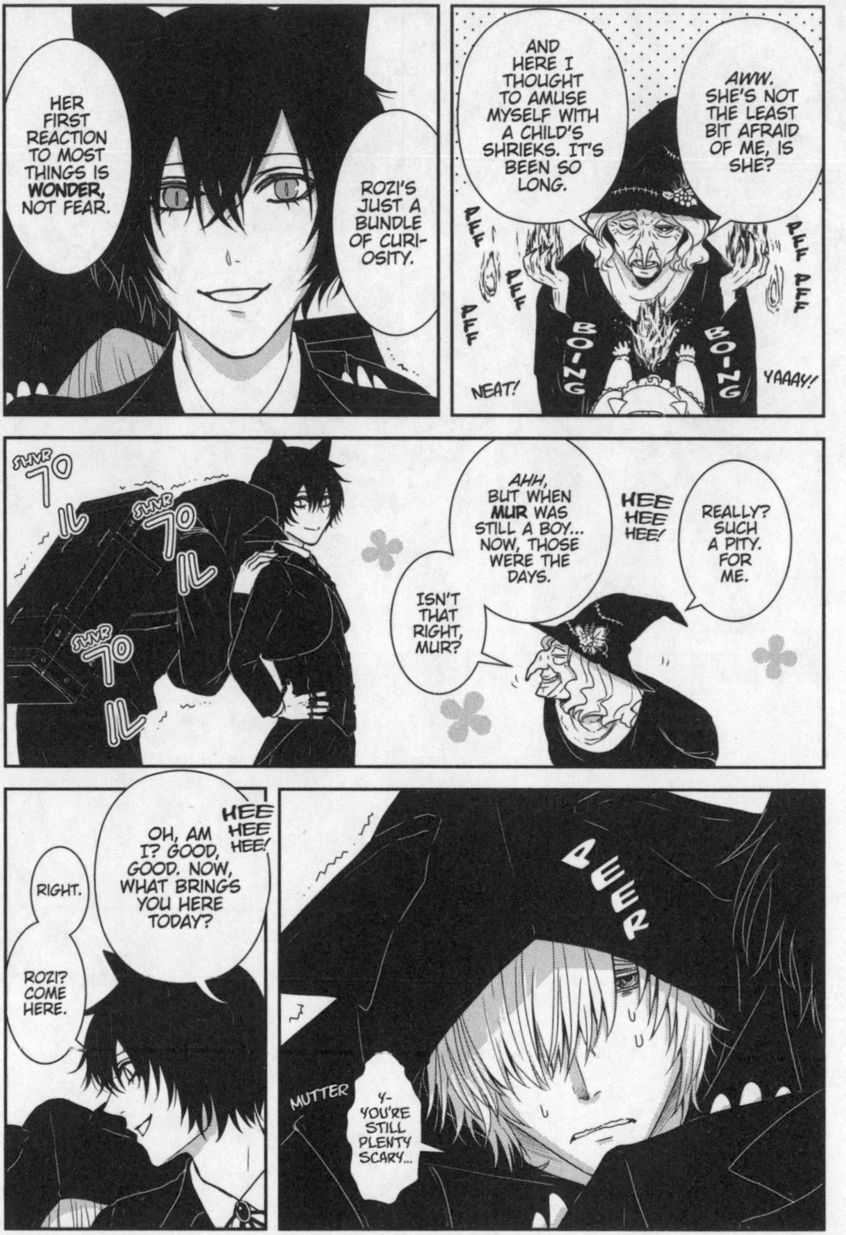
AWW. SHE'S NOT THE LEAST BIT AFRAID OF ME, IS SHE?
AND HERE I THOUGHT TO AMUSE MYSELF WITH A CHILD'S SHRIEKS. IT'S BEEN SO LONG.
PFF PFF
PFF PFF PFF
BOING BOING
YAAAY!
NEAT!
ROZI'S JUST A BUNDLE OF CURI-OSITY.
HER FIRST REACTION TO MOST THINGS IS **WONDER,** NOT FEAR.
REALLY? SUCH A PITY. FOR ME.
HEE HEE HEE!
AHH, BUT WHEN **MUR** WAS STILL A BOY... NOW, THOSE WERE THE DAYS.
ISN'T THAT RIGHT, MUR?
SHVR
SHVR
SHVR
PEER
Y-YOU'RE STILL PLENTY SCARY...
MUTTER
HEE HEE HEE!
OH, AM I? GOOD, GOOD. NOW, WHAT BRINGS YOU HERE TODAY?
RIGHT.
ROZI? COME HERE.

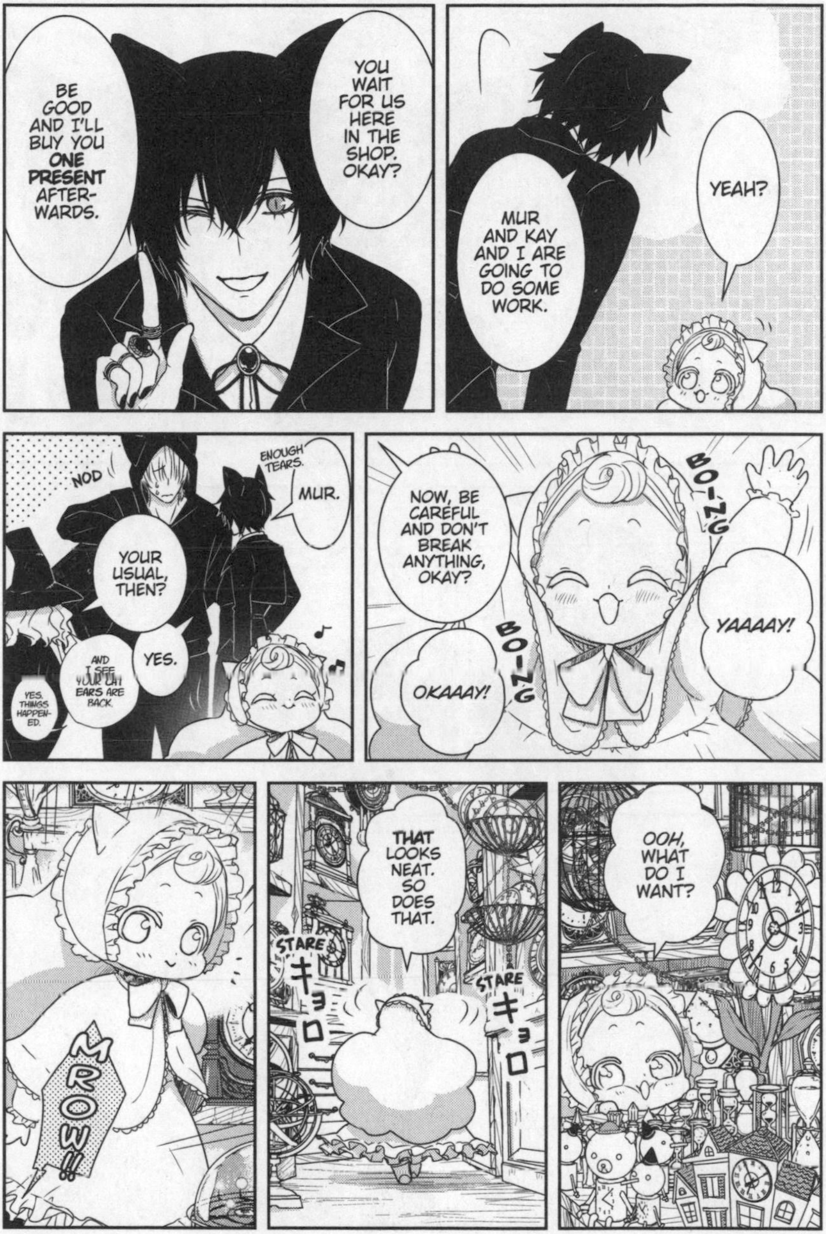
YEAH?
MUR AND KAY AND I ARE GOING TO DO SOME WORK.
YOU WAIT FOR US HERE IN THE SHOP. OKAY?
BE GOOD AND I'LL BUY YOU ONE PRESENT AFTER-WARDS.
BO-I-NG
YAAAAY!
NOW, BE CAREFUL AND DON'T BREAK ANYTHING, OKAY?
BO-I-NG
OKAAAY!
ENOUGH TEARS.
MUR.
NOD
YOUR USUAL, THEN?
YES.
AND I SEE YOUR CAT EARS ARE BACK.
YES. THINGS HAPPEN-ED.
OOH, WHAT DO I WANT?
THAT LOOKS NEAT. SO DOES THAT.
STARE キョロ
STARE キョロ
MROW!!

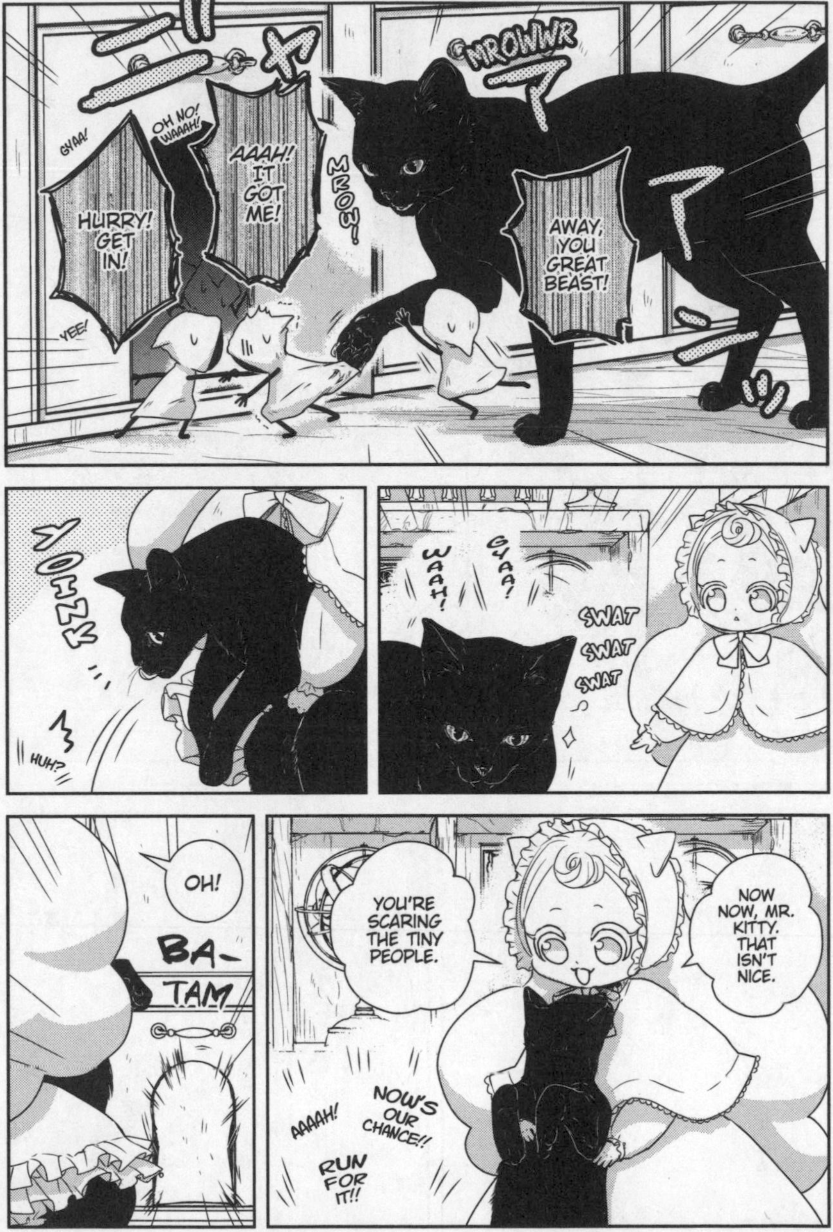
MROWWR
AWAY, YOU GREAT BEAST!
MROW!
AAAH! IT GOT ME!
OH NO! WAAAH!
GYAA!
HURRY! GET IN!
YEE!
GYAA!
WAAAH!
SWAT
SWAT
SWAT
YOINK
HUH?
NOW NOW, MR. KITTY. THAT ISN'T NICE.
YOU'RE SCARING THE TINY PEOPLE.
NOW'S OUR CHANCE!!
AAAAH!
RUN FOR IT!!
OH!
BA-
TAM

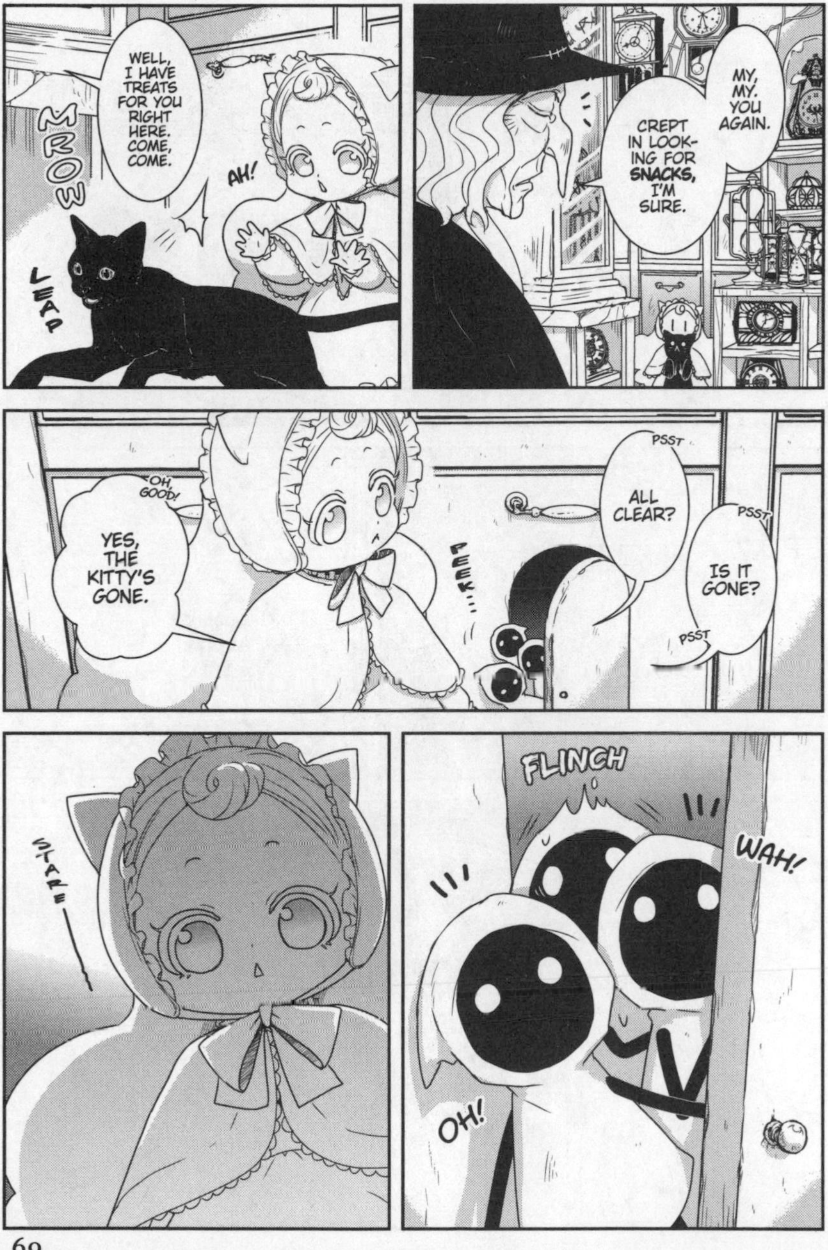
MY, MY. YOU AGAIN.
CREPT IN LOOKING FOR SNACKS, I'M SURE.
WELL, I HAVE TREATS FOR YOU RIGHT HERE. COME, COME.
MROW
AH!
LEAP
PSST
ALL CLEAR?
PSST
IS IT GONE?
PSST
PEEK...
OH, GOOD!
YES, THE KITTY'S GONE.
FLINCH
WAH!
OH!
STARE

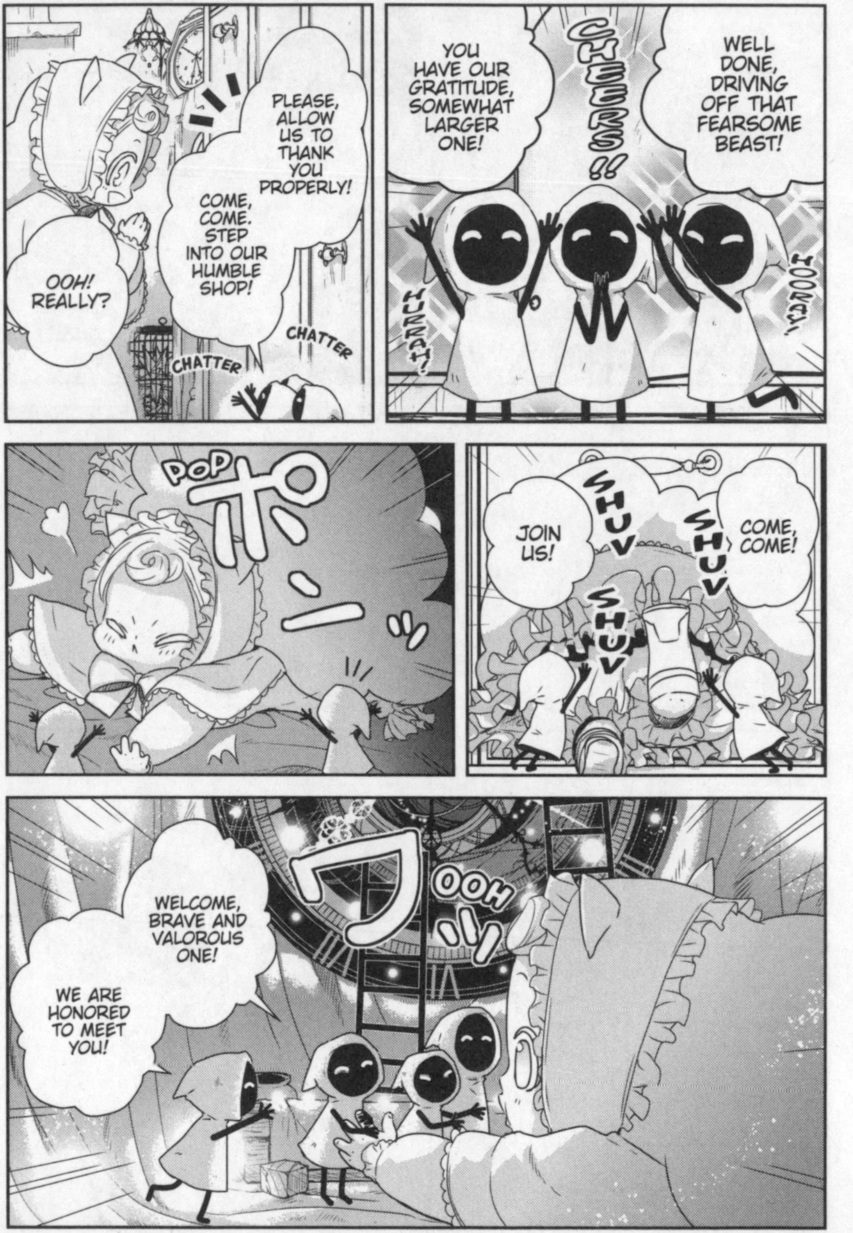
WELL DONE, DRIVING OFF THAT FEARSOME BEAST!
CHEERS!!
YOU HAVE OUR GRATITUDE, SOMEWHAT LARGER ONE!
HOORAY!
HURRAH!
PLEASE, ALLOW US TO THANK YOU PROPERLY!
COME, COME. STEP INTO OUR HUMBLE SHOP!
CHATTER
CHATTER
OOH! REALLY?
COME, COME!
SHUV
SHUV
JOIN US!
SHUV
POP
OOH
WELCOME, BRAVE AND VALOROUS ONE!
WE ARE HONORED TO MEET YOU!

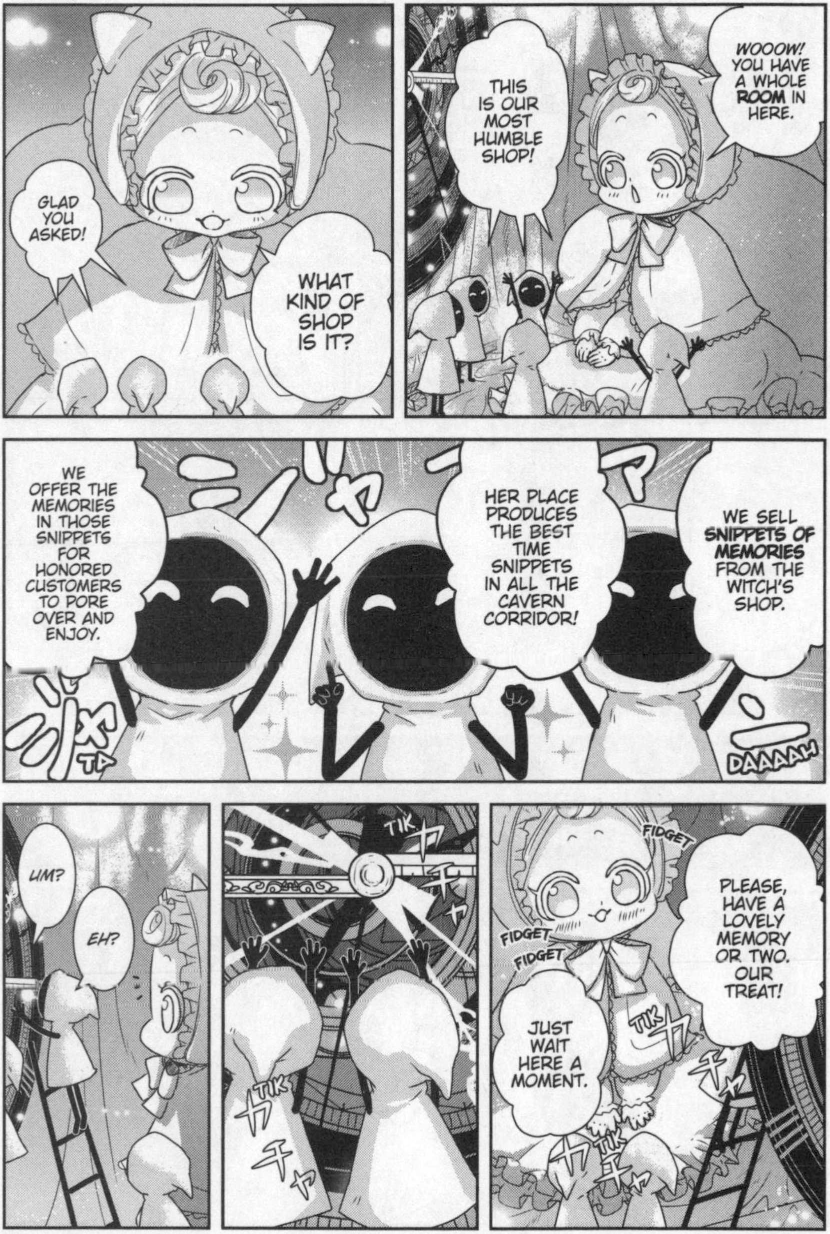
WOOOW! YOU HAVE A WHOLE ROOM IN HERE.
THIS IS OUR MOST HUMBLE SHOP!
WHAT KIND OF SHOP IS IT?
GLAD YOU ASKED!
WE SELL SNIPPETS OF MEMORIES FROM THE WITCH'S SHOP.
DAAAAH
HER PLACE PRODUCES THE BEST TIME SNIPPETS IN ALL THE CAVERN CORRIDOR!
WE OFFER THE MEMORIES IN THOSE SNIPPETS FOR HONORED CUSTOMERS TO PORE OVER AND ENJOY.
TA
FIDGET
PLEASE, HAVE A LOVELY MEMORY OR TWO. OUR TREAT!
FIDGET
FIDGET
JUST WAIT HERE A MOMENT.
TIK
TIK
TIK
TIK
UM?
EH?

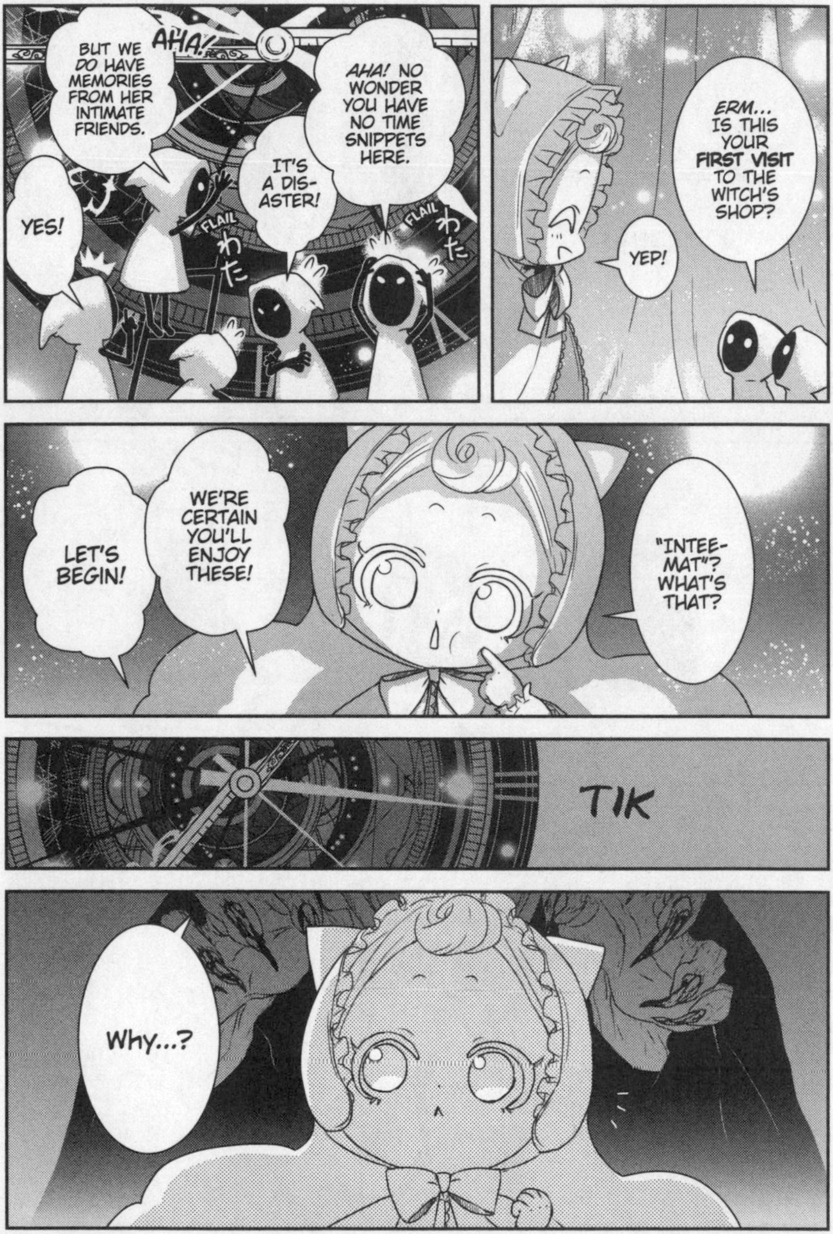
ERM... IS THIS YOUR FIRST VISIT TO THE WITCH'S SHOP?
YEP!
AHA! NO WONDER YOU HAVE NO TIME SNIPPETS HERE.
IT'S A DIS-ASTER!
FLAIL わた
FLAIL わた
AHA!
BUT WE DO HAVE MEMORIES FROM HER INTIMATE FRIENDS.
YES!
"INTEE-MAT"? WHAT'S THAT?
WE'RE CERTAIN YOU'LL ENJOY THESE!
LET'S BEGIN!
TIK
Why...?

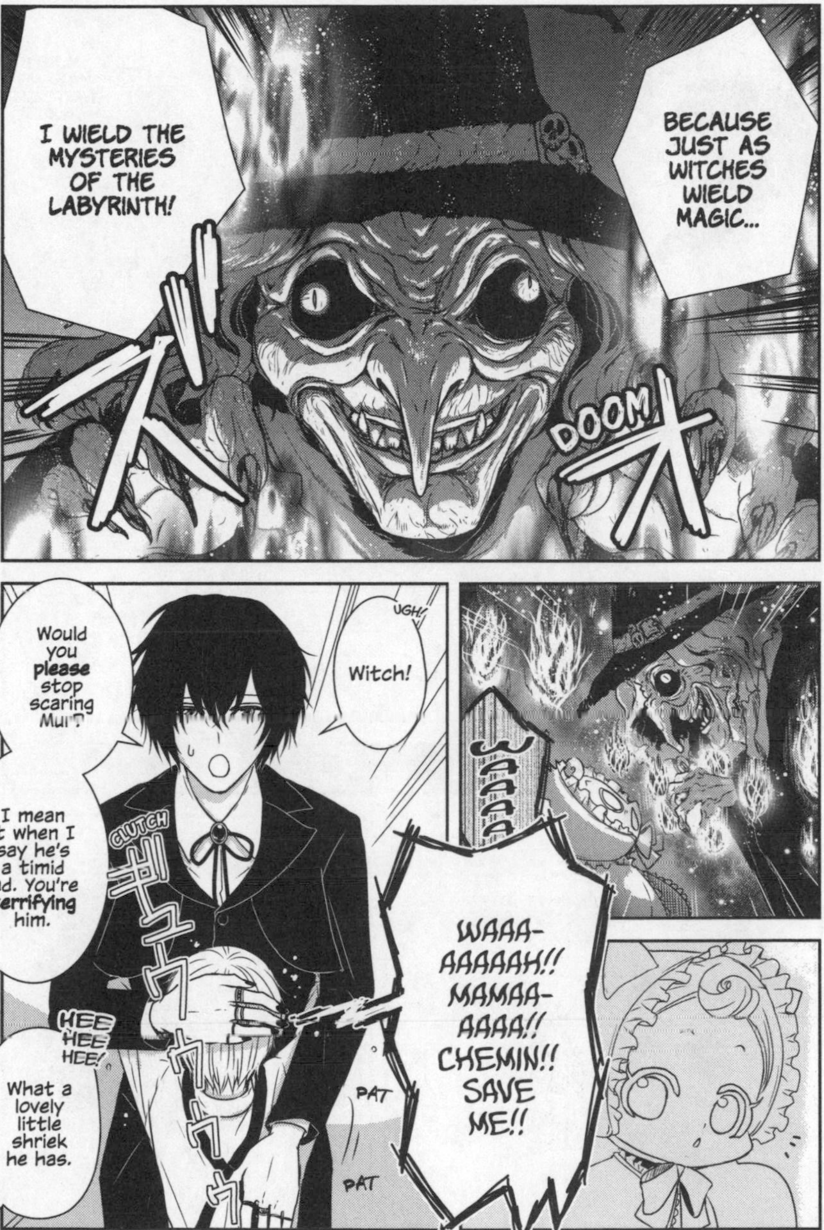
BECAUSE JUST AS WITCHES WIELD MAGIC...
I WIELD THE MYSTERIES OF THE LABYRINTH!
DOOM
WAAAAA
WAAA-AAAAAH!! MAMAA-AAAA!! CHEMIN!! SAVE ME!!
UGH!
Witch!
Would you please stop scaring Mui?
I mean it when I say he's a timid lad. You're terrifying him.
CLUTCH
HEE HEE HEE!
What a lovely little shriek he has.
PAT
PAT

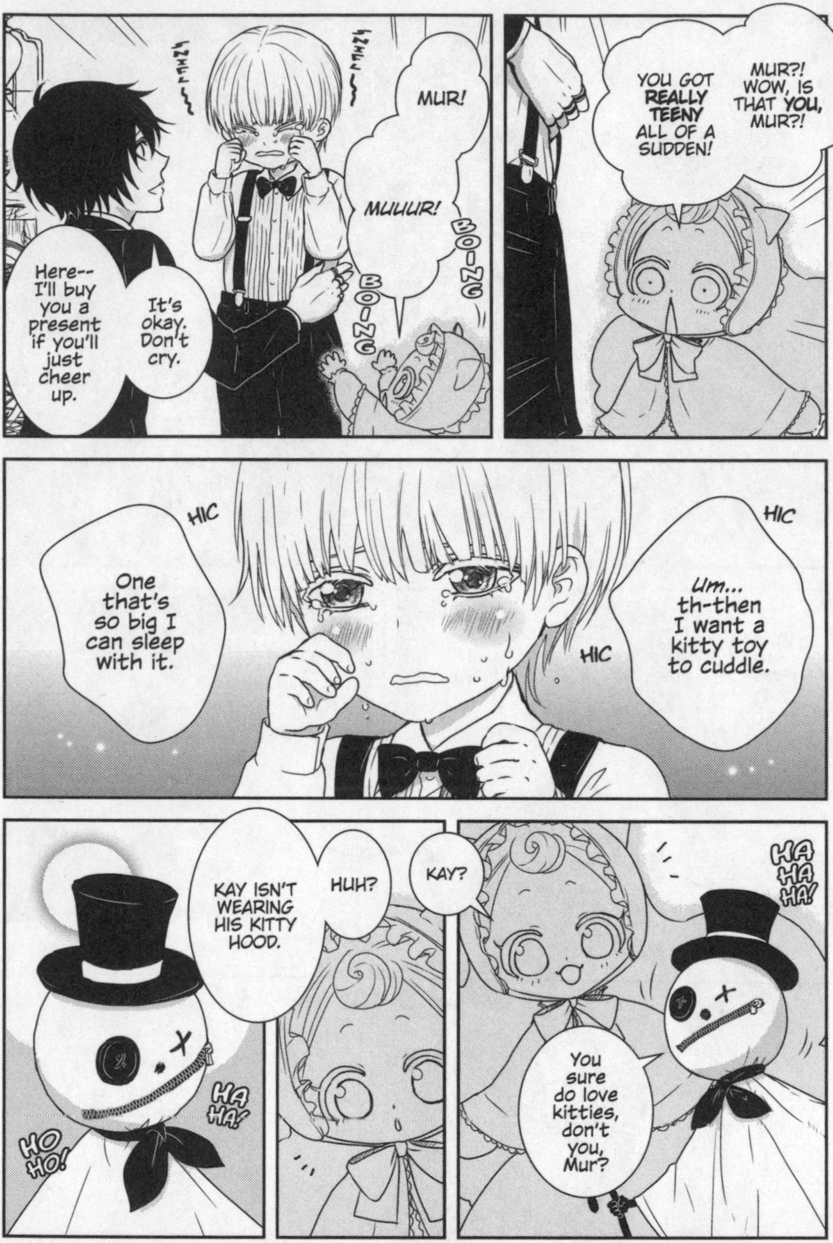
MUR?! WOW, IS THAT YOU, MUR?!
YOU GOT REALLY TEENY ALL OF A SUDDEN!
MUR!
MUUUR!
BOING
BOING
It's okay. Don't cry.
Here-- I'll buy you a present if you'll just cheer up.
HIC
Um... th-then I want a kitty toy to cuddle.
HIC
HIC
One that's so big I can sleep with it.
HA HA HA!
KAY?
You sure do love kitties, don't you, Mur?
HUH?
KAY ISN'T WEARING HIS KITTY HOOD.
HA HA!
HO HO!

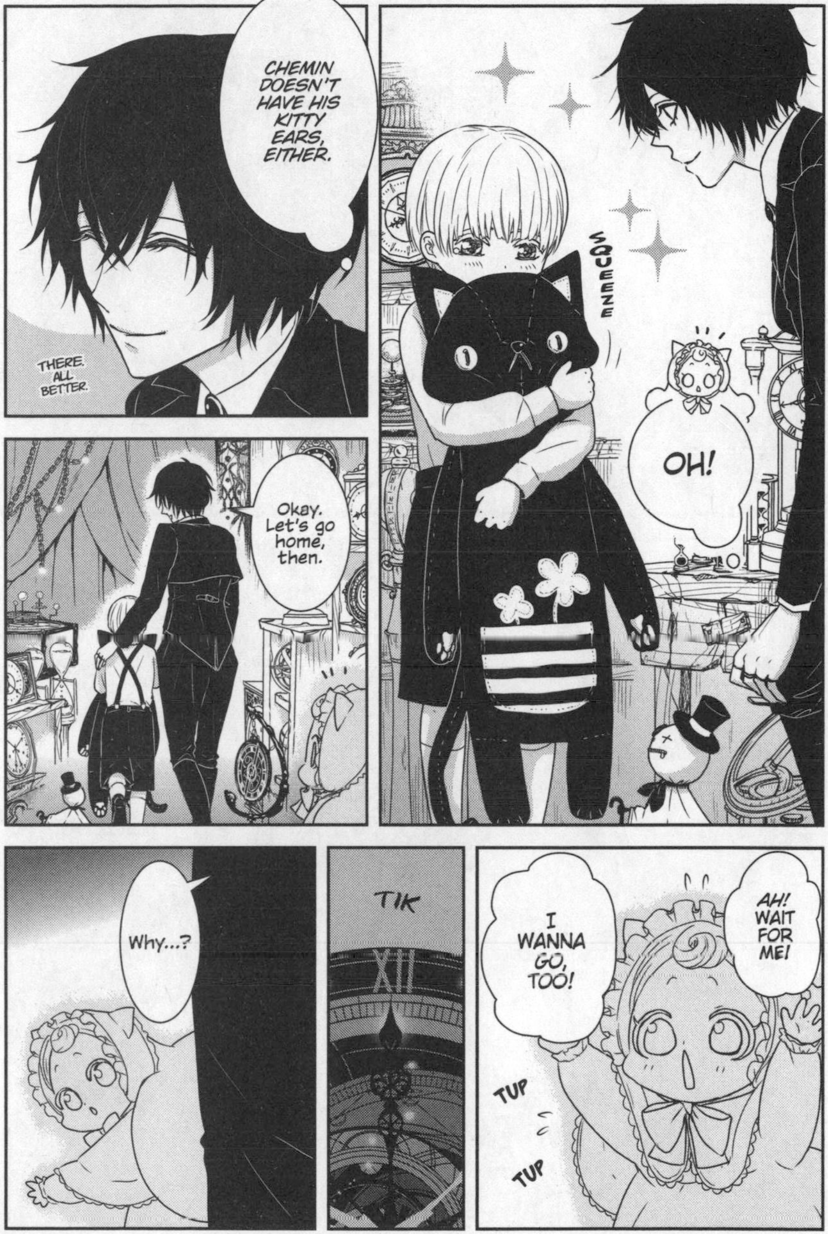
SQUEEZE
OH!
CHEMIN DOESN'T HAVE HIS KITTY EARS, EITHER.
THERE. ALL BETTER.
Okay. Let's go home, then.
AH! WAIT FOR ME!
I WANNA GO, TOO!
TUP
TUP
TIK
XII
Why...?

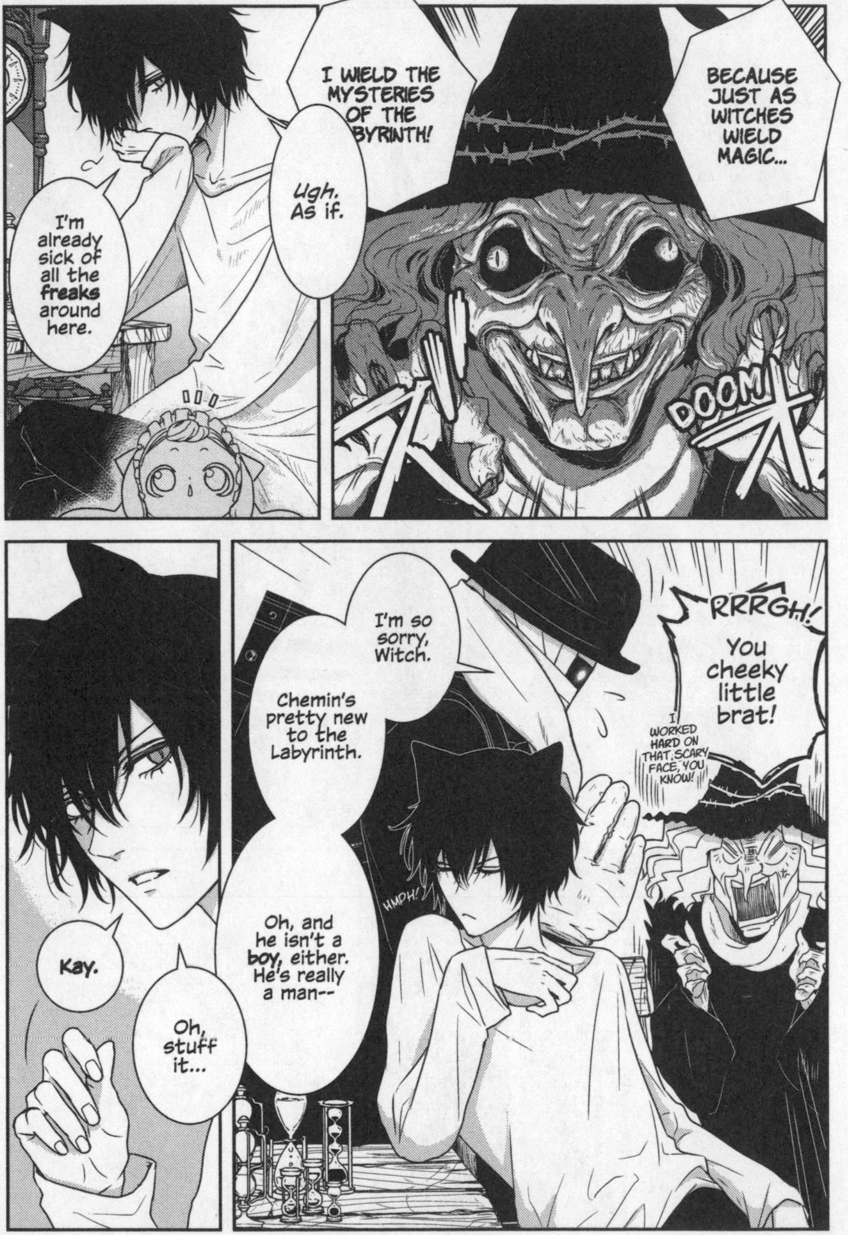
BECAUSE JUST AS WITCHES WIELD MAGIC...
I WIELD THE MYSTERIES OF THE ABYRINTH!
DOOM
Ugh. As if.
I'm already sick of all the freaks around here.
RRRGH!
You cheeky little brat!
I WORKED HARD ON THAT SCARY FACE, YOU KNOW!
I'm so sorry, Witch.
Chemin's pretty new to the Labyrinth.
HMPH!
Oh, and he isn't a boy, either. He's really a man--
Oh, stuff it...
Kay.

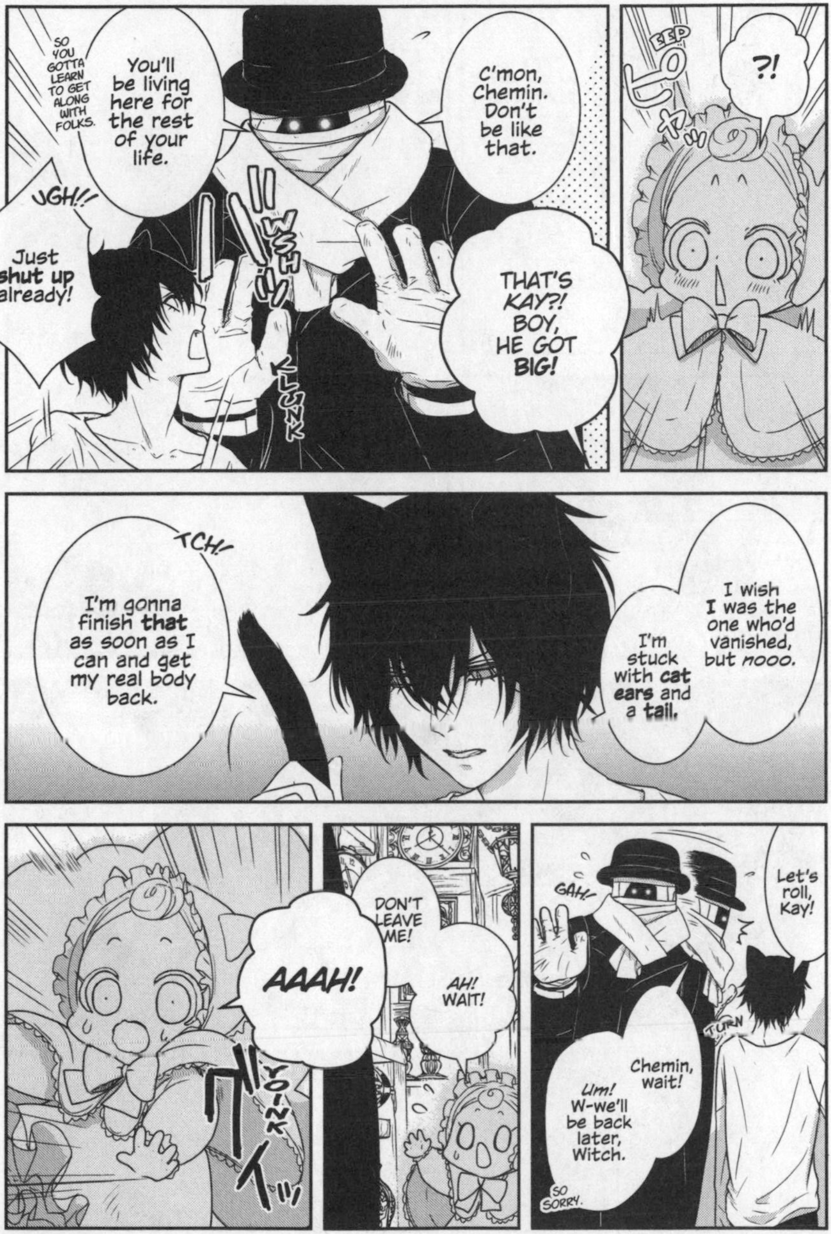
EEP
?!
C'mon, Chemin. Don't be like that.
You'll be living here for the rest of your life.
SO YOU GOTTA LEARN TO GET ALONG WITH FOLKS.
WSH
THAT'S KAY?! BOY, HE GOT BIG!
UGH!!
Just shut up already!
KLUNK
I wish I was the one who'd vanished, but nooo.
I'm stuck with cat ears and a tail.
TCH!
I'm gonna finish that as soon as I can and get my real body back.
Let's roll, Kay!
GAH!
TURN
Chemin, wait!
Um! W-we'll be back later, Witch.
SO SORRY.
DON'T LEAVE ME!
AH! WAIT!
AAAH!
YOINK

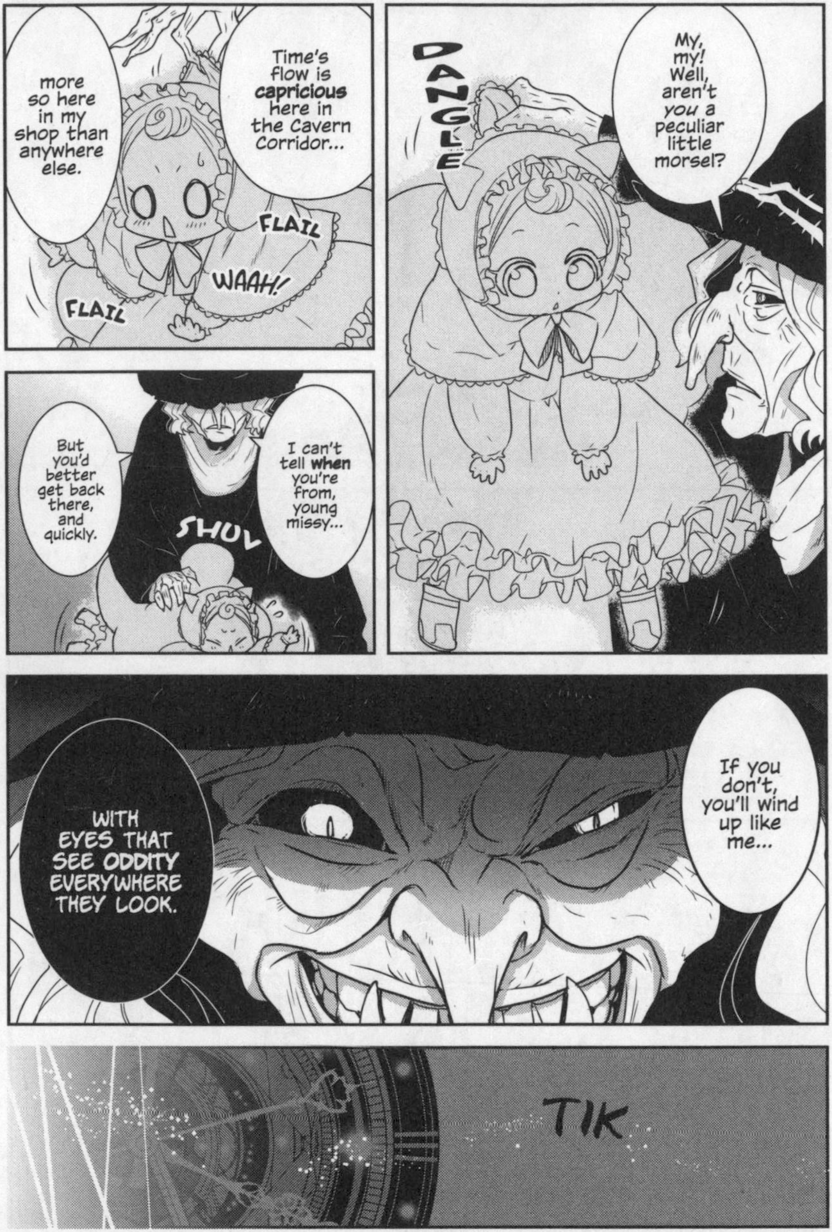
DANGLE
My, my! Well, aren't you a peculiar little morsel?
Time's flow is **capricious** here in the Cavern Corridor...
more so here in my shop than anywhere else.
FLAIL
WAAH!
FLAIL
I can't tell **when** you're from, young missy...
But you'd better get back there, and quickly.
SHUV
If you don't, you'll wind up like me...
WITH EYES THAT SEE **ODDITY** EVERYWHERE THEY LOOK.
TIK

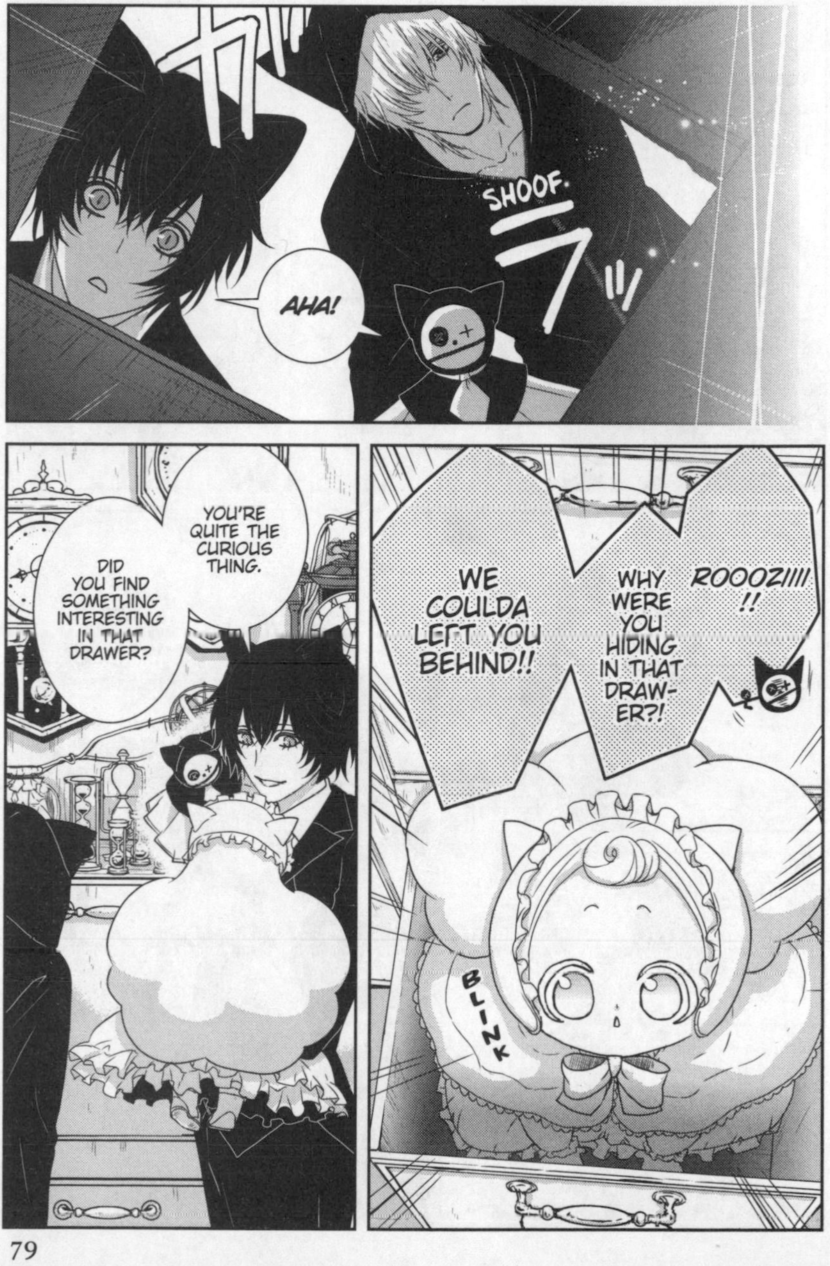
SHOOF
AHA!
ROOOZI!!!! !!
WHY WERE YOU HIDING IN THAT DRAWER?!
WE COULDA LEFT YOU BEHIND!!
BLINK
YOU'RE QUITE THE CURIOUS THING.
DID YOU FIND SOMETHING INTERESTING IN THAT DRAWER?

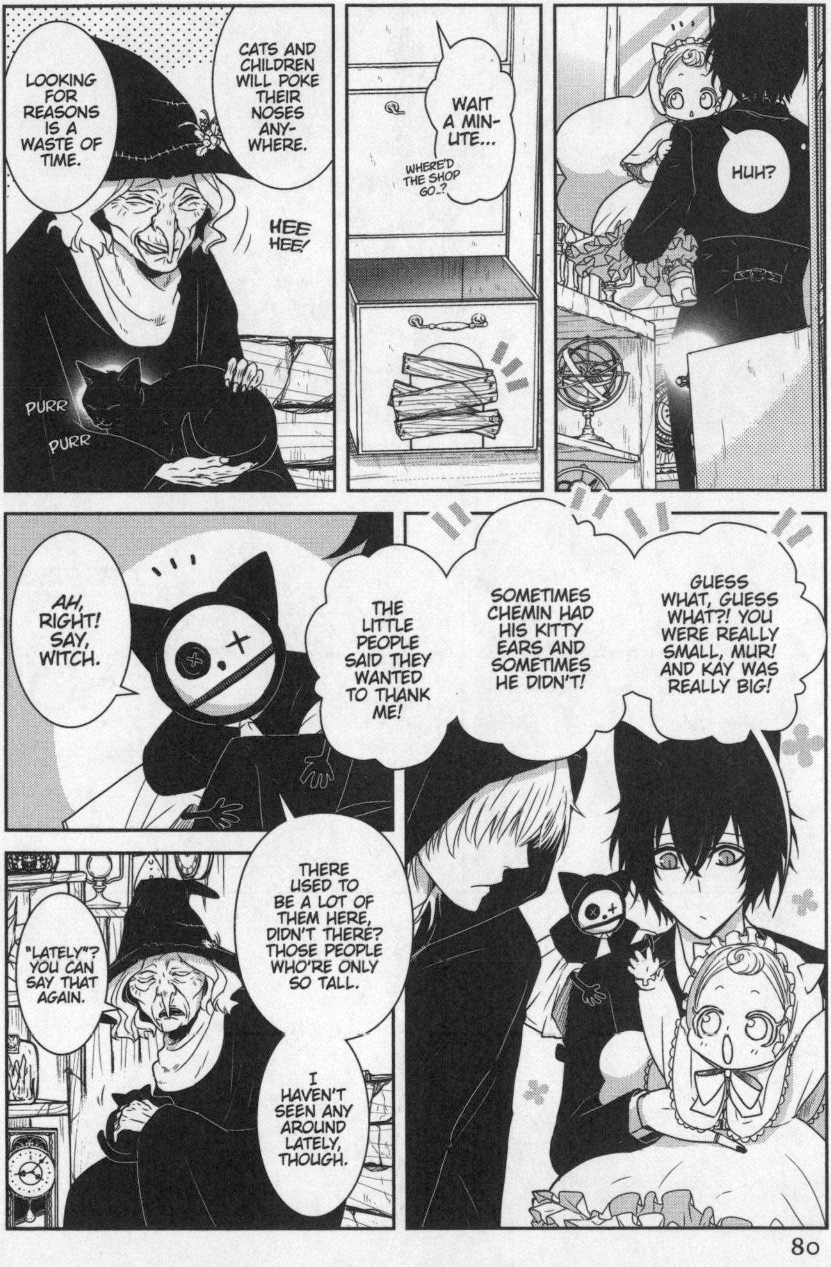
HUH?
WAIT A MIN-UTE...
WHERE'D THE SHOP GO..?
CATS AND CHILDREN WILL POKE THEIR NOSES ANY-WHERE.
LOOKING FOR REASONS IS A WASTE OF TIME.
HEE HEE!
PURR
PURR
GUESS WHAT, GUESS WHAT?! YOU WERE REALLY SMALL, MUR! AND KAY WAS REALLY BIG!
SOMETIMES CHEMIN HAD HIS KITTY EARS AND SOMETIMES HE DIDN'T!
THE LITTLE PEOPLE SAID THEY WANTED TO THANK ME!
AH, RIGHT! SAY, WITCH.
THERE USED TO BE A LOT OF THEM HERE, DIDN'T THERE? THOSE PEOPLE WHO'RE ONLY SO TALL.
I HAVEN'T SEEN ANY AROUND LATELY, THOUGH.
"LATELY"? YOU CAN SAY THAT AGAIN.

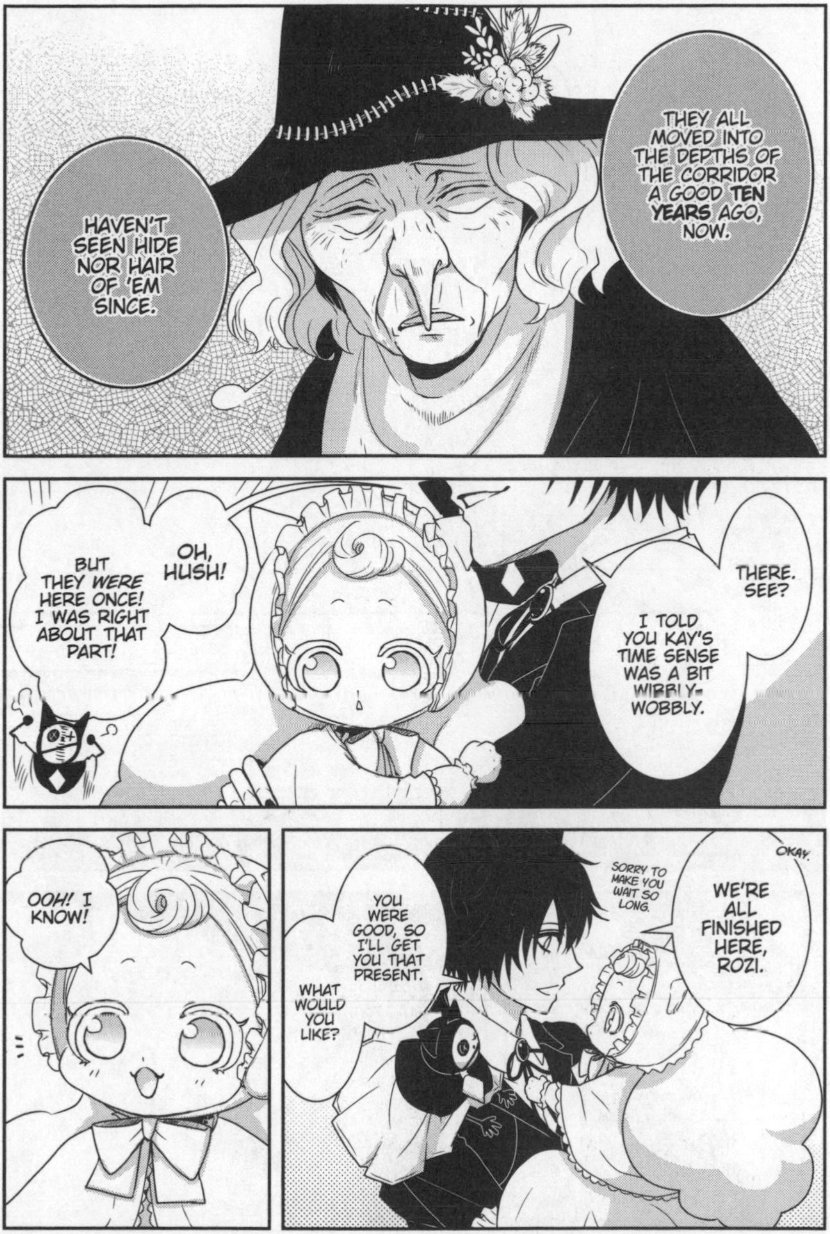
THEY ALL MOVED INTO THE DEPTHS OF THE CORRIDOR A GOOD **TEN YEARS** AGO, NOW.
HAVEN'T SEEN HIDE NOR HAIR OF 'EM SINCE.
THERE. SEE?
I TOLD YOU KAY'S TIME SENSE WAS A BIT WIBBLY-WOBBLY.
OH, HUSH!
BUT THEY *WERE* HERE ONCE! I WAS RIGHT ABOUT THAT PART!
OKAY.
WE'RE ALL FINISHED HERE, ROZI.
SORRY TO MAKE YOU WAIT SO LONG.
YOU WERE GOOD, SO I'LL GET YOU THAT PRESENT.
WHAT WOULD YOU LIKE?
OOH! I KNOW!

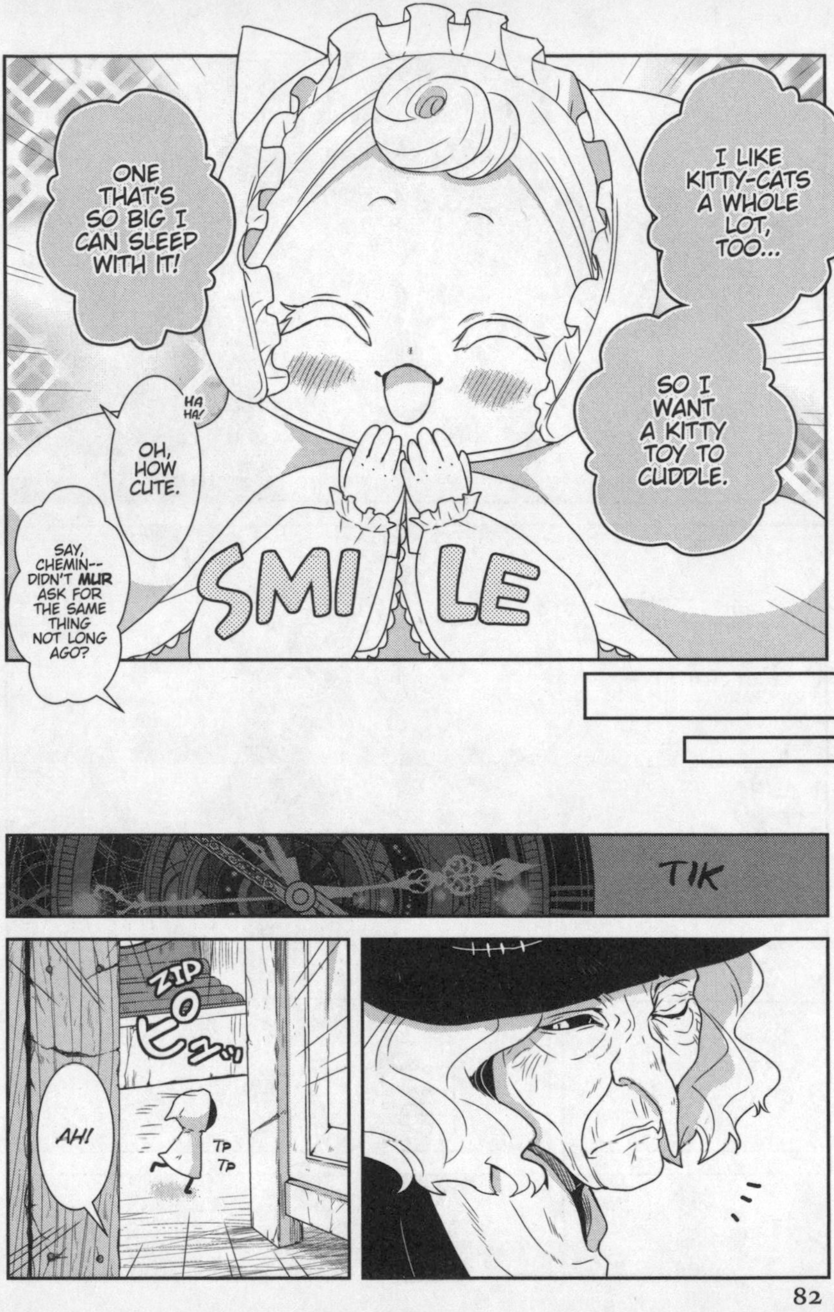
I LIKE KITTY-CATS A WHOLE LOT, TOO...
SO I WANT A KITTY TOY TO CUDDLE.
ONE THAT'S SO BIG I CAN SLEEP WITH IT!
SMILE
HA HA!
OH, HOW CUTE.
SAY, CHEMIN-- DIDN'T MUR ASK FOR THE SAME THING NOT LONG AGO?
TIK
ZIP
AH!
TP TP

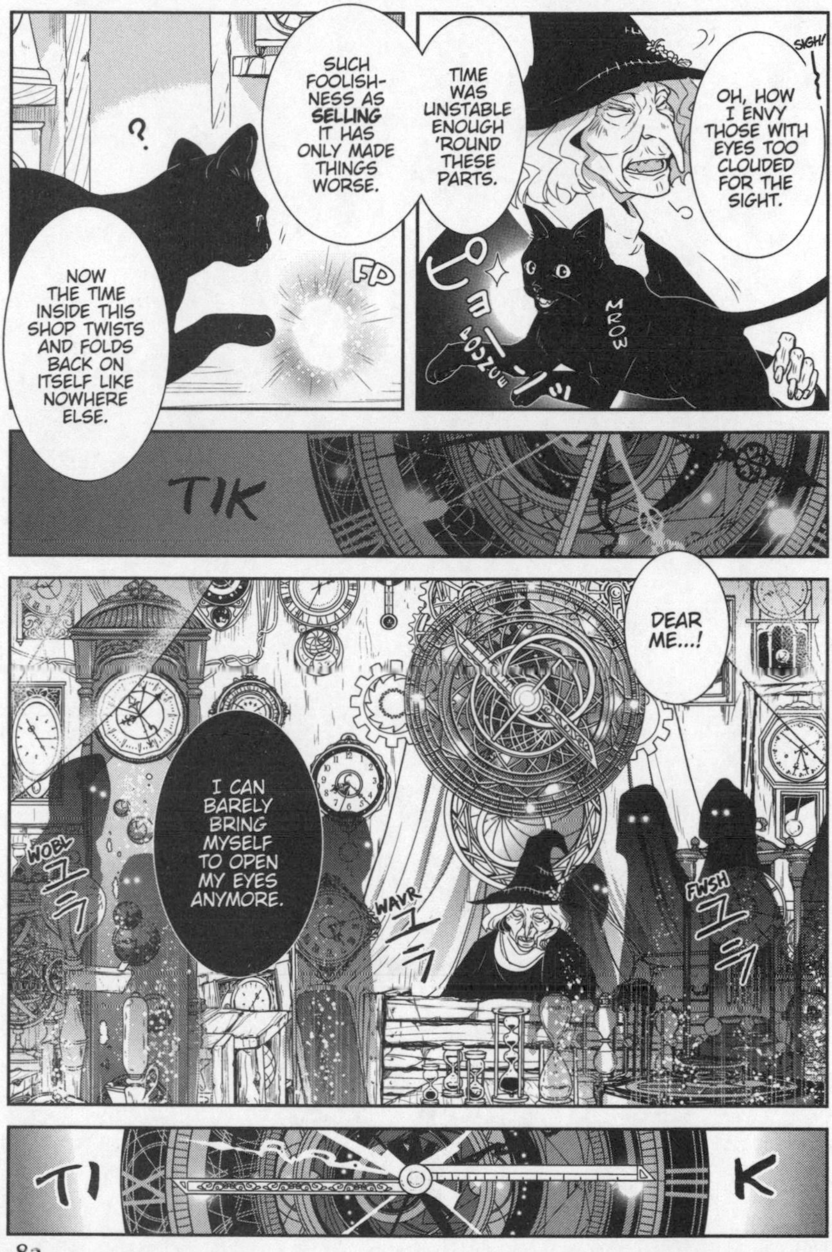
SIGH!
OH, HOW I ENVY THOSE WITH EYES TOO CLOUDED FOR THE SIGHT.
TIME WAS UNSTABLE ENOUGH 'ROUND THESE PARTS.
MROW
SUCH FOOLISH-NESS AS **SELLING** IT HAS ONLY MADE THINGS WORSE.
?
FP
NOW THE TIME INSIDE THIS SHOP TWISTS AND FOLDS BACK ON ITSELF LIKE NOWHERE ELSE.
TIK
DEAR ME...!
FWSH
WAVR
I CAN BARELY BRING MYSELF TO OPEN MY EYES ANYMORE.
WOBL
TI
K

3 The Monster and the Crow

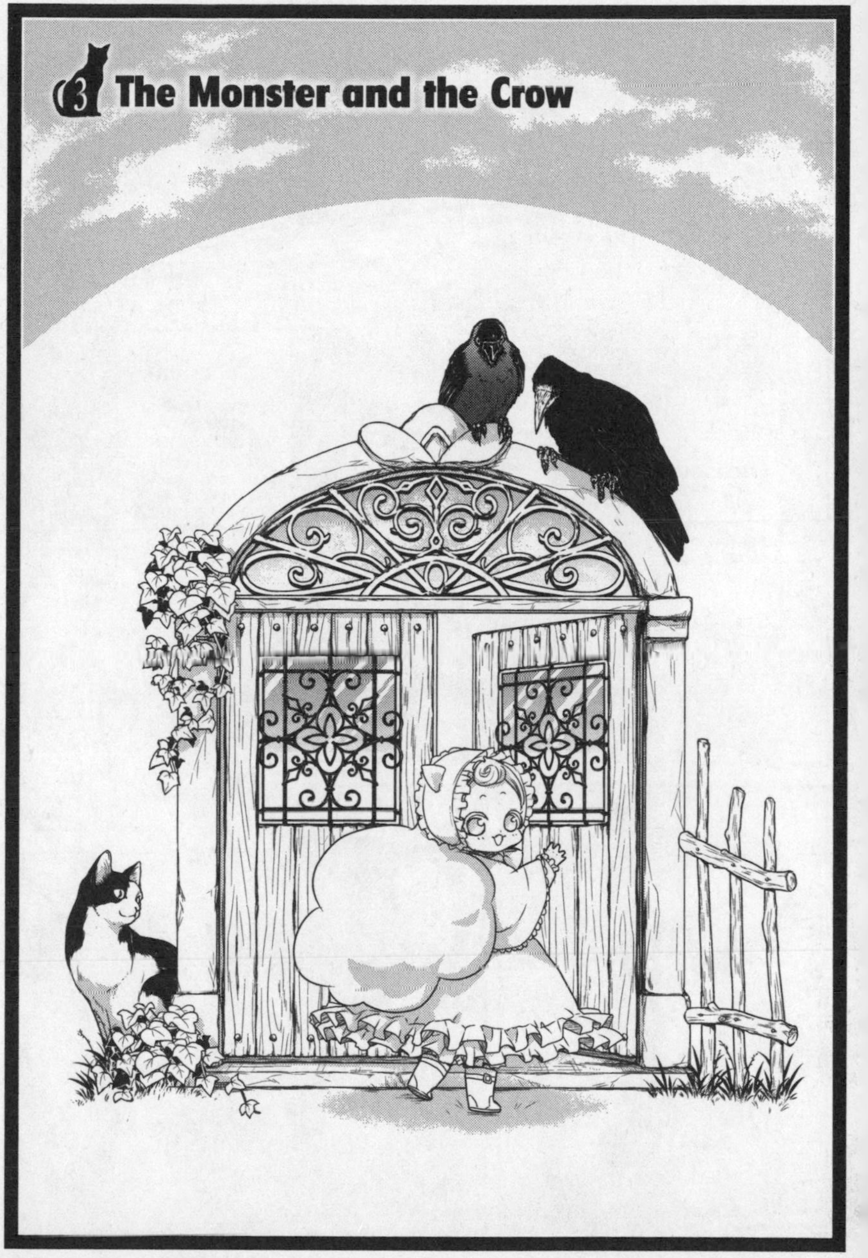

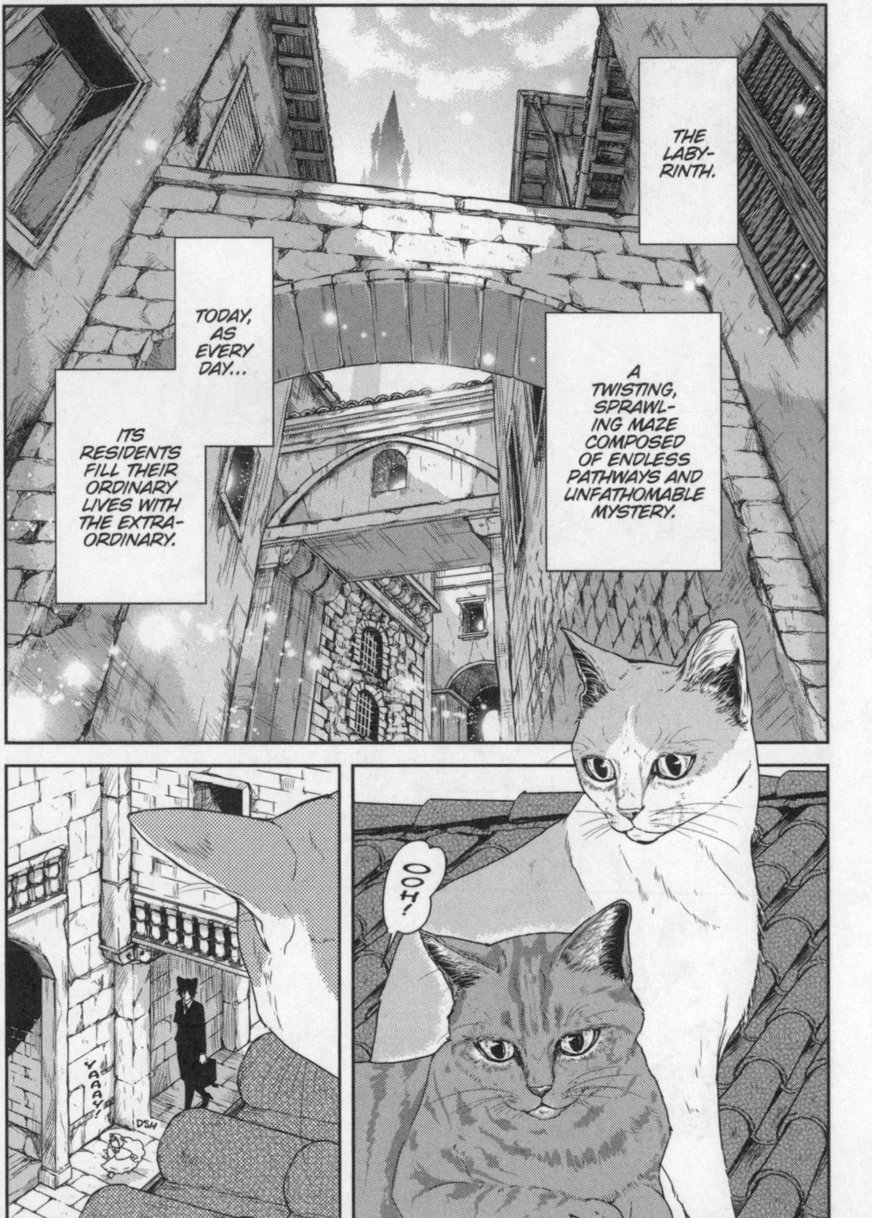
THE LABYRINTH.
A TWISTING, SPRAWLING MAZE COMPOSED OF ENDLESS PATHWAYS AND UNFATHOMABLE MYSTERY.
TODAY, AS EVERY DAY...
ITS RESIDENTS FILL THEIR ORDINARY LIVES WITH THE EXTRAORDINARY.
OOH?
YAAAAY!
DSH

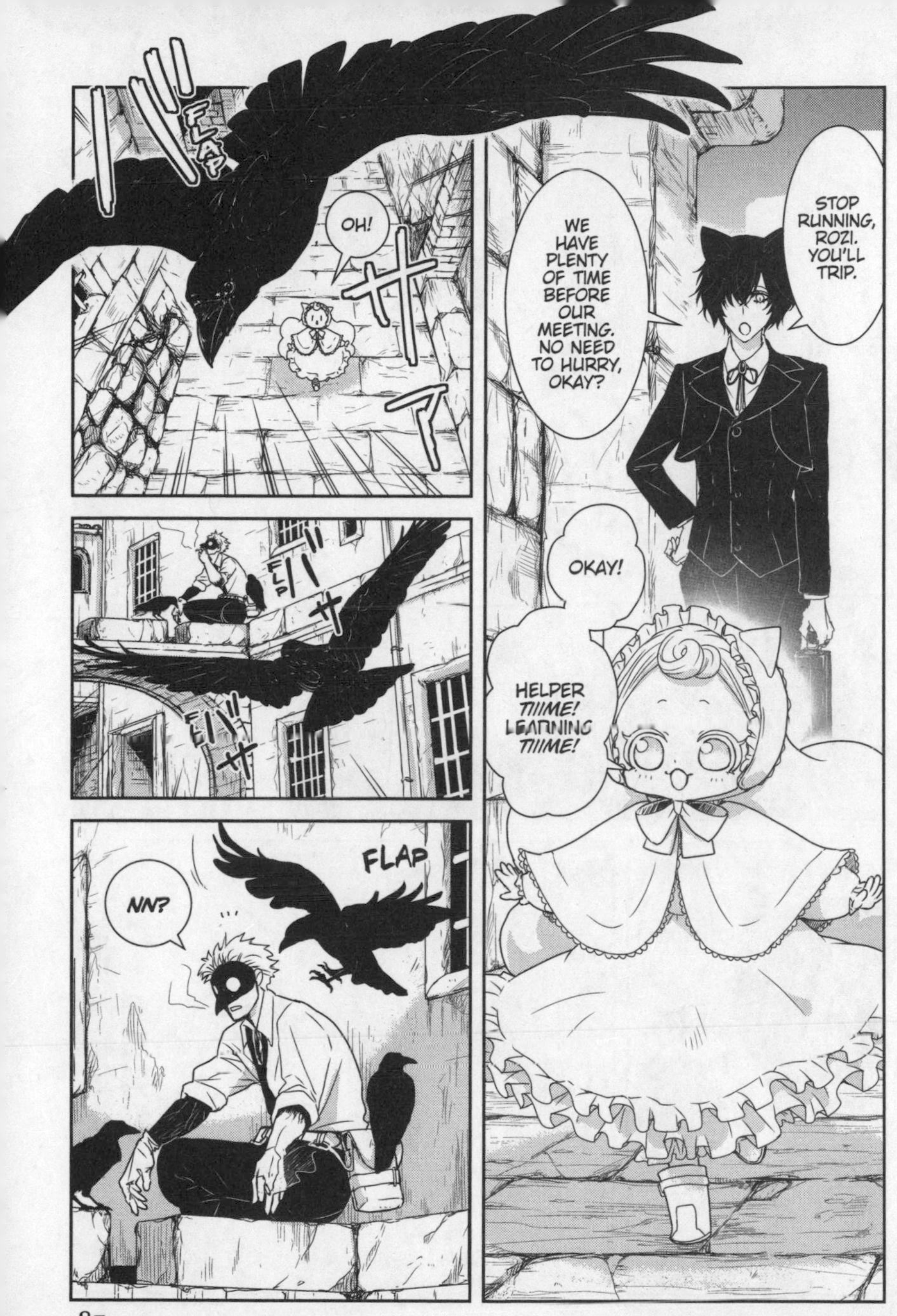
STOP RUNNING, ROZI. YOU'LL TRIP.
WE HAVE PLENTY OF TIME BEFORE OUR MEETING. NO NEED TO HURRY, OKAY?
OKAY!
HELPER TIIIME! LEARNING TIIIME!
FLAP
OH!
FLAP
FLAP
NN?

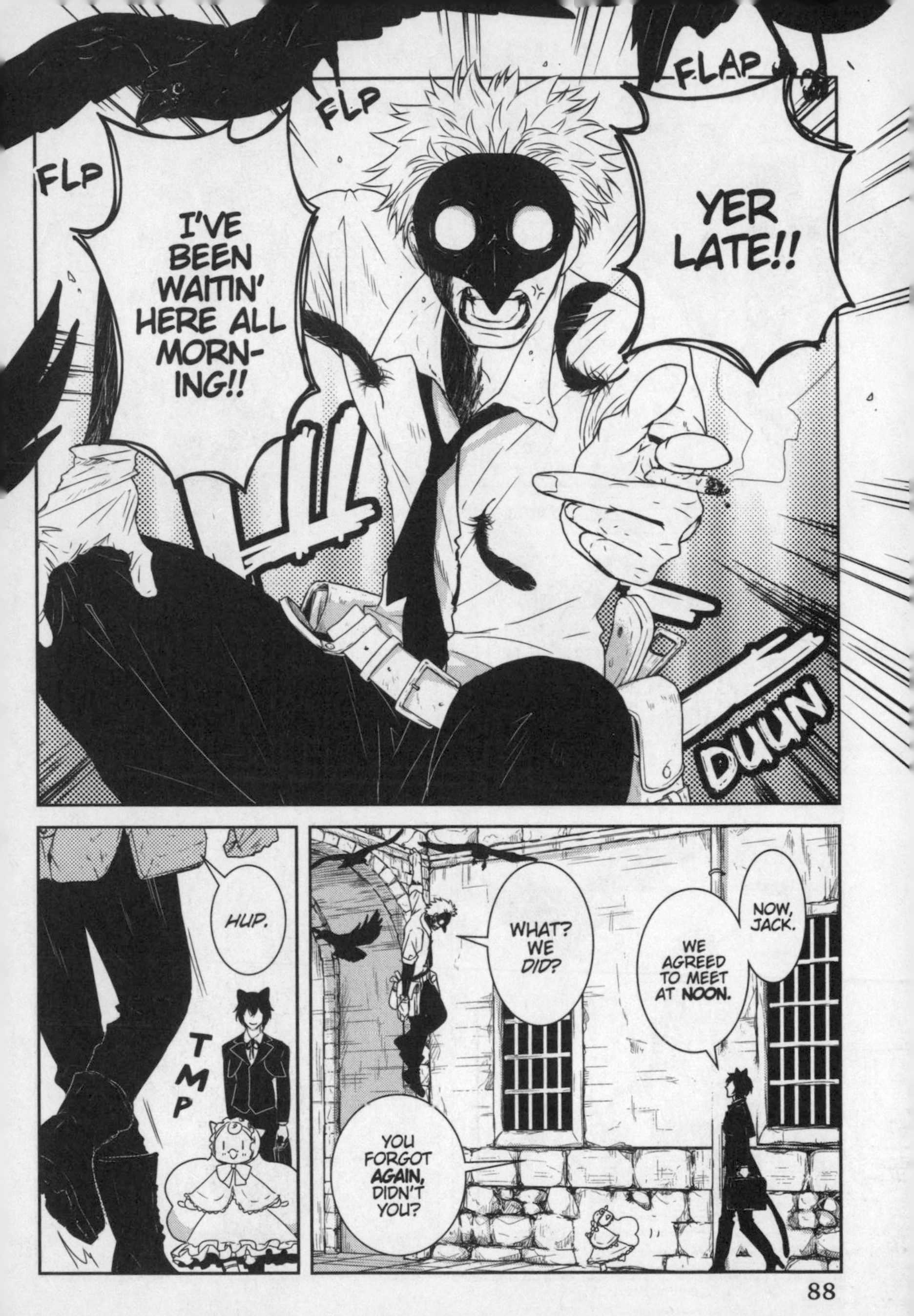
FLAP
YER LATE!!
FLP
FLP
I'VE BEEN WAITIN' HERE ALL MORN-ING!!
DUUN
NOW, JACK.
WE AGREED TO MEET AT NOON.
WHAT? WE DID?
YOU FORGOT AGAIN, DIDN'T YOU?
HUP.
TMP

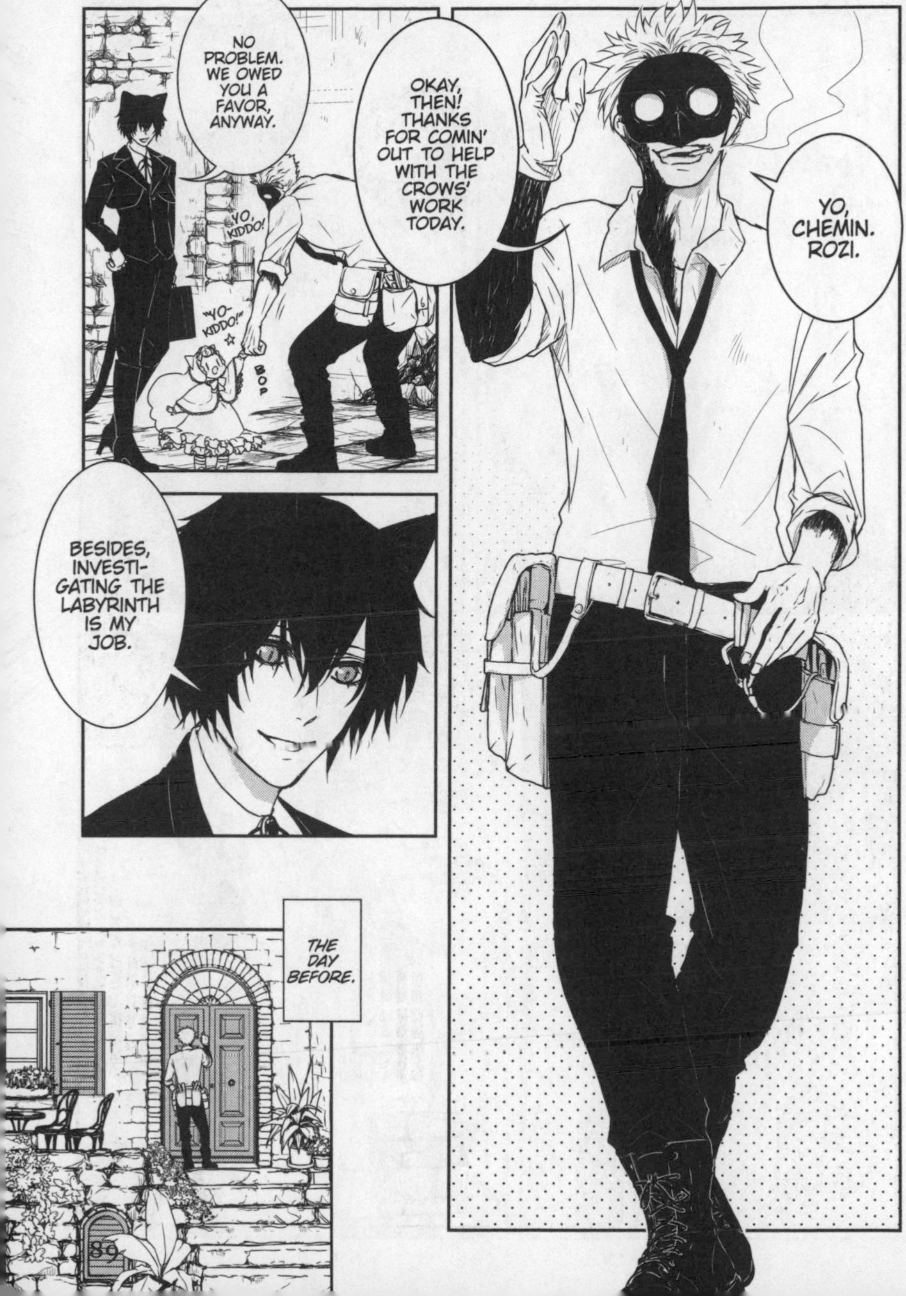
YO, CHEMIN. ROZI.
OKAY, THEN! THANKS FOR COMIN' OUT TO HELP WITH THE CROWS' WORK TODAY.
NO PROBLEM. WE OWED YOU A FAVOR, ANYWAY.
YO, KIDDO!
"YO-KIDDO!"
BOP
BESIDES, INVESTI-GATING THE LABYRINTH IS MY JOB.
THE DAY BEFORE.

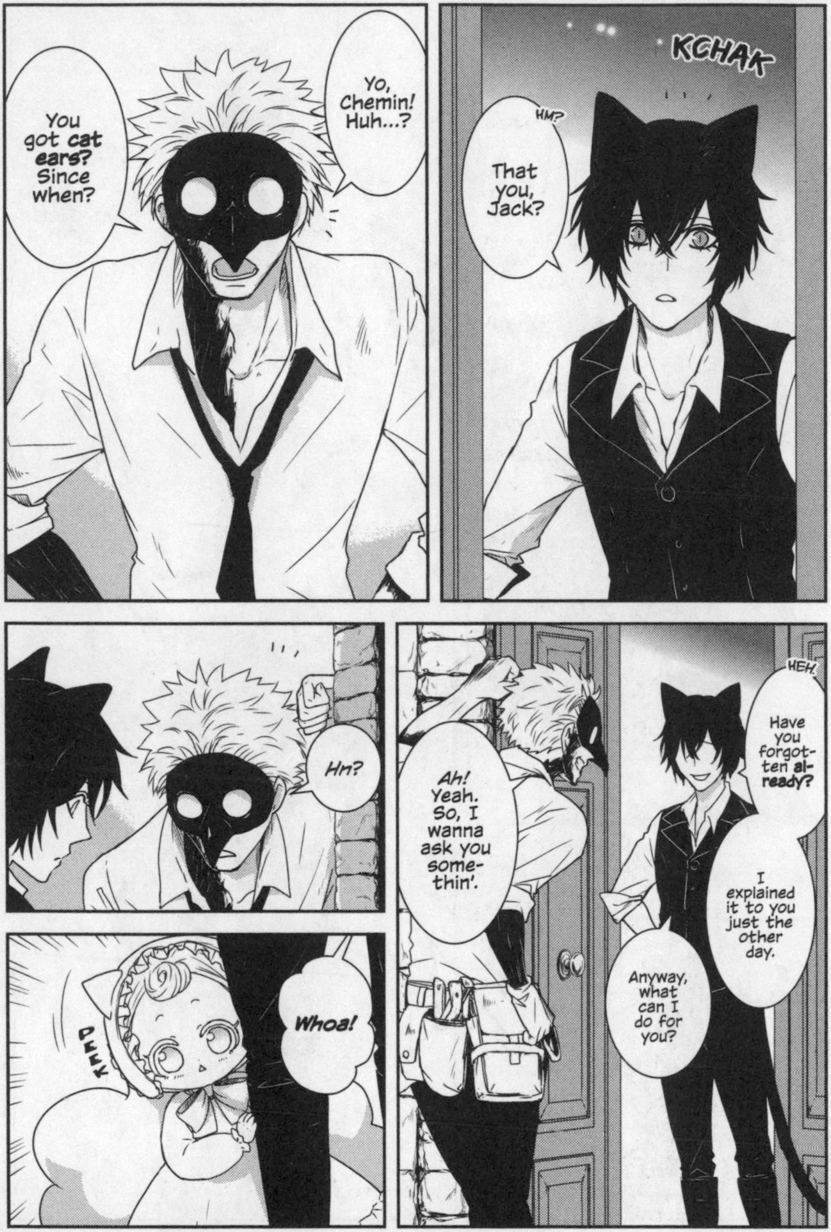
KCHAK
HM?
That you, Jack?
Yo, Chemin! Huh...?
You got cat ears? Since when?
HEH.
Have you forgot-ten already?
I explained it to you just the other day.
Anyway, what can I do for you?
Ah! Yeah. So, I wanna ask you some-thin'.
Hn?
Whoa!
PEEK

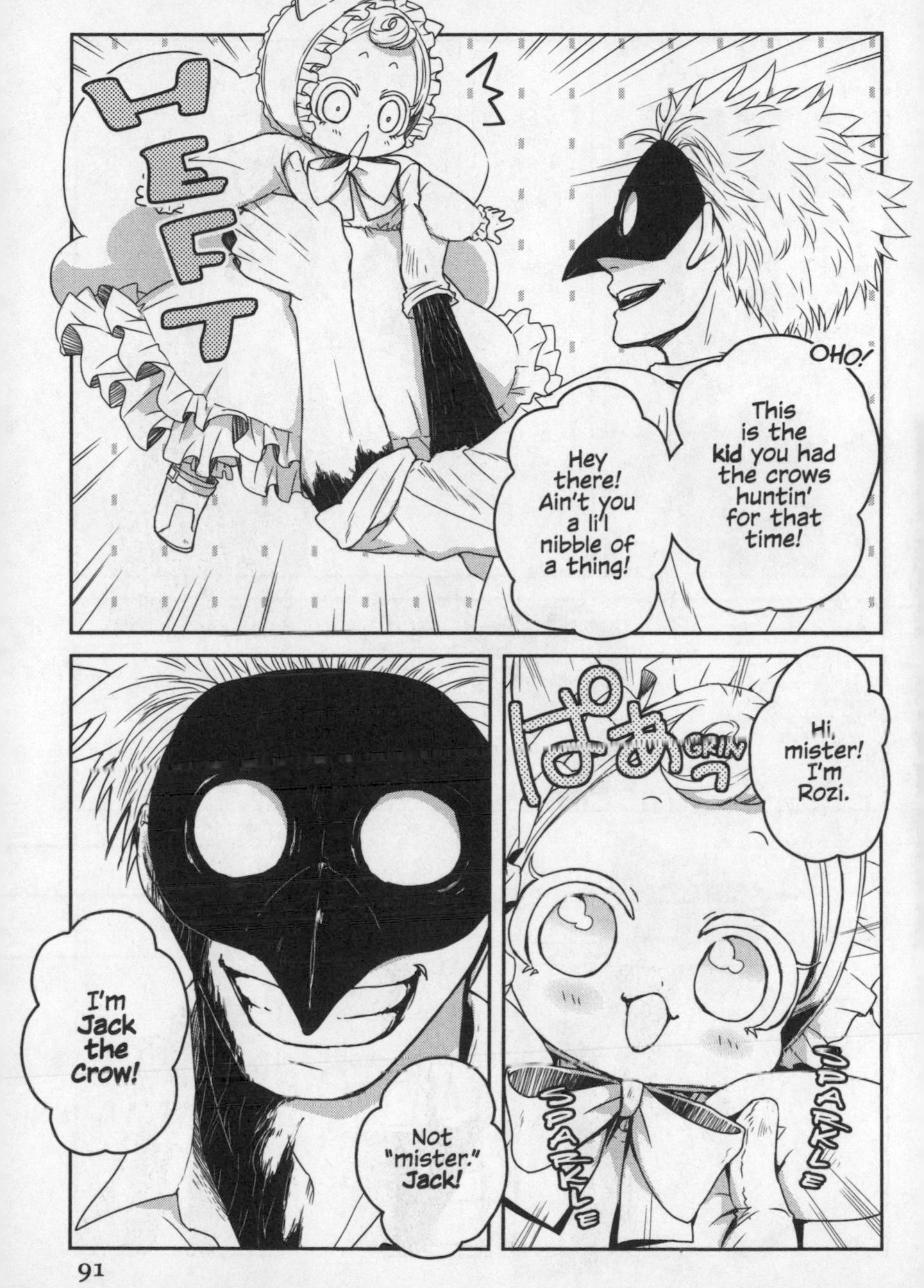
OHO!
This is the kid you had the crows huntin' for that time!
Hey there! Ain't you a li'l nibble of a thing!
HEFT
ぱあっ
GRIN
Hi, mister! I'm Rozi.
SPARKLE
SPARKLE
I'm Jack the Crow!
Not "mister." Jack!

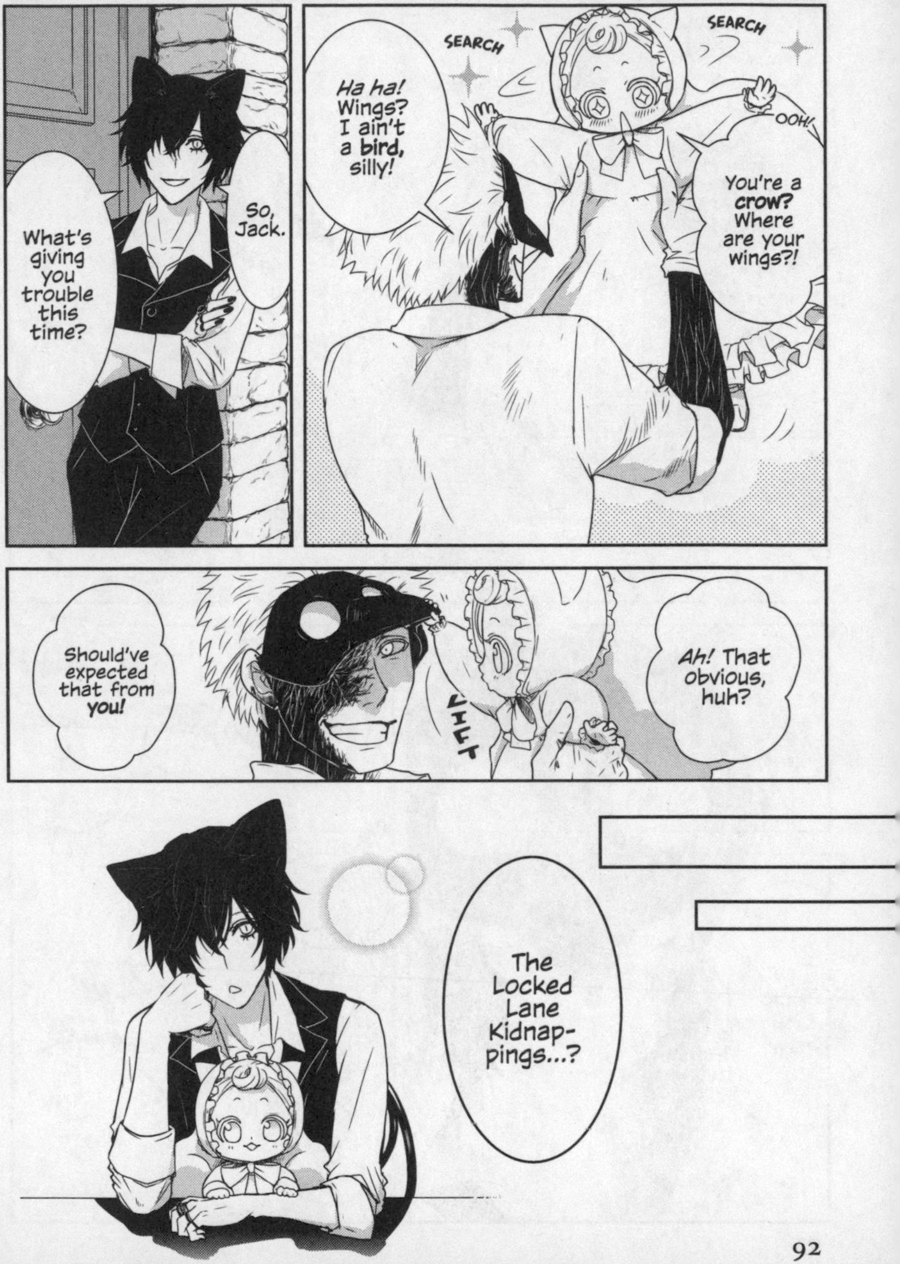
SEARCH
OOH!
You're a **crow?** Where are your wings?!
SEARCH
Ha ha! Wings? I ain't a **bird,** silly!
So, Jack.
What's giving you trouble this time?
Ah! That obvious, huh?
LIFT
Should've expected that from **you!**
The Locked Lane Kidnap-pings...?

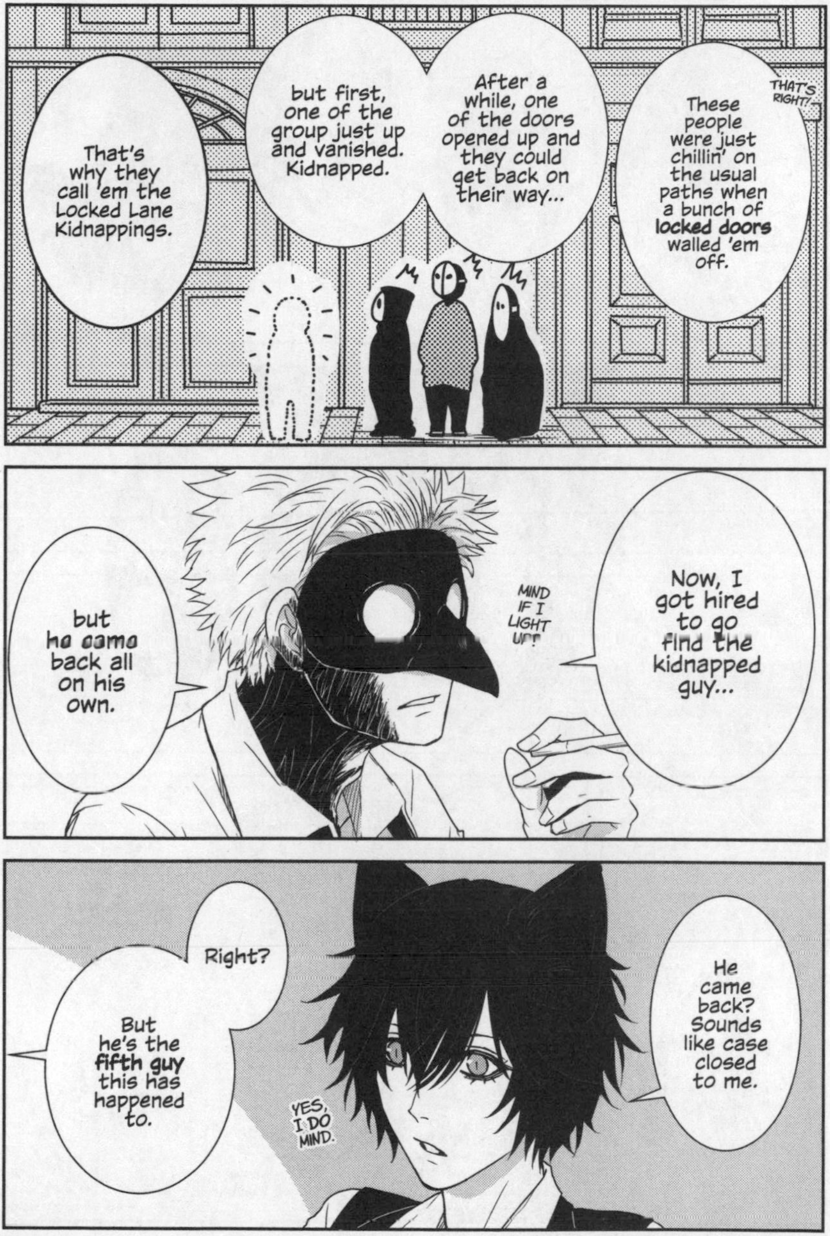
These people were just chillin' on the usual paths when a bunch of locked doors walled 'em off.
THAT'S RIGHT!
After a while, one of the doors opened up and they could get back on their way...
but first, one of the group just up and vanished. Kidnapped.
That's why they call 'em the Locked Lane Kidnappings.
Now, I got hired to go find the kidnapped guy...
MIND IF I LIGHT UP?
but he came back all on his own.
He came back? Sounds like case closed to me.
YES, I DO MIND.
Right?
But he's the fifth guy this has happened to.

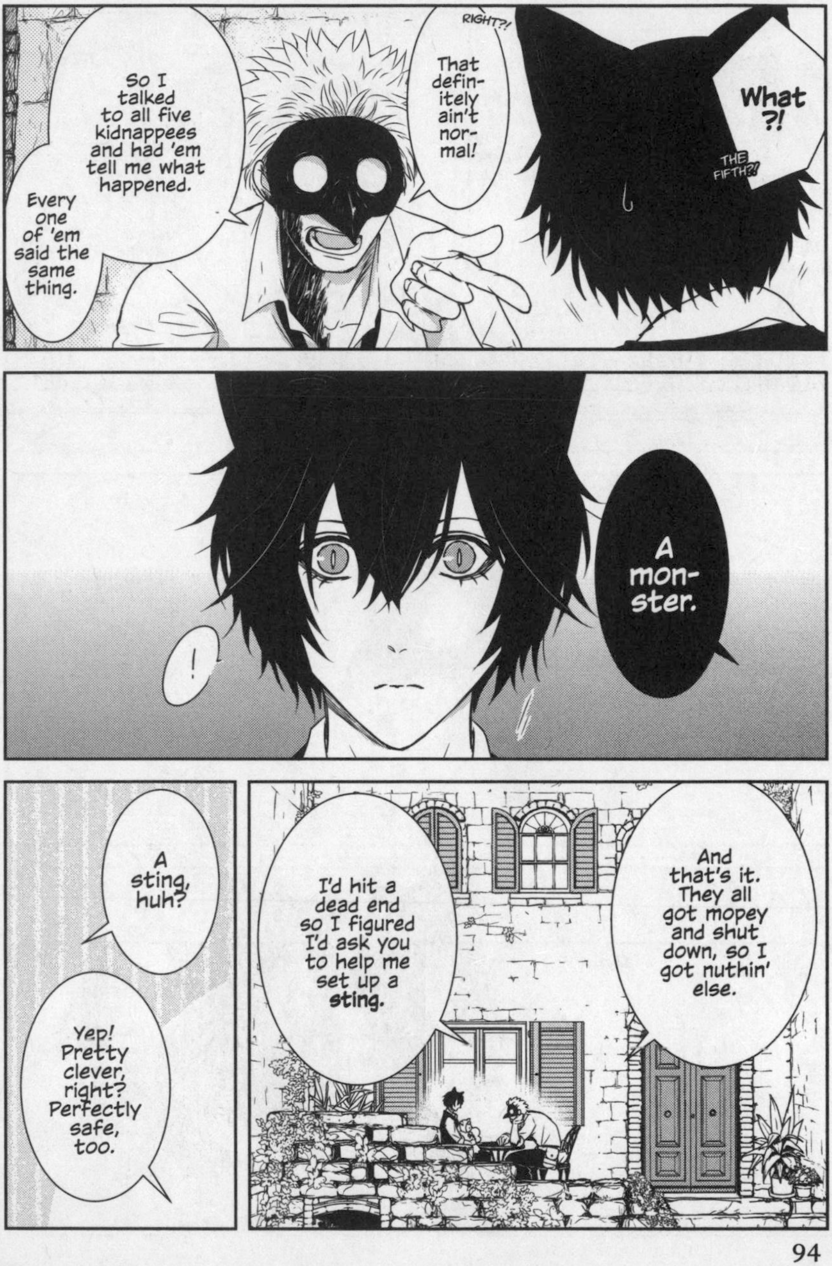
What ?!
THE FIFTH?!
RIGHT?!
That definitely ain't normal!
So I talked to all five kidnappees and had 'em tell me what happened.
Every one of 'em said the same thing.
A monster.
!
And that's it. They all got mopey and shut down, so I got nuthin' else.
I'd hit a dead end so I figured I'd ask you to help me set up a **sting.**
A sting, huh?
Yep! Pretty clever, right? Perfectly safe, too.

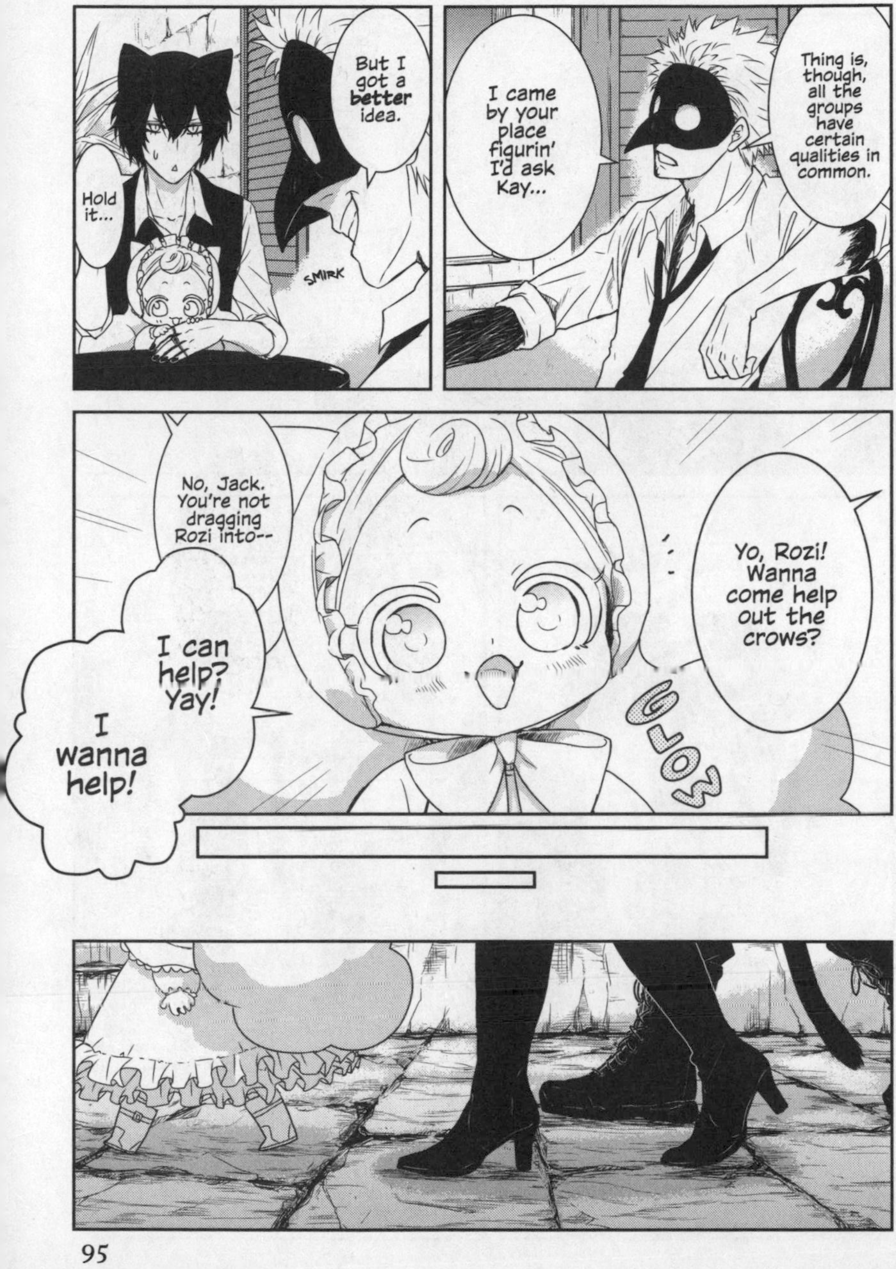
Thing is, though, all the groups have certain qualities in common.
I came by your place figurin' I'd ask Kay...
But I got a **better** idea.
SMIRK
Hold it...
Yo, Rozi! Wanna come help out the crows?
GLOW
No, Jack. You're not dragging Rozi into--
I can help? Yay!
I wanna help!

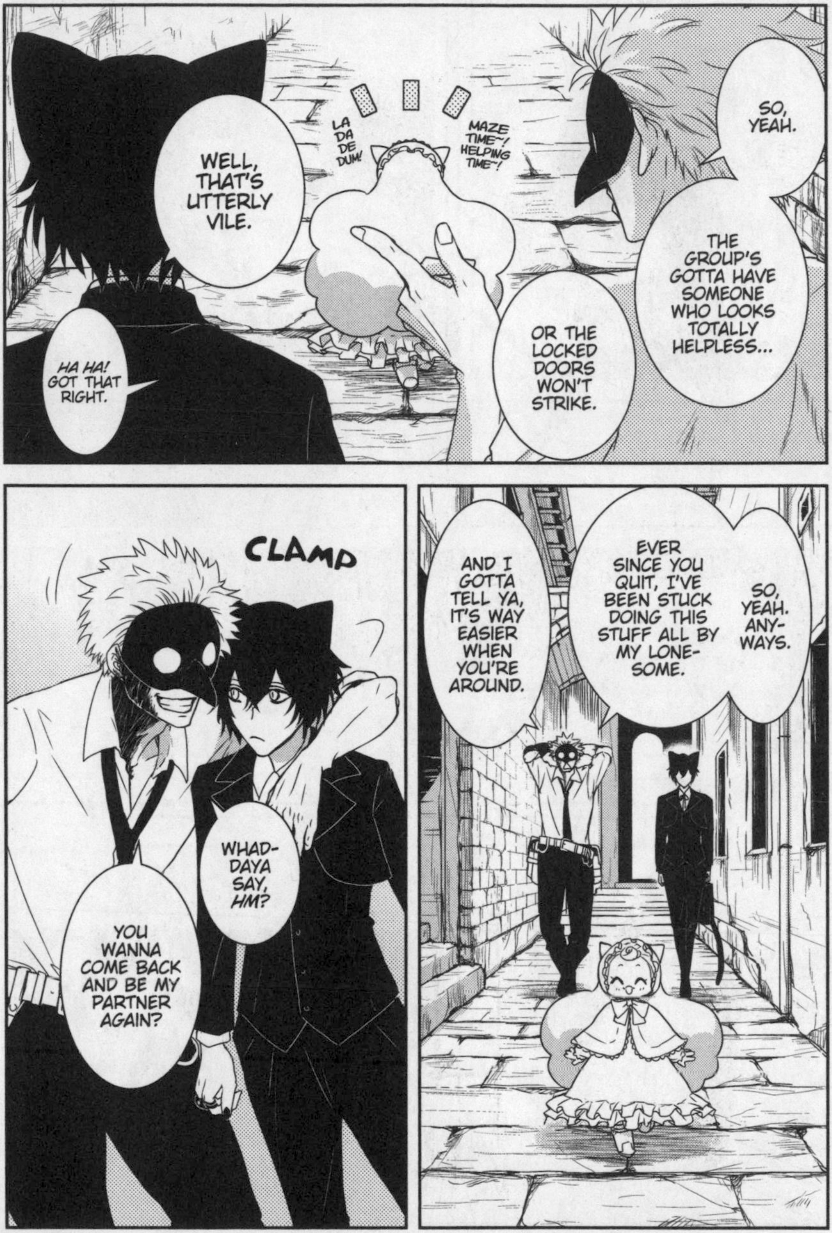
SO, YEAH.
THE GROUP'S GOTTA HAVE SOMEONE WHO LOOKS TOTALLY HELPLESS...
OR THE LOCKED DOORS WON'T STRIKE.
MAZE TIME~! HELPING TIME~!
LA DA DE DUM!
WELL, THAT'S UTTERLY VILE.
HA HA! GOT THAT RIGHT.
SO, YEAH. ANY-WAYS.
EVER SINCE YOU QUIT, I'VE BEEN STUCK DOING THIS STUFF ALL BY MY LONE-SOME.
AND I GOTTA TELL YA, IT'S WAY EASIER WHEN YOU'RE AROUND.
CLAMP
WHAD-DAYA SAY, HM?
YOU WANNA COME BACK AND BE MY PARTNER AGAIN?

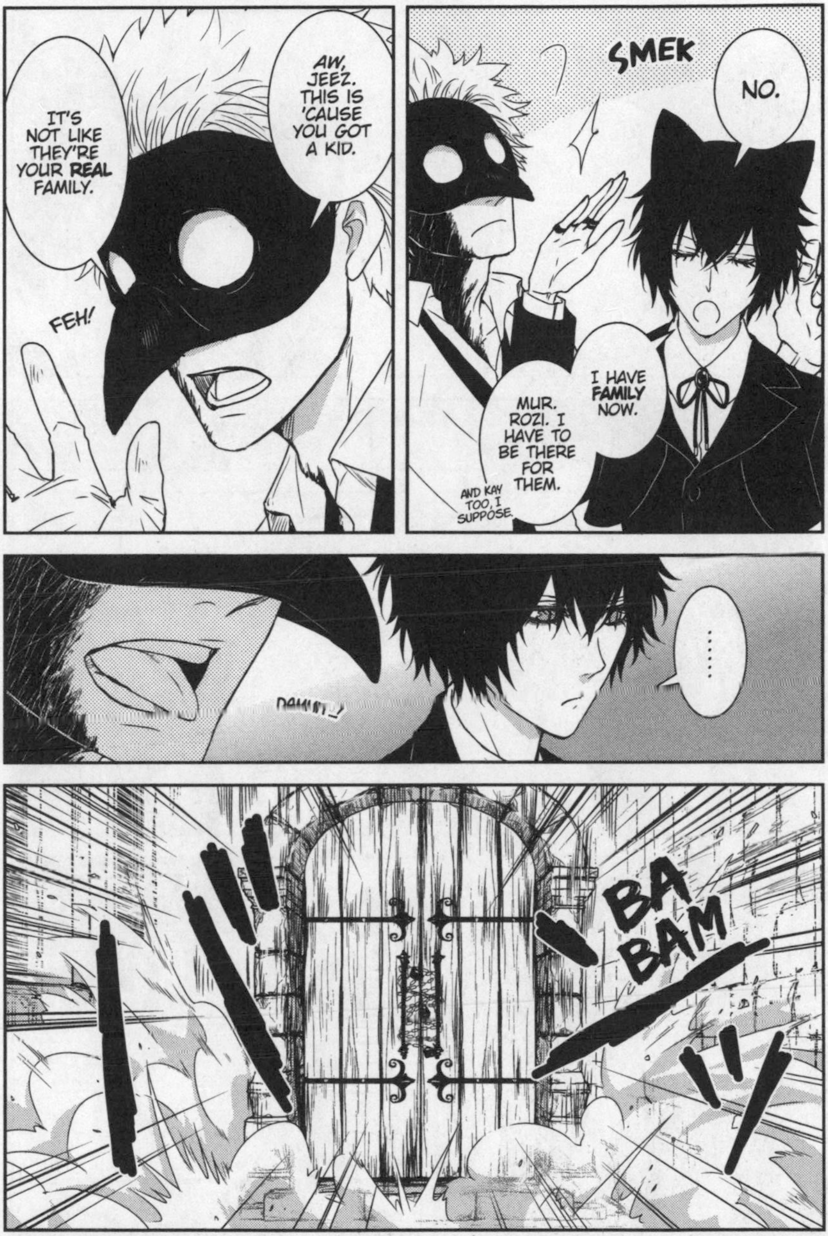
AW, JEEZ. THIS IS 'CAUSE YOU GOT A KID.
IT'S NOT LIKE THEY'RE YOUR REAL FAMILY.
FEH!
SMEK
NO.
I HAVE FAMILY NOW.
MUR. ROZI. I HAVE TO BE THERE FOR THEM.
AND KAY TOO, I SUPPOSE.
DAMMIT..!
......
BA BAM

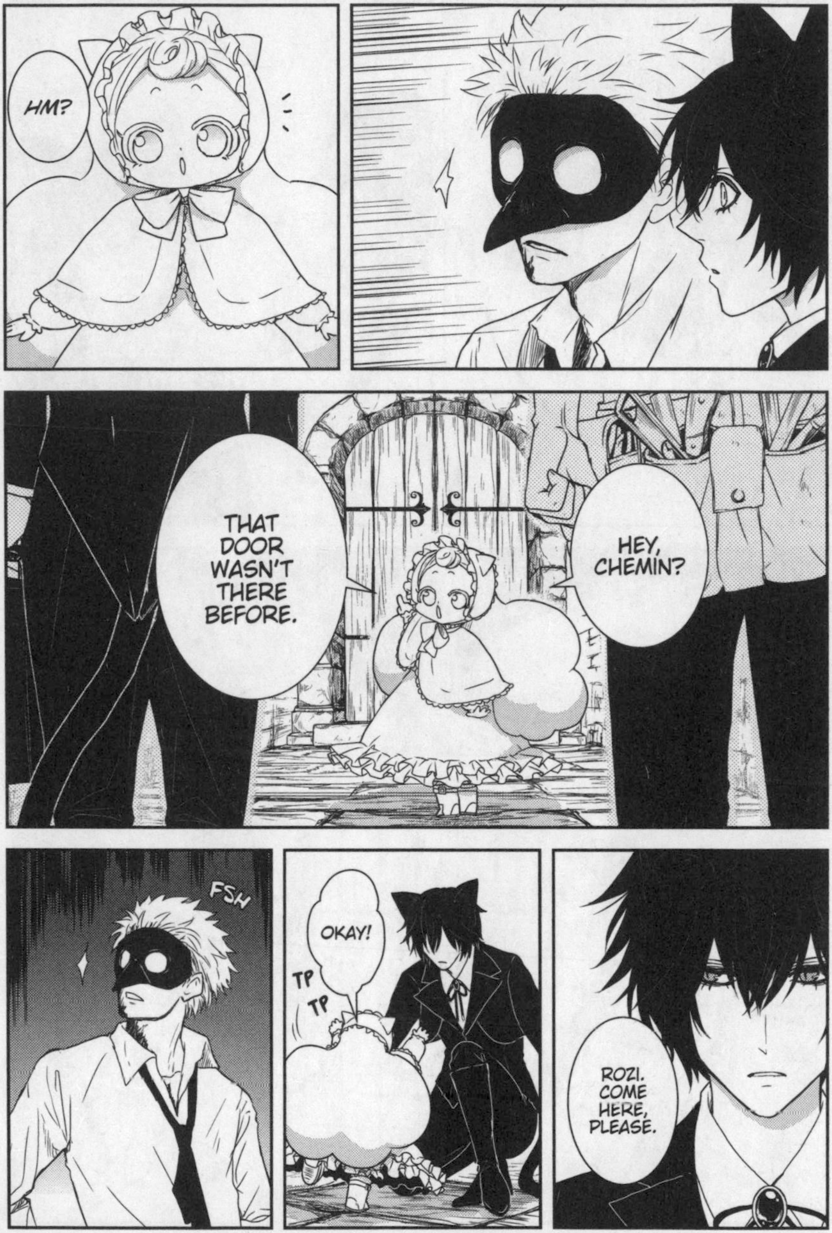
HM?
HEY, CHEMIN?
THAT DOOR WASN'T THERE BEFORE.
ROZI. COME HERE, PLEASE.
OKAY!
TP TP
FSH

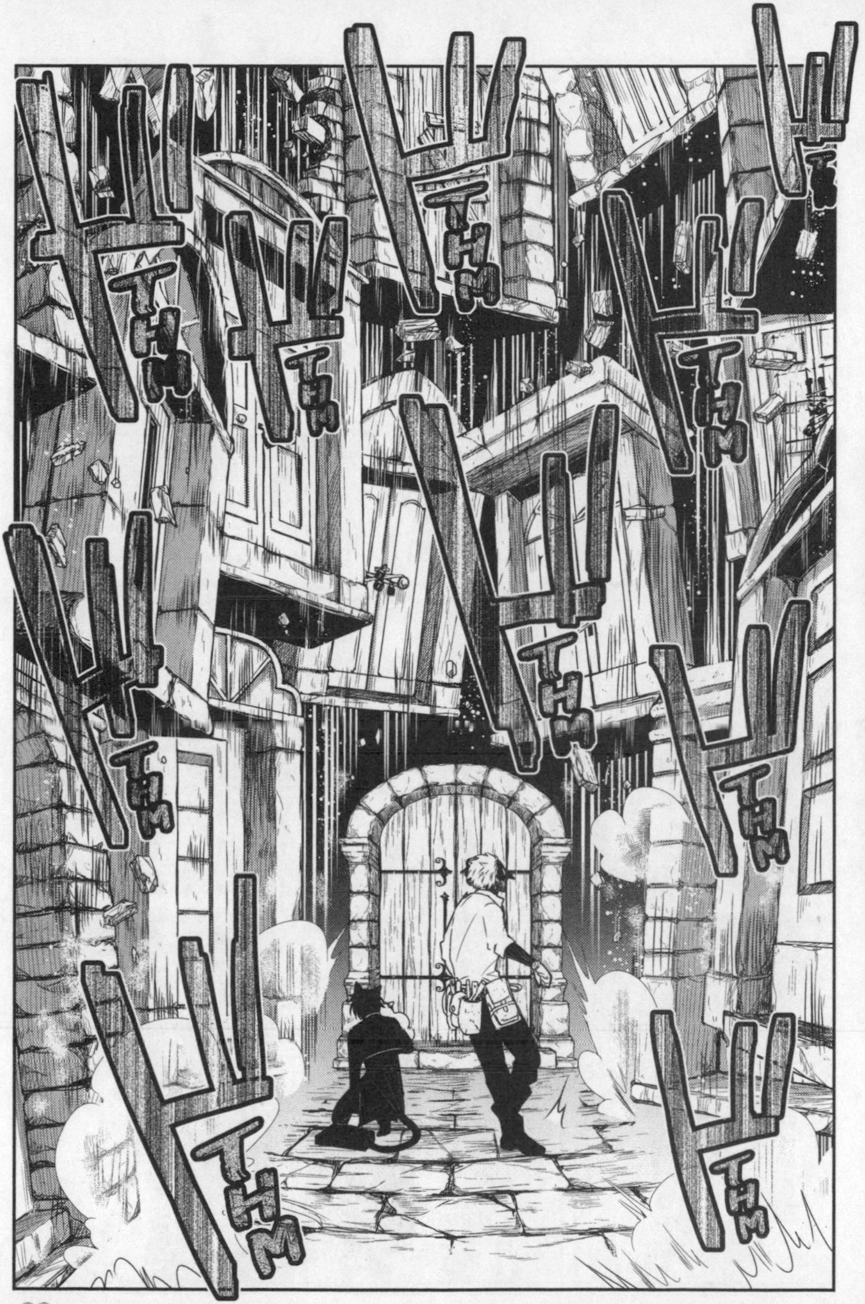
THM
THM
THM
THM
THM
THM
THM
THM
THM
THM

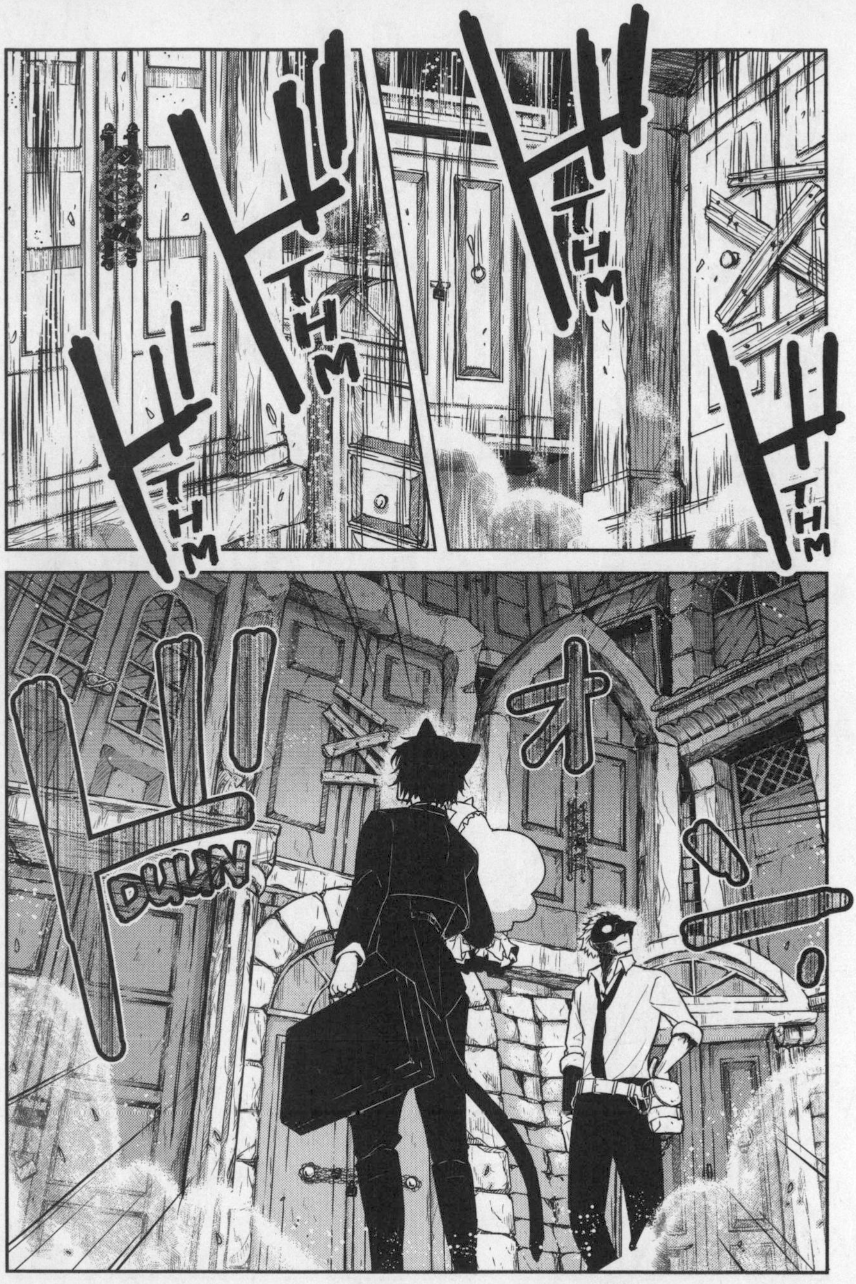
THM
THM
THM
THM
DUUN

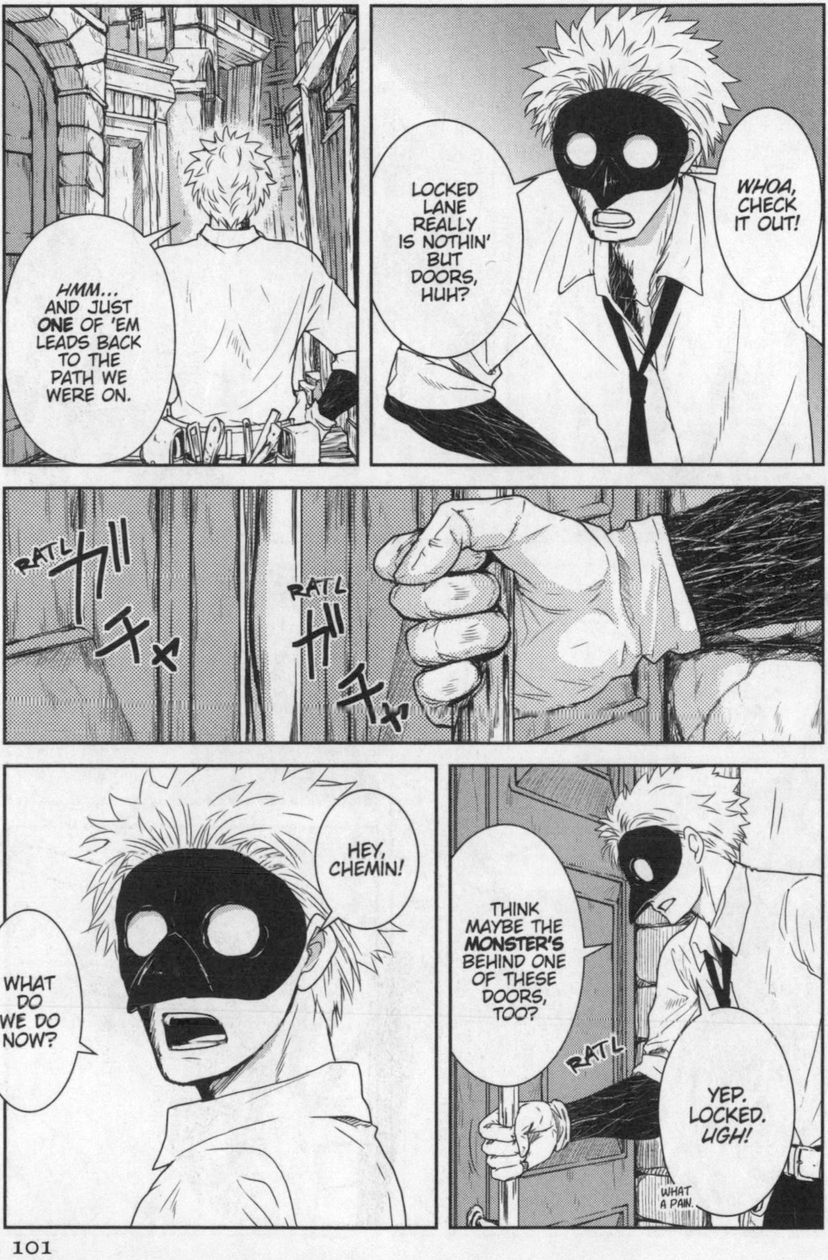

WHOA, CHECK IT OUT!
LOCKED LANE REALLY IS NOTHIN' BUT DOORS, HUH?
HMM... AND JUST ONE OF 'EM LEADS BACK TO THE PATH WE WERE ON.
RAT.L
ガチャ
RAT.L
ガチャ
THINK MAYBE THE MONSTER'S BEHIND ONE OF THESE DOORS, TOO?
RAT.L
YEP. LOCKED. UGH!
WHAT A PAIN.
HEY, CHEMIN!
WHAT DO WE DO NOW?

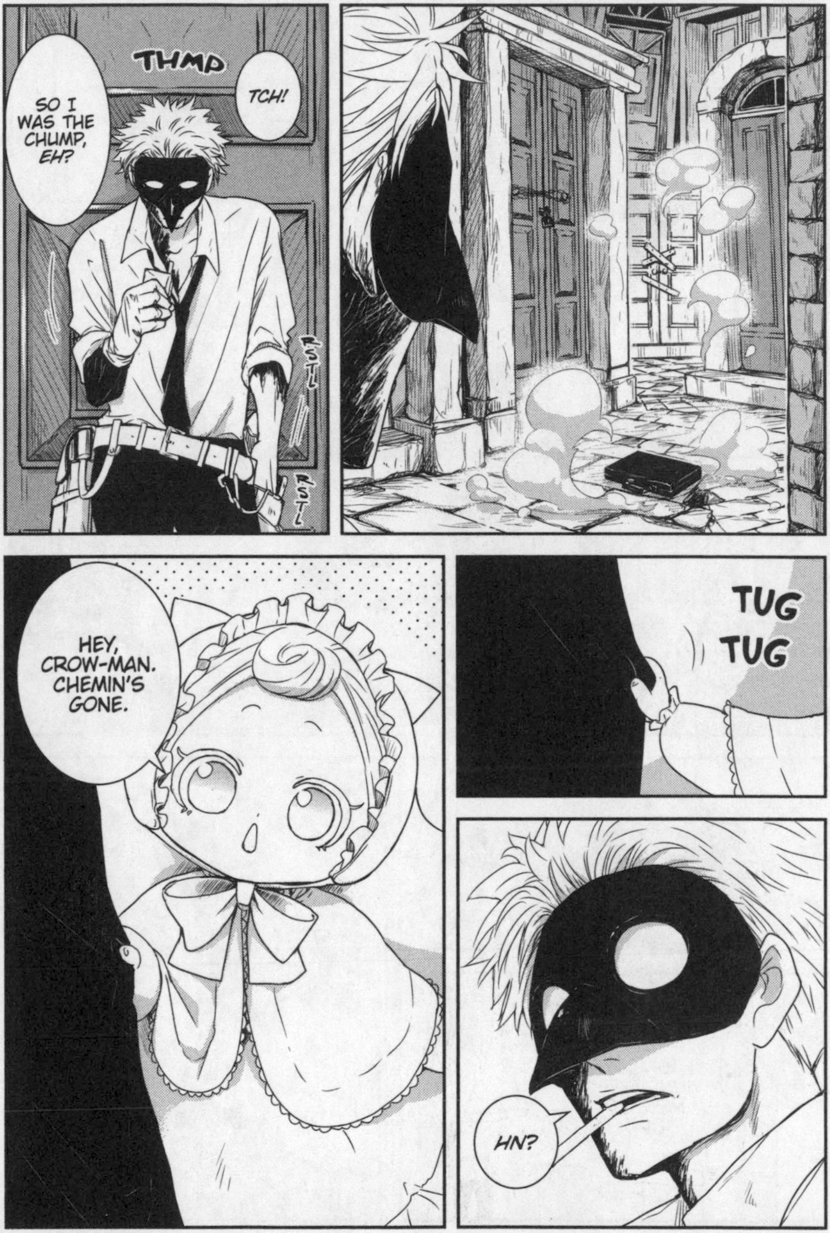
THMP
TCH!
SO I WAS THE CHUMP, EH?
R.S.T.L
R.S.T.L
TUG TUG
HN?
HEY, CROW-MAN. CHEMIN'S GONE.

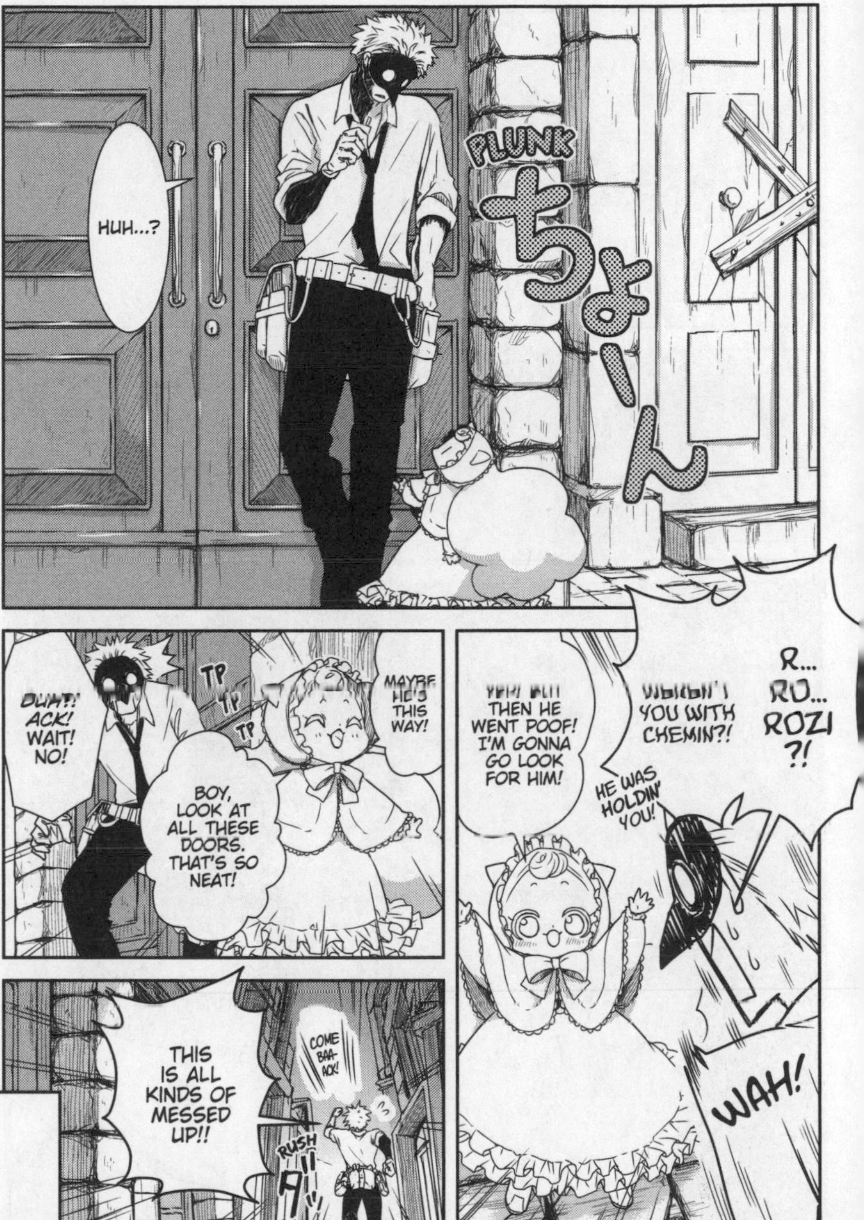

PLUNK
ちょ〜ん
HUH...?
R... RO... ROZI?!
YOU WITH CHEMIN?!
HE WAS HOLDIN' YOU!
THEN HE WENT POOF! I'M GONNA GO LOOK FOR HIM!
WAH!
MAYBE HE'S THIS WAY!
TP TP TP
BOY, LOOK AT ALL THESE DOORS. THAT'S SO NEAT!
ACK! WAIT! NO!
COME BAA-ACK!
THIS IS ALL KINDS OF MESSED UP!!
RUSH

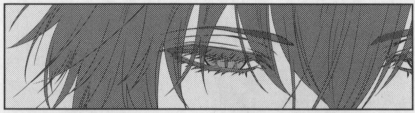

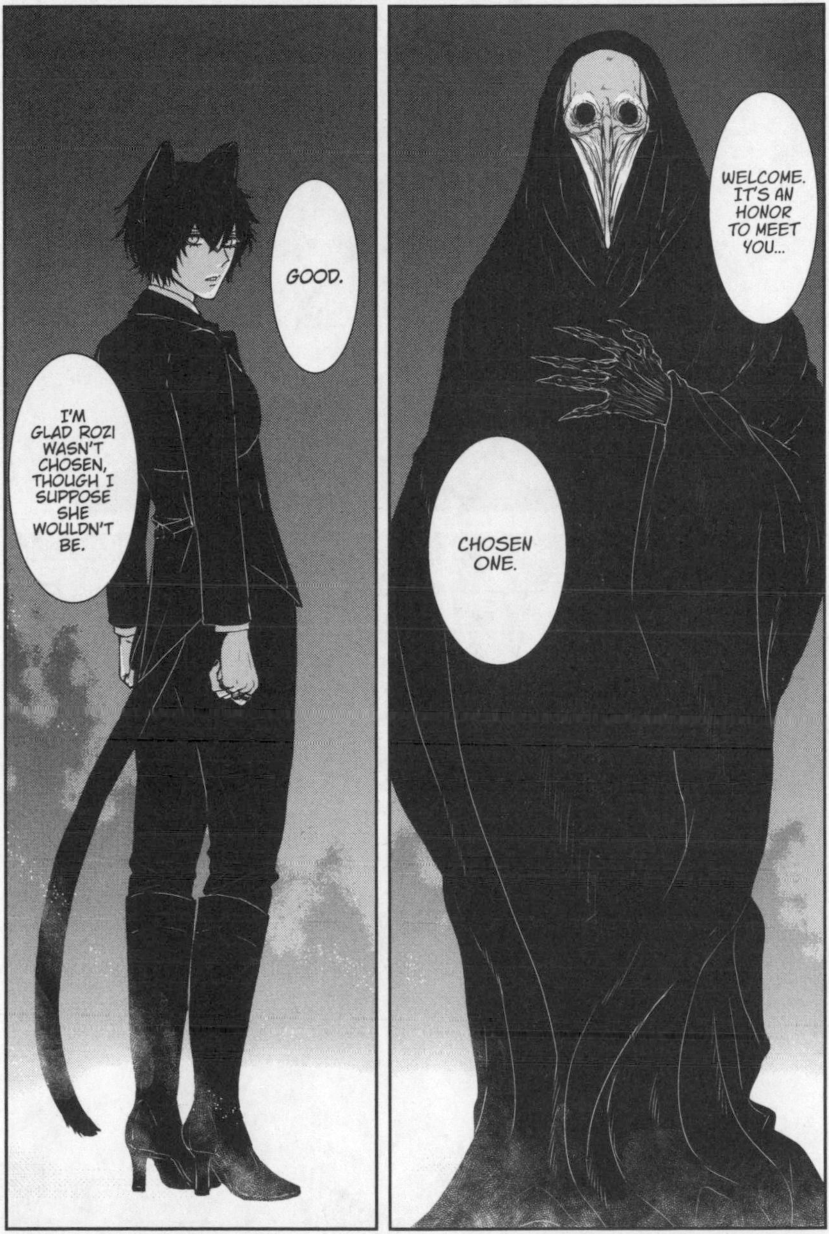
WELCOME. IT'S AN HONOR TO MEET YOU...
CHOSEN ONE.
GOOD.
I'M GLAD ROZI WASN'T CHOSEN, THOUGH I SUPPOSE SHE WOULDN'T BE.

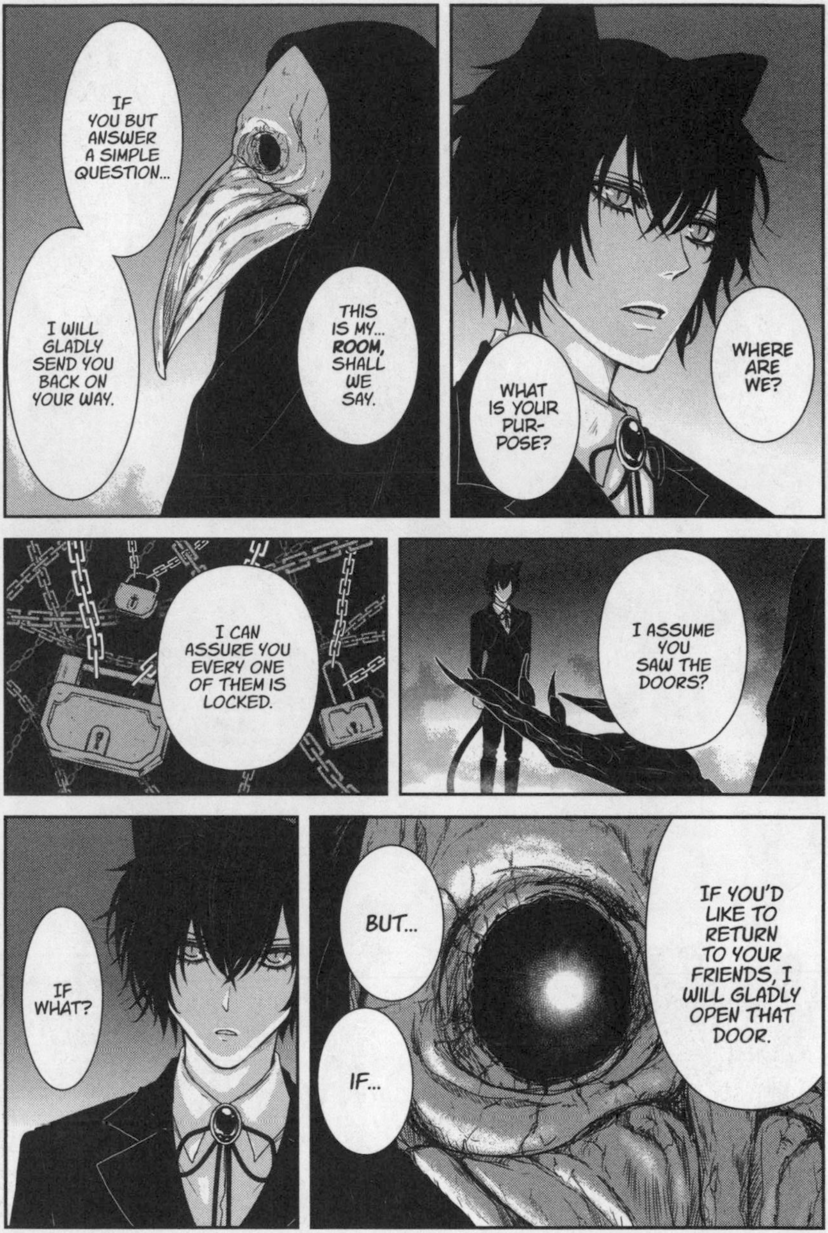
WHERE ARE WE?
WHAT IS YOUR PURPOSE?
THIS IS MY... **ROOM**, SHALL WE SAY.
IF YOU BUT ANSWER A SIMPLE QUESTION...
I WILL GLADLY SEND YOU BACK ON YOUR WAY.
I ASSUME YOU SAW THE DOORS?
I CAN ASSURE YOU EVERY ONE OF THEM IS LOCKED.
IF YOU'D LIKE TO RETURN TO YOUR FRIENDS, I WILL GLADLY OPEN THAT DOOR.
BUT...
IF...
IF WHAT?

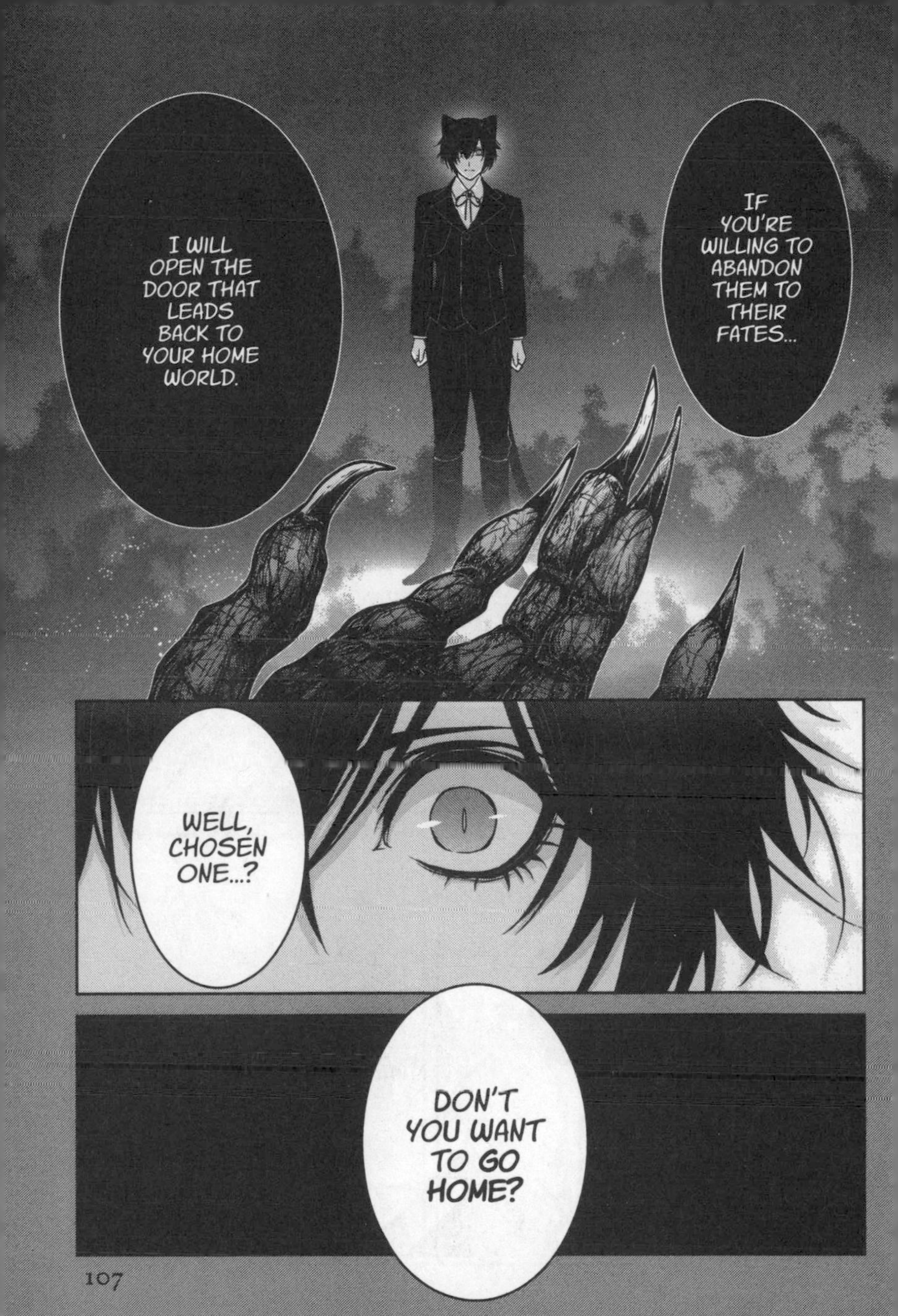
IF YOU'RE WILLING TO ABANDON THEM TO THEIR FATES...
I WILL OPEN THE DOOR THAT LEADS BACK TO YOUR HOME WORLD.
WELL, CHOSEN ONE...?
DON'T YOU WANT TO GO HOME?

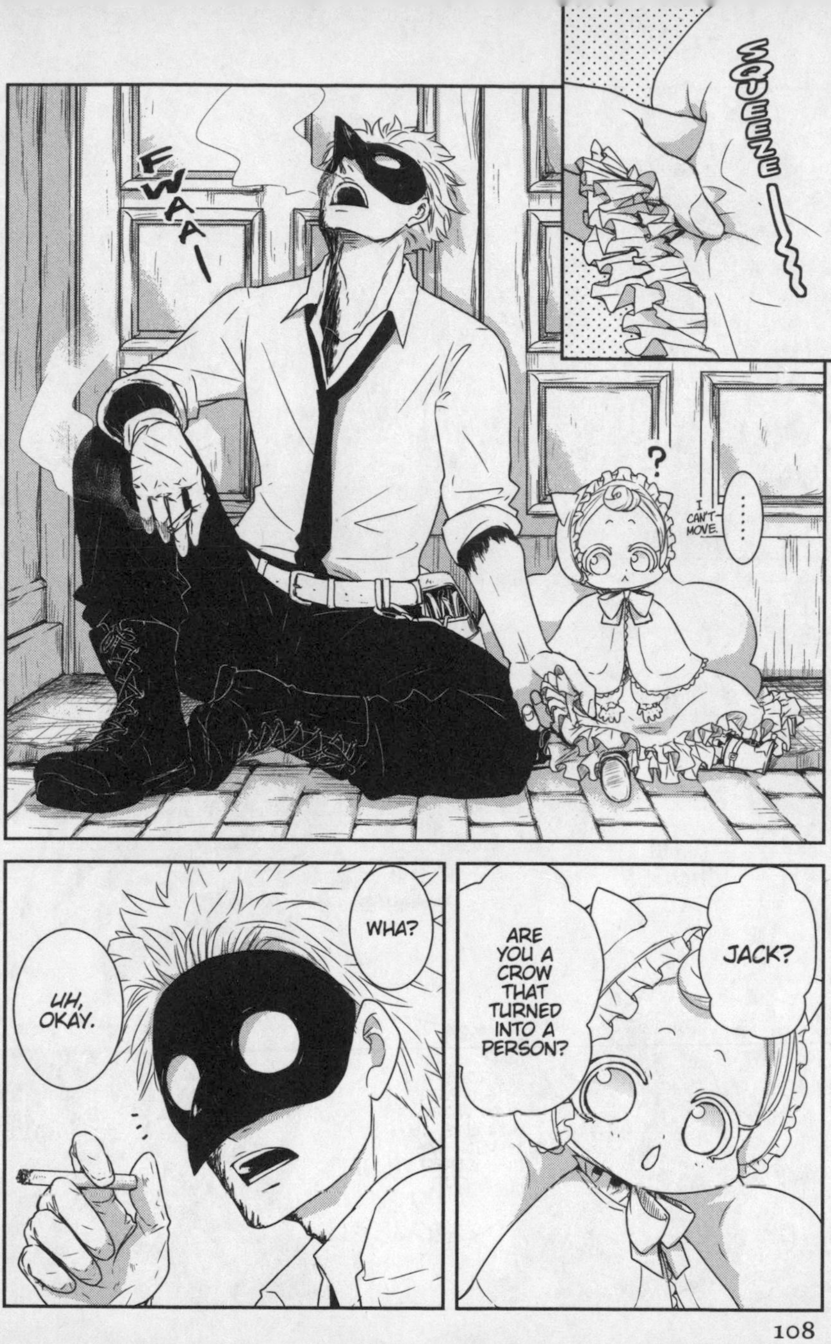
SQUEEZE
FWAA
?
I CAN'T MOVE.
......
JACK?
ARE YOU A CROW THAT TURNED INTO A PERSON?
WHA?
UH, OKAY.
...

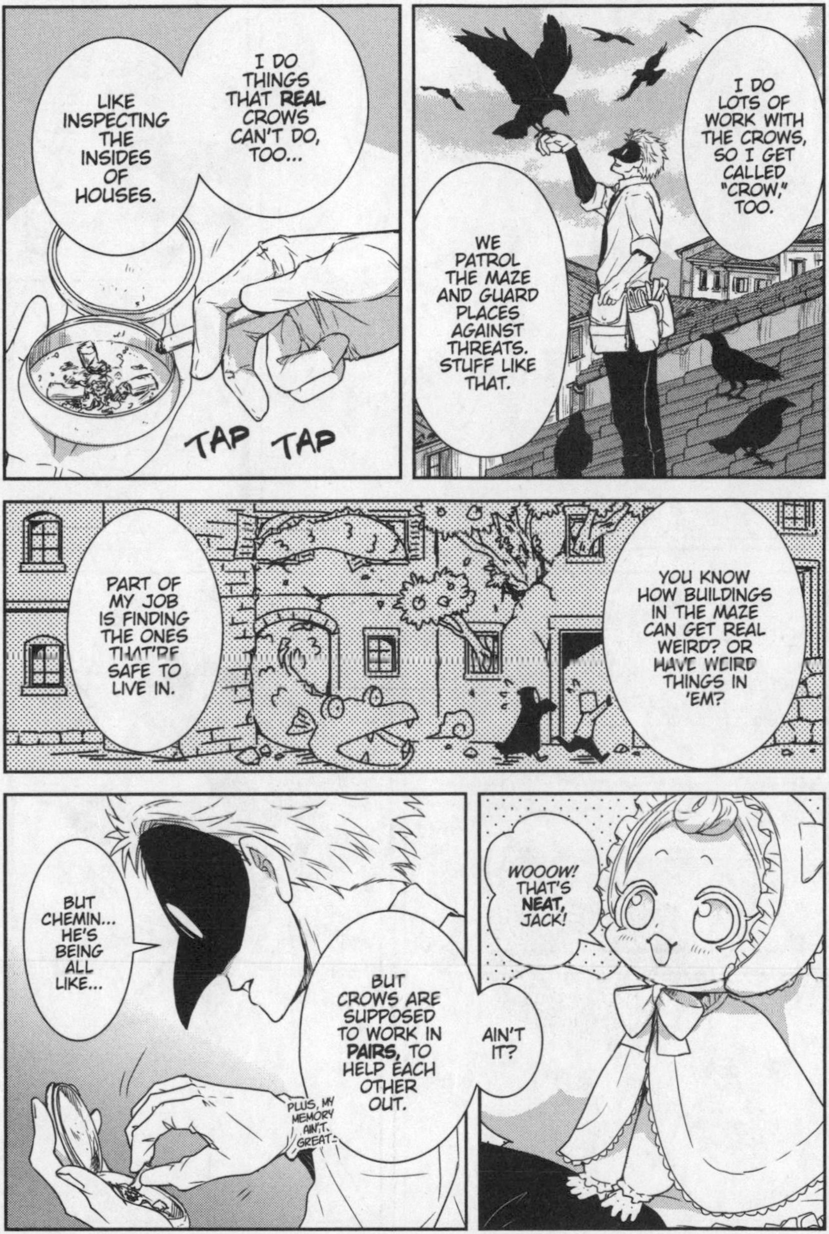
I DO LOTS OF WORK WITH THE CROWS, SO I GET CALLED "CROW," TOO.
WE PATROL THE MAZE AND GUARD PLACES AGAINST THREATS. STUFF LIKE THAT.
I DO THINGS THAT **REAL** CROWS CAN'T DO, TOO...
LIKE INSPECTING THE INSIDES OF HOUSES.
TAP TAP
YOU KNOW HOW BUILDINGS IN THE MAZE CAN GET REAL WEIRD? OR HAVE WEIRD THINGS IN 'EM?
PART OF MY JOB IS FINDING THE ONES THAT'RE SAFE TO LIVE IN.
WOOOW! THAT'S ***NEAT,*** *JACK!*
AIN'T IT?
BUT CROWS ARE SUPPOSED TO WORK IN **PAIRS,** TO HELP EACH OTHER OUT.
BUT CHEMIN... HE'S BEING ALL LIKE...
PLUS, MY MEMORY AIN'T GREAT.

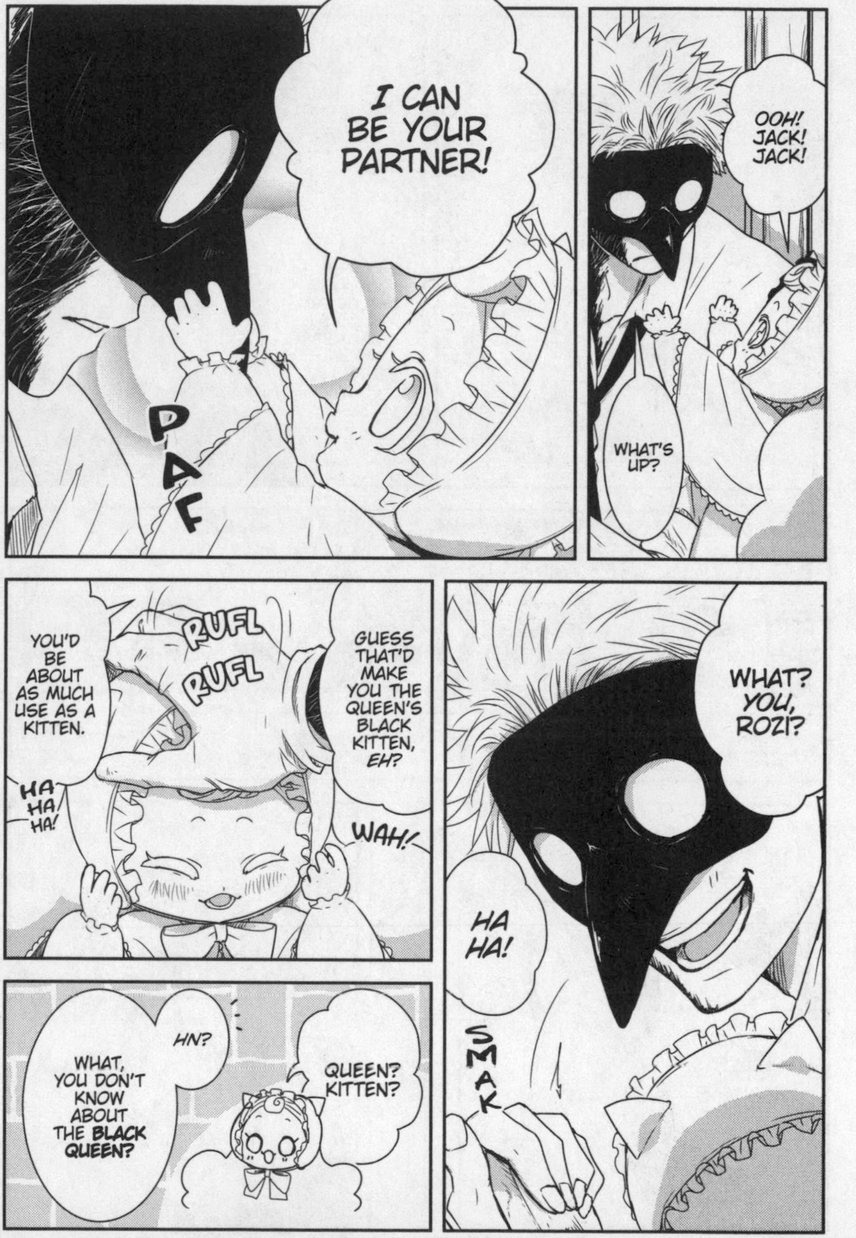
OOH! JACK! JACK!
WHAT'S UP?
I CAN BE YOUR PARTNER!
PAF
WHAT? *YOU*, ROZI?
HA HA!
SMAK
GUESS THAT'D MAKE YOU THE QUEEN'S BLACK KITTEN, *EH?*
RUFL
RUFL
YOU'D BE ABOUT AS MUCH USE AS A KITTEN.
WAH!
HA HA HA!
QUEEN? KITTEN?
HN?
WHAT, YOU DON'T KNOW ABOUT THE **BLACK QUEEN?**

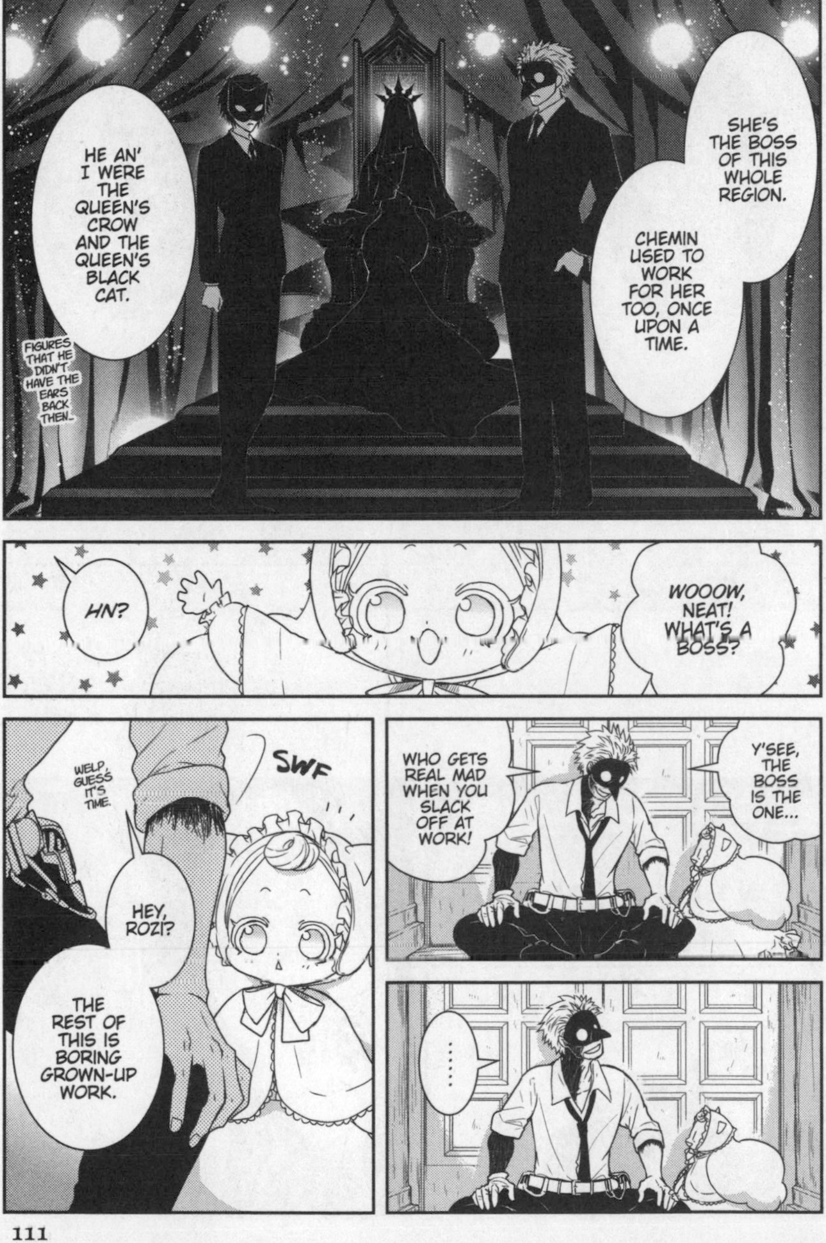
SHE'S THE BOSS OF THIS WHOLE REGION.
CHEMIN USED TO WORK FOR HER TOO, ONCE UPON A TIME.
HE AN' I WERE THE QUEEN'S CROW AND THE QUEEN'S BLACK CAT.
FIGURES THAT HE DIDN'T HAVE THE EARS BACK THEN...
WOOOW, NEAT! WHAT'S A BOSS?
HN?
Y'SEE, THE BOSS IS THE ONE...
WHO GETS REAL MAD WHEN YOU SLACK OFF AT WORK!
......
SWF
WELP, GUESS IT'S TIME.
HEY, ROZI?
THE REST OF THIS IS BORING GROWN-UP WORK.

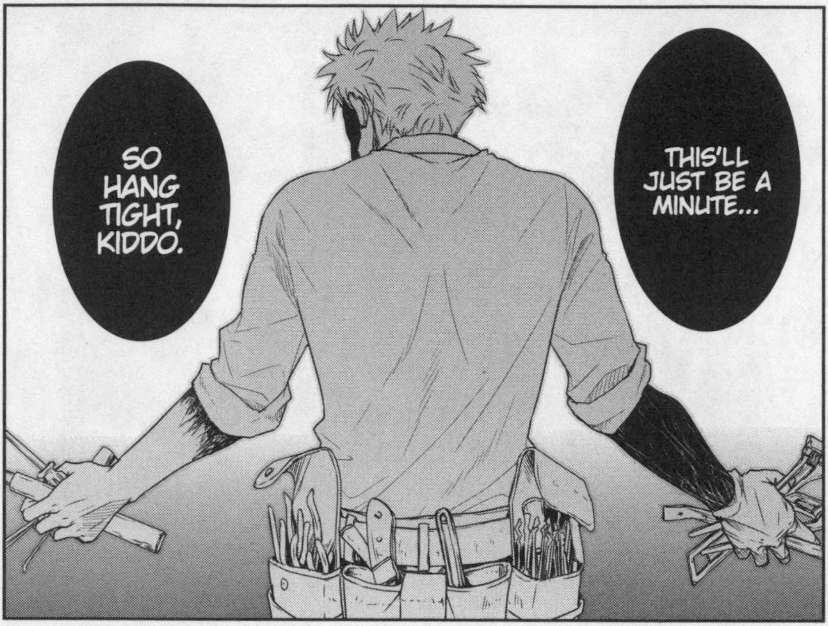
THIS'LL JUST BE A MINUTE...
SO HANG TIGHT, KIDDO.

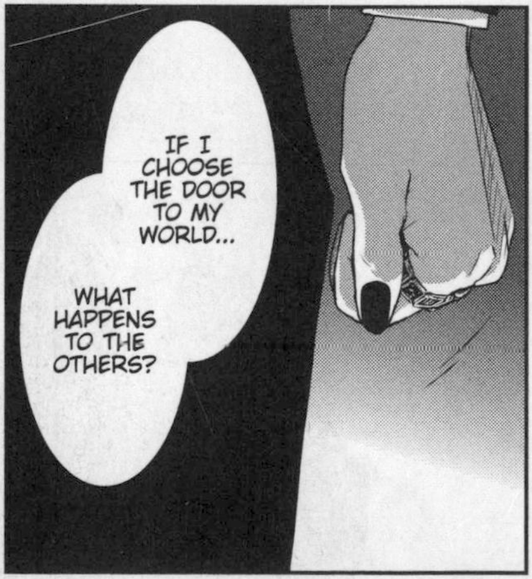
IF I CHOOSE THE DOOR TO MY WORLD...
WHAT HAPPENS TO THE OTHERS?

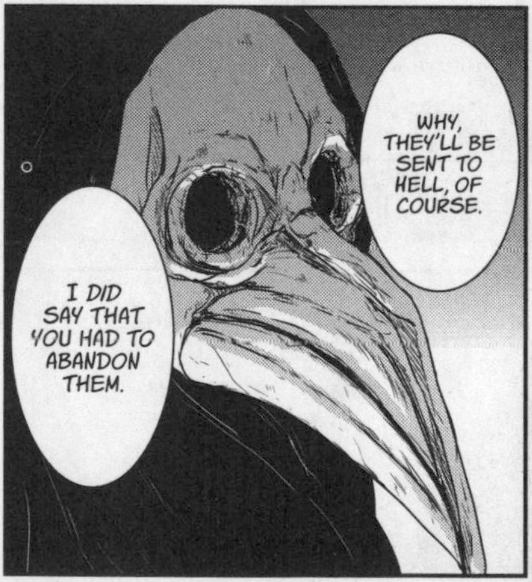
WHY, THEY'LL BE SENT TO HELL, OF COURSE.
I *DID* SAY THAT YOU HAD TO ABANDON THEM.

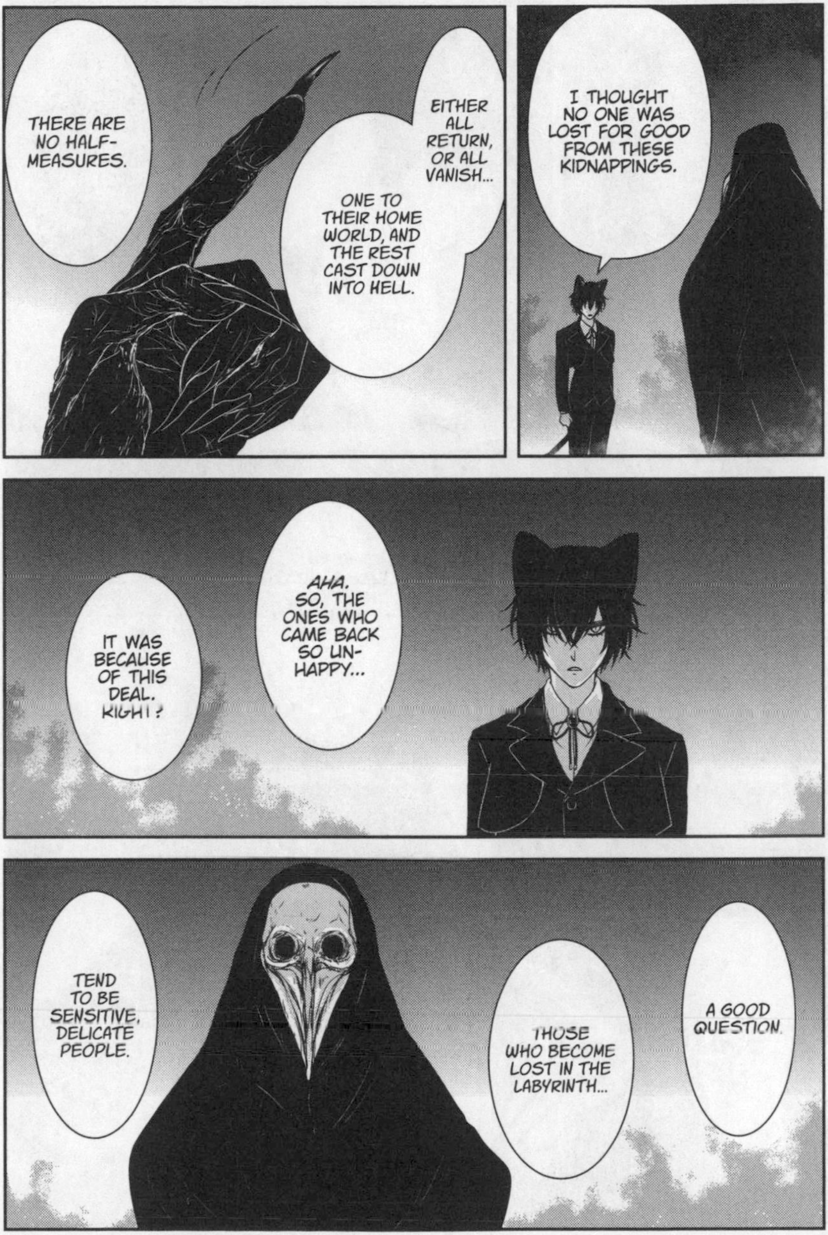
I THOUGHT NO ONE WAS LOST FOR GOOD FROM THESE KIDNAPPINGS.
EITHER ALL RETURN, OR ALL VANISH...
ONE TO THEIR HOME WORLD, AND THE REST CAST DOWN INTO HELL.
THERE ARE NO HALF-MEASURES.
AHA. SO, THE ONES WHO CAME BACK SO UN-HAPPY...
IT WAS BECAUSE OF THIS DEAL. RIGHT?
A GOOD QUESTION.
THOSE WHO BECOME LOST IN THE LABYRINTH...
TEND TO BE SENSITIVE, DELICATE PEOPLE.

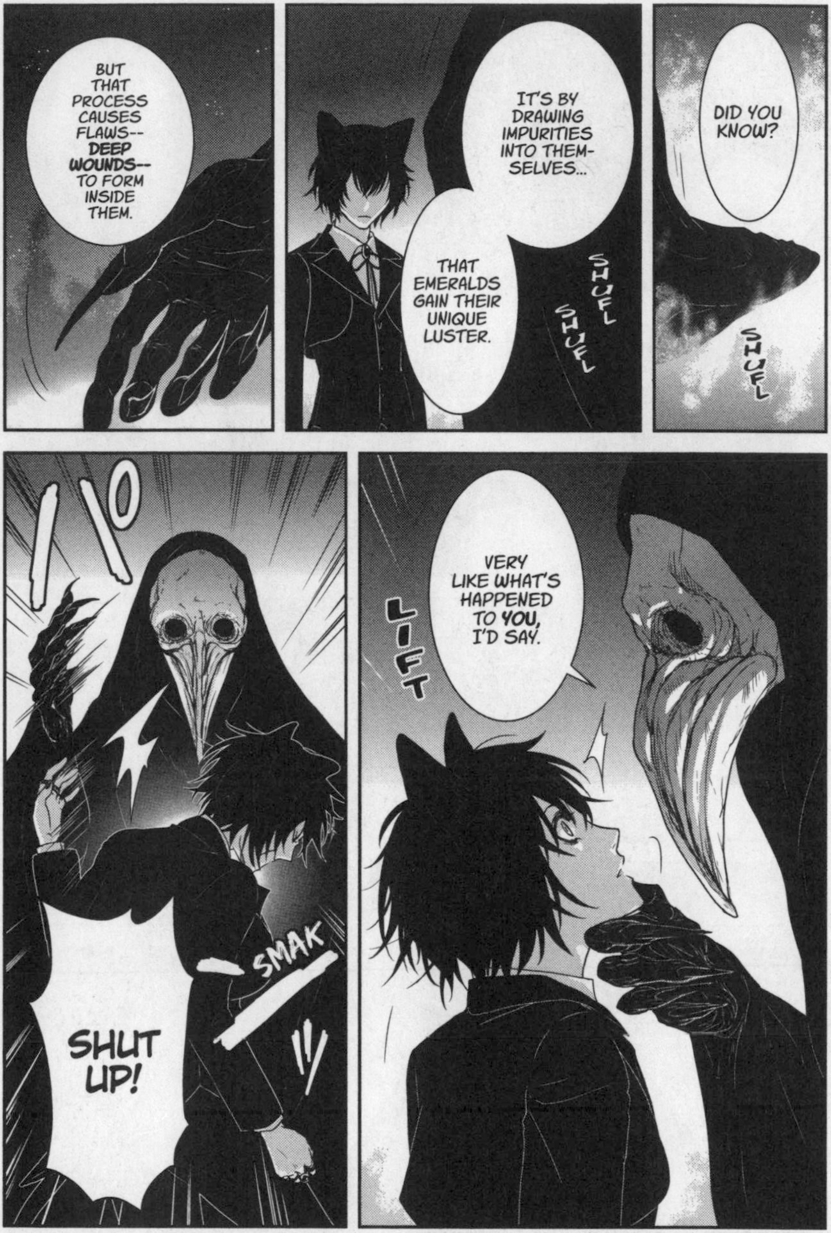
DID YOU KNOW?
SHUFL
IT'S BY DRAWING IMPURITIES INTO THEMSELVES...
THAT EMERALDS GAIN THEIR UNIQUE LUSTER.
SHUFL
SHUFL
BUT THAT PROCESS CAUSES FLAWS-- DEEP WOUNDS-- TO FORM INSIDE THEM.
LIFT
VERY LIKE WHAT'S HAPPENED TO YOU, I'D SAY.
SMAK
SHUT UP!

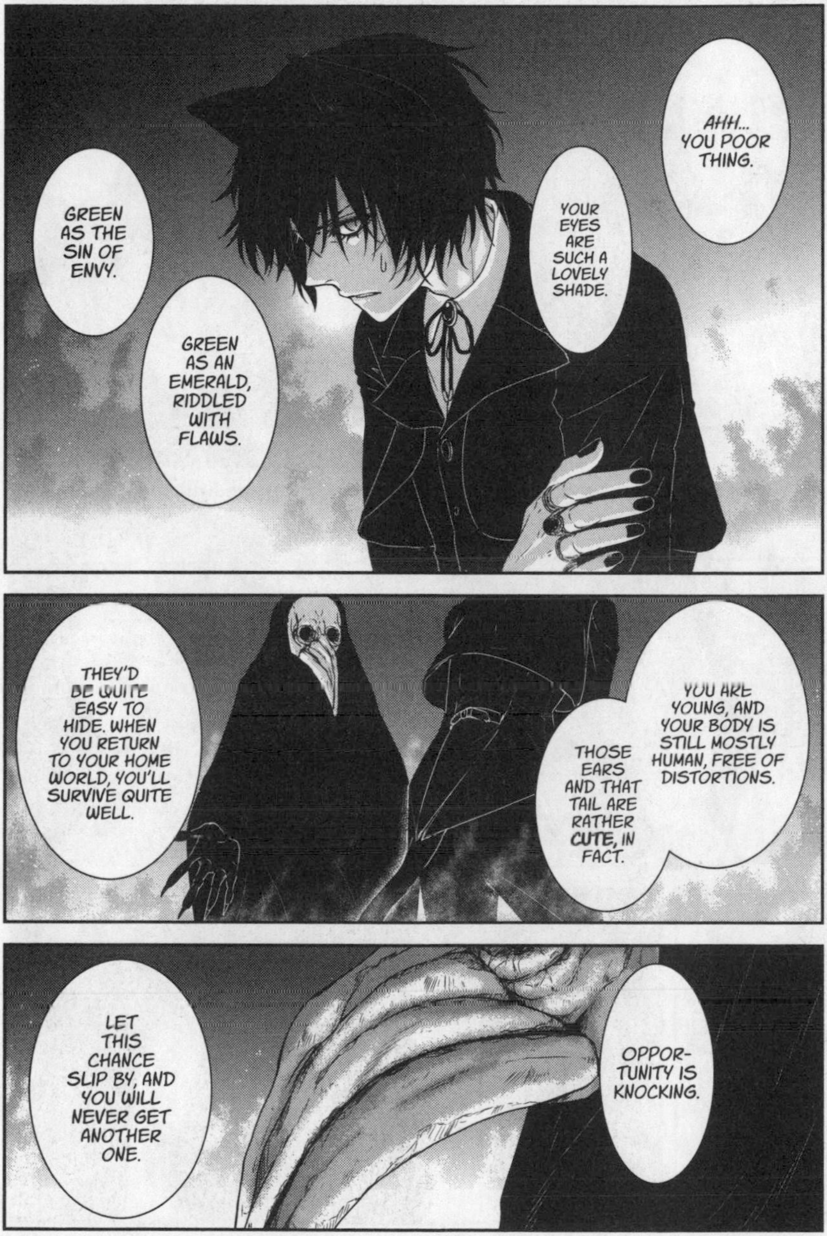
AHH... YOU POOR THING.
YOUR EYES ARE SUCH A LOVELY SHADE.
GREEN AS THE SIN OF ENVY.
GREEN AS AN EMERALD, RIDDLED WITH FLAWS.
YOU ARE YOUNG, AND YOUR BODY IS STILL MOSTLY HUMAN, FREE OF DISTORTIONS.
THOSE EARS AND THAT TAIL ARE RATHER CUTE, IN FACT.
THEY'D BE QUITE EASY TO HIDE. WHEN YOU RETURN TO YOUR HOME WORLD, YOU'LL SURVIVE QUITE WELL.
OPPORTUNITY IS KNOCKING.
LET THIS CHANCE SLIP BY, AND YOU WILL NEVER GET ANOTHER ONE.

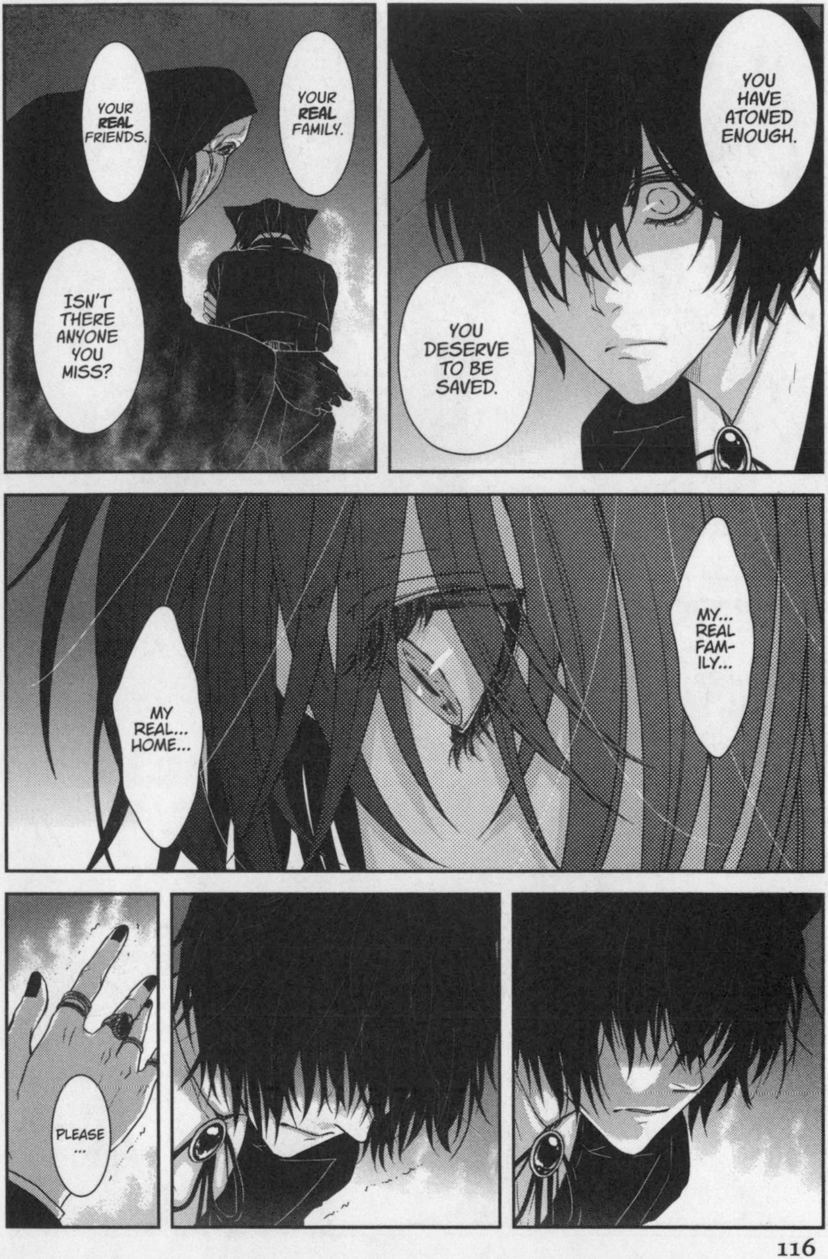
YOU HAVE ATONED ENOUGH.
YOU DESERVE TO BE SAVED.
YOUR **REAL** FAMILY.
YOUR **REAL** FRIENDS.
ISN'T THERE ANYONE YOU MISS?
MY... REAL FAM-ILY...
MY REAL... HOME...
PLEASE ...

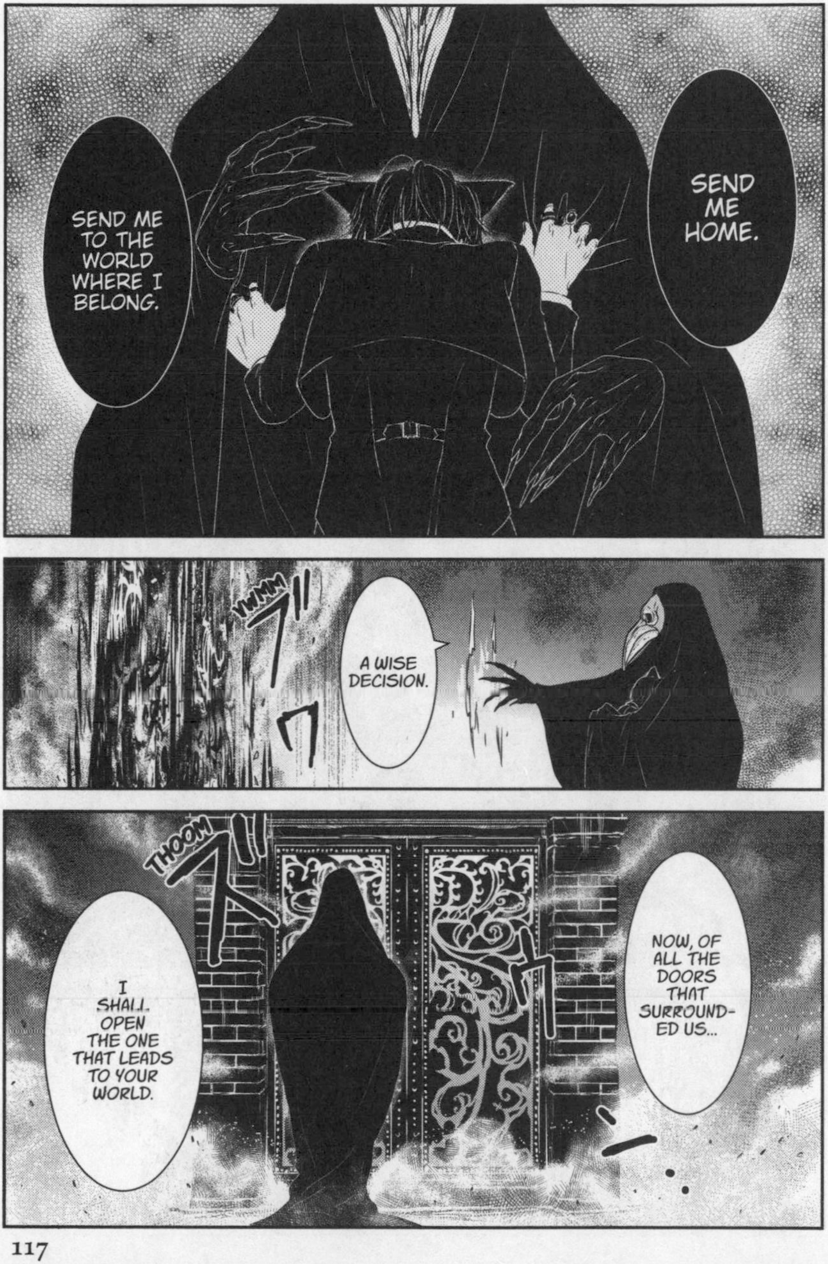
SEND ME HOME.
SEND ME TO THE WORLD WHERE I BELONG.
A WISE DECISION.
VWMM
NOW, OF ALL THE DOORS THAT SURROUNDED-ED US...
THOOM
I SHALL OPEN THE ONE THAT LEADS TO YOUR WORLD.

REACH
TWCH
CHAK
RATL KLIK
RATL
SNAK
THNK
WHUMP
WHAT ?!

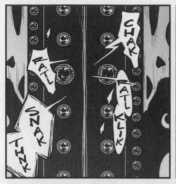

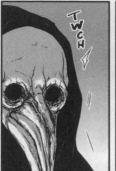

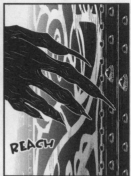

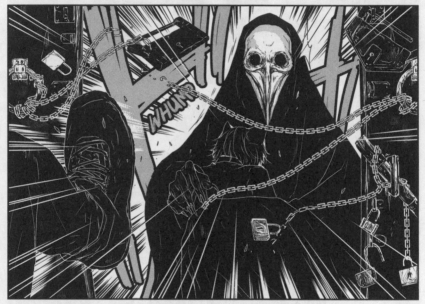

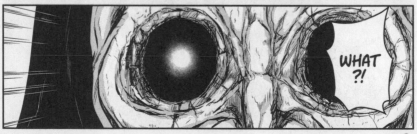

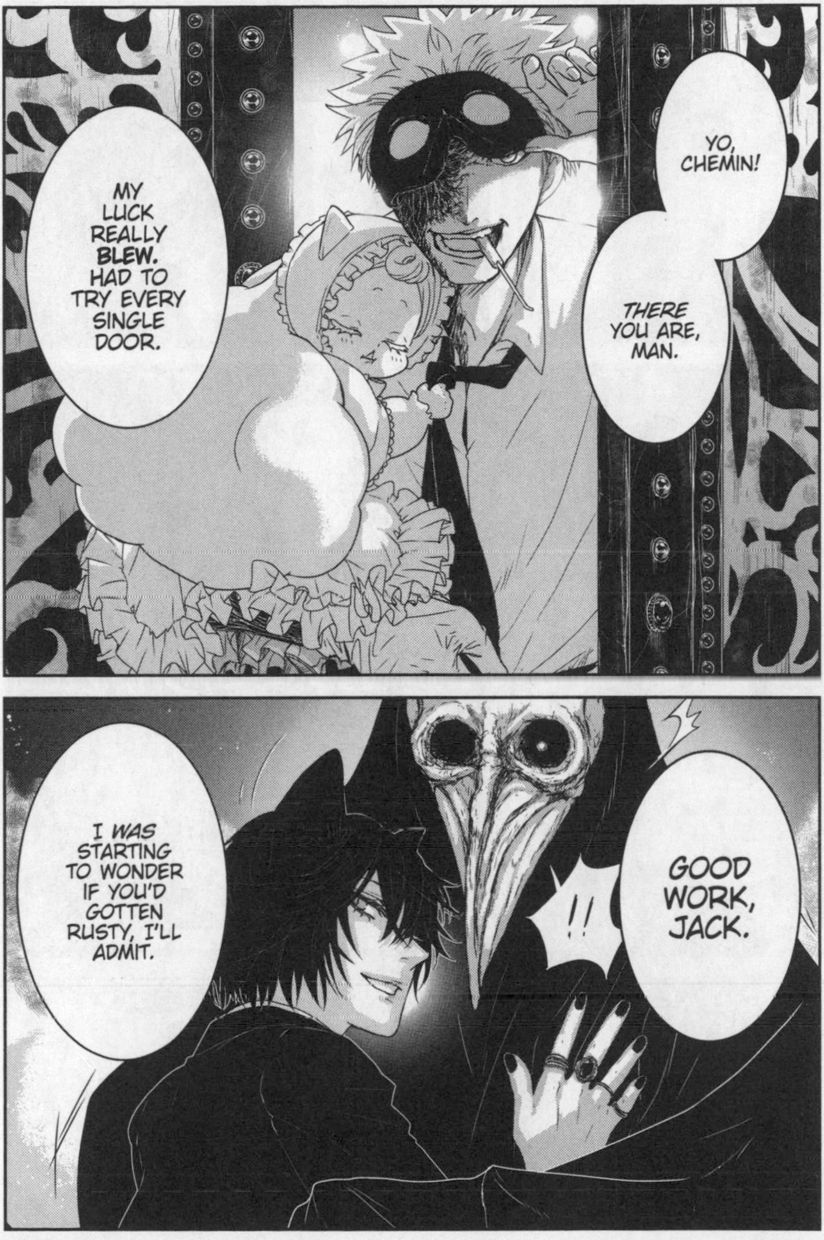
YO, CHEMIN!
THERE YOU ARE, MAN.
MY LUCK REALLY BLEW. HAD TO TRY EVERY SINGLE DOOR.
GOOD WORK, JACK.
!!
I WAS STARTING TO WONDER IF YOU'D GOTTEN RUSTY, I'LL ADMIT.

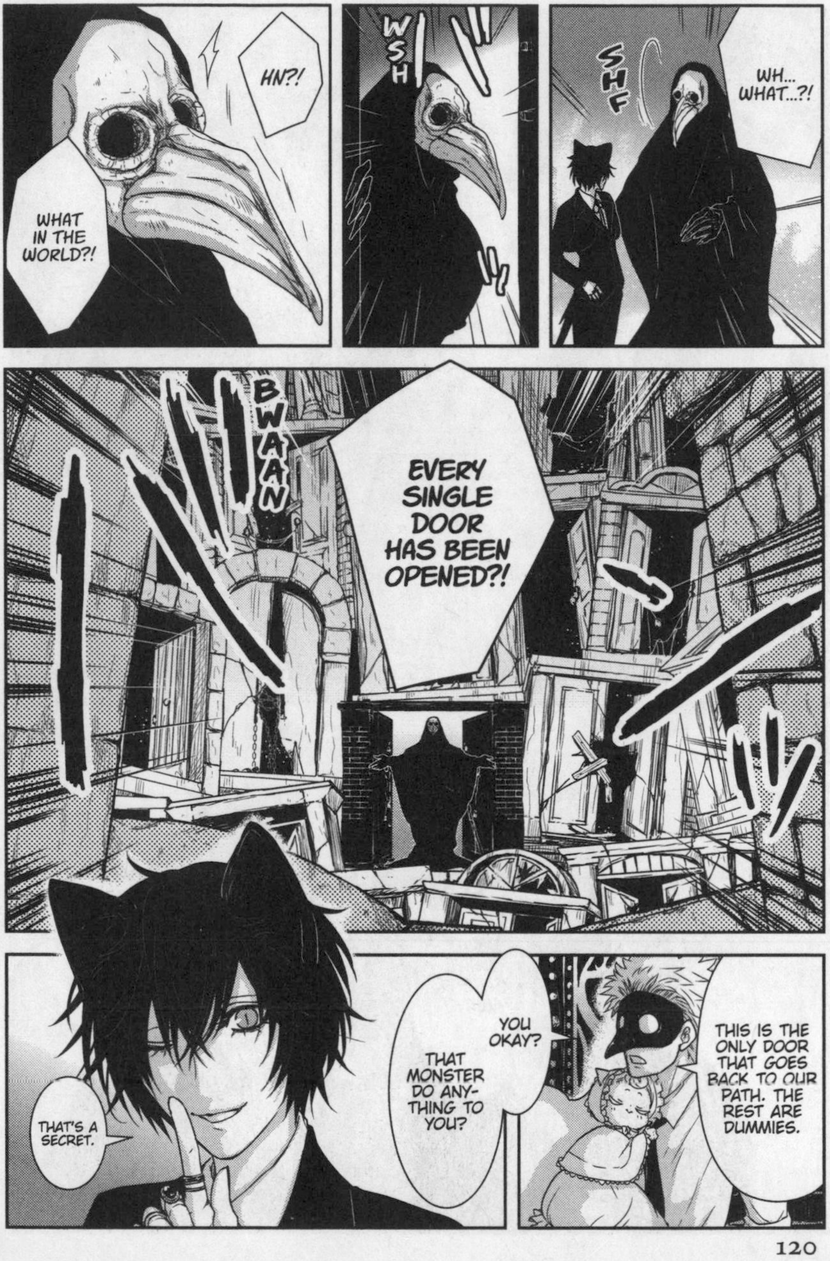
SHF
WH... WHAT...?!
WSH
HN?!
WHAT IN THE WORLD?!
BWAAN
EVERY SINGLE DOOR HAS BEEN OPENED?!
THIS IS THE ONLY DOOR THAT GOES BACK TO OUR PATH. THE REST ARE DUMMIES.
YOU OKAY?
THAT MONSTER DO ANY-THING TO YOU?
THAT'S A SECRET.

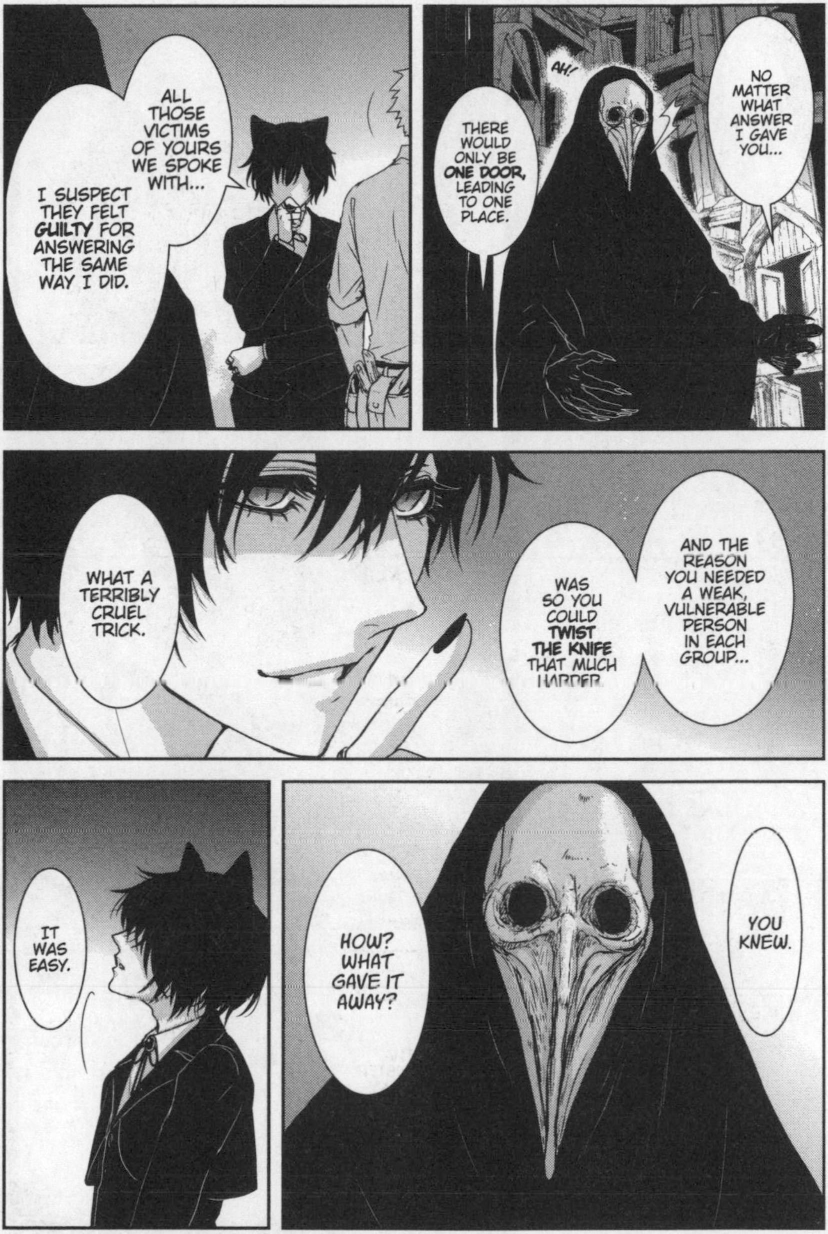
NO MATTER WHAT ANSWER I GAVE YOU...
AH!
THERE WOULD ONLY BE **ONE DOOR,** LEADING TO ONE PLACE.
ALL THOSE VICTIMS OF YOURS WE SPOKE WITH...
I SUSPECT THEY FELT **GUILTY** FOR ANSWERING THE SAME WAY I DID.
AND THE REASON YOU NEEDED A WEAK, VULNERABLE PERSON IN EACH GROUP...
WAS SO YOU COULD **TWIST THE KNIFE** THAT MUCH HARDER.
WHAT A TERRIBLY CRUEL TRICK.
YOU KNEW.
HOW? WHAT GAVE IT AWAY?
IT WAS EASY.

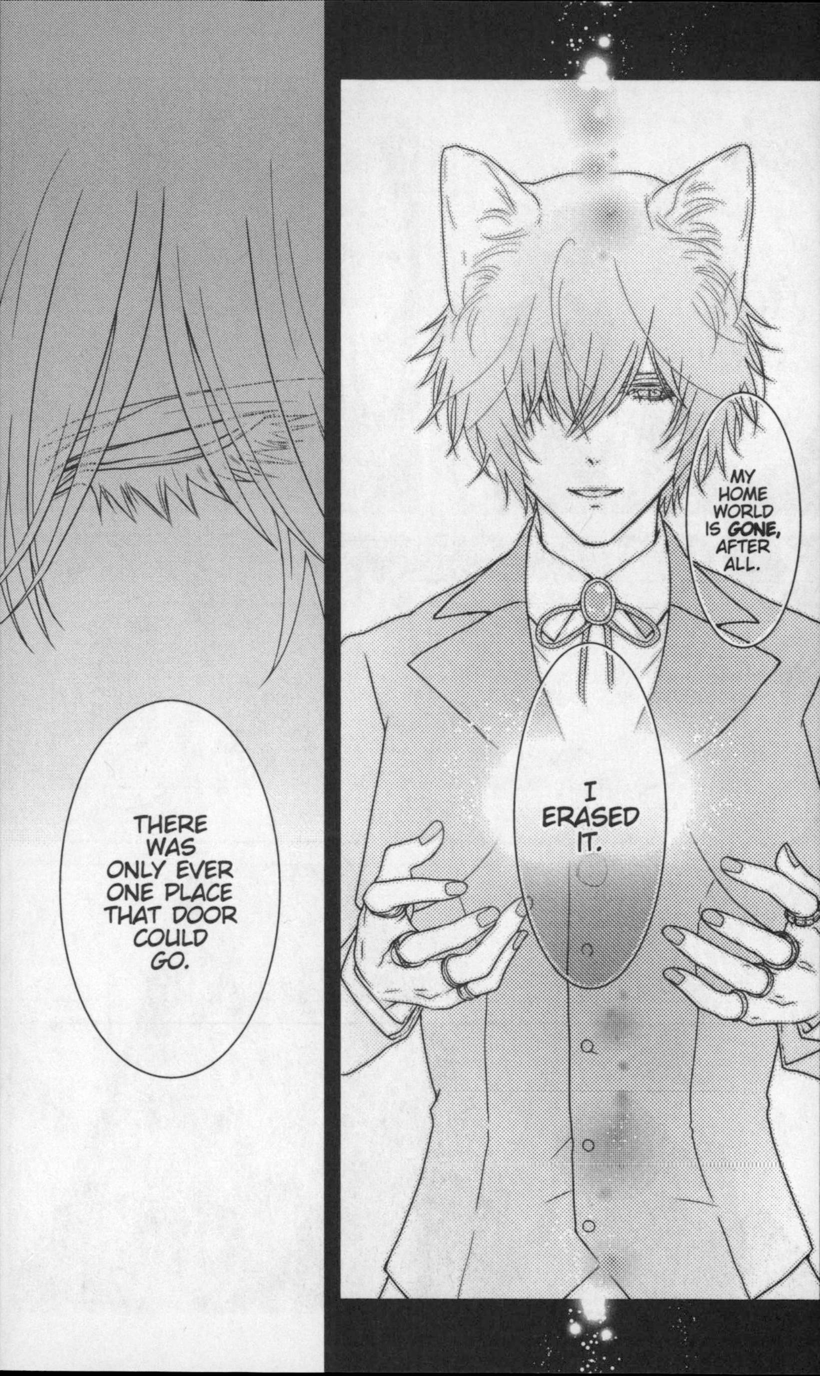
MY HOME WORLD IS **GONE**, AFTER ALL.
I ERASED IT.
THERE WAS ONLY EVER ONE PLACE THAT DOOR COULD GO.

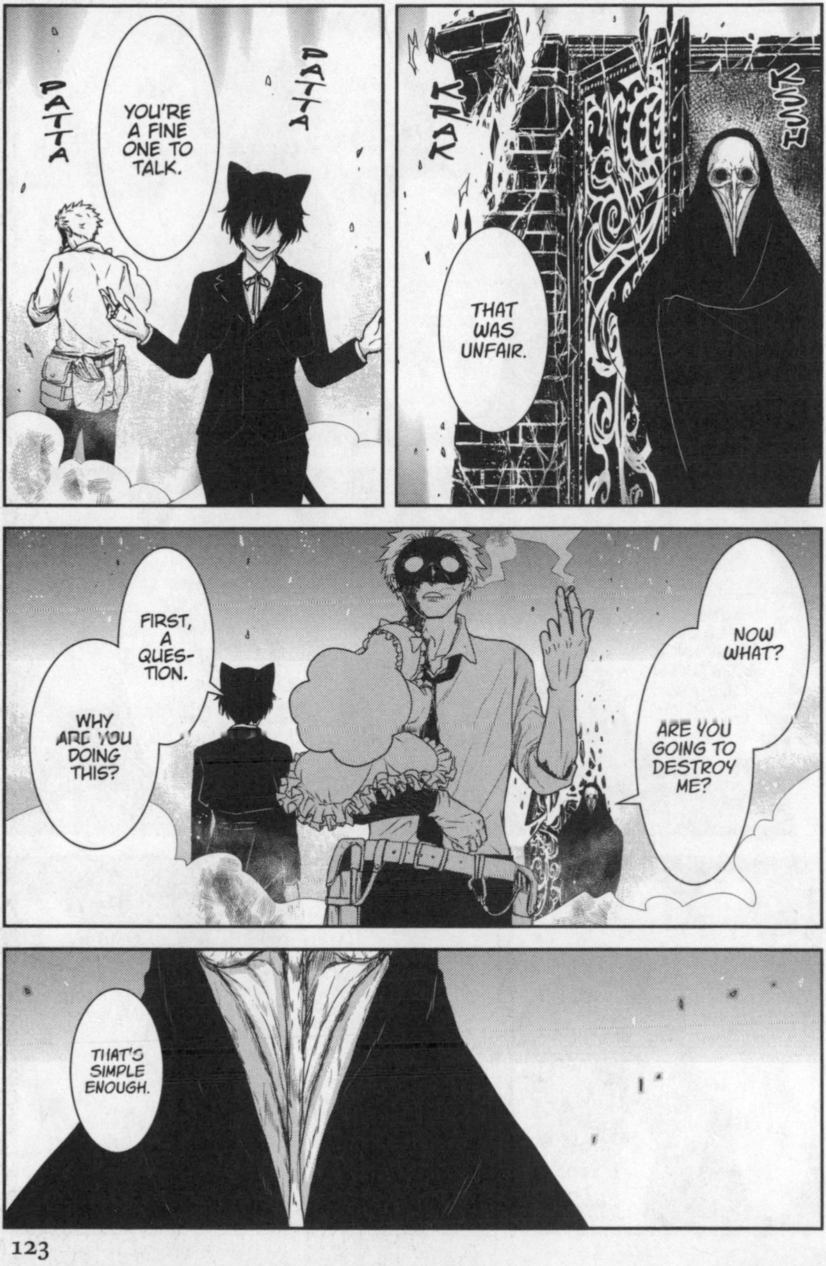
KSSH
KRAK
THAT WAS UNFAIR.
PATTA
YOU'RE A FINE ONE TO TALK.
PATTA
NOW WHAT?
ARE YOU GOING TO DESTROY ME?
FIRST, A QUES-TION.
WHY ARE YOU DOING THIS?
THAT'S SIMPLE ENOUGH.

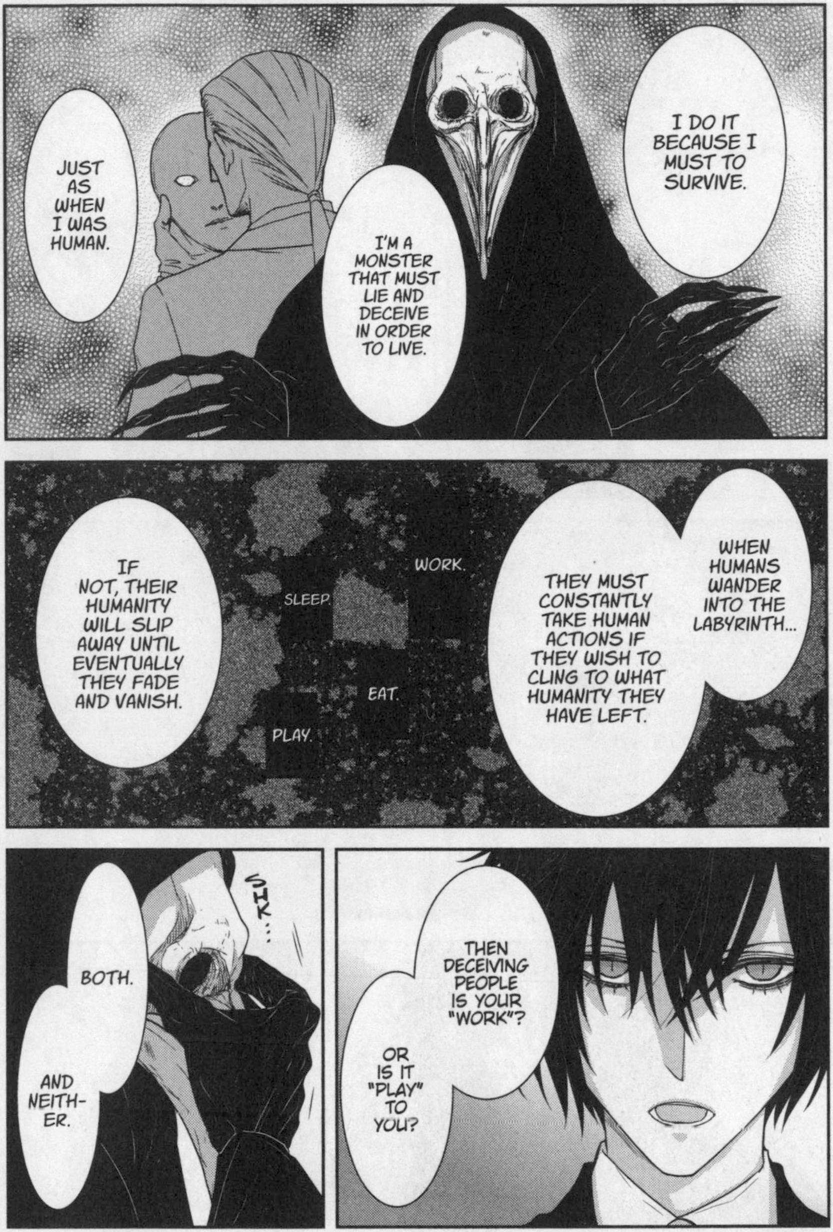
I DO IT BECAUSE I MUST TO SURVIVE.
I'M A MONSTER THAT MUST LIE AND DECEIVE IN ORDER TO LIVE.
JUST AS WHEN I WAS HUMAN.
WHEN HUMANS WANDER INTO THE LABYRINTH...
THEY MUST CONSTANTLY TAKE HUMAN ACTIONS IF THEY WISH TO CLING TO WHAT HUMANITY THEY HAVE LEFT.
WORK.
SLEEP.
EAT.
PLAY.
IF NOT, THEIR HUMANITY WILL SLIP AWAY UNTIL EVENTUALLY THEY FADE AND VANISH.
THEN DECEIVING PEOPLE IS YOUR "WORK"?
OR IS IT "PLAY" TO YOU?
SHK...
BOTH.
AND NEITH-ER.

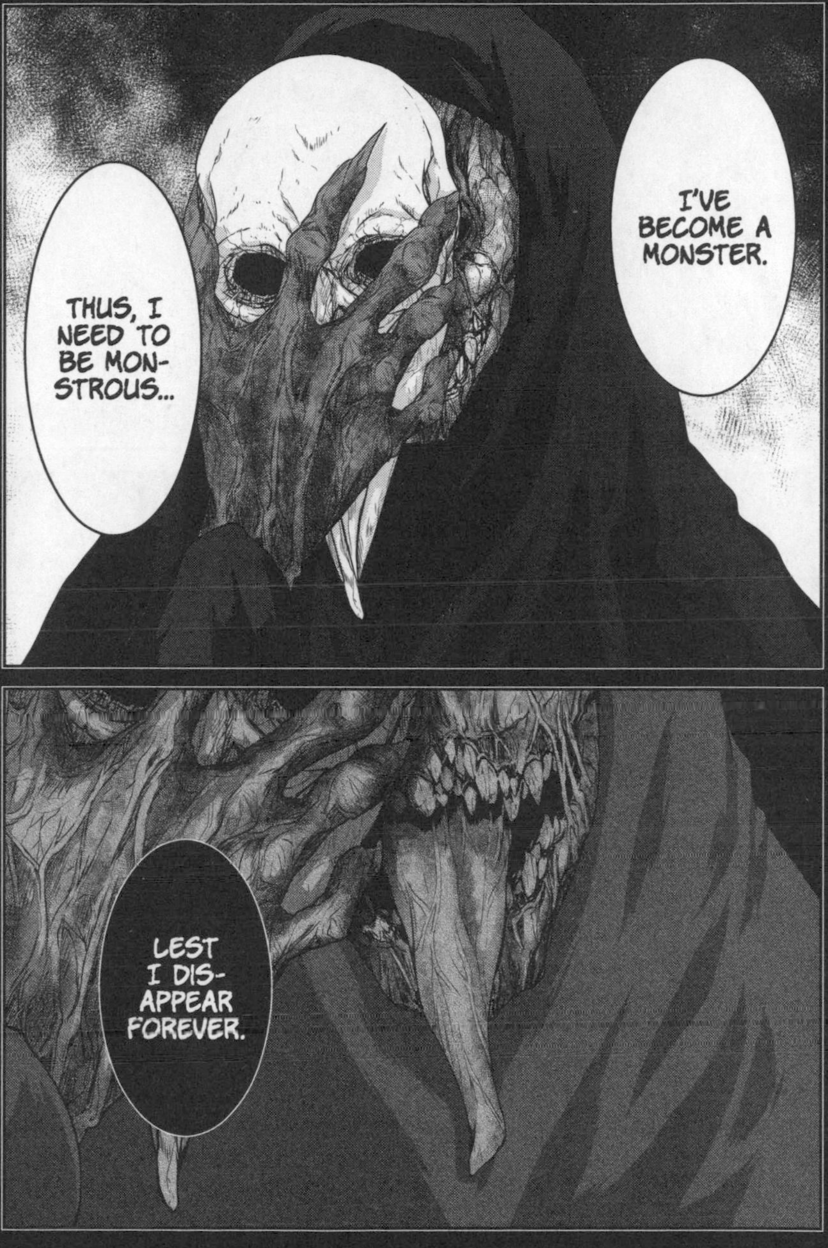
I'VE BECOME A MONSTER.
THUS, I NEED TO BE MONSTROUS...
LEST I DISAPPEAR FOREVER.

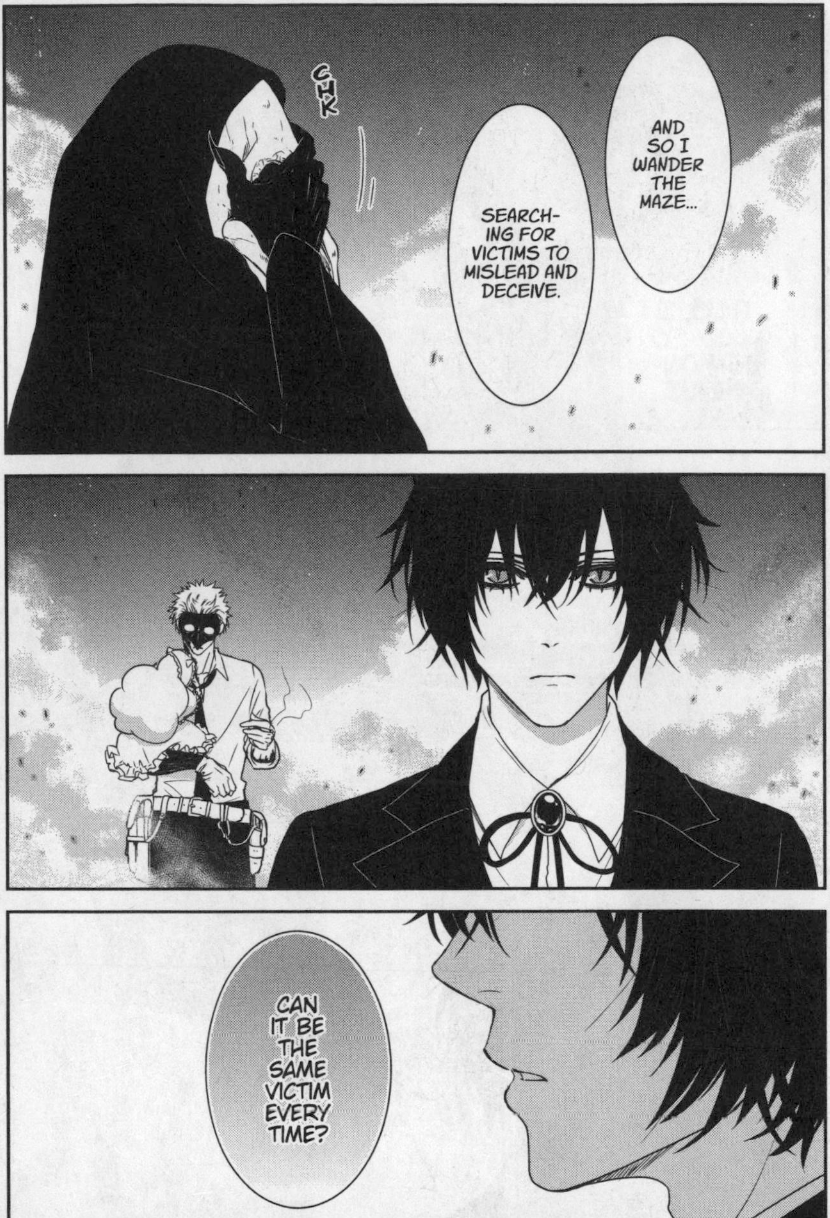
AND SO I WANDER THE MAZE...
SEARCH-ING FOR VICTIMS TO MISLEAD AND DECEIVE.
CHK
CAN IT BE THE SAME VICTIM EVERY TIME?

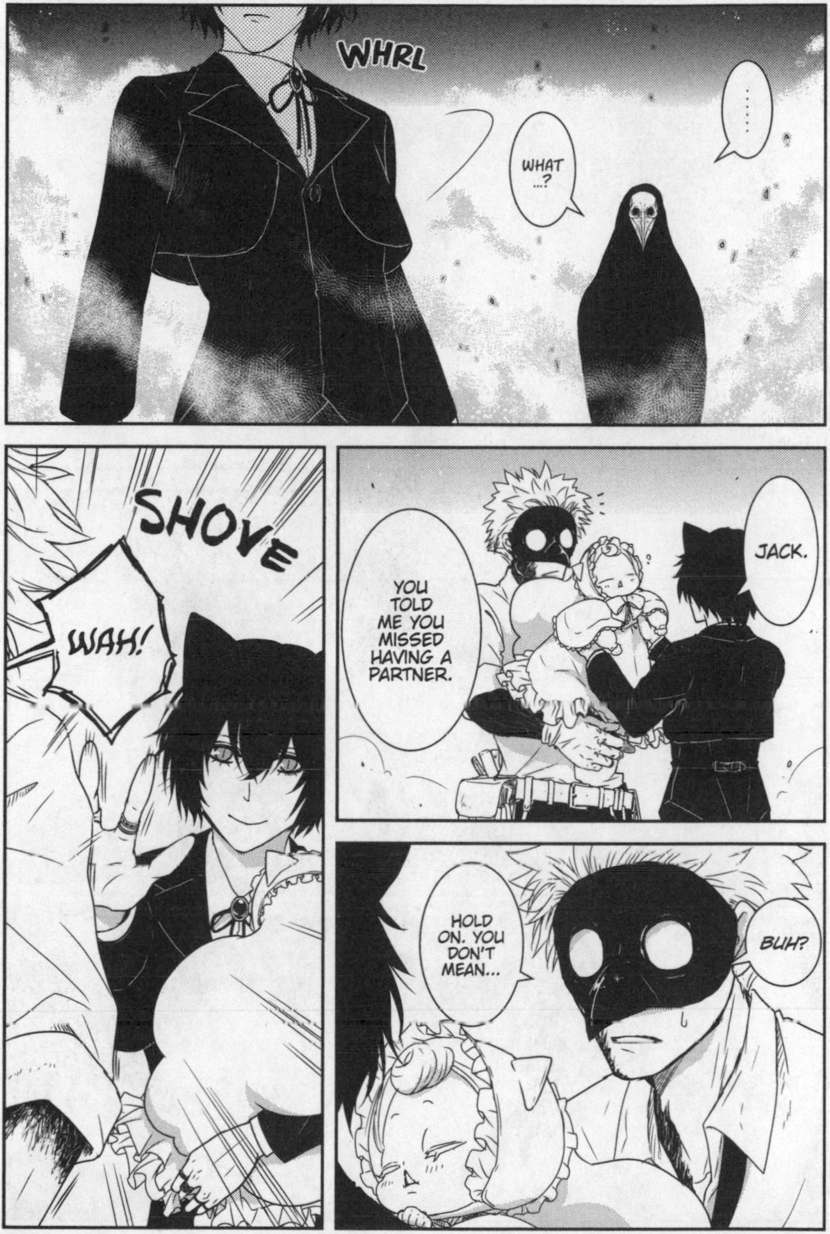

......
WHRL
WHAT ...?
JACK.
YOU TOLD ME YOU MISSED HAVING A PARTNER.
BUH?
HOLD ON. YOU DON'T MEAN...
SHOVE
WAH!

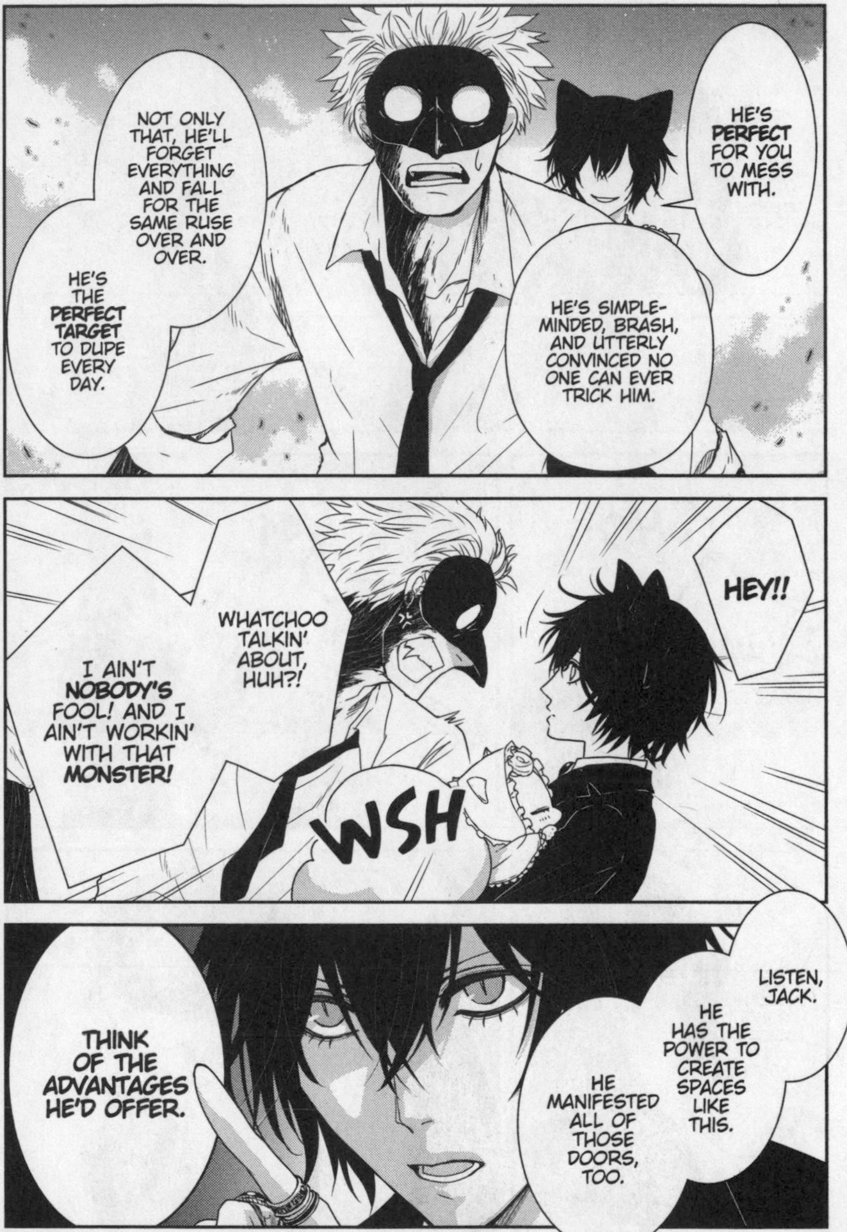
HE'S PERFECT FOR YOU TO MESS WITH.
HE'S SIMPLE-MINDED, BRASH, AND UTTERLY CONVINCED NO ONE CAN EVER TRICK HIM.
NOT ONLY THAT, HE'LL FORGET EVERYTHING AND FALL FOR THE SAME RUSE OVER AND OVER.
HE'S THE PERFECT TARGET TO DUPE EVERY DAY.
HEY!!
WHATCHOO TALKIN' ABOUT, HUH?!
I AIN'T NOBODY'S FOOL! AND I AIN'T WORKIN' WITH THAT MONSTER!
WSH
LISTEN, JACK.
HE HAS THE POWER TO CREATE SPACES LIKE THIS.
HE MANIFESTED ALL OF THOSE DOORS, TOO.
THINK OF THE ADVANTAGES HE'D OFFER.

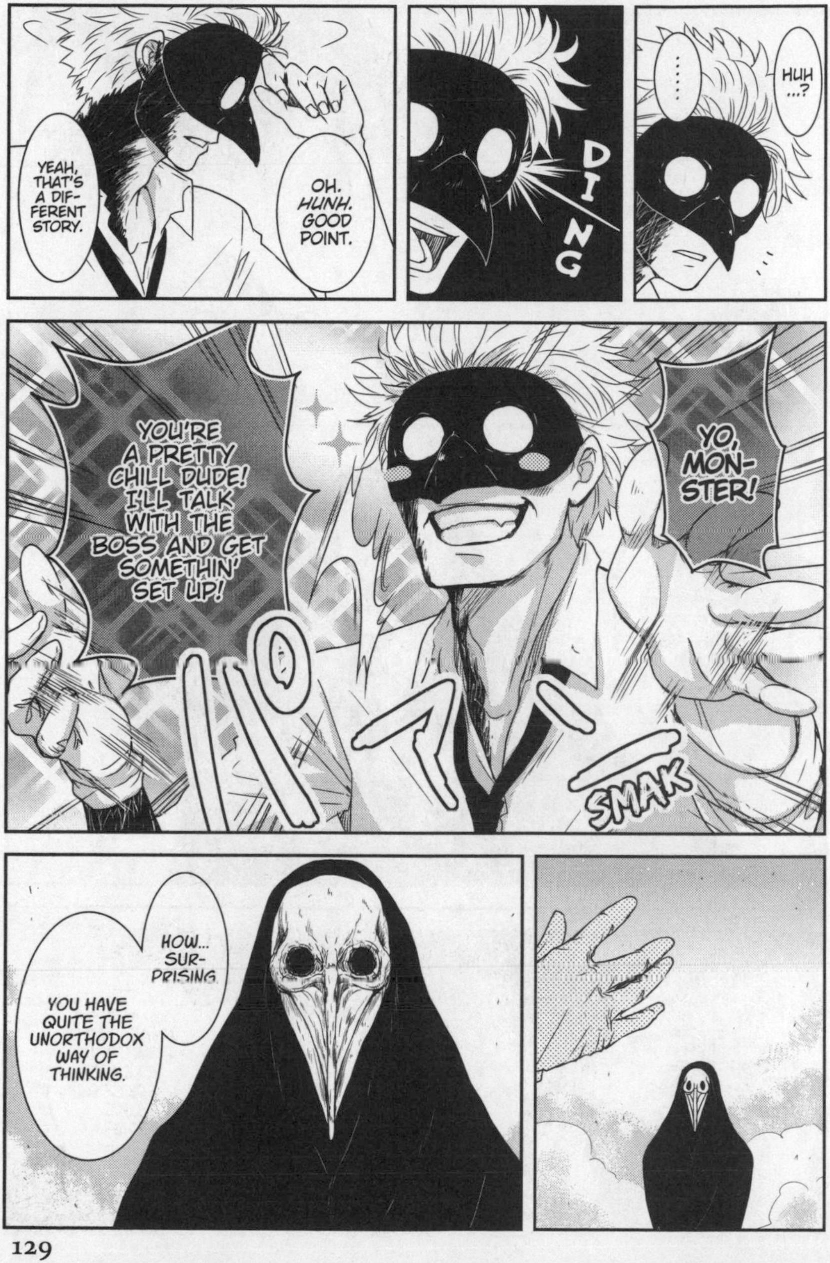
HUH ...?
......
DING
OH. HUNH. GOOD POINT.
YEAH, THAT'S A DIFFERENT STORY.
YO, MONSTER!
YOU'RE A PRETTY CHILL DUDE! I'LL TALK WITH THE BOSS AND GET SOMETHIN' SET UP!
SMAK
HOW... SURPRISING.
YOU HAVE QUITE THE UNORTHODOX WAY OF THINKING.

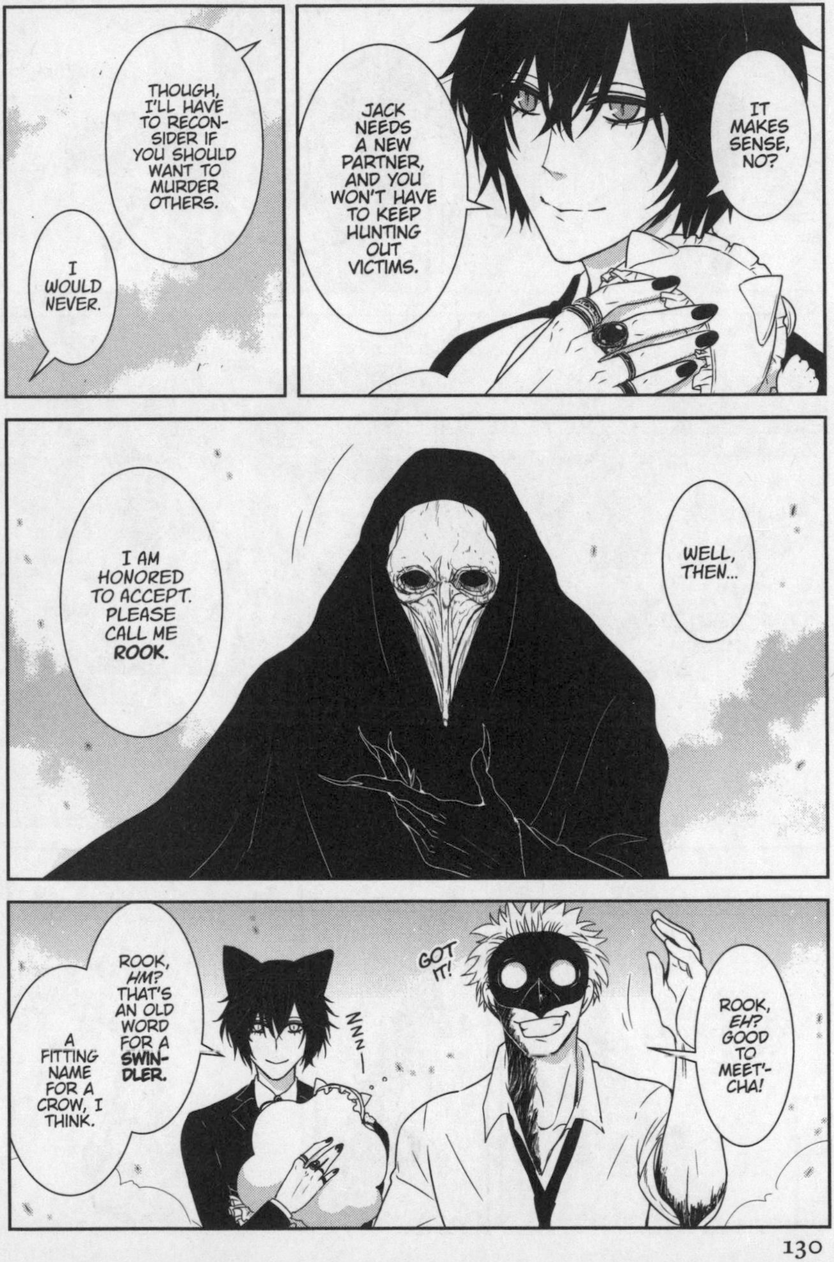
IT MAKES SENSE, NO?
JACK NEEDS A NEW PARTNER, AND YOU WON'T HAVE TO KEEP HUNTING OUT VICTIMS.
THOUGH, I'LL HAVE TO RECON-SIDER IF YOU SHOULD WANT TO MURDER OTHERS.
I WOULD NEVER.
WELL, THEN...
I AM HONORED TO ACCEPT. PLEASE CALL ME **ROOK.**
ROOK, *EH?* GOOD TO MEET'-CHA!
GOT IT!
ZZZ
ROOK, *HM?* THAT'S AN OLD WORD FOR A **SWIN-DLER.**
A FITTING NAME FOR A CROW, I THINK.

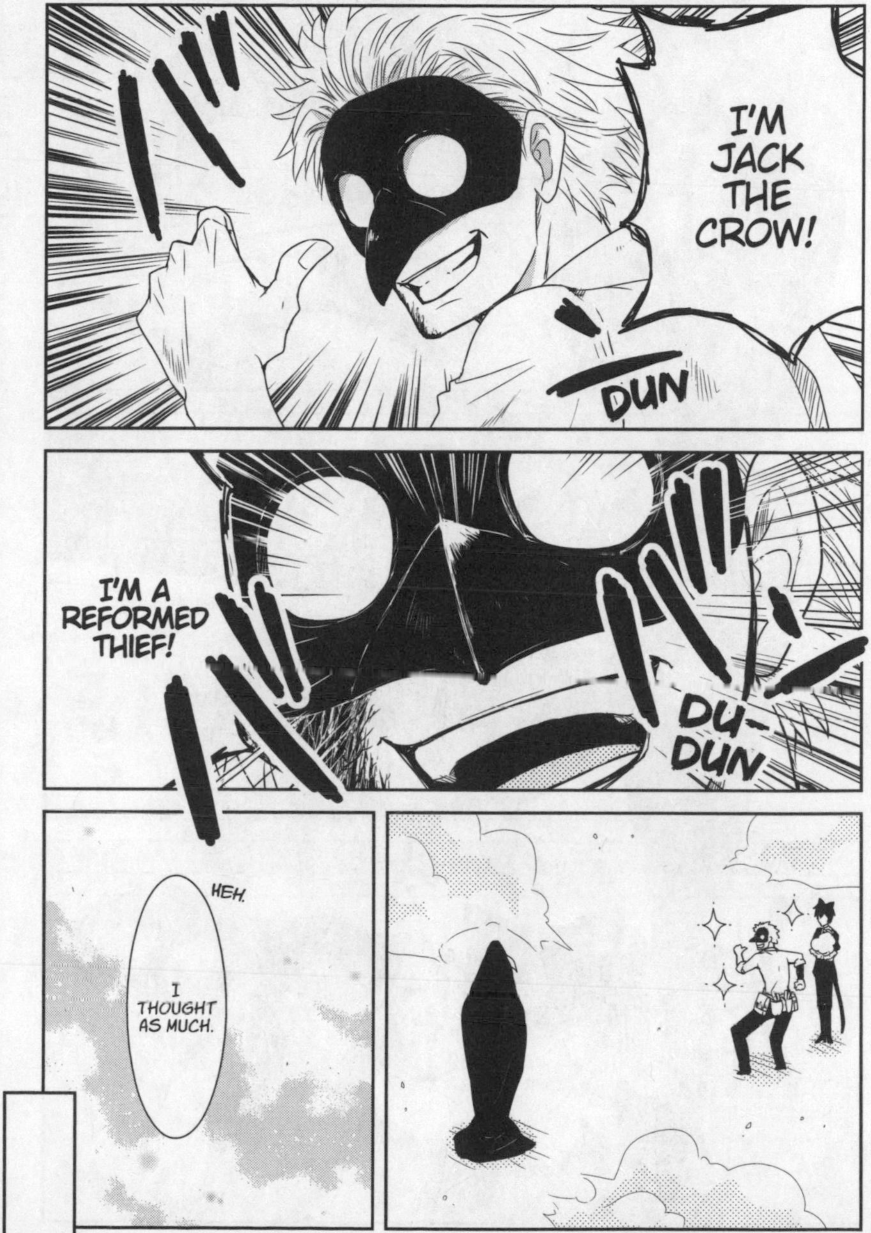
I'M JACK THE CROW!
DUN
I'M A REFORMED THIEF!
DU-DUN
HEH.
I THOUGHT AS MUCH.

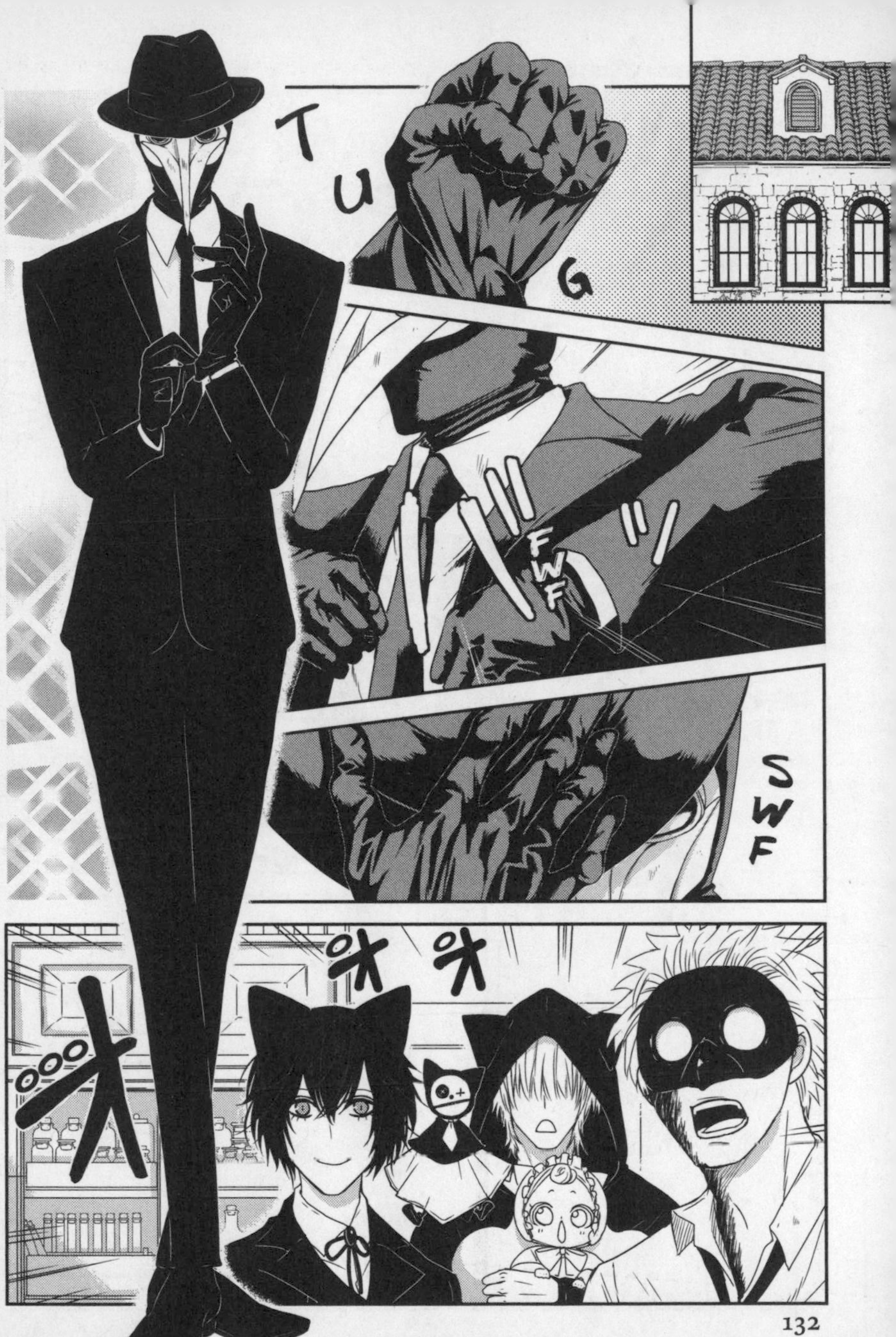
TUG
FWF
SWF

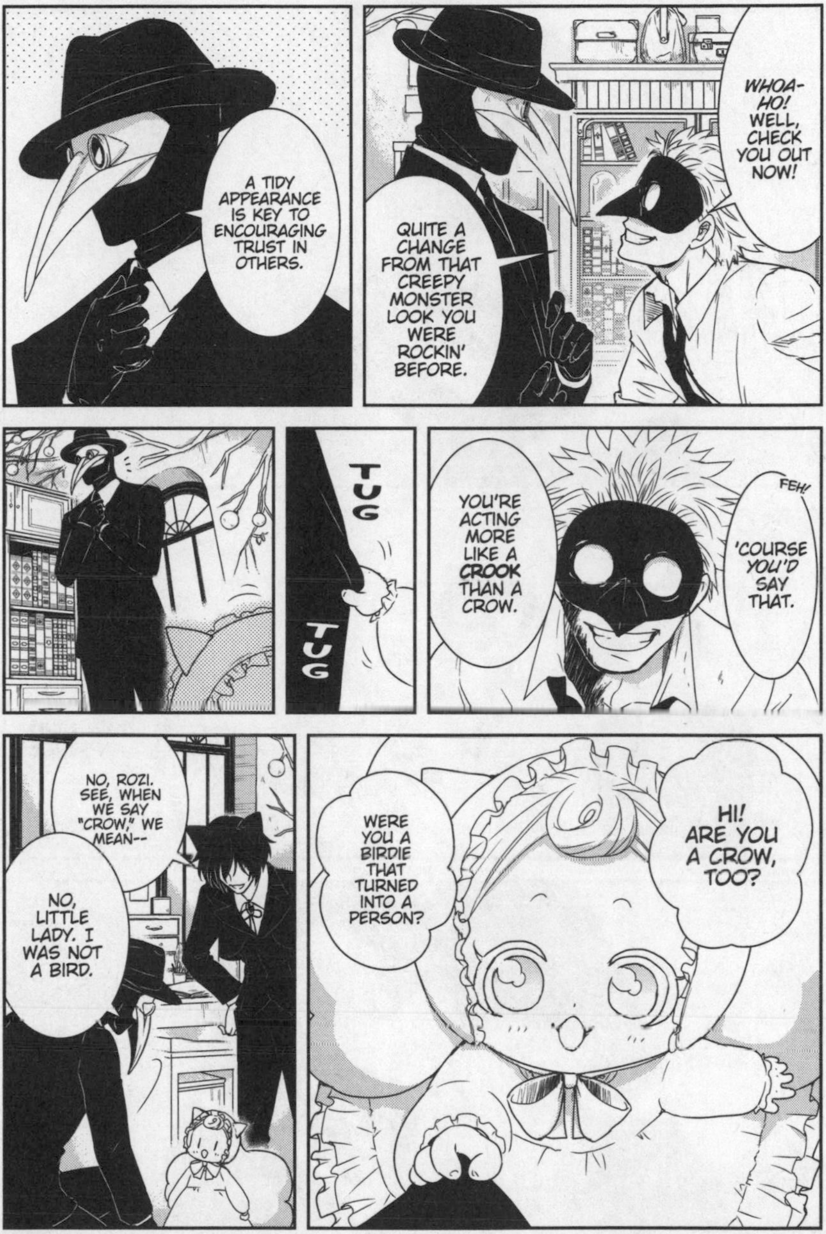
WHOA-HO! WELL, CHECK YOU OUT NOW!
QUITE A CHANGE FROM THAT CREEPY MONSTER LOOK YOU WERE ROCKIN' BEFORE.
A TIDY APPEARANCE IS KEY TO ENCOURAGING TRUST IN OTHERS.
FEH!
'COURSE YOU'D SAY THAT.
YOU'RE ACTING MORE LIKE A CROOK THAN A CROW.
TUG
TUG
HI! ARE YOU A CROW, TOO?
WERE YOU A BIRDIE THAT TURNED INTO A PERSON?
NO, ROZI. SEE, WHEN WE SAY "CROW," WE MEAN--
NO, LITTLE LADY. I WAS NOT A BIRD.

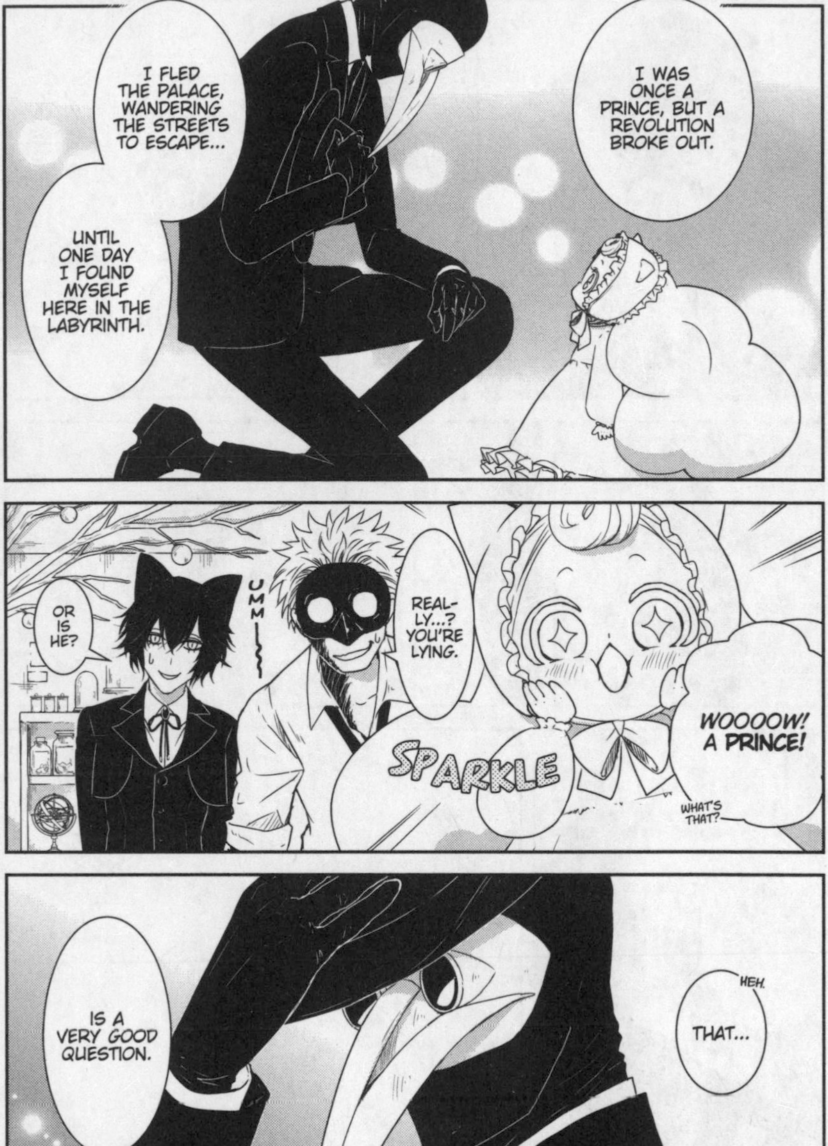
I WAS ONCE A PRINCE, BUT A REVOLUTION BROKE OUT.
I FLED THE PALACE, WANDERING THE STREETS TO ESCAPE...
UNTIL ONE DAY I FOUND MYSELF HERE IN THE LABYRINTH.
WOOOOW! A PRINCE!
WHAT'S THAT?
SPARKLE
REAL-LY...? YOU'RE LYING.
UMM...
OR IS HE?
HEH.
THAT...
IS A VERY GOOD QUESTION.

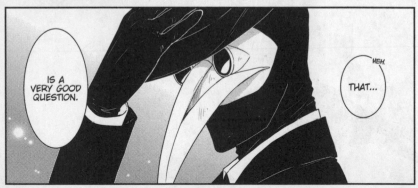

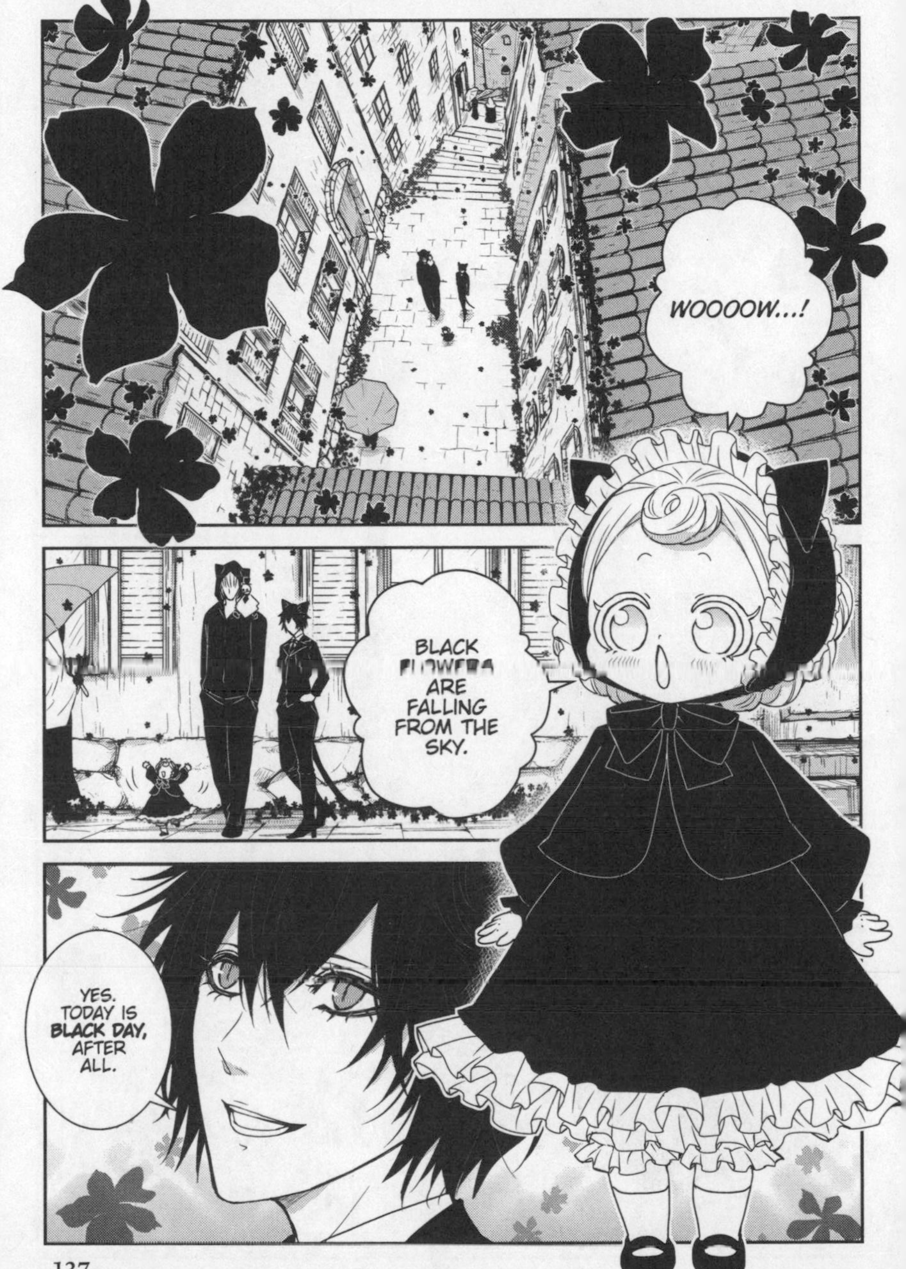
WOOOOW...!
BLACK FLOWERS ARE FALLING FROM THE SKY.
YES. TODAY IS **BLACK DAY,** AFTER ALL.

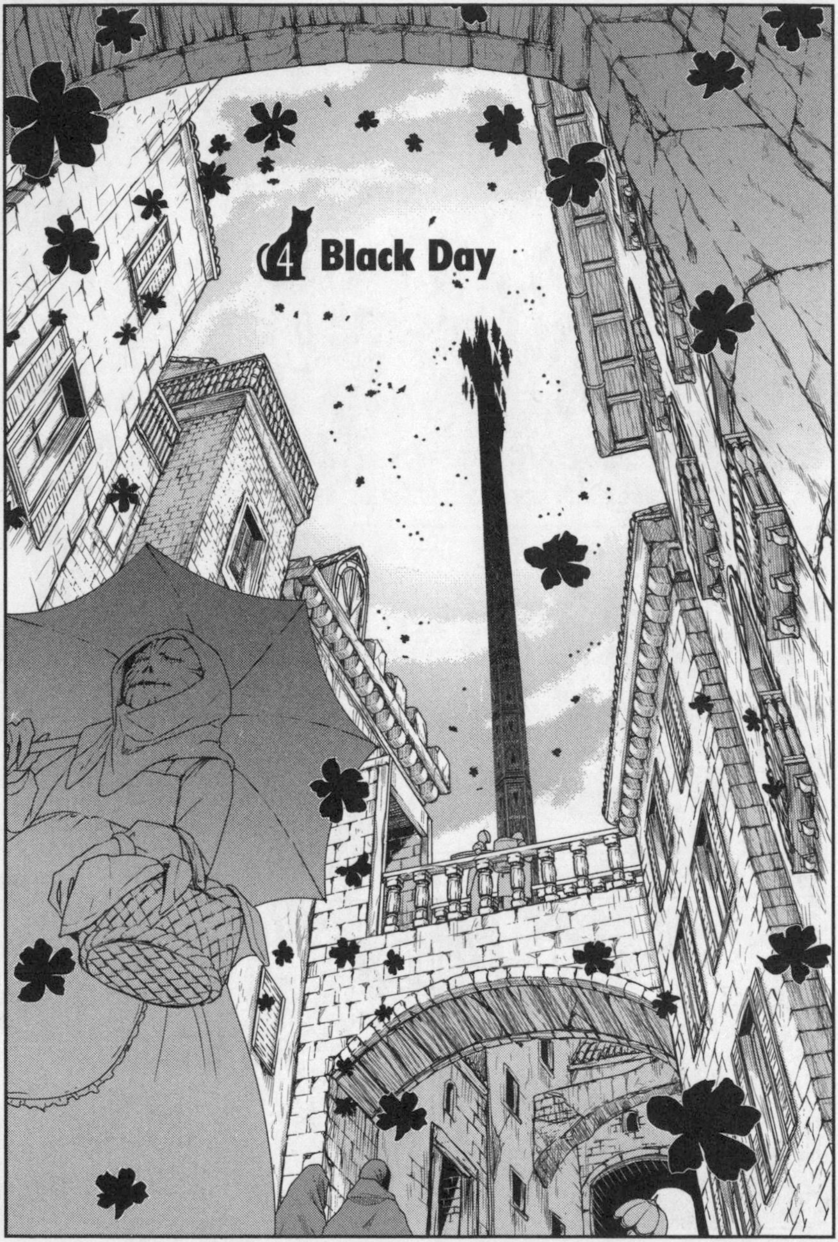
4 Black Day

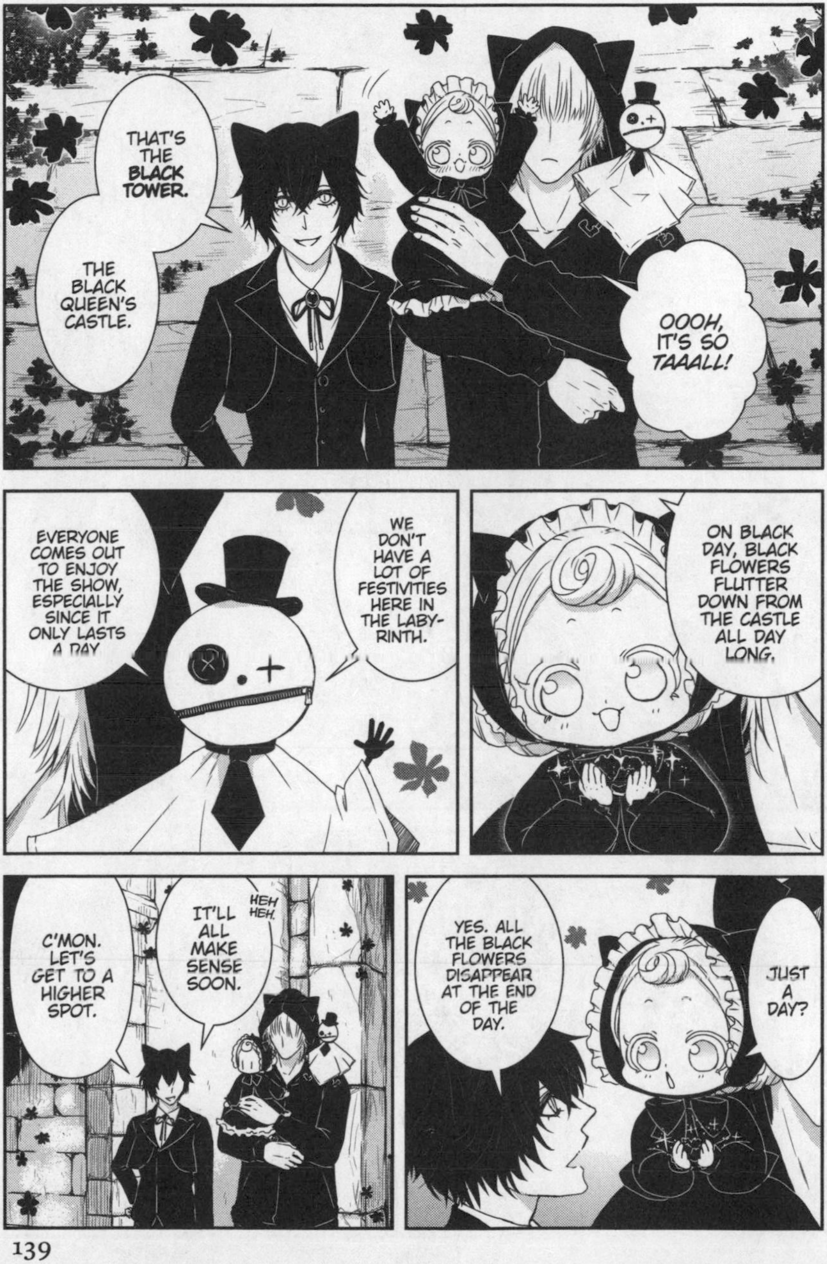
THAT'S THE BLACK TOWER.
THE BLACK QUEEN'S CASTLE.
OOOH, IT'S SO TAAALL!
ON BLACK DAY, BLACK FLOWERS FLUTTER DOWN FROM THE CASTLE ALL DAY LONG.
WE DON'T HAVE A LOT OF FESTIVITIES HERE IN THE LABY-RINTH.
EVERYONE COMES OUT TO ENJOY THE SHOW, ESPECIALLY SINCE IT ONLY LASTS A DAY.
JUST A DAY?
YES. ALL THE BLACK FLOWERS DISAPPEAR AT THE END OF THE DAY.
HEH HEH.
IT'LL ALL MAKE SENSE SOON.
C'MON. LET'S GET TO A HIGHER SPOT.

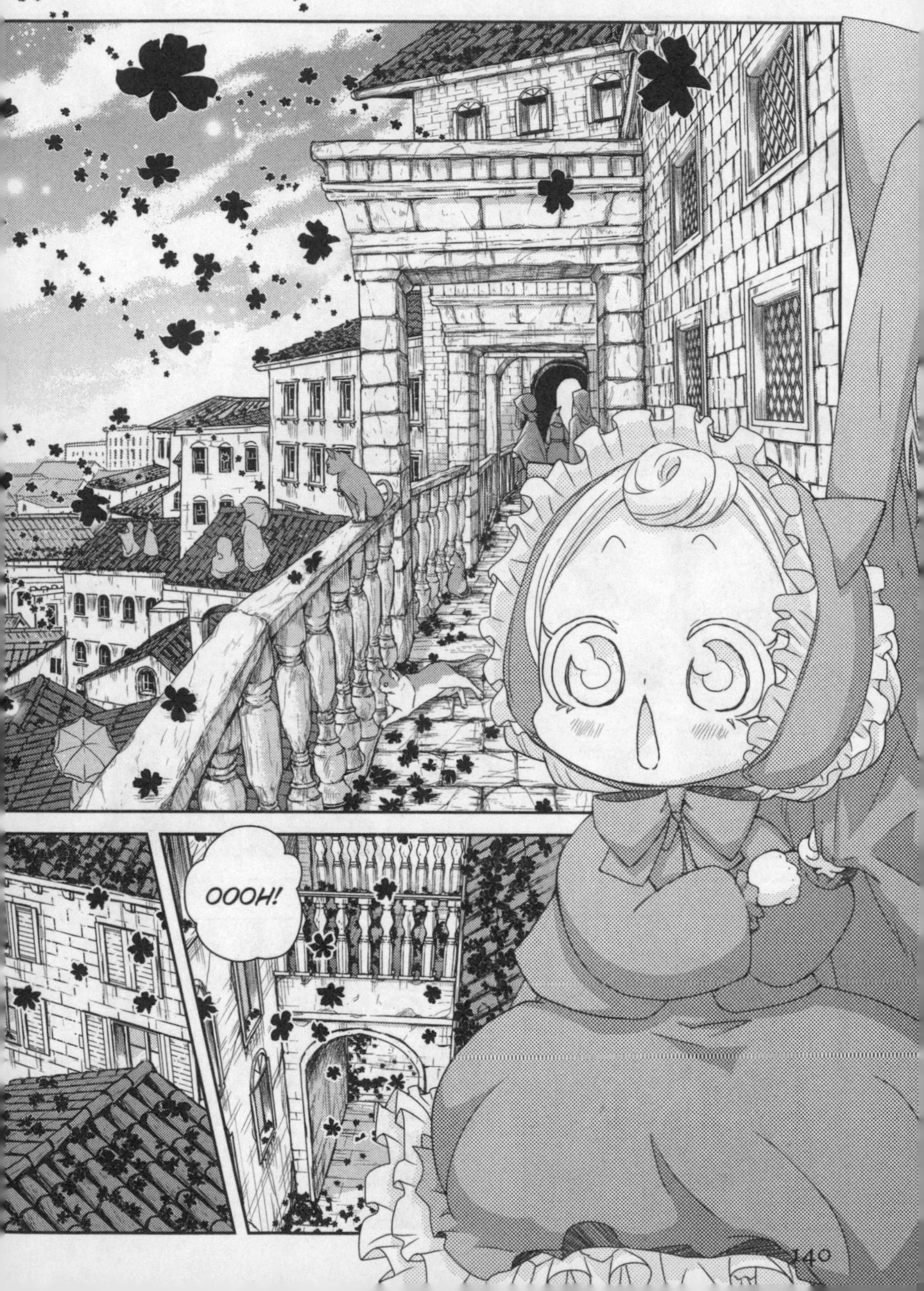
OOOH!

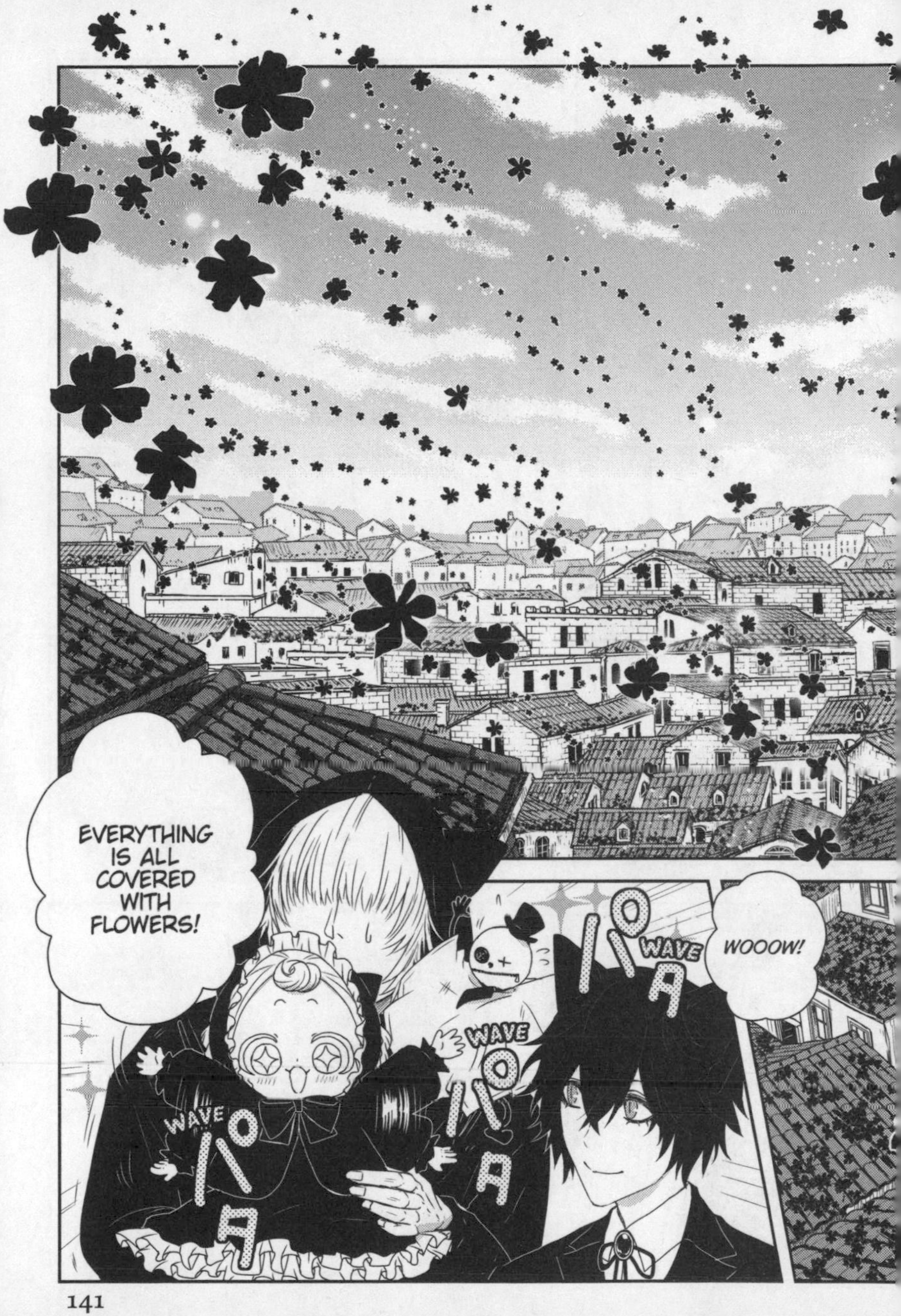
WOOOW!
パタ WAVE
EVERYTHING IS ALL COVERED WITH FLOWERS!
WAVE パタ
WAVE パタ

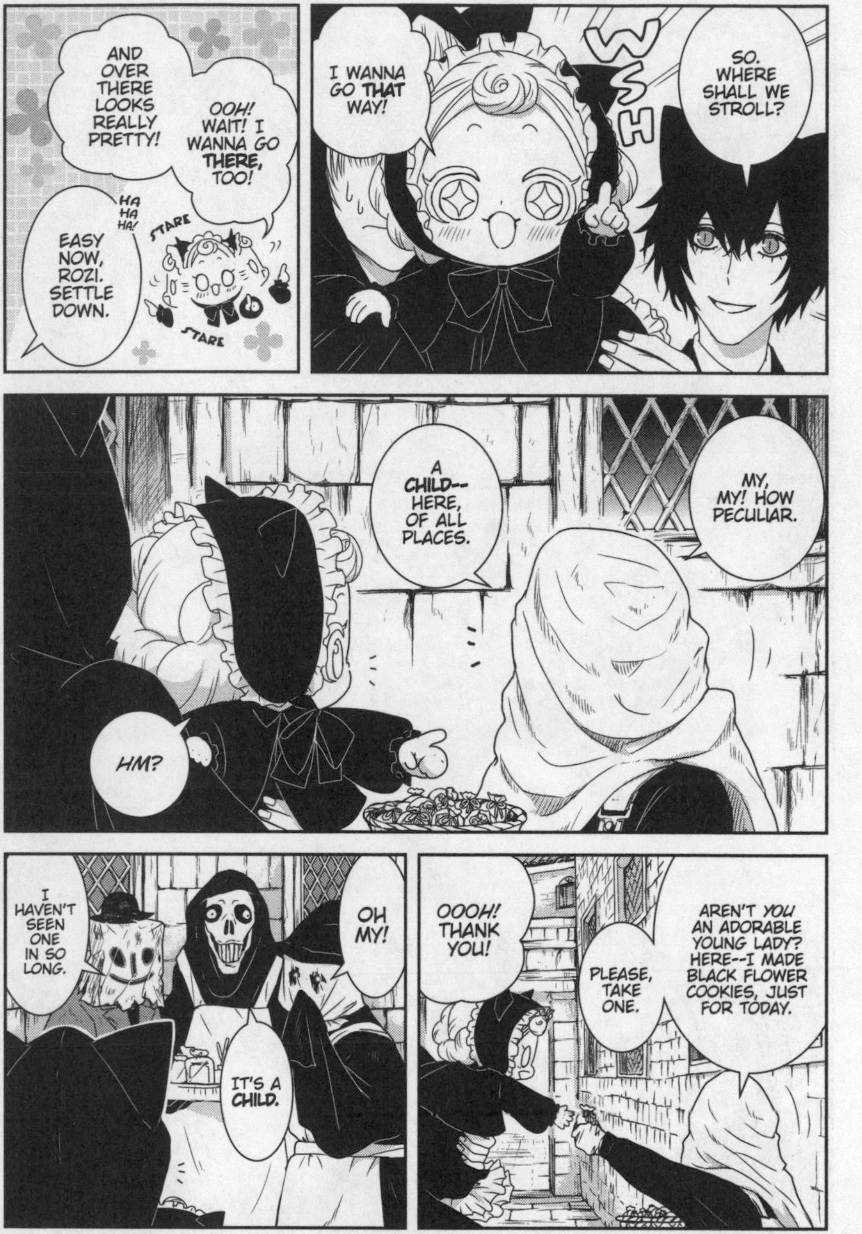
SO. WHERE SHALL WE STROLL?
WSH
I WANNA GO THAT WAY!
OOH! WAIT! I WANNA GO THERE, TOO!
AND OVER THERE LOOKS REALLY PRETTY!
HA HA HA!
EASY NOW, ROZI. SETTLE DOWN.
STARE
STARE
MY, MY! HOW PECULIAR.
A CHILD-- HERE, OF ALL PLACES.
HM?
AREN'T YOU AN ADORABLE YOUNG LADY? HERE--I MADE BLACK FLOWER COOKIES, JUST FOR TODAY.
PLEASE, TAKE ONE.
OOOH! THANK YOU!
OH MY!
I HAVEN'T SEEN ONE IN SO LONG.
IT'S A CHILD.

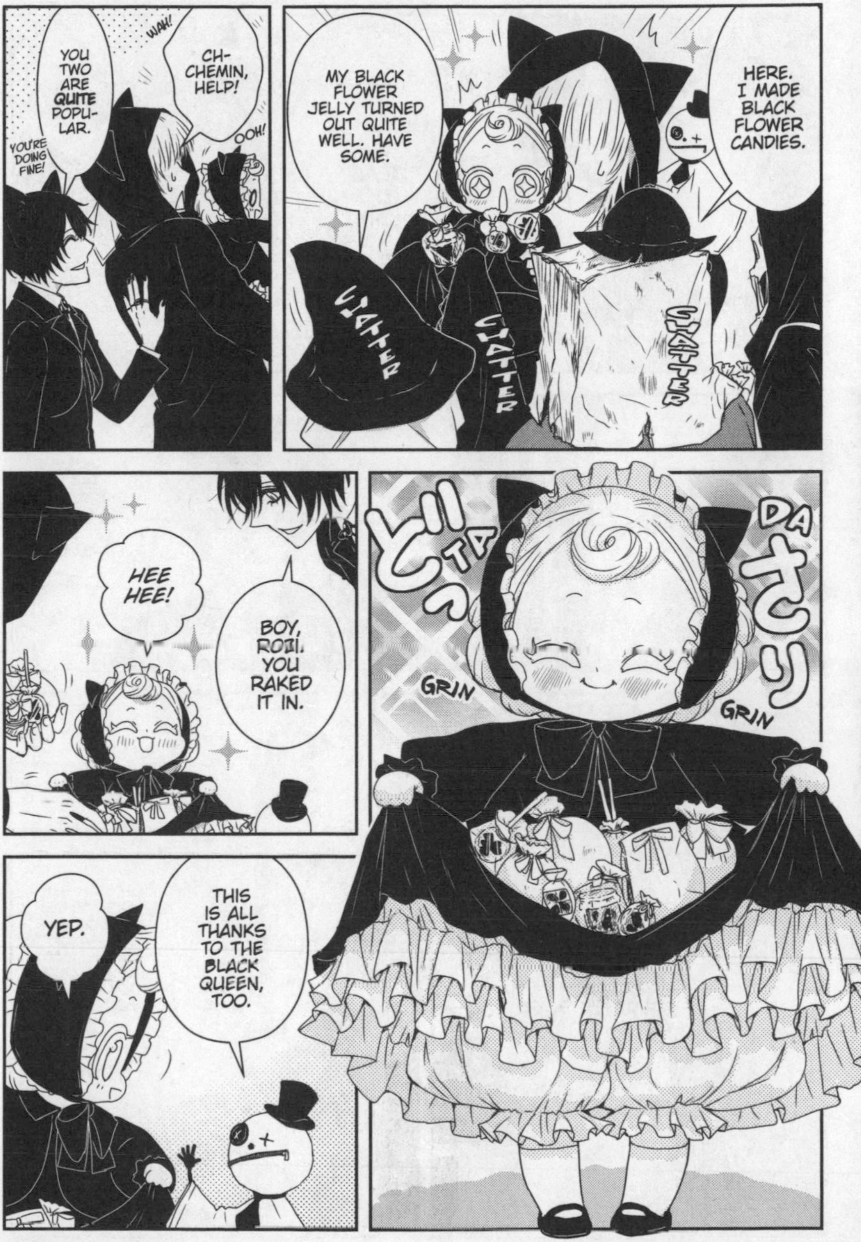
HERE. I MADE BLACK FLOWER CANDIES.
MY BLACK FLOWER JELLY TURNED OUT QUITE WELL. HAVE SOME.
CHATTER
CHATTER
CHATTER
CH-CHEMIN, HELP!
WAH!
YOU TWO ARE QUITE POPU-LAR.
OOH!
YOU'RE DOING FINE!
DA さり
TA どっ
GRIN
GRIN
BOY, ROII. YOU RAKED IT IN.
HEE HEE!
THIS IS ALL THANKS TO THE BLACK QUEEN, TOO.
YEP.

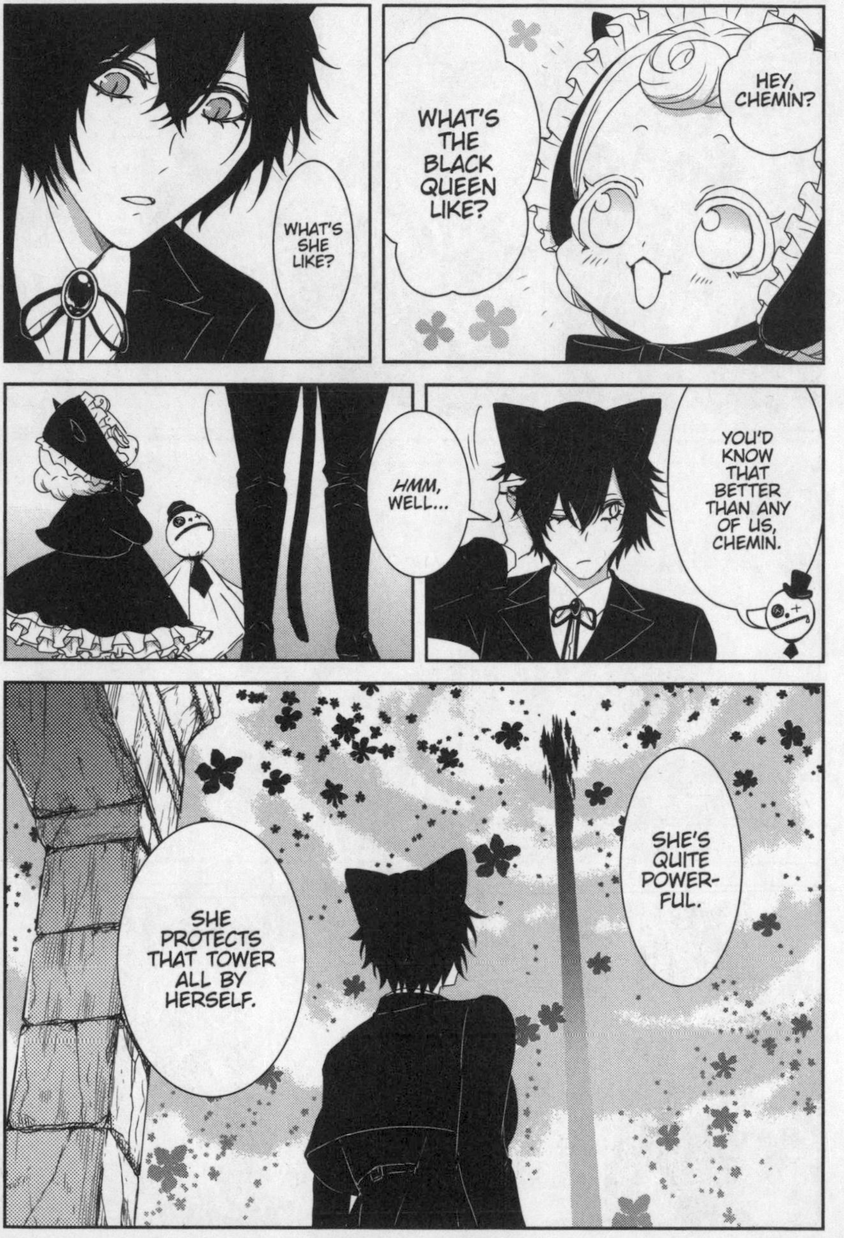
HEY, CHEMIN?
WHAT'S THE BLACK QUEEN LIKE?
WHAT'S SHE LIKE?
YOU'D KNOW THAT BETTER THAN ANY OF US, CHEMIN.
HMM, WELL...
SHE'S QUITE POWER-FUL.
SHE PROTECTS THAT TOWER ALL BY HERSELF.

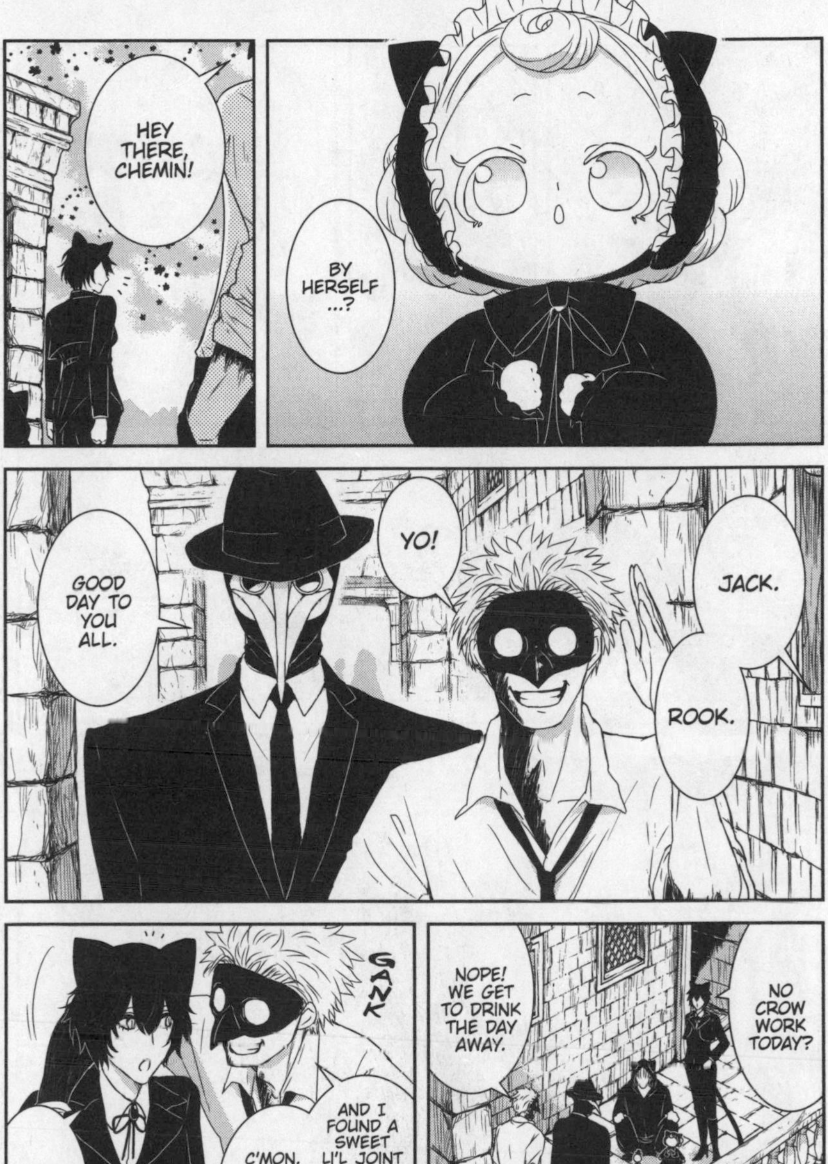

BY HERSELF ...?
HEY THERE, CHEMIN!
JACK.
ROOK.
YO!
GOOD DAY TO YOU ALL.
NO CROW WORK TODAY?
NOPE! WE GET TO DRINK THE DAY AWAY.
GANK
AND I FOUND A SWEET LI'L JOINT THAT'S GOT THE GOOD STUFF, TOO.
C'MON. LET'S DRINK TO THE FLOWERS.
WHAT, NOW?

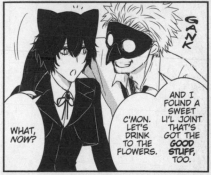

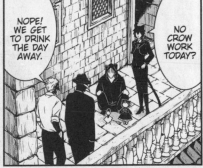

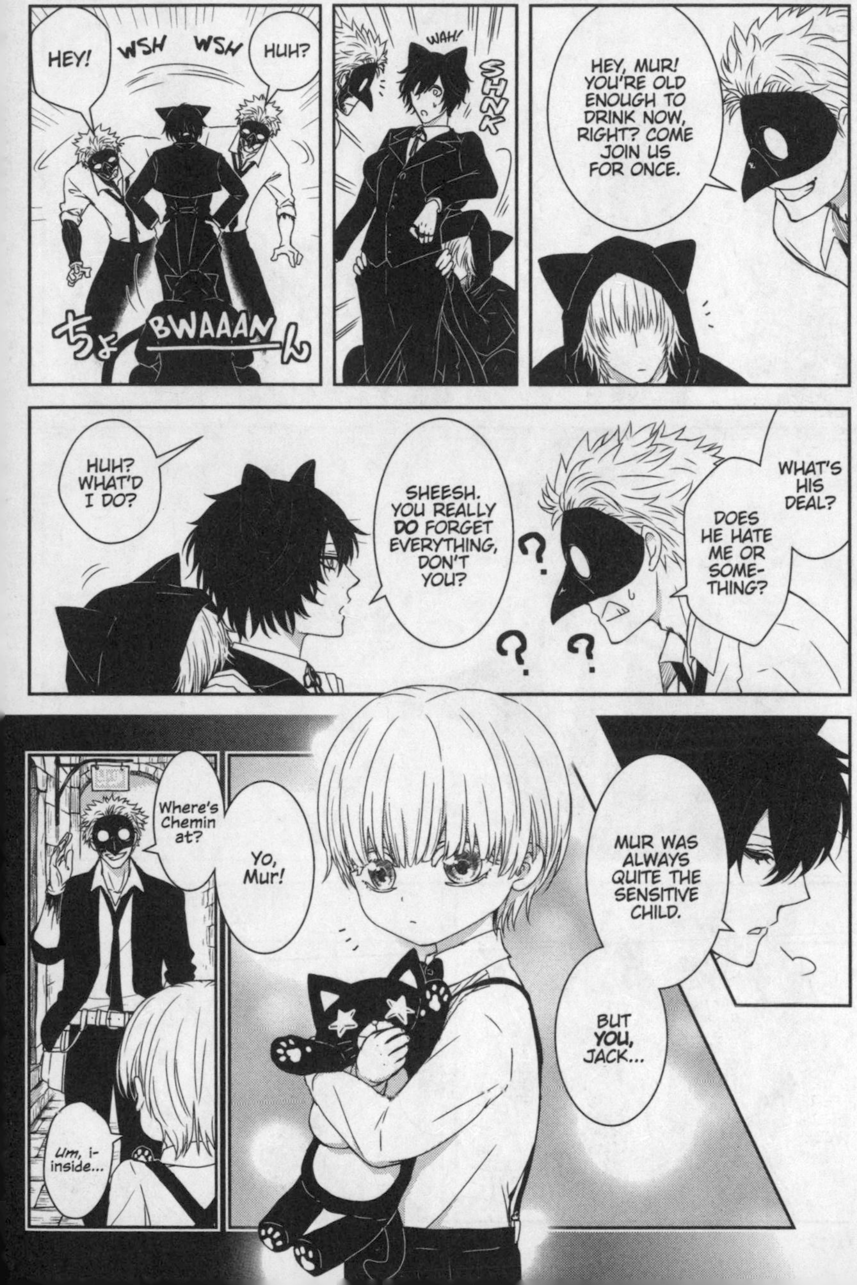
HEY, MUR! YOU'RE OLD ENOUGH TO DRINK NOW, RIGHT? COME JOIN US FOR ONCE.
WAH!
SHNK
HUH?
WSH WSH
HEY!
ちょ BWAAAN ん
WHAT'S HIS DEAL?
DOES HE HATE ME OR SOME-THING?
? ? ?
SHEESH. YOU REALLY DO FORGET EVERYTHING, DON'T YOU?
HUH? WHAT'D I DO?
MUR WAS ALWAYS QUITE THE SENSITIVE CHILD.
BUT YOU, JACK...
Yo, Mur!
Where's Chemin at?
Um, i-inside...

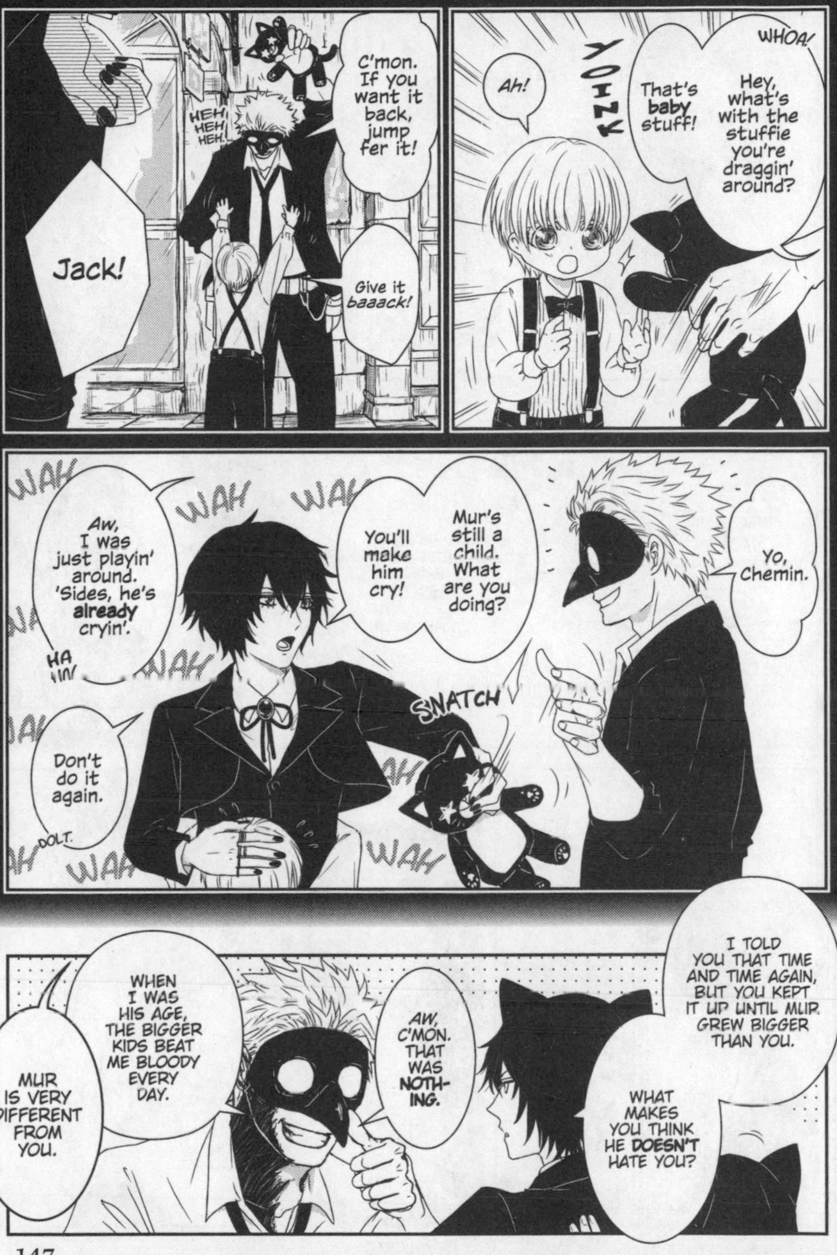
WHOA!
Hey, what's with the stuffie you're draggin' around?
That's baby stuff!
YOINK
Ah!
C'mon. If you want it back, jump fer it!
HEH HEH HEH.
Give it baaack!
Jack!
Yo, Chemin.
Mur's still a child. What are you doing?
You'll make him cry!
WAH WAH WAH
SNATCH
Aw, I was just playin' around. 'Sides, he's already cryin'.
Don't do it again.
DOLT.
WAH WAH
I TOLD YOU THAT TIME AND TIME AGAIN, BUT YOU KEPT IT UP UNTIL MUR GREW BIGGER THAN YOU.
WHAT MAKES YOU THINK HE DOESN'T HATE YOU?
AW, C'MON. THAT WAS NOTHING.
WHEN I WAS HIS AGE, THE BIGGER KIDS BEAT ME BLOODY EVERY DAY.
MUR IS VERY DIFFERENT FROM YOU.

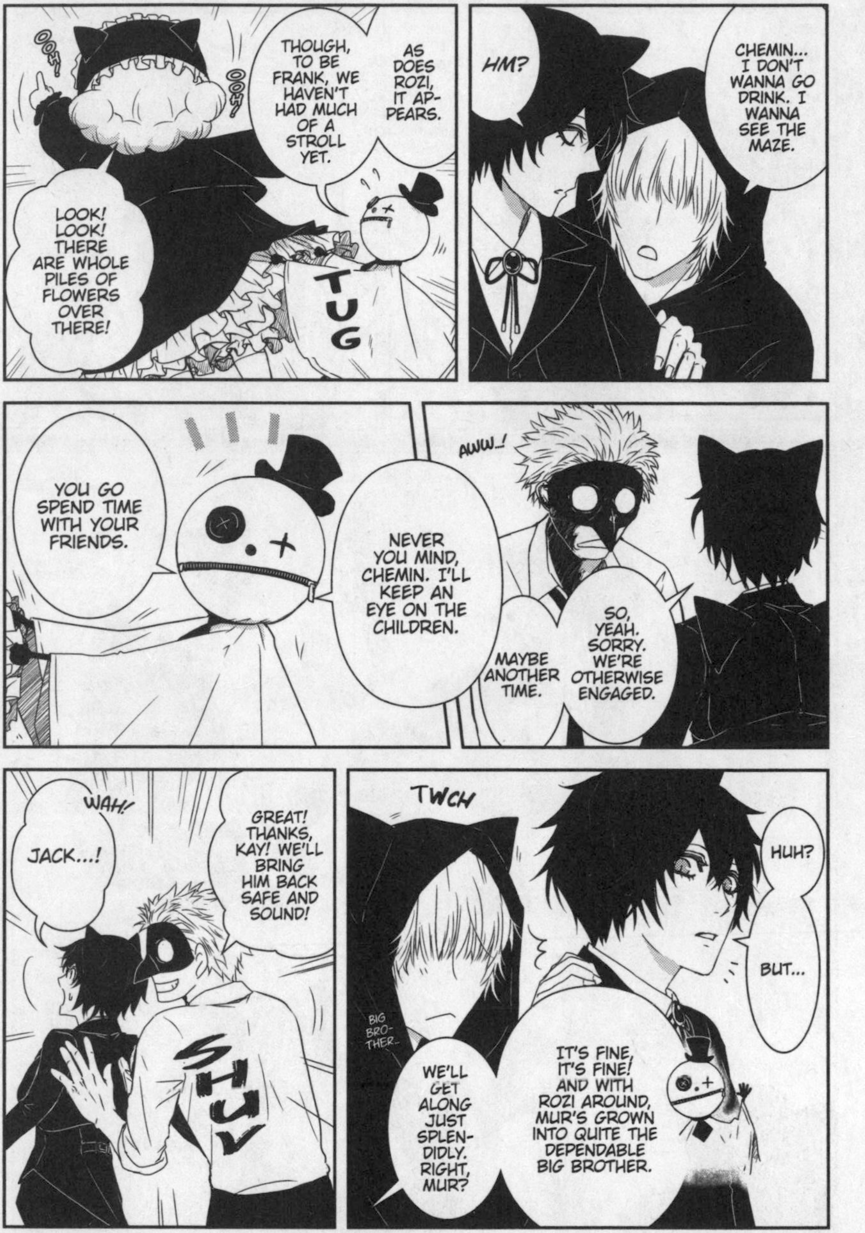
CHEMIN... I DON'T WANNA GO DRINK. I WANNA SEE THE MAZE.
HM?
AS DOES ROZI, IT APPEARS.
THOUGH, TO BE FRANK, WE HAVEN'T HAD MUCH OF A STROLL YET.
OOH! OOH!
LOOK! LOOK! THERE ARE WHOLE PILES OF FLOWERS OVER THERE!
TUG
AWW..!
SO, YEAH. SORRY. WE'RE OTHERWISE ENGAGED.
MAYBE ANOTHER TIME.
NEVER YOU MIND, CHEMIN. I'LL KEEP AN EYE ON THE CHILDREN.
YOU GO SPEND TIME WITH YOUR FRIENDS.
TWCH
HUH?
BUT...
IT'S FINE, IT'S FINE! AND WITH ROZI AROUND, MUR'S GROWN INTO QUITE THE DEPENDABLE BIG BROTHER.
BIG BROTHER...
WE'LL GET ALONG JUST SPLENDIDLY. RIGHT, MUR?
GREAT! THANKS, KAY! WE'LL BRING HIM BACK SAFE AND SOUND!
WAH!
JACK...!
SHUV

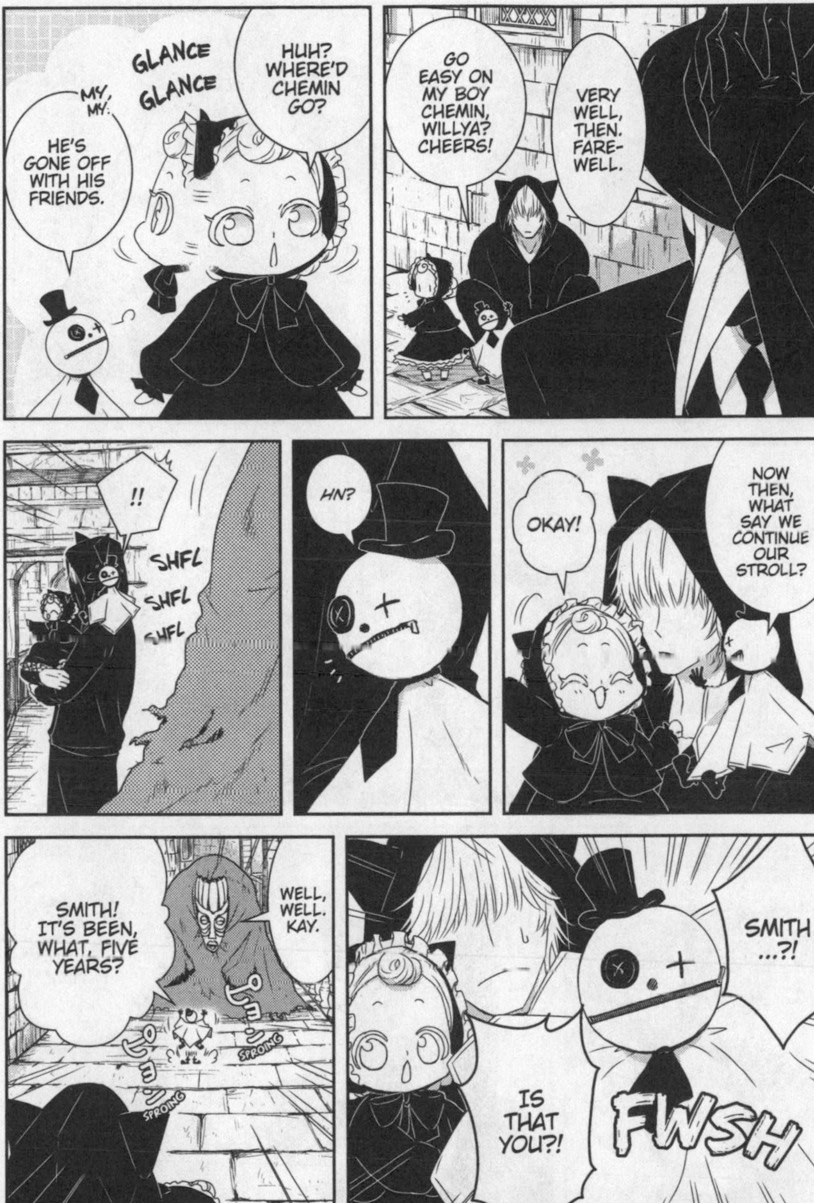
VERY WELL, THEN. FARE-WELL.
GO EASY ON MY BOY CHEMIN, WILLYA? CHEERS!
HUH? WHERE'D CHEMIN GO?
GLANCE GLANCE
MY, MY.
HE'S GONE OFF WITH HIS FRIENDS.
NOW THEN, WHAT SAY WE CONTINUE OUR STROLL?
OKAY!
HN?
!!
SHFL SHFL SHFL
SMITH ...?!
FWSH
IS THAT YOU?!
WELL, WELL. KAY.
SMITH! IT'S BEEN, WHAT, FIVE YEARS?
SPROING
SPROING

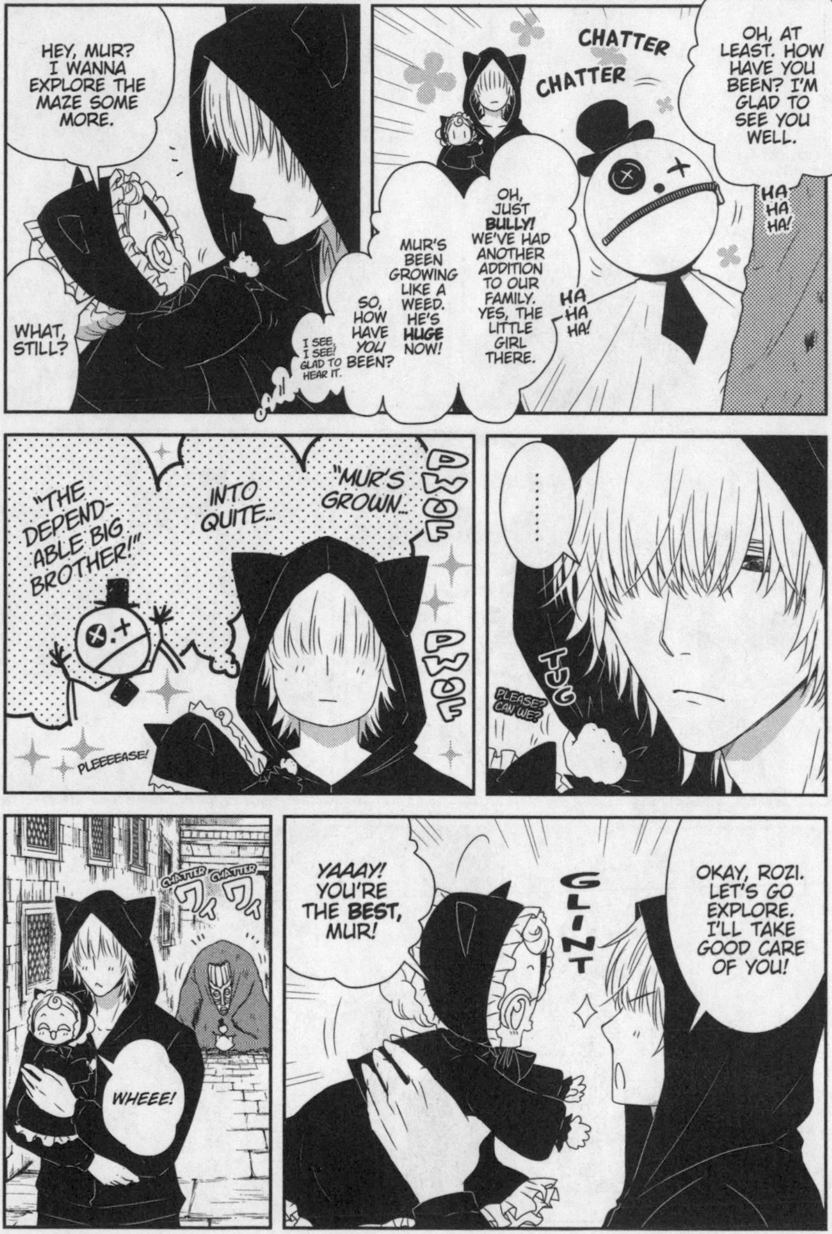
CHATTER
CHATTER
OH, AT LEAST. HOW HAVE YOU BEEN? I'M GLAD TO SEE YOU WELL.
HA HA HA!
OH, JUST BULLY! WE'VE HAD ANOTHER ADDITION TO OUR FAMILY. YES, THE LITTLE GIRL THERE.
HA HA HA!
MUR'S BEEN GROWING LIKE A WEED. HE'S HUGE NOW!
SO, HOW HAVE YOU BEEN?
I SEE, I SEE! GLAD TO HEAR IT.
HEY, MUR? I WANNA EXPLORE THE MAZE SOME MORE.
WHAT, STILL?
......
TUG
PLEASE? CAN WE?
"MUR'S GROWN...
INTO QUITE...
"THE DEPENDABLE BIG BROTHER!"
PWOF
PWOF
PLEEEEASE!
OKAY, ROZI. LET'S GO EXPLORE. I'LL TAKE GOOD CARE OF YOU!
GLINT
YAAAY! YOU'RE THE BEST, MUR!
CHATTER CHATTER
ワイ ワイ
WHEEE!

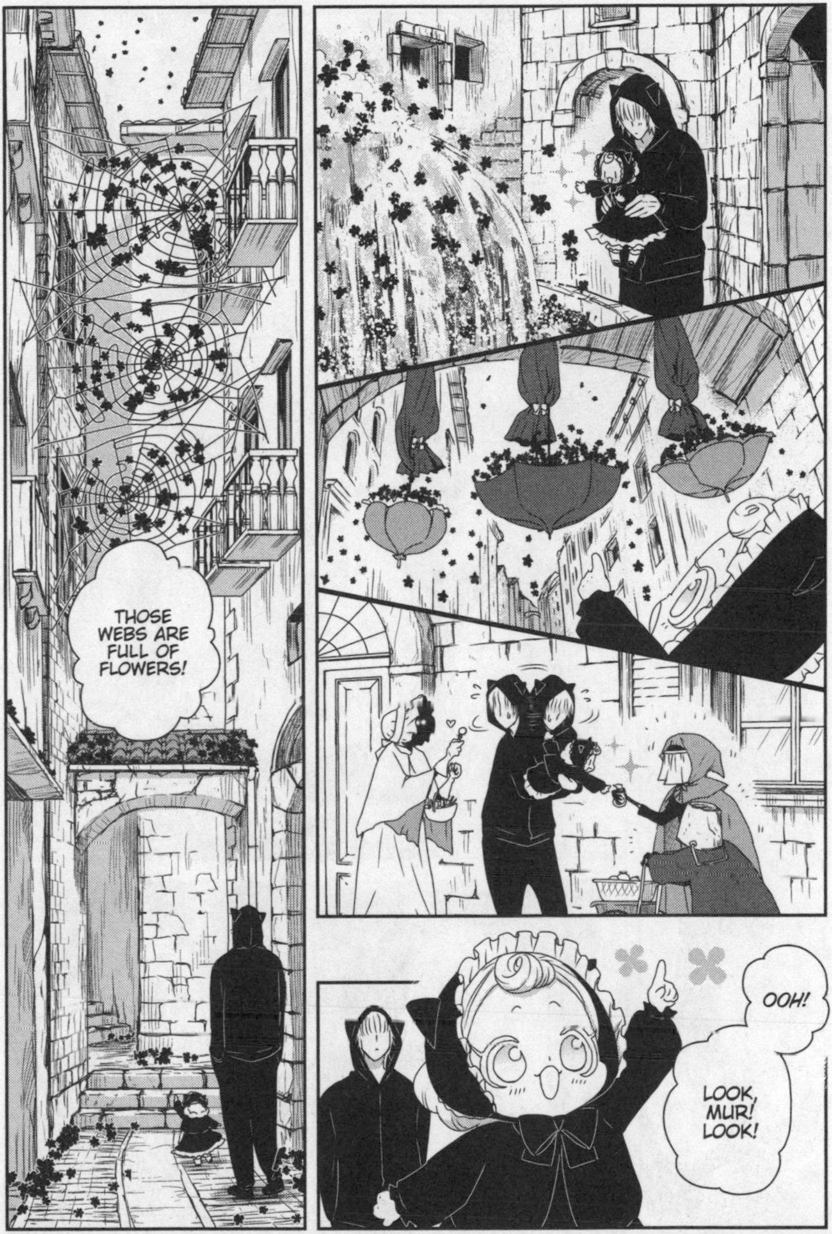
OOH!
LOOK, MUR! LOOK!
THOSE WEBS ARE FULL OF FLOWERS!

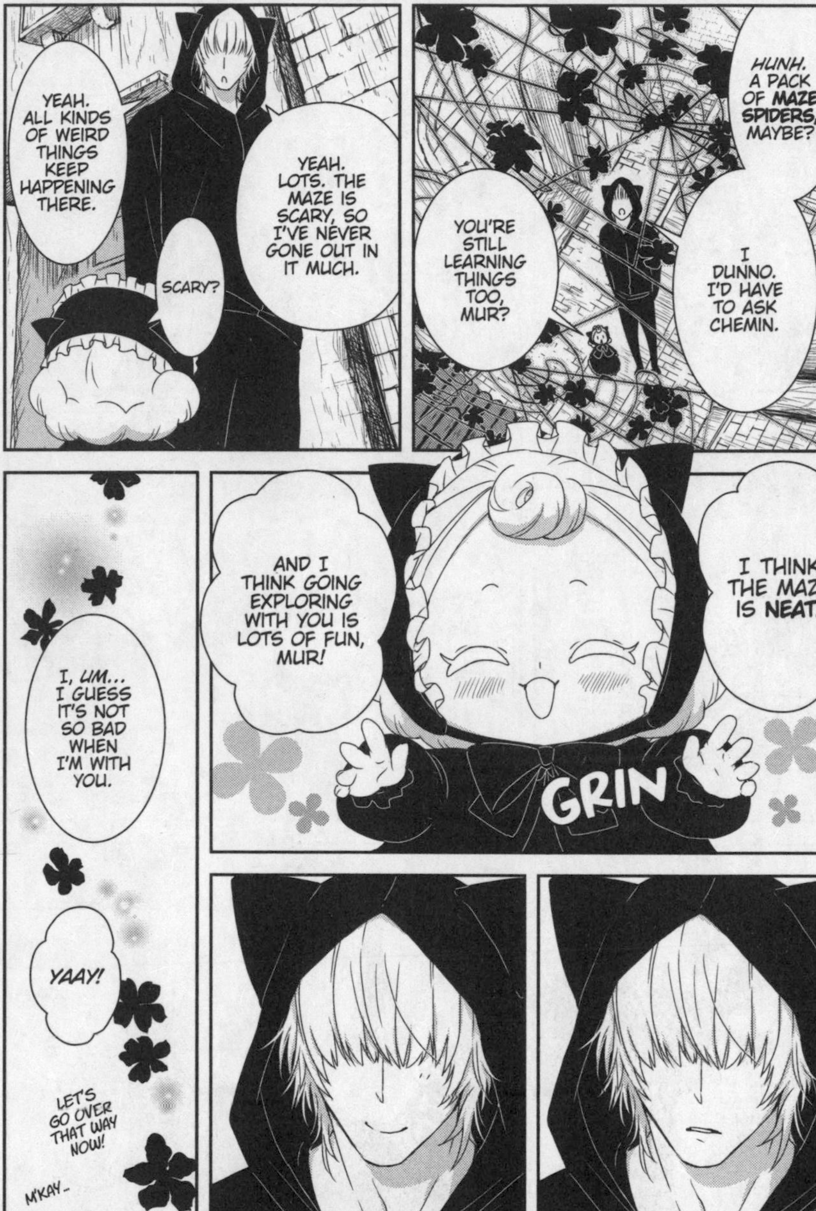
HUNH. A PACK OF MAZE SPIDERS, MAYBE?
YOU'RE STILL LEARNING THINGS TOO, MUR?
I DUNNO. I'D HAVE TO ASK CHEMIN.
YEAH. ALL KINDS OF WEIRD THINGS KEEP HAPPENING THERE.
YEAH. LOTS. THE MAZE IS SCARY, SO I'VE NEVER GONE OUT IN IT MUCH.
SCARY?
I THINK THE MAZE IS NEAT!
AND I THINK GOING EXPLORING WITH YOU IS LOTS OF FUN, MUR!
GRIN
I, UM... I GUESS IT'S NOT SO BAD WHEN I'M WITH YOU.
YAAY!
LET'S GO OVER THAT WAY NOW!
M'KAY...

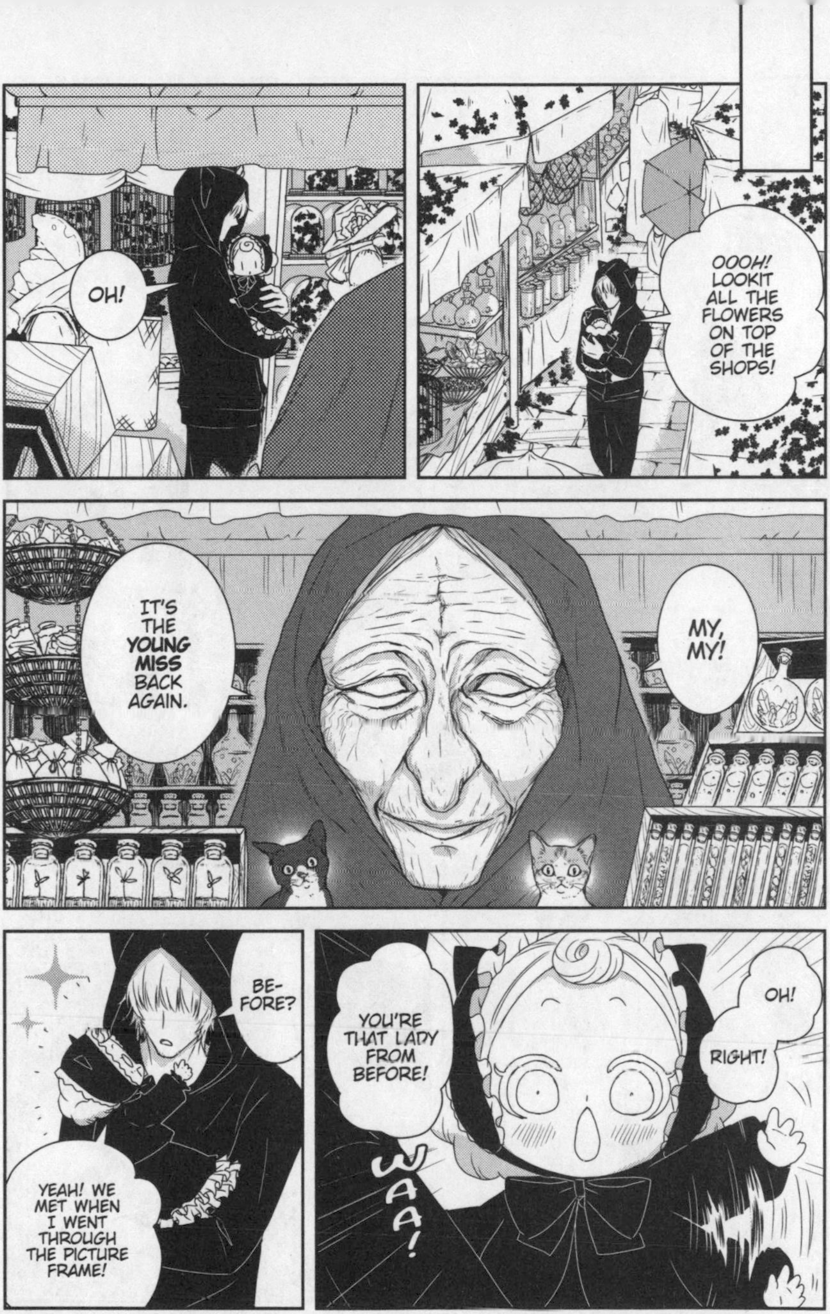
OOOH! LOOKIT ALL THE FLOWERS ON TOP OF THE SHOPS!
OH!
MY, MY!
IT'S THE YOUNG MISS BACK AGAIN.
OH!
RIGHT!
YOU'RE THAT LADY FROM BEFORE!
WAA!
BE-FORE?
YEAH! WE MET WHEN I WENT THROUGH THE PICTURE FRAME!

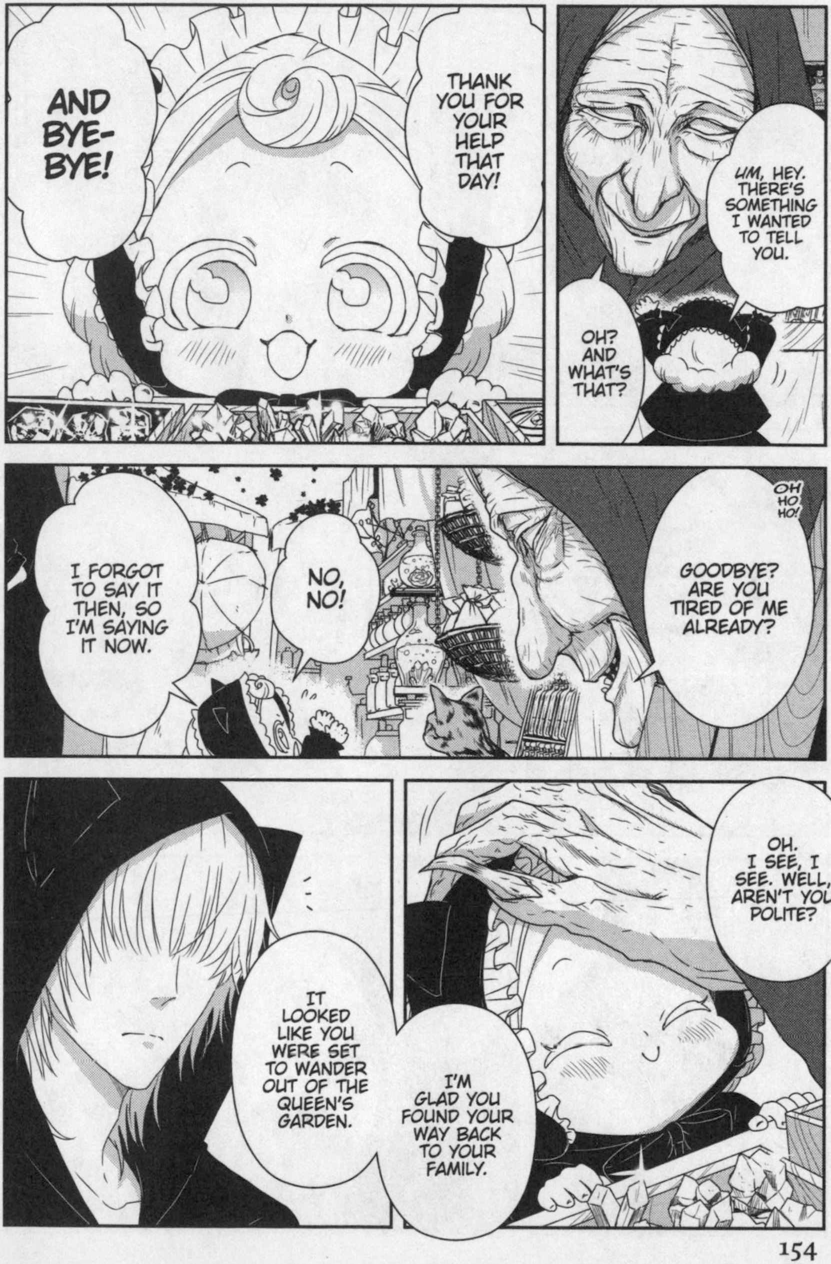
UM, HEY. THERE'S SOMETHING I WANTED TO TELL YOU.
OH? AND WHAT'S THAT?
THANK YOU FOR YOUR HELP THAT DAY!
AND BYE-BYE!
OH HO HO!
GOODBYE? ARE YOU TIRED OF ME ALREADY?
NO, NO!
I FORGOT TO SAY IT THEN, SO I'M SAYING IT NOW.
OH. I SEE, I SEE. WELL, AREN'T YOU POLITE?
IT LOOKED LIKE YOU WERE SET TO WANDER OUT OF THE QUEEN'S GARDEN.
I'M GLAD YOU FOUND YOUR WAY BACK TO YOUR FAMILY.

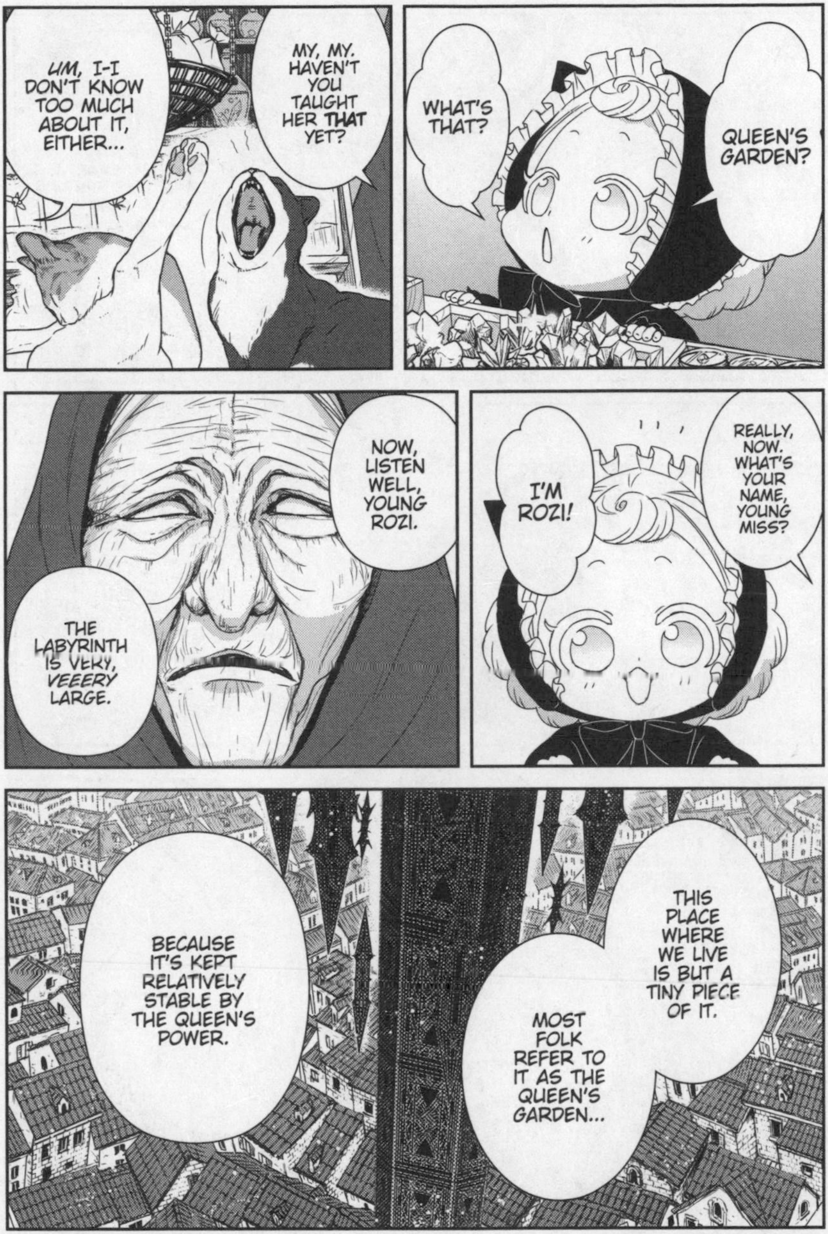
QUEEN'S GARDEN?
WHAT'S THAT?
MY, MY. HAVEN'T YOU TAUGHT HER THAT YET?
UM, I-I DON'T KNOW TOO MUCH ABOUT IT, EITHER...
REALLY, NOW. WHAT'S YOUR NAME, YOUNG MISS?
I'M ROZI!
NOW, LISTEN WELL, YOUNG ROZI.
THE LABYRINTH IS VERY, VEEERY LARGE.
THIS PLACE WHERE WE LIVE IS BUT A TINY PIECE OF IT.
MOST FOLK REFER TO IT AS THE QUEEN'S GARDEN...
BECAUSE IT'S KEPT RELATIVELY STABLE BY THE QUEEN'S POWER.

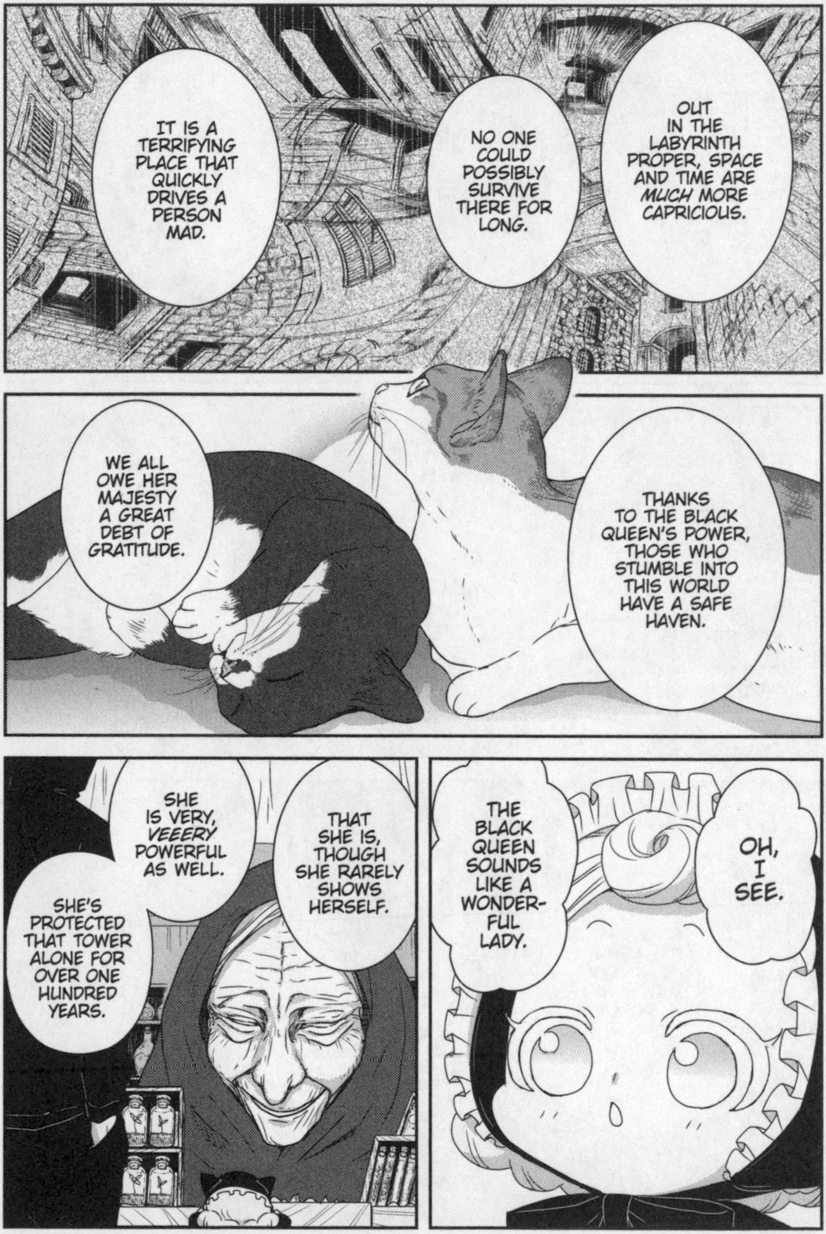
OUT IN THE LABYRINTH PROPER, SPACE AND TIME ARE *MUCH* MORE CAPRICIOUS.
NO ONE COULD POSSIBLY SURVIVE THERE FOR LONG.
IT IS A TERRIFYING PLACE THAT QUICKLY DRIVES A PERSON MAD.
THANKS TO THE BLACK QUEEN'S POWER, THOSE WHO STUMBLE INTO THIS WORLD HAVE A SAFE HAVEN.
WE ALL OWE HER MAJESTY A GREAT DEBT OF GRATITUDE.
OH, I SEE.
THE BLACK QUEEN SOUNDS LIKE A WONDER-FUL LADY.
THAT SHE IS, THOUGH SHE RARELY SHOWS HERSELF.
SHE IS VERY, *VEEERY* POWERFUL AS WELL.
SHE'S PROTECTED THAT TOWER ALONE FOR OVER ONE HUNDRED YEARS.

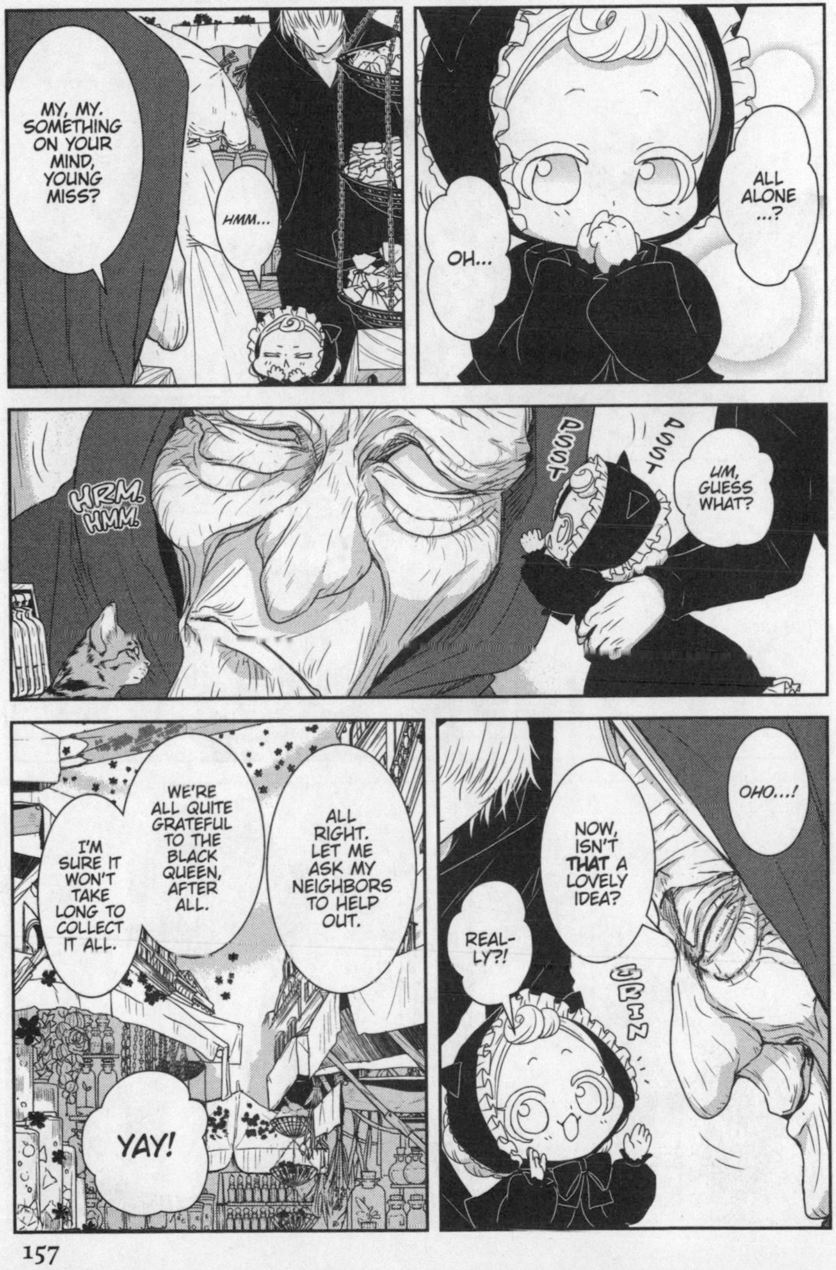
ALL ALONE ...?
OH...
HMM...
MY, MY. SOMETHING ON YOUR MIND, YOUNG MISS?
PSST
PSST
UM, GUESS WHAT?
HRM. HMM.
OHO...!
NOW, ISN'T THAT A LOVELY IDEA?
GRIN
REAL-LY?!
ALL RIGHT. LET ME ASK MY NEIGHBORS TO HELP OUT.
WE'RE ALL QUITE GRATEFUL TO THE BLACK QUEEN, AFTER ALL.
I'M SURE IT WON'T TAKE LONG TO COLLECT IT ALL.
YAY!

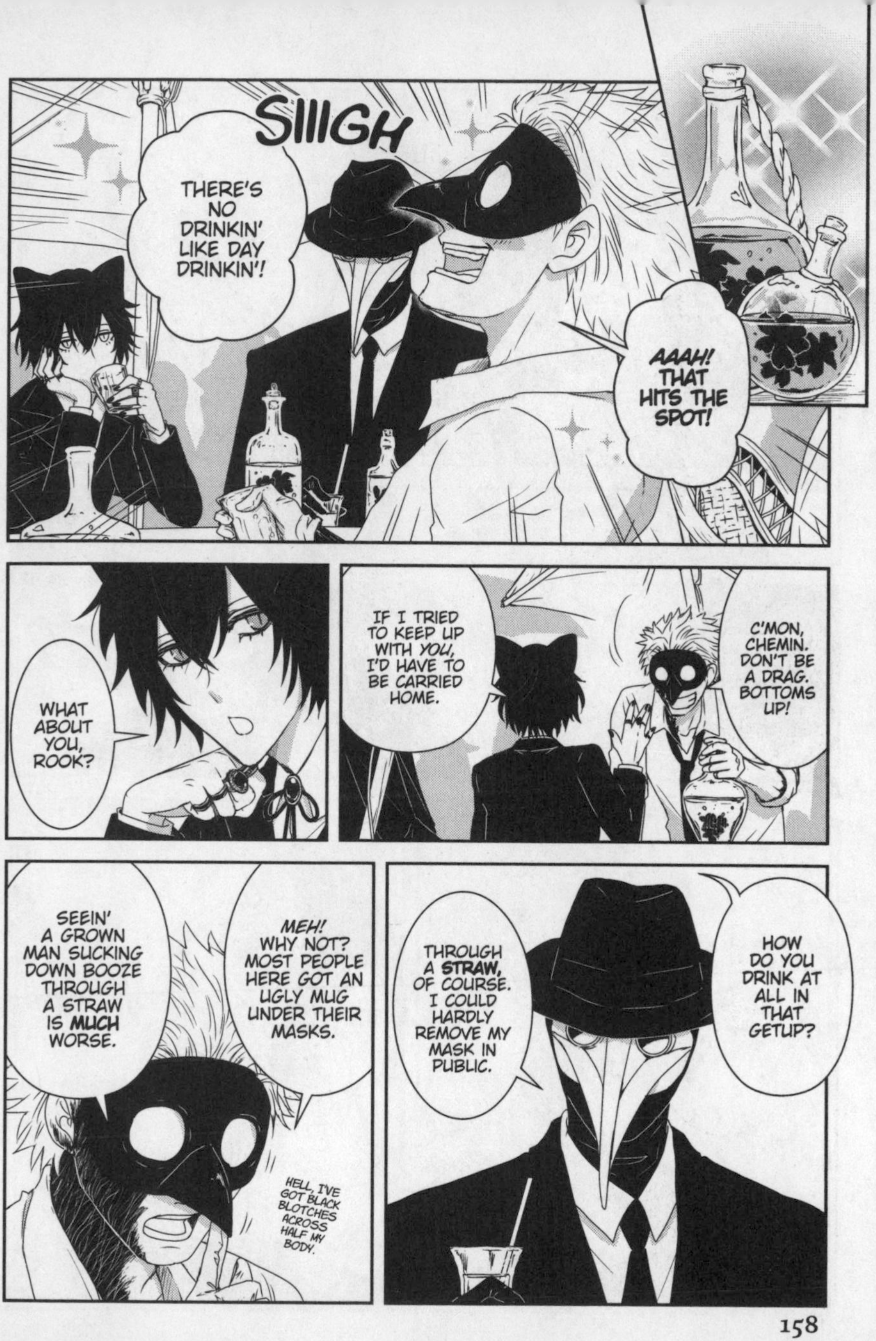
AAAH! THAT HITS THE SPOT!
SIIIGH
THERE'S NO DRINKIN' LIKE DAY DRINKIN'!
C'MON, CHEMIN. DON'T BE A DRAG. BOTTOMS UP!
IF I TRIED TO KEEP UP WITH *YOU*, I'D HAVE TO BE CARRIED HOME.
WHAT ABOUT YOU, ROOK?
HOW DO YOU DRINK AT ALL IN THAT GETUP?
THROUGH A **STRAW,** OF COURSE. I COULD HARDLY REMOVE MY MASK IN PUBLIC.
MEH! WHY NOT? MOST PEOPLE HERE GOT AN UGLY MUG UNDER THEIR MASKS.
SEEIN' A GROWN MAN SUCKING DOWN BOOZE THROUGH A STRAW IS **MUCH** WORSE.
HELL, I'VE GOT BLACK BLOTCHES ACROSS HALF MY BODY.

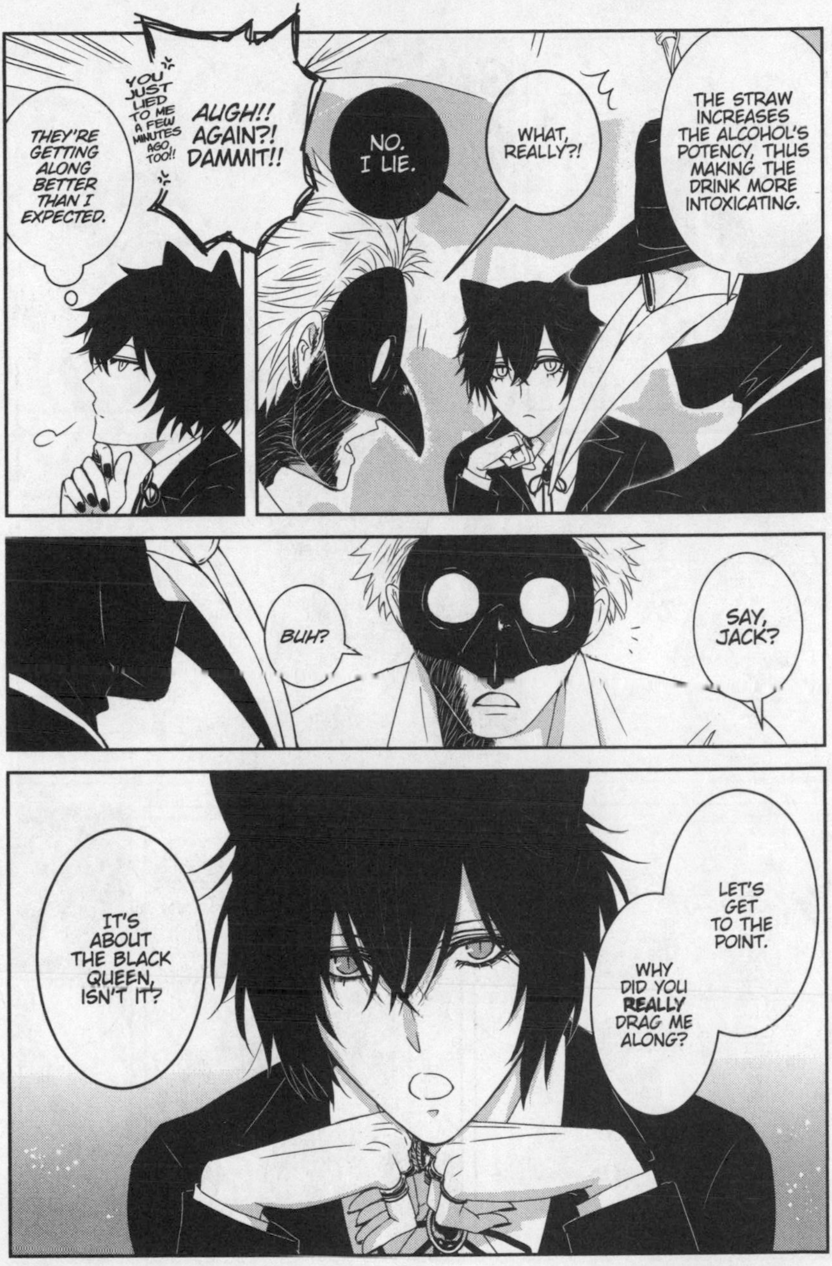
THE STRAW INCREASES THE ALCOHOL'S POTENCY, THUS MAKING THE DRINK MORE INTOXICATING.
WHAT, REALLY?!
NO. I LIE.
AUGH!! AGAIN?! DAMMIT!!
YOU JUST LIED TO ME A FEW MINUTES AGO TOO!!
THEY'RE GETTING ALONG BETTER THAN I EXPECTED.
SAY, JACK?
BUH?
LET'S GET TO THE POINT.
WHY DID YOU REALLY DRAG ME ALONG?
IT'S ABOUT THE BLACK QUEEN, ISN'T IT?

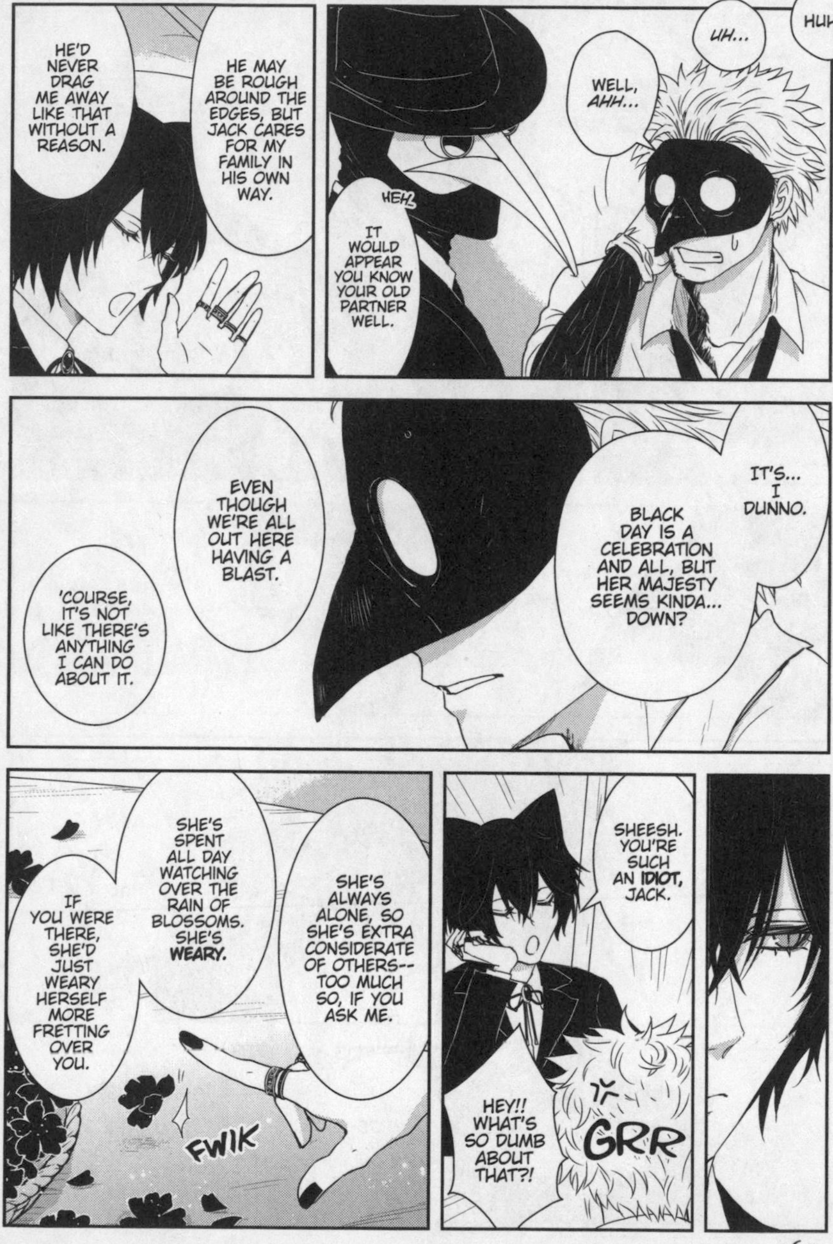
HUH?
UH...
WELL, AHH...
HEH
IT WOULD APPEAR YOU KNOW YOUR OLD PARTNER WELL.
HE MAY BE ROUGH AROUND THE EDGES, BUT JACK CARES FOR MY FAMILY IN HIS OWN WAY.
HE'D NEVER DRAG ME AWAY LIKE THAT WITHOUT A REASON.
IT'S... I DUNNO.
BLACK DAY IS A CELEBRATION AND ALL, BUT HER MAJESTY SEEMS KINDA... DOWN?
EVEN THOUGH WE'RE ALL OUT HERE HAVING A BLAST.
'COURSE, IT'S NOT LIKE THERE'S ANYTHING I CAN DO ABOUT IT.
SHEESH. YOU'RE SUCH AN **IDIOT**, JACK.
HEY!! WHAT'S SO DUMB ABOUT THAT?!
GRR
SHE'S ALWAYS ALONE, SO SHE'S EXTRA CONSIDERATE OF OTHERS-- TOO MUCH SO, IF YOU ASK ME.
SHE'S SPENT ALL DAY WATCHING OVER THE RAIN OF BLOSSOMS. SHE'S **WEARY.**
IF YOU WERE THERE, SHE'D JUST WEARY HERSELF MORE FRETTING OVER YOU.
FWIK

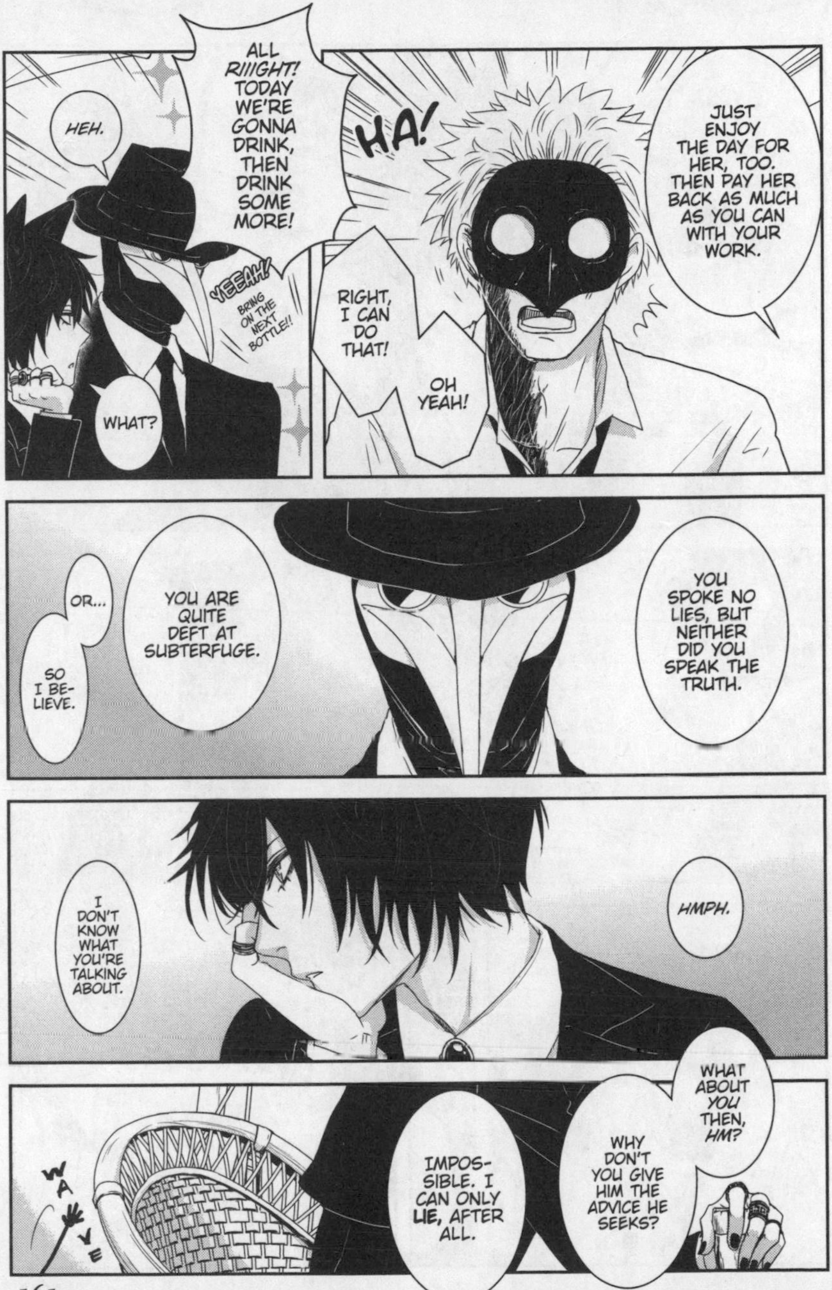
JUST ENJOY THE DAY FOR HER, TOO. THEN PAY HER BACK AS MUCH AS YOU CAN WITH YOUR WORK.
HA!
RIGHT, I CAN DO THAT!
OH YEAH!
ALL RIIIGHT! TODAY WE'RE GONNA DRINK, THEN DRINK SOME MORE!
YEEAH!
BRING ON THE NEXT BOTTLE!!
HEH.
WHAT?
YOU SPOKE NO LIES, BUT NEITHER DID YOU SPEAK THE TRUTH.
YOU ARE QUITE DEFT AT SUBTERFUGE.
OR...
SO I BE-LIEVE.
HMPH.
I DON'T KNOW WHAT YOU'RE TALKING ABOUT.
WHAT ABOUT YOU THEN, HM?
WHY DON'T YOU GIVE HIM THE ADVICE HE SEEKS?
IMPOS-SIBLE. I CAN ONLY LIE, AFTER ALL.
WAVE

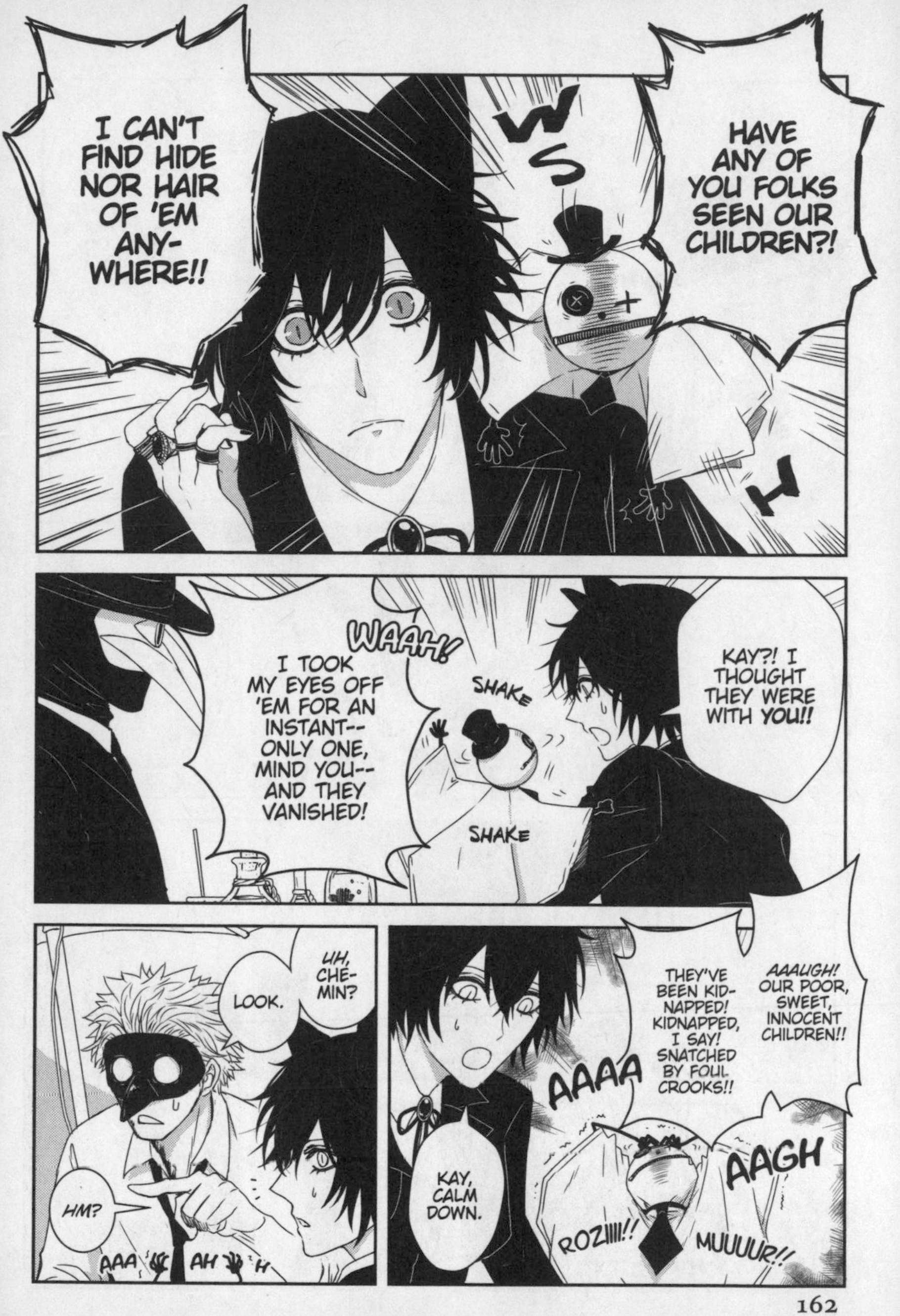
HAVE ANY OF YOU FOLKS SEEN OUR CHILDREN?!
WS
H
I CAN'T FIND HIDE NOR HAIR OF 'EM ANYWHERE!!
KAY?! I THOUGHT THEY WERE WITH YOU!!
SHAKE
WAAH!
I TOOK MY EYES OFF 'EM FOR AN INSTANT-- ONLY ONE, MIND YOU-- AND THEY VANISHED!
SHAKE
AAAUGH! OUR POOR, SWEET, INNOCENT CHILDREN!!
THEY'VE BEEN KIDNAPPED! KIDNAPPED, I SAY! SNATCHED BY FOUL CROOKS!!
AAAA
AAGH
KAY, CALM DOWN.
ROZIIII!!
MUUUUR!!
UH, CHE-MIN?
LOOK.
HM?
AAA
AH
H

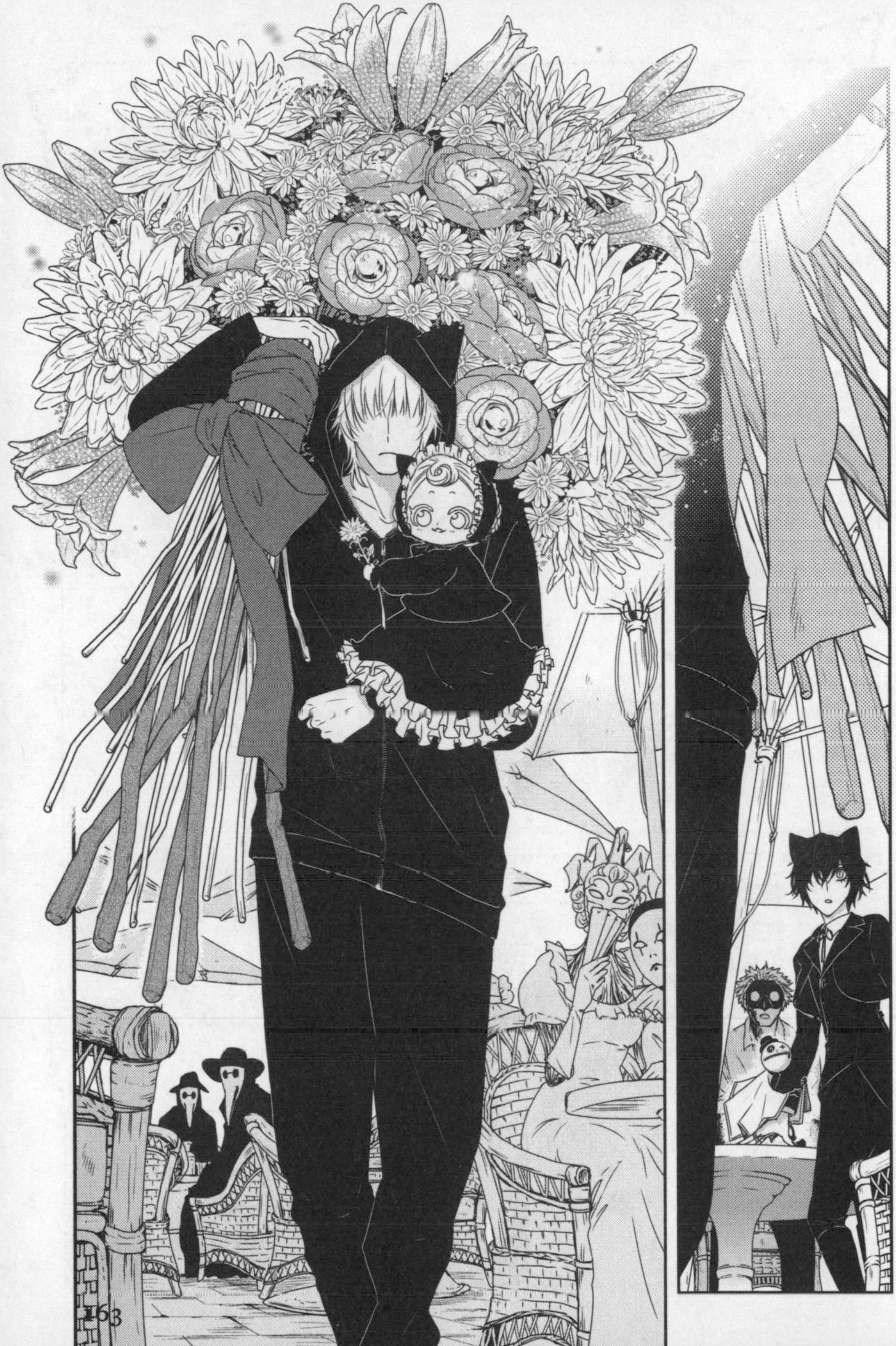

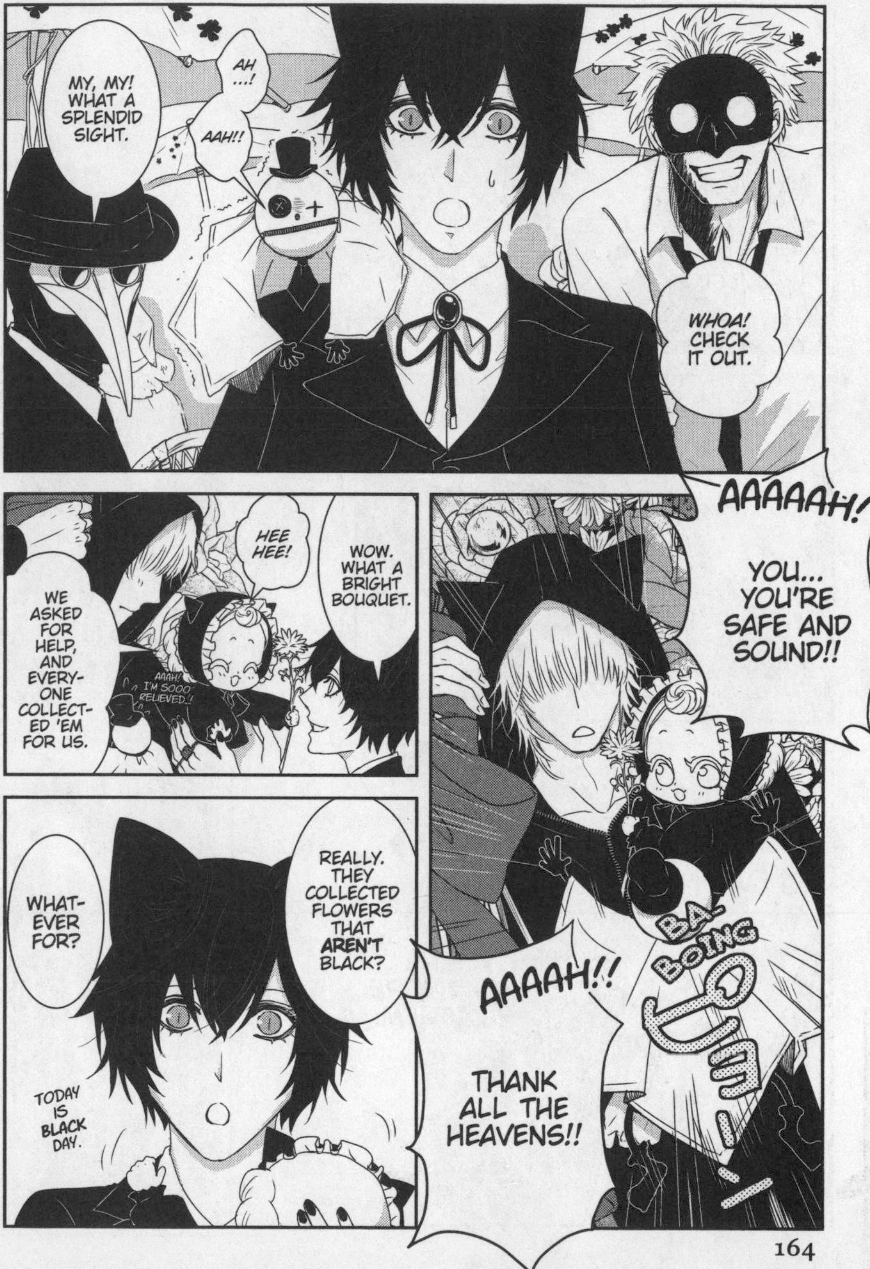
WHOA! CHECK IT OUT.
AH ...!
AAH!!
MY, MY! WHAT A SPLENDID SIGHT.
AAAAAH!
YOU... YOU'RE SAFE AND SOUND!!
BA-BOING
AAAAH!!
THANK ALL THE HEAVENS!!
WOW. WHAT A BRIGHT BOUQUET.
HEE HEE!
WE ASKED FOR HELP, AND EVERY-ONE COLLECT-ED 'EM FOR US.
AAAH! I'M SOOO RELIEVED!!
REALLY. THEY COLLECTED FLOWERS THAT AREN'T BLACK?
WHAT-EVER FOR?
TODAY IS BLACK DAY.

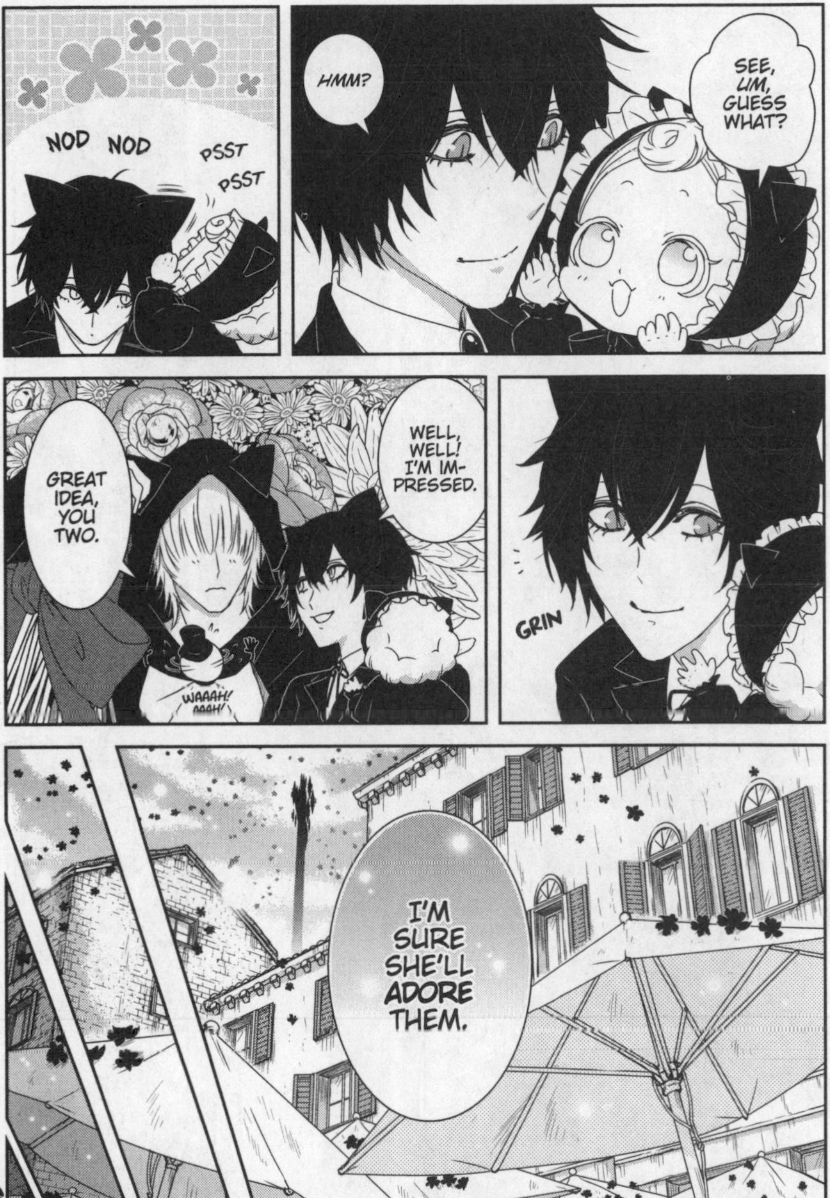
SEE, UM, GUESS WHAT?
HMM?
NOD NOD
PSST PSST
GRIN
WELL, WELL! I'M IM-PRESSED.
GREAT IDEA, YOU TWO.
WAAAH!
I'M SURE SHE'LL ADORE THEM.

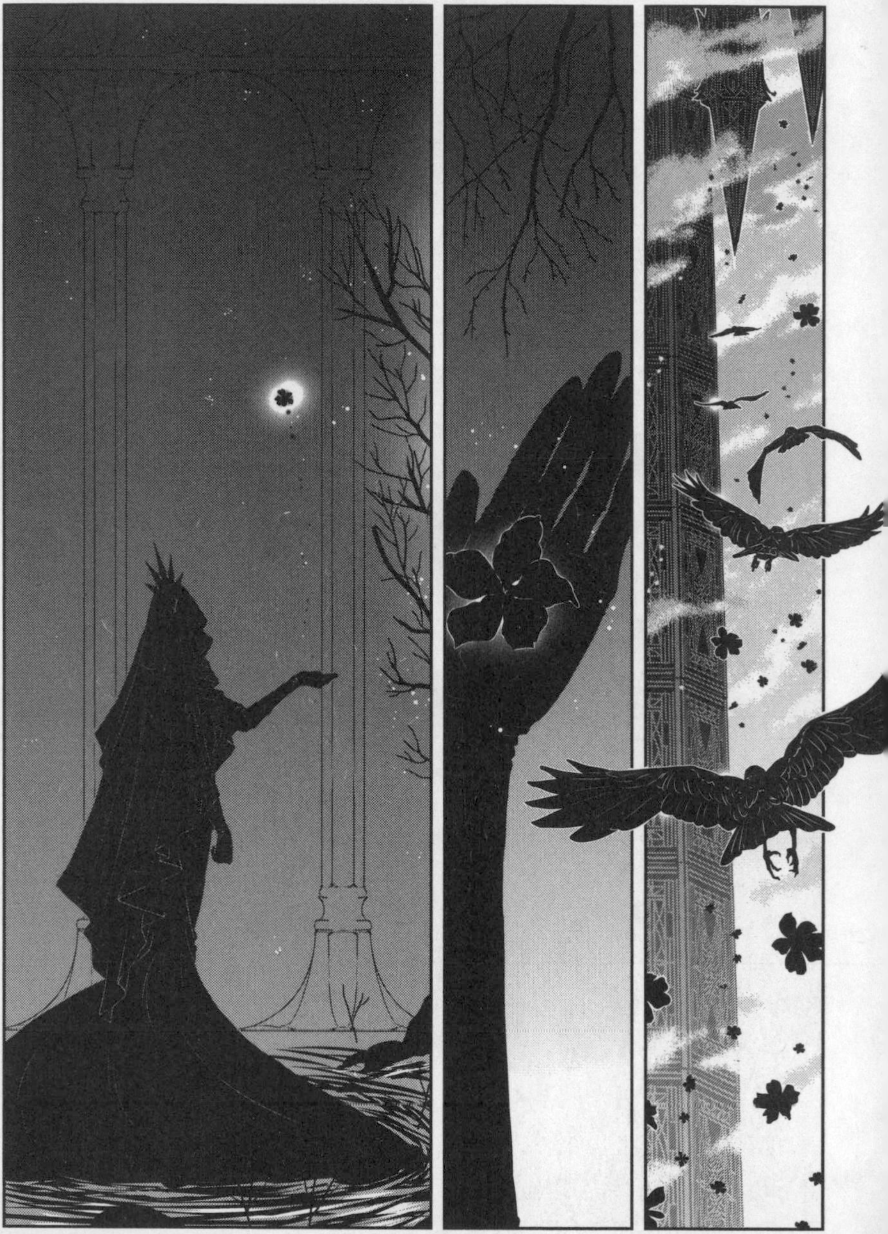

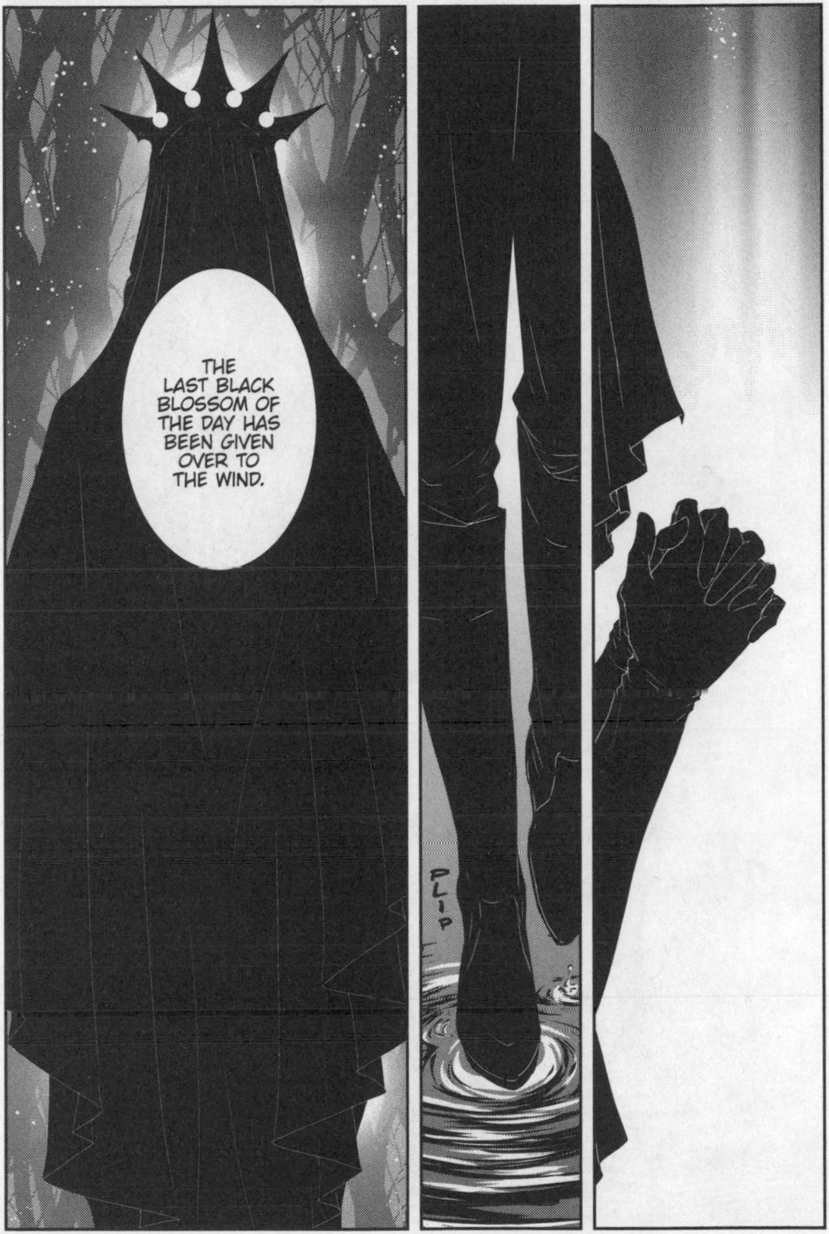
PLIP
THE LAST BLACK BLOSSOM OF THE DAY HAS BEEN GIVEN OVER TO THE WIND.

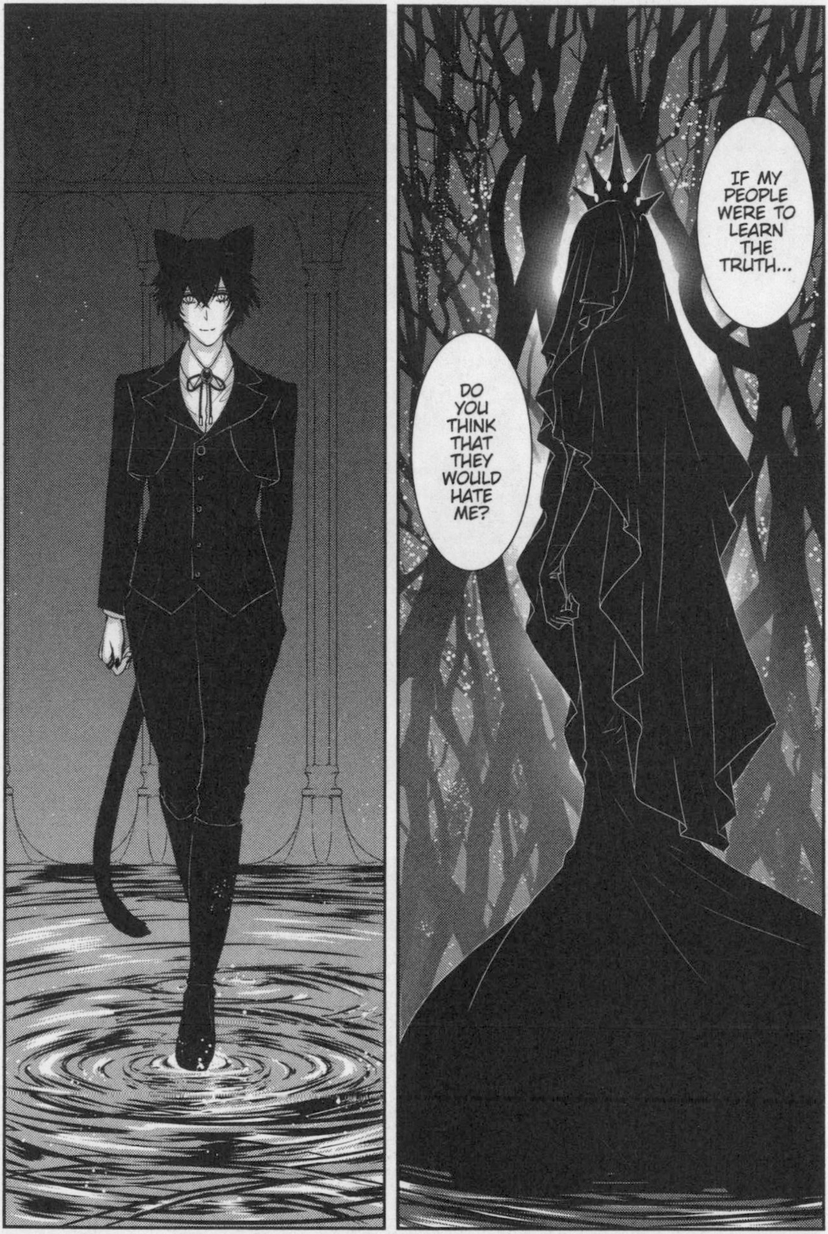
IF MY PEOPLE WERE TO LEARN THE TRUTH...
DO YOU THINK THAT THEY WOULD HATE ME?

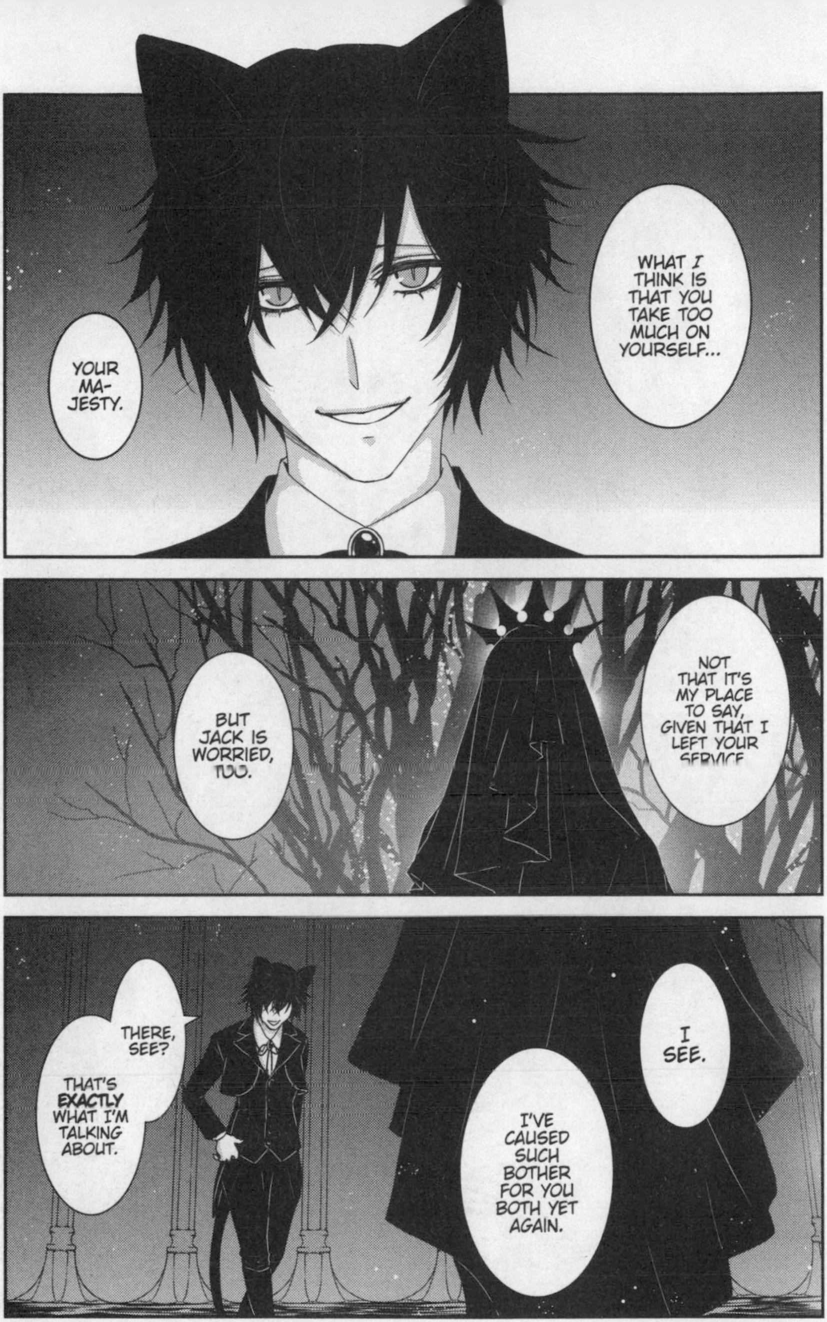
WHAT *I* THINK IS THAT YOU TAKE TOO MUCH ON YOURSELF...
YOUR MA-JESTY.
NOT THAT IT'S MY PLACE TO SAY, GIVEN THAT I LEFT YOUR SERVICE
BUT JACK IS WORRIED, TOO.
I SEE.
I'VE CAUSED SUCH BOTHER FOR YOU BOTH YET AGAIN.
THERE, SEE?
THAT'S **EXACTLY** WHAT I'M TALKING ABOUT.

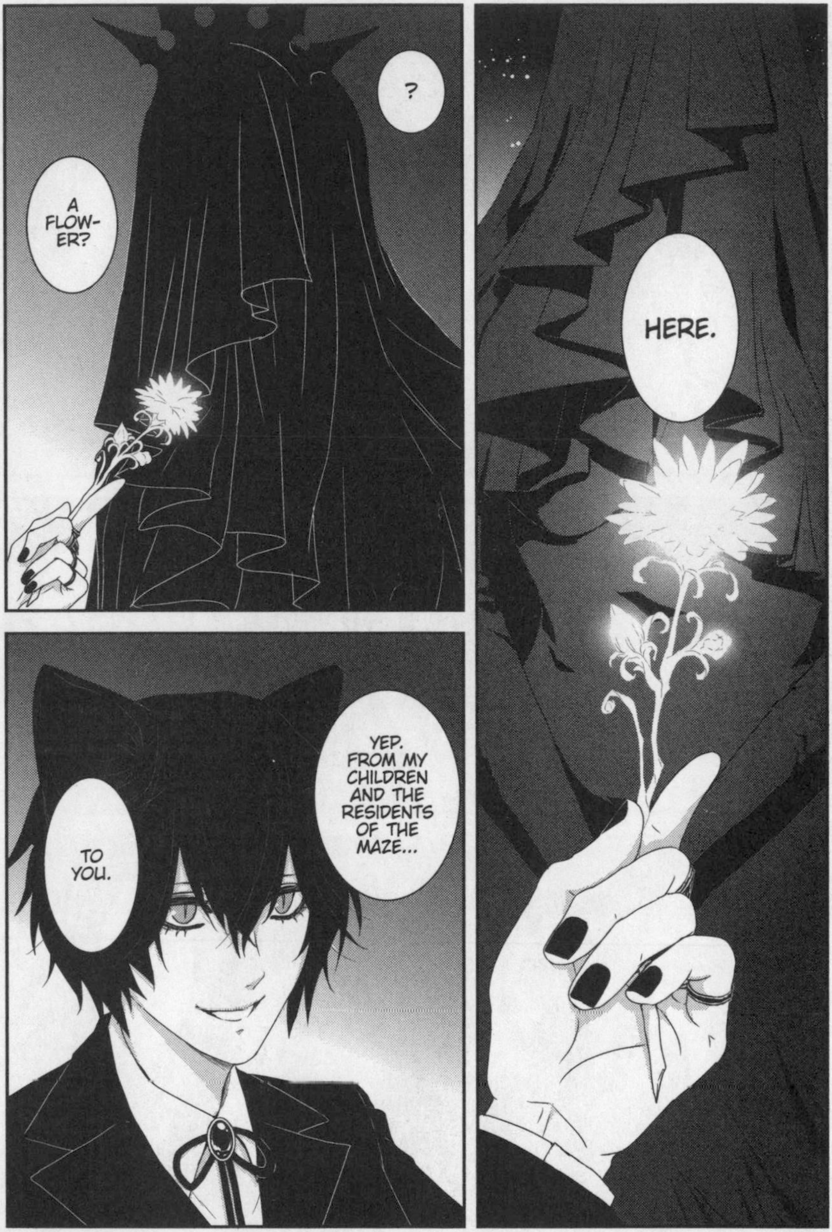
HERE.
?
A FLOW-
ER?
YEP. FROM MY CHILDREN AND THE RESIDENTS OF THE MAZE...
TO YOU.

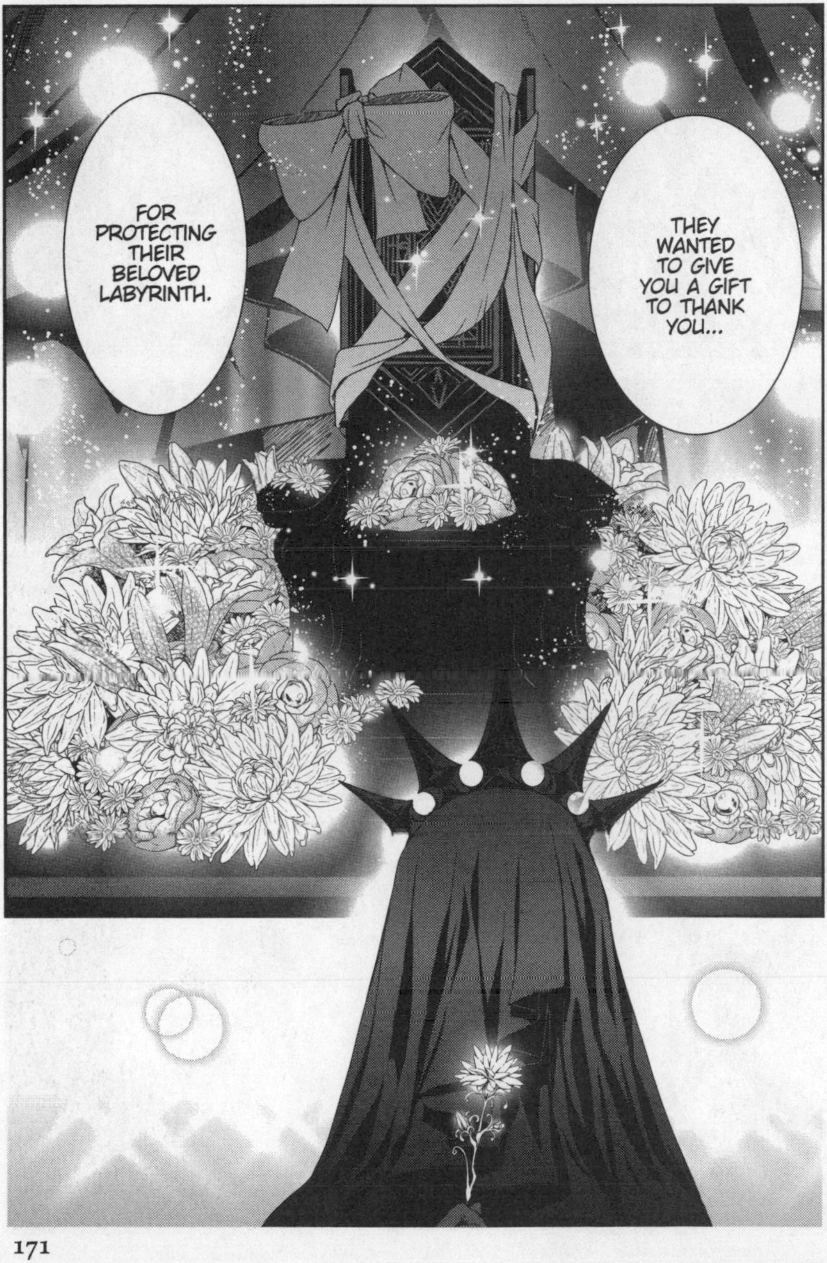
THEY WANTED TO GIVE YOU A GIFT TO THANK YOU...
FOR PROTECTING THEIR BELOVED LABYRINTH.

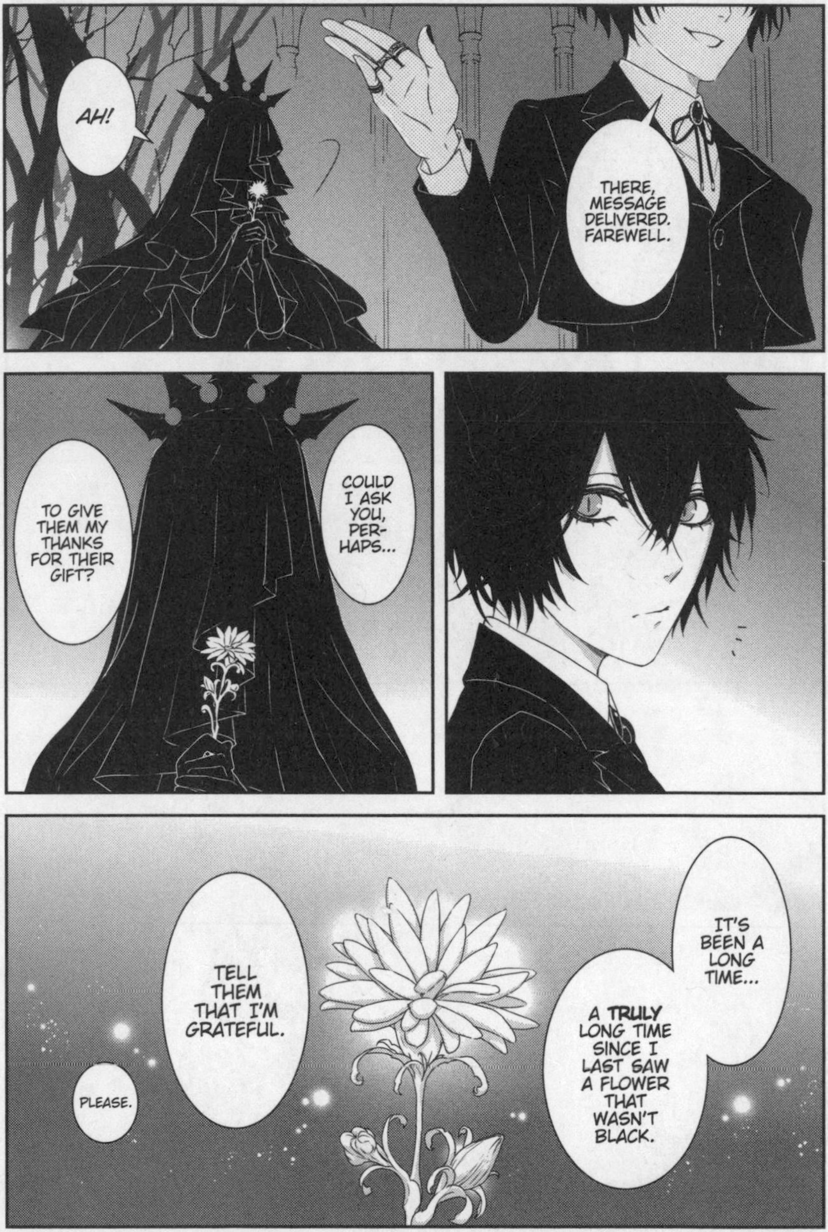
THERE, MESSAGE DELIVERED. FAREWELL.
AH!
COULD I ASK YOU, PER-HAPS...
TO GIVE THEM MY THANKS FOR THEIR GIFT?
IT'S BEEN A LONG TIME...
A TRULY LONG TIME SINCE I LAST SAW A FLOWER THAT WASN'T BLACK.
TELL THEM THAT I'M GRATEFUL.
PLEASE.

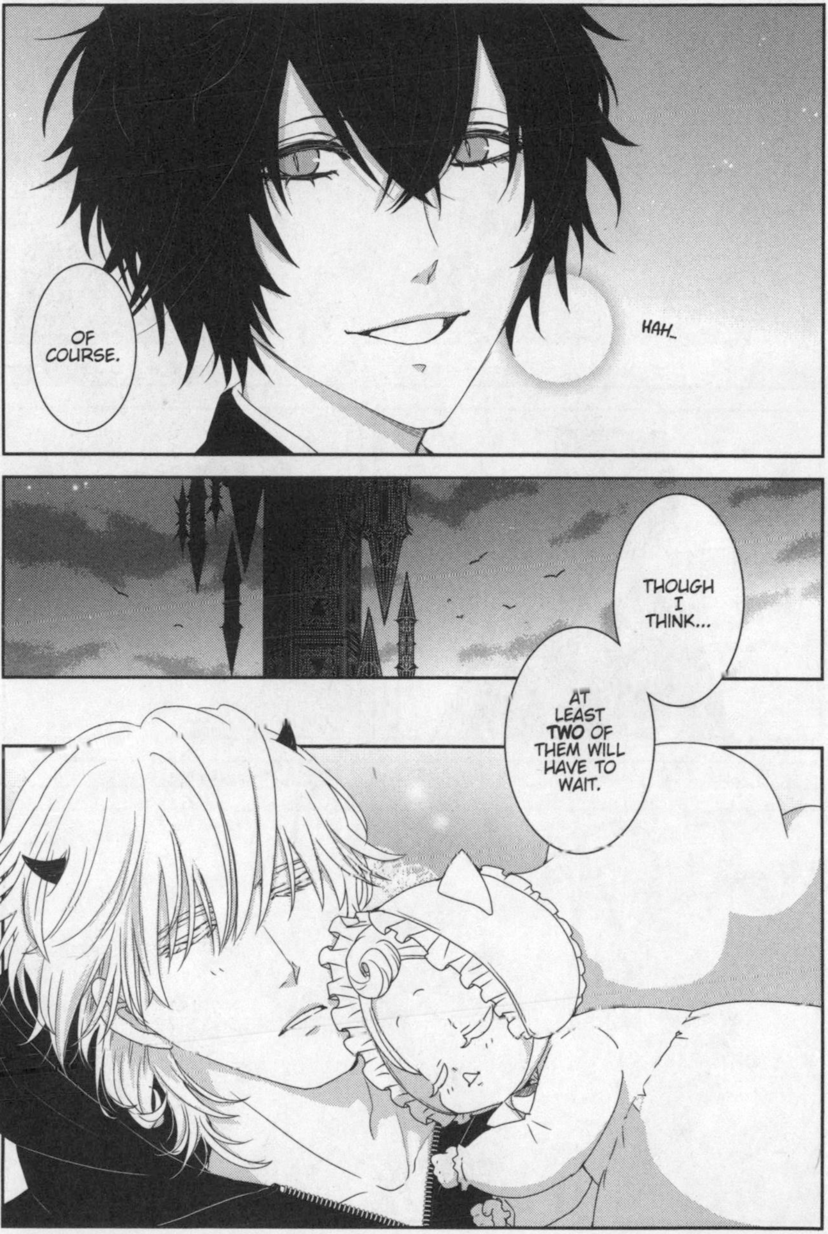
HAH..
OF COURSE.
THOUGH I THINK...
AT LEAST TWO OF THEM WILL HAVE TO WAIT.

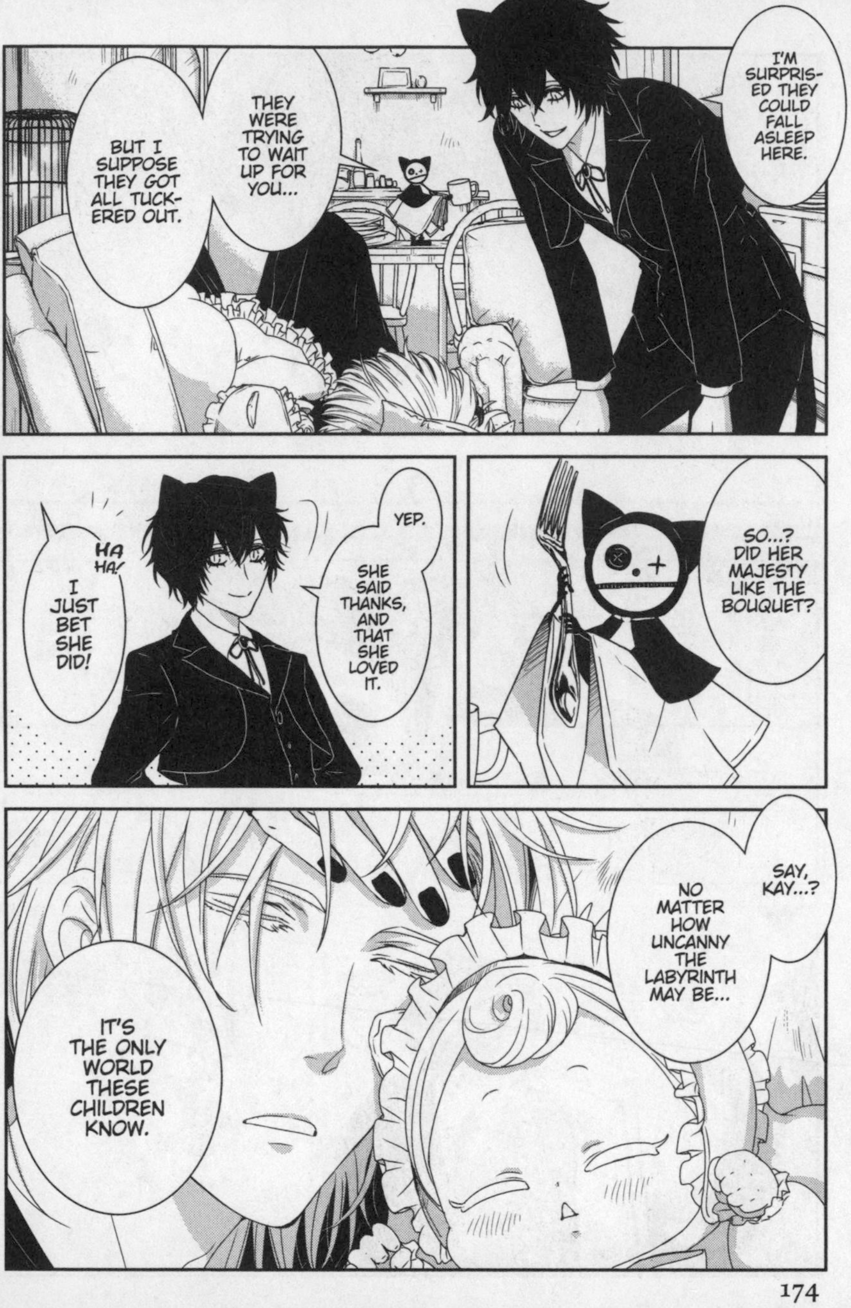

I'M SURPRISED THEY COULD FALL ASLEEP HERE.
THEY WERE TRYING TO WAIT UP FOR YOU...
BUT I SUPPOSE THEY GOT ALL TUCKERED OUT.
SO...? DID HER MAJESTY LIKE THE BOUQUET?
YEP.
SHE SAID THANKS, AND THAT SHE LOVED IT.
HA HA!
I JUST BET SHE DID!
SAY, KAY...?
NO MATTER HOW UNCANNY THE LABYRINTH MAY BE...
IT'S THE ONLY WORLD THESE CHILDREN KNOW.

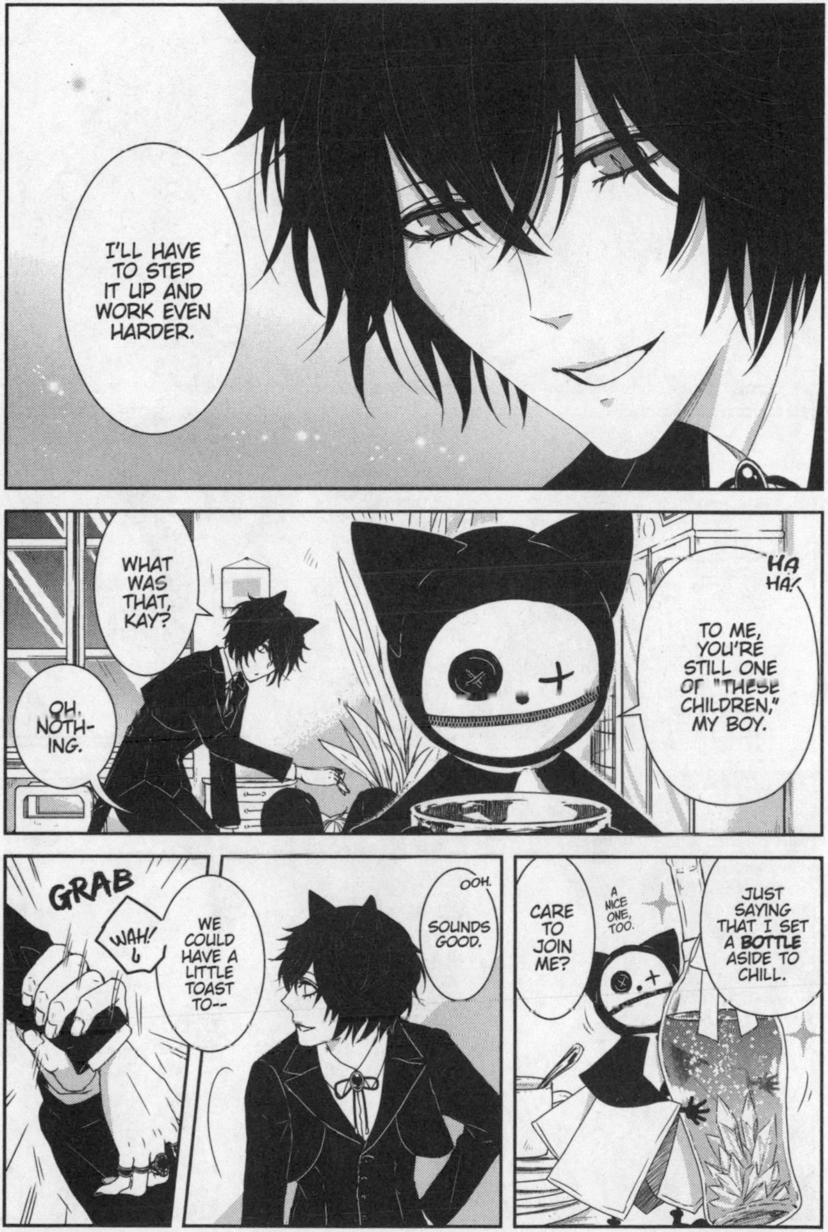
I'LL HAVE TO STEP IT UP AND WORK EVEN HARDER.
HA HA!
TO ME, YOU'RE STILL ONE OF "THESE CHILDREN," MY BOY.
WHAT WAS THAT, KAY?
OH, NOTHING.
JUST SAYING THAT I SET A BOTTLE ASIDE TO CHILL.
A NICE ONE, TOO.
CARE TO JOIN ME?
OOH.
SOUNDS GOOD.
WE COULD HAVE A LITTLE TOAST TO--
WAH!
GRAB

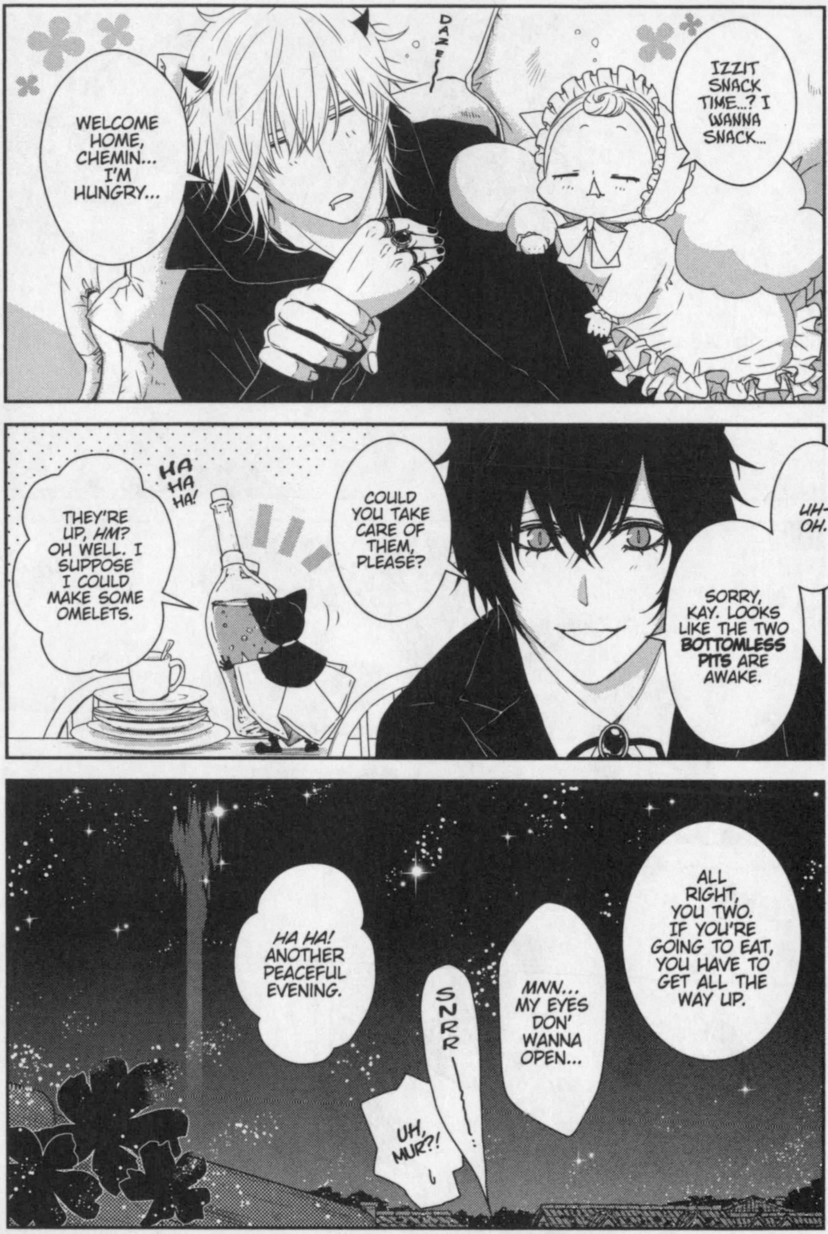
IZZIT SNACK TIME...? I WANNA SNACK...
DAZE—
WELCOME HOME, CHEMIN... I'M HUNGRY...
UH-OH.
SORRY, KAY. LOOKS LIKE THE TWO **BOTTOMLESS PITS** ARE AWAKE.
COULD YOU TAKE CARE OF THEM, PLEASE?
HA HA HA!
THEY'RE UP, *HM*? OH WELL. I SUPPOSE I COULD MAKE SOME OMELETS.
ALL RIGHT, YOU TWO. IF YOU'RE GOING TO EAT, YOU HAVE TO GET ALL THE WAY UP.
MNN... MY EYES DON' WANNA OPEN...
SNRR—
UH, MUR?!
HA HA! ANOTHER PEACEFUL EVENING.

Rozi in the Labyrinth 1 END

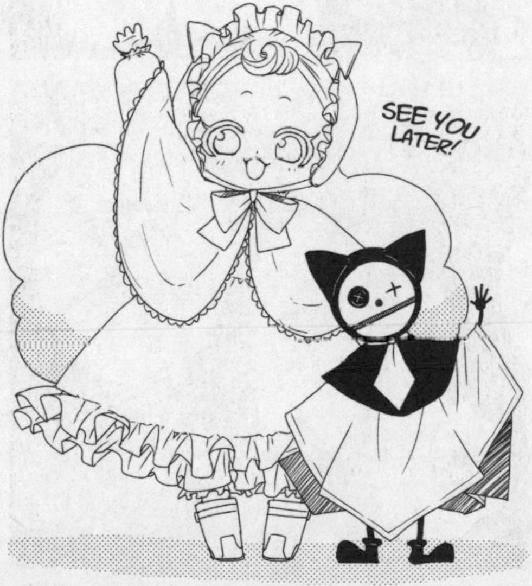
SEE YOU LATER!

Rozi in the Labyrinth Volume 1

Thank you very much for reading this far! The Labyrinth is a world inspired by my experiences visiting a certain foreign city and walking its streets. It felt like I'd wandered into a different world, and that those roads might go on forever.

I can admire the old streets and alleys of foreign cities for hours. They feel as though strange and mysterious things could happen along them, and I wonder what lies at their end.

When the roads beckon to you, making you want to lose yourself amongst them...but a little corner of your mind is scared that if you do, you might never find your way home again...I think that's the point where the Labyrinth begins. Little Rozi's fun and slightly strange everyday life will continue on. I invite you to keep exploring the Labyrinth's mysteries along with her and her family in the next volume, too.

Shiya
Totsuki

SEVEN SEAS ENTERTAINMENT PRESENTS

ROZI in the Labyrinth

story and art by SHIYA TOTSUKI

VOLUME 1

TRANSLATION
Adrienne Beck

LETTERING AND RETOUCH
Jennifer Skarupa

COVER DESIGN
KC Fabellon

PROOFREADER
Danielle King

EDITOR
Shanti Whitesides

PREPRESS TECHNICIAN
Rhiannon Rasmussen-Silverstein

PRODUCTION ASSISTANT
Christa Miesner

PRODUCTION MANAGER
Lissa Pattillo

MANAGING EDITOR
Julie Davis

ASSOCIATE PUBLISHER
Adam Arnold

PUBLISHER
Jason DeAngelis

ROZI IN THE LABYRINTH VOL. 1
©Shiya Totsuki 2019
All rights reserved.
Originally published in Japan in 2019 by MAG Garden Corporation, TOKYO.
English translation rights arranged through TOHAN CORPORATION, Tokyo.

Seven Seas press and purchase enquiries can be sent to Marketing Manager Lianne Sentar at press@gomanga.com. Information regarding the distribution and purchase of digital editions is available from Digital Manager CK Russell at digital@gomanga.com.

Seven Seas and the Seven Seas logo are trademarks of Seven Seas Entertainment. All rights reserved.

ISBN: 978-1-64505-943-1

Printed in Canada

FOLLOW US ONLINE: w   m

READING DIRECTIONS

This book reads from *right to left*, Japanese style. If this is your first time reading manga, you start reading from the top right panel on each page and take it from there. If you get lost, just follow the numbered diagram here. It may seem backwards at first, but you'll get the hang of it! Have fun!!

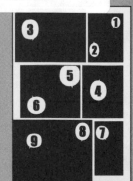